**W9-AEE-407**

A history of American architecture

To my son Alexander

# A HISTORY OF

BUILDINGS IN THEIR CULTURAL

# AMERICAN

AND TECHNOLOGICAL CONTEXT

# ARCHITECTURE

Mark Gelernter

UNIVERSITY PRESS OF NEW ENGLAND

Hanover and London

UNIVERSITY PRESS OF NEW ENGLAND

publishes books under its own imprint and is the publisher for Brandeis University
Press, Dartmouth College, Middlebury College Press, University of New Hampshire,
Tufts University, and Wesleyan University Press.

University Press of New England, Hanover, NH 03755

Simultaneously published in Great Britain
by Manchester University Press

Printed in Great Britain    5    4    3    2    1

Every effort has been made to trace all copyright holders for the illustrations in this book,
but if any have been overlooked inadvertently, please contact Manchester University Press,
Oxford Road, Manchester M13 9NR, UK.

*Library of Congress Cataloging-in-Publication Data*
Gelernter, Mark, 1951–
       A history of American architecture : buildings in their cultural
   and technological context / Mark Gelernter.
          p.    cm.
       Includes bibliographical references.
       ISBN 0–87451–940–3 (cloth)
       1. Architecture—United States.   2. Architecture and society—
   United States.   I. Title.
   NA705.G35   1999
   720′.973—dc21                                        98–51812

Designed in Apollo with Eras display
by Max Nettleton FCSD

Typeset in Hong Kong by Graphicraft Limited

Printed in Great Britain
by Biddles Limited, Guildford and King's Lynn

# Contents

# List of illustrations

LIST OF ILLUSTRATIONS

LIST OF ILLUSTRATIONS

# Foreword

Although we all use buildings and towns every day, seldom do we consciously think about where they came from, or why they possess a particular shape or style. Buildings are so integral to our daily existence that they often retreat invisibly into the background as we concentrate on our more immediate concerns. But in many significant ways, buildings and towns help shape our lives. They structure how we move about, how we perform our tasks, and how we meet other people. Our buildings and towns also express our values and aspirations, and provide one of the primary means by which we visualize ourselves and our society. Allowing a little exaggeration, we are our buildings, and our buildings are us.

With this relationship in mind, buildings from the past raise fascinating questions about our ancestors and their lifestyles, values and outlooks. Why did our colonial forebears give over a significant part of their homes to a grand staircase, and to a parlor which was seldom used but which contained the home's most valued possessions? Why did the Victorians cover their homes in elaborately ornate decoration? Why are so many American towns – and all of the land west of the Mississippi River – laid out on a gridiron plan? Why did buildings become so tall in the last decades of the nineteenth century? And why did Americans build cozy English Tudor houses before the Second World War, and stripped Ranch houses afterwards? These architectural ideas and others express powerful cultural forces at play. They embody deeply felt ideas about a number of fundamental issues, including our relationship with nature, our social relations with others, the importance of the individual, the value of science and technology, and our political role in the world.

Of course, the most powerful cultural forces in the world could not construct an idea beyond the technological and material means available at the time. Although occasionally in the history of America and Europe we find artists proposing unbuildable forms for philosophical reasons, most of our ancestors had to balance their cultural desires with their technological and financial abilities. Sometimes the desire for a particular architectural form drove individuals to invent new technologies by which the form could be realized, while other times individuals reshaped their desires in order to use a particular technology.

This book is going to study this fascinating relationship between buildings and the cultures in which they were conceived and constructed. It will concentrate on the geographical area of the present day continental United States, although the first few chapters will dip down into Mesoamerica and the area of present day Mexico, where we find the origins of ideas that subsequently influenced the architecture of North America. The architectural developments on this continent from their prehistoric beginnings to the present will also be explored. This means studying the Native American architecture that predated the European invasion in the fifteenth century. Many American architectural history books omit this indigenous architecture, on the grounds that it exerted so little influence on subsequent architectural developments. Yet there are several important reasons why a history of Native American architecture should begin our study. First, architectural ideas are interesting in themselves, whether others adopt them or not. Second, research in recent years has shown that the Native American civilizations and architecture were far more sophisticated than we formerly believed. The Europeans could have learned much from the Native American builders about how to adapt buildings to the demanding geographies and climates of the Americas. And third, as we will see in the next chapter, comparing the Native American and European cultures provides a unique opportunity to see how two independently developing civilizations addressed the basic problems of architecture.

To understand the history of American architecture, we must also understand the history of Europe. Although American architects periodically sought a separate national style for the new country, the reality remains that America's ideas have largely followed European ones through most of its history. Even the genuinely original American developments make more sense when we see them in the larger context of the prevailing tastes and fashions, and these were usually dictated by Europe. This book will explore American and European developments in parallel, so that we may see how and when these influenced each other. Although America is emphasized, on occasion we must devote a fair amount of space to significant European developments like the Enlightenment or the Industrial Revolution that later shaped the American outlook.

Each chapter addresses an identifiable historical period, like the era surrounding the American Revolution, or the era after the Civil War, or the Postmodern period following the Vietnam War. These historical periods begin and end with significant social, political or philosophical changes, and often possess characteristic social, technical and aesthetic viewpoints. Each chapter first explores the major factors that shaped the conditions and outlook of the period, and then examines the architectural ideas that emerged within this context. Because the book attempts to highlight the relationship between buildings and their culture, it concentrates on the big picture rather than on enumerating many details. So instead of cataloguing a number of good examples of a particular type or style, often just one characteristic example that most clearly explains the idea is discussed. Using this overview as a framework, a reader who wishes to explore further examples can then consult other sources.

Some architectural historians in recent years have begun to study the specific details surrounding the commission, design and construction of individual buildings, trying to show how particular personalities, deed restrictions, and so on, helped shape the design and its construction. Although much of this material is fascinating and instructive, it sometimes misses the forest for the trees. Despite their local and peculiar circumstances, most buildings still sufficiently follow broader cultural impulses that they can readily be seen as possessing an identifiable style common to other buildings in the period. The local circumstances of an individual building did not usually invent its style, although local circumstances may influence why that particular style was chosen, or how that particular style was employed. Since this book mainly wants to explore why the broader styles were developed, it discusses the particular details surrounding a particular building only when those resulted in ideas which subsequently changed the style.

In setting out the broader cultural and technological context for each chronological period, only limited previous knowledge of American and European social and political history is presumed. In the last two decades of teaching undergraduate and graduate architecture students in both England and America, I have found that those who are attracted to the field of architecture do not typically bring with them an equivalent enthusiasm for history. Most appreciate some helpful reminders of their rusty social and political history when they see that this information can help them understand the architectural ideas in which they have more inherent interest. I have tried to offer only the broadest picture of social and political history, concentrating mainly on those aspects that particularly influenced architecture. On occasion, though, I have thrown in well-known roadmarkers, like references to monarchs, presidents and famous writers or artists, which can help readers relate a period more vividly to their previous historical knowledge. A few times I have necessarily discussed some political developments in even greater detail, to help understand an important architectural development. For example, the British Whigs in the eighteenth century supported a Neo-Palladian movement in architecture that eventually killed off the prevalent English Baroque in both Britain and America. We will understand why these politicians championed a particular architectural style only if we understand a little of their political beliefs.

Although it is quite impossible to write an architectural history without injecting my own biases and preferences, I have tried to refrain from a traditional form of architectural writing that stressed connoisseurship. Following an older model of art history and criticism, many of the pioneering architectural historians like Pevsner and Hitchcock selected buildings according to their own sense of good taste, or according to a stylistic agenda they wished to advance. They then justified their choices by showing how the particular visual or formal characteristics of each building answered their standards. They might say, for example, that a building possessed particularly fine proportions, or honestly expressed its construction. The historians in this tradition ignored or disparaged buildings that did not fit their aesthetic scheme. However, the late twentieth century no longer enjoys a common set of standards against which we can judge buildings in this manner. In today's atmosphere of multiple and competing points of view, the best we can do is to explain the architectural ideas in a given period within their own terms, discuss their pros and cons, and then let the reader decide for him- or herself if the ideas make sense.

In this spirit, I have particularly tried to render a more balanced view of the period from about 1880 to 1945. Most architectural history books written after 1945 tried to portray this period as a great battle between the Modernists and the traditionalists. The former were usually represented as clear-thinking visionaries in tune with the new century, while the latter were dismissed as reactionaries who stood in the way of progress. Most histories written after 1945 hardly discuss a traditional building after 1910, when the first Modernist essays by Gropius and Le Corbusier appeared on the scene. However, with the decline of the Modernist style itself in the 1980s, we are able to re-examine this period free from the Modernist agenda. A very different story emerges when we read the contemporary books and magazines written between 1885 and 1945. Almost all European and American buildings in this period were designed in the traditional styles, while the few Modernist buildings were hardly discussed even by the professional architecture magazines. The early Modernists were not engaged in a great battle as much as they were largely ignored. Only in the 1930s did the professional architectural magazines begin to shift allegiance to the new style, and even then most clients still preferred – and insisted on building in – the traditional styles. To say that hundreds were tuned into the true spirit of the twentieth century while millions were not is certainly a curious way to view history. I have tried to counteract this common interpretation by looking more sympathetically at the traditional styles of the period, and explaining how the traditional architects also addressed the conditions of the new century. Readers can decide for themselves if the Modernists or the traditionalists most had their thumbs on the pulse of early twentieth-century culture.

I have supplemented the photographic illustrations with a number of my own line drawings. Although photographs offer a most realistic view of buildings, they are so ubiquitous in modern life that we often give them only a passing glance. Line drawings, in contrast, like miniaturized dollhouses or ship models, irresistably draw the viewer into their universe. Drawings seem to present the material in sharper contrast and with greater detail, even though they usually contain less information than a photograph. And as I learned when I drew the new illustrations for the nineteenth edition of Banister Fletcher's *History of Architecture*, a thoughtfully constructed line drawing can direct the viewer's attention to the salient features of the building composition and details while suppressing less important or even distracting information. I have randomly mixed photos and drawings throughout the book, to keep the reader juggling back and forth between these two different ways of viewing three-dimensional objects in two dimensions. I hope this variety will help the viewer to address each image with fresh eyes.

I could not write a book like this without standing on the shoulders of many authors who came before me. Many fine comprehensive histories of American architecture precede this one, from which I have drawn extensively for factual material and conceptual insights. The four-volume series, *American Buildings and their Architects* by William Pierson, Jr and William Jordy remains one of the best detailed studies of our American architectural heritage. Marcus Whiffen and Frederick Koeper's *American Architecture 1607–1976*, Vincent Scully's *American Architecture and Urbanism*, and Leland Roth's *Concise History of American Architecture* all pack equally rich material into concisely written single volumes. Richard Longstreth's *On the Edge of the World* helped me understand the complex period at the turn of the twentieth century, particularly the nature and history of the traditional styles that he appropriately called 'academic eclectic'. These and many other books listed in the bibliography have enriched our understanding of American architecture, each contributing a different perspective on the buildings we should value and the reasons why. I am also indebted to John M. Blum and his colleagues for their comprehensive book, *The National Experience: A History of the United States*. Although I supplemented this with numerous other readings, their work remained the reliable source to which I returned time and again for concise insights into American history and the American outlook. Richard Bushman's book, *The Refinement of America: Persons, Houses, Cities*, introduced me to the important concept of gentility in post-Renaissance Western culture, without which we cannot make sense of a number of significant stylistic and spatial changes in European and American architecture. I am also indebted to Stuart Fiedel's *Prehistory of the Americas*, and to Peter Nabokov and Robert Easton's *Native American Architecture*, both of which opened pioneering windows onto the cultures and architecture of the Native Americans.

I also wish to acknowledge the invaluable help of my own colleagues and friends who have materially participated in the development of this book. I owe the greatest debt to my former editor at Manchester University Press, Katharine Reeve, who first suggested the idea for this book and commissioned me to write it. When Katharine moved on to undertake her own research, my current editor Vanessa Graham and her team at MUP, including Matthew Frost, Stephanie Sloan and Lauren McAllister, ably helped me complete the project. I would like to thank Jeffrey Limerick for his advice and guidance throughout this project, and in particular for his substantial contributions to chapters 6, 7, 8 and 9. His own primary and secondary research into the period from 1880 to 1945 provided valuable insights into a period that is only recently coming out from under the shadow of Modernist scholarship. We spent a number of happy hours discussing this period, buried in the rare books collection at the University of Colorado library. I also benefited from extensive discussions with Keith Loftin on a number of architectural topics, in particular the Romantic characteristics of Jefferson's University of Virginia, and the broader implications of deconstructivism. Joan Draper's own high standards of scholarship and personal interests in non-traditional histories continually inspired me to look beyond the usual high fashion architects. Her close reading of an earlier draft helped sharpen my arguments and presentation. I also thank William Pierson, Jr for his helpful correspondence regarding the Baroque and Georgian periods. Other colleagues and friends who helped with suggestions and additional source materials include Roger Stonehouse, Betty Naster, Myra Rich, Gordon Brown, Cameron Kruger, Terry Mulholland and Stefan Hampden.

Robin Manteuffel and Beth Henrik superbly managed the immensely difficult task of gathering photographs and copyright permissions. Robin is now on speaking terms with practically every archivist in America, while Beth astutely talked her way into the Smithsonian when all of Washington, DC, was closed during a budget crisis. Dean Lindsey offered invaluable help in maintaining the computer database of images, in tracking down obscure references, and in drawing most of the plans. Lynn Lickteig and Carole Cardon provided their usual outstanding photographic services. Jeff Fleischer gathered a number of excellent photographs from his colleagues in the graduate school and, along with Tom Zavadil, helped draw several of the line illustrations. B. C. Holicky undertook the daunting task of drafting the glossary. Lisa Miller, Tonia Hobaugh-Toca, Joe Hosek, Todd Vandenburg and Talby Reyner all helped with the countless but essential tasks attending a project of this scale. I would also like to thank the students in my graduate seminar on the History of American Architecture, who read and discussed early drafts of this book. I substantially redrafted several chapters in light of their questions and comments, immeasurably improving the final manuscript as a consequence. My wife Janet provided excellent editorial support, preparing the bibliography and catching errant typos and verbosity. To Janet and my other family members George, Wendie, Ben and Alex, I owe the greatest debt of all. By providing moral support in the low periods, and enthusiastic cheering in the high periods, they kept me working when I really wanted to go skiing instead.

# 1

# FIRST CIVILIZATIONS
## 12,000 BC–AD 1500

THE HISTORY of American architecture begins with a story of two worlds. The one with which we are most familiar originated in Europe and forcibly entered the American continents with the arrival of Christopher Columbus in the fifteenth century AD. The other one inhabited the American continents from prehistoric times,

1 First civilizations before
AD 1500

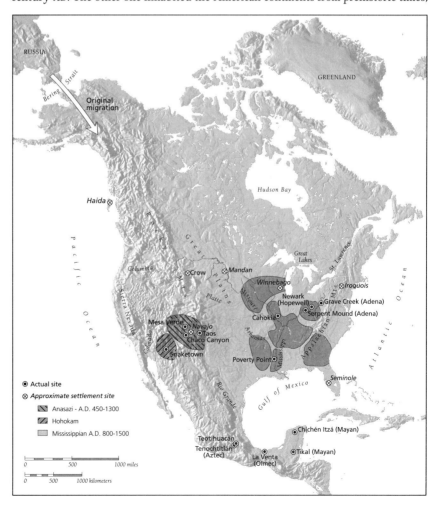

RUSSIA

Bering Strait

Original migration

GREENLAND

Hudson Bay

Haida ⊗

Rocky Mountains

Great Plains

Great Lakes

St. Lawrence

Columbia

Crow ⊗ ⊗Mandan

Winnebago ⊗ ⊗Iroquois

Platte

Newark (Hopewell) ⊗Grave Creek (Adena)

Missouri

Cahokia ⊗ Serpent Mound (Adena)

Pacific Ocean

Sierra Nevada

Mesa Verde ⊗Navajo ⊗Taos Chaco Canyon

Colorado

Arkansas

Mississippi

Appalachian Mountains

Atlantic Ocean

Snaketown

Poverty Point⊗

Rio Grande

Seminole ⊗

Gulf of Mexico

◉ Actual site
⊗ Approximate settlement site

▨ Anasazi - A.D. 450-1300
▨ Hohokam
▒ Mississippian A.D. 800-1500

0     500     1000 miles

0     500     1000 kilometers

Teotihuacán Tenochtitlán (Aztec)

Chichén Itzá (Mayan)

La Venta (Olmec)

Tikal (Mayan)

and then almost disappeared completely under the weight of the European invasion. Most of this book concentrates on the former, since it largely defined the American culture and architectural heritage with which we live today. But the history of the Native American civilizations and architecture also offers a fascinating story. Thanks to new research and a maturing attitude in America towards its aboriginal heritage, we are now more aware of the sophisticated levels these earlier cultures attained. For example, when Hernán Cortés entered the Aztec capital of Tenochtitlán in 1519, he gazed upon an imperial city of 400,000 people, larger than any contemporary European city, five times larger than London. Its central pyramid stood 200 feet tall, just short of the ancient Egyptian pyramid of Mykerinos at Gizeh. Less familiar but no less remarkable was the Mississippian civilization with its capital at Cahokia, near present day East St Louis, Illinois. At its peak around AD 1100, Cahokia spread over six square miles and housed 40,000 people, over half the size of contemporary London. It boasted the largest pyramid in North America, and for almost half a millennium the culture of which it was a part either directly controlled or influenced a region from the present day eastern Dakotas to Georgia. No modern history of American architecture would be complete without discussing these remarkable Native American civilizations.

Since the European world almost completely replaced the Native American one, acquiring in the process only the slightest traces of the vanquished civilizations, it is tempting to treat the two worlds in sequential chapters. Those books which address the subject typically begin with a survey of ancient American cultures leading up to the time of the European invasion, and then switch to the state of European culture at that time. But this treatment misses several opportunities. First, although it explains the origins of cultural and architectural ideas in the Native American world, it leaves us wondering where the European ideas originated and how they developed before the fifteenth century. We suddenly have to accept as givens, without a clear under-standing of their origins, architectural types like churches, palaces, marketplaces, cities and suburbs, and architectural styles like Classical and Gothic. A deeper appreciation of the origin and development of these ideas would help us understand more fully their subsequent development in American architecture.

Second, by treating European and Native American histories separately, we miss an opportunity to explore a fascinating question in the history of culture and architecture. A number of architectural theories and styles in the history of the West claimed to have discovered the universal principles of architecture which hold true for all times and all people. We can test these assertions by studying a fortuitous occurrence at the very beginning of architecture's development in prehistoric times. The European and Native American cultures both originated in a common culture on the steppes of Siberia in the last Ice Age. Before cities or permanent architecture had been invented, one group split off and entered the hitherto uninhabited American continents. When rising seas in the Bering Strait cut off contact between the two worlds, each culture developed completely independently of the other. So what cultural and architectural ideas did they subsequently invent in common, and what ideas uniquely emerged in response to local conditions? Those ideas that appear on both continents we might reasonably assume derive from universal human abilities and needs, and from the inherent nature of making buildings.

Studying the two cultures together will help us answer yet another perplexing question in the history of American culture and architecture. Why did the Europeans so completely reject the Native American cultures and architectural ideas they found, even though a number of the Native American architectural ideas better suited the

American climate and geography than the imported European ideas? What made these two worlds so fundamentally different and even hostile at the time of contact, given their common ancestry? This chapter will examine the origins and development of the two civilizations together, looking in particular for the similarities and differences in the cultural and technological ideas that shaped their respective cities and buildings.

## Prehistoric culture and architecture

### The Neolithic hunters

The common ancestors of the European and Native American civilizations inhabited the tundra at the edge of the glaciers during the last Ice Age. They probably lived in small bands of half a dozen nuclear families, roaming a traditional territory in search of the large game which provided their primary subsistence. They also distributed their responsibilities and material possessions fairly evenly among the members of the band. Since even the best hunters could return empty handed, the welfare of the band as a whole depended on collectively sharing the good and bad times. Informal leadership fell to an individual who was particularly skilled at hunting game, while responsibility for communicating with the spirits of the animals and thus ensuring a steady supply of game fell to the shaman or medicine man.

To counter the harsh tundra climate, these hunters typically lived in pit houses, shallow depressions dug into the subsoil and roofed over with a frame of mammoth tusks or bones and a covering of sewn hides or bundled grass [2]. Sometimes they added central posts to support the roof, while other times they simply arched the tusks over the pit to meet at a ridge. This sensible design strategy employed a readily available and renewable material, sheltered them from the winds, and took advantage of the earth's natural insulating properties. Several families probably lived in each pit house, and as many as fifty people might have lived in the community. At a site in Kostienki, Russia, 22,000 years ago, a large pit 110 feet by 49 feet held nine hearths, although other sites reveal more modestly sized houses of 10 to 15 feet. The hunters in this late glacial period also constructed tents by stretching hides over a wooden framework, when they could find suitably long and straight tree branches

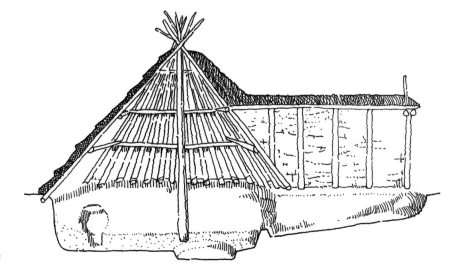

**2** Prehistoric pit house,
Pan-p'o-ts'un, China, 4000 BC

3 Plateau Parrain, Dordogne
region, France, 15,000 BC

[3]. Both the pit house and the tent became important architectural prototypes for subsequent building in the Old and New Worlds.

The glaciers in this period covered one-third of the earth at their greatest extent, reaching down over much of northern Europe and to the Great Lakes in North America. They trapped so much water that the world's oceans dropped as much as 300 feet, opening up a land bridge at the Bering Strait between present day Siberia and Alaska. Prehistoric herds of North American horses strayed across and eventually made their way to Europe, while woolly mammoths and mastodons migrated in the other direction. Some time between 35,000 and 11,500 years ago, bands of Siberian hunters followed the herds into North America. Only a few families, interestingly, might have made this crossing. Recent genetic studies reveal that most contemporary Native Americans share a common ancestor dating back 15,000 to 30,000 years ago. These first Americans, now known as the Clovis from an archeological site in New Mexico, continued the big game hunting tradition of their Siberian predecessors and spread throughout the Americas.

The hunters in the Old World and New witnessed one of the great ecological transformations in history. The world began to warm up around 14,000 years ago, eventually leading to the current temperate Holocene era. Ten thousand years ago, the rising oceans flooded the land bridge, cutting off communication with the Old World. The game rich tundra disappeared, eventually replaced by diverse ecological regions ranging from rain forests to deserts. A mass extinction of animals followed, since particularly the large species failed to adapt to the changing climate. On the American continent, ground sloths, giant beavers, horses, camels, mammoths, mastodons, and musk-oxen all disappeared. After 9000 BC the culture of big game hunting died out, its way of life gone.

### Archaic civilizations

Around the world, people adapted to these dramatic changes in climate and ecology by changing their subsistence patterns. They had to rely more on small game, birds, fish, shellfish and wild plants. Foraging for nuts, berries and wild grains became an important part of their survival system. Groups learned to manage the resources of their territory more carefully, scheduling their movements through the area to take advantage of seasonal availability of game and plants. They adapted to the opportunities and challenges in their own regions and, since the regions were now more diverse ecologically, the once universal hunting culture began to split into regional variations of hunter/gatherers. The period saw greater social and eventually linguistic diversity.

In some regions, food sources were widely spread throughout the area, and camps had to be moved regularly. In other areas richer in flora and fauna, food sources were so closely available that camps moved little or never. Throughout the world, the transition from big game hunting to hunting/gathering led to the establishment of the first permanent settlements. With sedentary living and diversified food sources came other momentous cultural changes. Now it was possible to store food surpluses as insurance against the times of poor game or failed wild crops. Someone had to control the redistribution of the surplus, and so we see the emergence in this period of a social hierarchy. The person who controlled the community's surplus resources received a higher proportion of goods, and was given a more elaborate burial. Surpluses also meant that some individuals could be freed from the responsibility of food gathering, and specialize in skills like arrow making and pottery. In some areas, the status of women increased, since they were the ones responsible for foraging and gathering. In a number of regions, for example in the southwest of the present day United States, a matriarchal system eventually emerged in which the women owned the homes and their husbands moved in with them. The women in these cultures took responsibility for the layout and construction of the buildings. The world population rose dramatically as food supplies became more secure.

Different ecological zones presented different opportunities for building. As we will see throughout much of subsequent architectural history, local cultures in each region developed architectural forms and building systems which exploited local resources and adapted to the local climate. In forested regions around the world, for example, many early builders continued to construct versions of the prehistoric tent with a wooden frame and external covering. When large animal hides were no longer available for the covering, builders substituted bundled grass or wattle and daub. The latter consisted of mud plastered over woven mats of small branches. This system of a frame and cover used materials efficiently, providing a light yet sturdy structure that could be sheathed with any convenient materials. Indeed, the concept proved so adaptable that we will find it appearing time and again throughout the history of architecture, eventually evolving into Gothic cathedrals and twentieth-century skyscrapers.

A good early example of the system can be found in the Koster settlement in southern Illinois, around 5500 BC. By this time a thick deciduous forest covered the eastern seaboard and Great Lakes region, replacing the coniferous spruces and pines which had retreated to the colder north. The Koster builders erected stout wooden posts in foundation trenches, forming rectangular houses 8 to 10 feet wide and 20 to 35 feet long, and covered in wattle and daub. This was not the only way to build with wood, however. Some Europeans in this early period built the predecessor to the ubiquitous log cabin of the American frontier, by laying up horizontal logs interlocked at the corners. This system ultimately proved less popular because it required more trees for the same size structure.

Those cultures in regions devoid of trees developed another construction strategy, the load-bearing masonry wall. We find many such structures in the early villages of the ancient Near East, and a little later in the dry regions of the Americas. Starting with the ancient pit house idea, the early masons piled up heavy walls of local stone or sun-dried clay bricks around a shallow depression in the ground. These massive masonry walls provided effective insulation in climates where the temperatures fluctuated widely. In the early masonry houses of the Near East, we also find an interesting evolution from circular plans to rectangular ones [4]. Perhaps these early masons built in circles at first to follow an old pit house prototype, or to provide additional structural strength to the masonry walls. But as the populations increased they chose to pack their huts closer together rather than to spread them further afield, eventually creating villages of tightly packed and more geometrically efficient rectangular houses. Çatal Hüyük in present day Turkey (7000–6000 BC) shows the results of close geometrical packing and load-bearing construction [5]. The layout of this village also reveals two other significant characteristics of these early permanent settlements. Numerous shrines are freely intermixed with the living rooms, and no house clearly stands out from the rest as grander or richer. In other words, we see no centralized temples or palaces, implying no specialized priesthoods or central political authority. Those social concepts and building types had to await further cultural developments.

4 Beidha, Jordan, 7000–6000 BC

5 Çatal Hüyük, Turkey, 7000–6000 BC

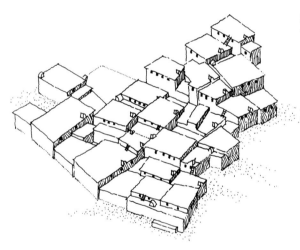

## The rise of chiefdoms and cities

### The transition to greater complexity

In the Old World and the New, agriculture developed hand in hand with sedentary living and the increasing level of social complexity. Larger populations required larger and more reliable food sources, and the women had more time to experiment with the planting and cross-breeding that eventually produced high yield foodstuffs and an agricultural revolution. Larger food supplies then fueled population growths, which in turn demanded more complex social arrangements. The subsequent development of all major civilization in the Old World, and most of them in the New, depended on the development of agriculture. Uniquely in the New World, how-ever, a number of highly complex and sophisticated cultures emerged on the basis of hunting/gathering alone. These appeared in areas of natural abundance, namely the Pacific Northwest, California and the temperate forests of the Southeast.

Responding to these cyclical relationships among stable food supplies, popula-tion growth and increasingly complex societies, many archaic cultures throughout the world grew into chiefdoms and eventually states. One individual emerged as a permanent leader and based his or her authority on some connection with the ancestral spirits, claiming in one stroke permanent and irrefutable authority for both secular and religious affairs. The leader – eventually king or queen – now derived his or her role from inheritance rather than from personal skills. Around the leader gathered an entourage of high status individuals, and sometimes a priesthood grown out of the shaman system. Now the priesthood aimed to intervene with the gods who influenced agriculture or natural foodstuffs, including the gods of sun and rain. As before, the leader organized the storage and redistribution of food surpluses, negotiated with neighbors, and arranged expeditions for raw materials.

Architecturally, the new social arrangements demanded a central community of high status in which lived the chief and his or her entourage, and where the com-munal surpluses were stored. A ceremonial precinct usually stood at the center of the community. Here the chief could hold redistribution banquets, and the priests could publicly worship the gods or spirits. A new architectural type, the religious monument or temple, emerged to stand over the ceremonial precinct as a symbol of authority and as a connection to the spirit world. The chief's high status also demanded increasingly elaborate burials, often under massive earthworks like mounds. Along with the need for these large public works came the organizational ability to build them. A centralized authority with a secure food supply could free a large labor force from responsibility for gathering food, and then direct its building efforts for the benefit of the entire community.

The close packing of forms in the small archaic settlements like Çatal Hüyük meant that access to each house had to be gained through openings in the roof. As settlements grew larger, streets were developed to provide easier circulation through the town, and to give easier access to each dwelling through a door off the street. In many of these more complex towns throughout the world, we also find the appearance of courtyard houses which opened up the center of the house to light and breezes while still obtaining a close packing of forms. Courtyards worked particularly well in hot climates, when a water fountain or a pool in the center of the court naturally cooled the breezes wafting into the surrounding house. This eventually became the universal house type for the cultures in the Near East, for the cultures surrounding the Mediterranean sea, and for the cultures inhabiting the hot areas of the Americas.

### Developments in the Old World

After 3500 BC, the towns in Mesopotamia began to reflect these social changes. They suddenly grew much larger, eventually into cities. Grand palaces emerged to support the king and queen and accompanying bureaucrats, while temples rose to provide a central setting for the ritual ceremonies conducted by the priesthood. These temples usually took the form of a mound. Ziggurats in Mesopotamia piled progress-ively smaller platforms on top of each other, and capped the top with a temple. A similar stepped pyramid of King Zoser at Saqqara in Egypt eventually gave way to the familiar square-based, regular solid pyramids of Chefren, Cheops and Mykerinos at Gizeh around 2570 BC, although these latter Egyptian forms abandoned the temple at the top. We might view the invention of these pyramids as a natural tendency to reach to the heavens, to stand closer to the forces that the gatherers and farmers wished to understand and control. Mounds and pyramids no doubt also served as potent symbols of authority and control for the new aristocracy and priesthood.

The new formalities in culture also led to orthogonal planning and bilateral symmetries in town and building layouts, particularly for the major monuments like palaces, temples, and public squares. The mortuary temple of Queen Hatshepsut shows the new idea [6]. Compared to the informal geometries we noted earlier in Çatal Hüyük, increasingly these early civilizations based their important designs on rectangles and squares whose sides are proportioned according to exact mathematical ratios like 1:2, 3:4 and 5:8, and whose sides intersect at precisely right angles. Elements like rooms also balance each other on opposites sides of a central axis. Why did the earliest civilizations abandon the informal spatial arrangements of the earlier archaic cultures, and impose instead this formal geometry? We have learned one reason from the records of the Greeks, who conceived of their temples as earthly homes for divine gods, and who therefore needed to provide suitably divine architectural forms. For them, rationally precise geometry represented the perfection of the gods. We might also see the new interest in formal geometry as following from their desire to chart nature's patterns and recurring cycles in order to anticipate growing seasons. Powerful geometry in buildings and towns certainly helped express the central authority now exerted by the aristocracy and priesthood. And perhaps rational geometry represented a thrilling ability, for the first time, to impose human will and intellect upon a natural world previously uncontrolled. More prosaically, orthogonal planning also emerged as a rational and convenient way to survey and organize large projects under central control.

In a number of early Near Eastern cities, the strictly orthogonal and geometrically formal arrangements of the major public areas did not extend into the residential neighborhoods. Although the streets roughly followed an orthogonal grid, they occasionally deformed to accommodate natural contours or obstacles, or dead-ended into buildings which had encroached into the public domain. The houses typically followed the courtyard idea, admitting light and fresh air into the centers of houses otherwise tightly packed together. Around this basic idea, the houses grew informally and without the self-conscious proportions and symmetries of the public buildings. This distinction between public buildings designed according to formal or abstract principles, and private dwellings growing more informally, appeared in most subsequent cities throughout the world.

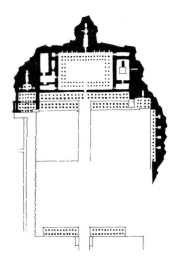

**6** Funerary temple of Queen Hatshepsut, Deir el-Bahri, Egypt, 1480 BC

### Developments in the New World

Lagging only a little behind the Old World descendants of their common ancestors, the Native Americans independently developed these same ideas about culture and architecture. Around 2000 BC at several coastal sites in present day Peru, they built monumental structures including a U-shaped complex of platform temples 20 feet high at El Paraíso. Constructed three hundred years later at La Florida near present day Lima, a gigantic platform 840 feet long and 110 feet high – 10 stories tall and almost three American football fields long – continued the impulse of these early civilizations in the Old World and New to mark as grandly as possible their ceremonial centers. The workforce required to construct this platform implies some system of centralized control and a stable food supply.

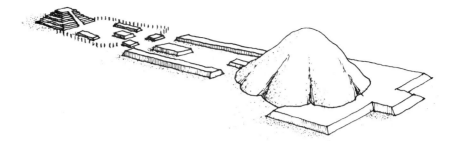

**7** La Venta, Mexico, 800–400 BC

Around 1200 BC, about the time of Rameses II and Moses in the Old World, the Olmec civilization dramatically arose in the humid lowlands of the Mexican Gulf Coast. Like the roughly contemporary Old World civilizations, the Olmecs depended on agriculture, and therefore placed great weight on understanding or controlling the natural phenomena like the sun, water and the changing seasons. Although they developed a complex calendar based on astronomical observations with which to mark the seasons and plan their agricultural activities, they also established a priesthood that took responsibility for understanding and appeasing the gods whom they believed controlled the natural events. Massive public works again suggest a centralized authority.

The town of La Venta, the primary Olmec center after 900 BC, displays the same architectural ideas that we saw in the ancient Near East and in Egypt, probably invented for the same reasons of religious and political expression. The town designers symmetrically aligned a series of mounds, platforms, ceremonial courtyards, and two pyramids along a geometrical axis 8 degrees west of north [7]. This axis pointed possibly to a constellation, or perhaps to the sun's orientation at noon. One can only speculate if this arrangement supported astronomical observations, as has been suggested for Stonehenge in England, or simply acknowledged important orientations in the natural world. The smaller pyramid stood on a square base, and stepped back in four terraces to a flat top, much like the Step Pyramid of Zoser in Egypt. A ramp on

**8** Poverty Point, Louisiana, 1200 BC

the main axis suggests that the priests performed ceremonies at the top. The larger pyramid took the form of a fluted cone, 110 feet high and 420 feet across its base. This shape, some have suggested, intentionally referred to the volcanic cones in the nearby mountains from which perhaps the Olmecs migrated, and therefore stood as a sign for their ancient homeland. But we can also see both the pyramids and the orthogonal geometry of the site as deriving from the same impulses that generated these architectural ideas in the Old World, a desire to mediate with the gods and to help exert control over the local population.

North America in this period lay at the fringe of these emerging civilizations. Most groups continued archaic subsistence patterns and social arrangements. The Mississippi river valley, however, offered conditions that could support a more complex society. With its tributaries including the Missouri and Ohio rivers, this extensive waterway drained half of America, from the Appalachians to the Rockies. The river not only provided a relatively easy transportation system, but it offered a rich diet of fish, shellfish, wild plants and animals for the hunter/gatherers who lived on its banks. The extensive forests provided ready building materials, and the fecund soil in the valley bottom lay ready for agricultural experiments. Around 1200 BC, a more complex society emerged on the banks of the lower Mississippi, at Poverty Point in northeastern Louisiana. Like the other civilizations we have examined in the Old World and New, it also built extensive earthworks including a mound 70 feet high and 600 feet across, and six concentric embankments with an outer perimeter extending two-thirds of a mile [8]. The embankments alone required approximately 3 million hours of work to construct. From the air the complex unmistakably forms a giant bird. Since the design is far easier to discern from the air than from ground level, we might speculate that it was meant to be seen by the celestial gods or spirits who were presumed to orchestrate the natural phenomena. That is, it possibly functioned much like the pyramids in Mexico, the Near East and Egypt in mediating between the humans and their gods. After a brief florescence the site was abandoned, and North American groups returned to the archaic way of life for another half a millennium.

## The European divergence

Most civilizations throughout the Old World and New continued to develop broadly along the lines we have just examined. Although we have no space to discuss it here, early civilizations in India and China also developed roughly similar social, religious, and architectural systems. In the next sections, we will explore how the later Native American civilizations elaborated variations on these themes in the diverse regions of the North American continent. However, before doing so, we will examine here a conceptual revolution that eventually diverted the European civilizations away from this world-wide pattern of development. In the sixth century BC, just as the Olmec civilization in Mexico was waning, the ancient Greeks invented a set of philosophical, aesthetic and political ideas quite unlike those held by the other ancient civilizations. These ideas eventually formed the fundamental outlook of the European and then European-American civilizations. We often take their ideas for granted, and even assume that the Greeks had simply discovered the real and natural order of things. But their innovations were by no means inevitable. The social, intellectual and aesthetic world they invented remained a minority conception throughout the subsequent history of the world, occasionally fading away even in the Western cultures themselves.

The following three sections briefly summarize the history of European culture and architecture from ancient Greece to the eve of the Renaissance in the fifteenth century. This summary can, at best, offer only a cursory overview of a long and complex story. But at the risk of oversimplification, there are several reasons why this story needs to be reviewed here. First, by seeing this history in its broadest terms, we can more easily compare its salient features to the general world pattern discussed above. This will help us to understand some of the essential differences between the indigenous populations of the Americas and the European invaders. Second, a quick survey of this history allows us to review a number of important cultural and architectural concepts that were originally developed in this long period, and that later exerted considerable influence on post-Renaissance Europe and America. For example, generations of European and later American architects periodically revived Classical and then Gothic outlooks and architectural expressions. To understand these ideas, we need to understand their origins and the values that they embodied. Readers who are already familiar with the main features of Western cultural and architectural history may skip these three sections and begin again with the section 'Civilizations in the New World', but readers whose European cultural and architectural history is a little rusty may find this a useful summary of the main ideas.

### The Greek revolution

The Greeks, in essence, invented the idea of the individual. In all of the other societies we have so far examined, people lived according to the rule of authorities outside themselves. The king or queen and cultural traditions told them what to do, the priests and religious canons told them what to think, and ancient rules of thumb and tradition told them how to build. Personal opinions, particularly those that opposed the dominant views or cultural traditions, were not encouraged. The Greeks reversed this emphasis and celebrated the individual perception. They believed in the powers and the right of the individual to think and reason for him- or herself, even when personal beliefs countered the majority view.

A number of important consequences followed from this new idea. First, the Greeks developed an unprecedented interest in physical nature, looking for the causes of natural events in nature itself rather than solely in pre-ordained myths. This was the beginning of Western philosophy and, later, Western natural science. Second, the new interest in sensory nature transformed the nature of art. Previous art portrayed abstractions in which, for example, a figure of higher social rank was made much larger in a picture. The Greeks contrarily began to represent what they actually perceived, attending as closely as possible to every detail. This was the beginning of Western representational art. Third, the priority given to the individual could not tolerate an authoritarian king or queen. Each individual's views counted, and government had to rule according to the wishes of those who were governed. This was the beginning of Western democracy.

Although the Greeks themselves never pressed their conception of the individual to its logical extreme, their Western successors often did. From the Greek invention ultimately derives a uniquely Western concept of the individual as a social or economic entity more fundamental than the community. At its best, this attitude encouraged great risk-taking and innovation; at its worst, it encouraged individuals to pursue personal gain at the expense of the larger community. The Greek invention also led their successors to a uniquely Western concept of the artist or architect as a creative genius, one who actively works to overthrow cultural traditions in favor of personal visions. Where most other world civilizations were content to reproduce or gradually to adapt successful architectural traditions, the inheritors of the Greek legacy often strained to invent new ideas for their own sake.

The Greek emphasis on individual sensory perception also led to a fundamental duality that framed most subsequent Western thinking about the nature of art and architecture. From the heritage of the ancient world the Greeks had acquired an interest in rationality and order, and so they continued to value the common ancient world ideas about orthogonal geometry, axial symmetry, and precise mathematical proportions. But at the same time, they focused new attention on the aesthetic delights of dramatic and changing sensory experience. Rather than rationally and predictably approaching their buildings on the main central axis as many ancient civilizations had done, for example, they often established winding routes in which the viewers glimpsed a building from a number of angles before approaching it obliquely. In this way the viewer formed a number of different impressions of the building, each one varied in size, in proportion, in its relation to the sun, and so on. This approach made it more difficult to understand at first glance the intellectual order of the building, but it heightened a sensory and emotional reaction to the experience. Although the Greeks sought a balance between the intellectual and the sensory, and between the rational and the picturesque, the Western successors to the Greek tradition more often fell into one extreme and then the other. Sometimes an entire generation stressed the rational, for example, followed by a generation stressing the picturesque. Other times a given culture or age split between acrimonious advocates of the opposite tendencies. Many of the stylistic battles that we will examine in this history can be traced back to this duality in the Greek outlook.

The new Greek ideas also transformed one of the main building types of the ancient world, the temple. As part of their new emphasis on the distinct personality and on democratic equality, they humanized their gods and made them more approachable to individuals. A specialized priesthood consequently diminished in importance. Temples no longer needed to stand over the community as symbols of power and authority, but rather could serve more as earthly houses for humanized gods, and as centers for shared community ritual ceremonies. The Greeks consequently designed their temples as houses, with one or two rectangular rooms surrounded by a colonnade and capped by a simple gable roof [9]. So powerful was this image, and so representative of the Greek outlook, that it eventually became a prototype for much Western architecture both religious and secular.

The Greeks based their temple designs on the ancient idea of the wooden structural frame, now built more durably in stone. The main architectural components of the temple derive from the structural elements themselves. First are the regular rows of columns with their bases, shafts and capitals. Next are the beams – commonly referred to in this Greek system as the entablatures – resting on the tops of the columns; these entablatures are decoratively divided into three horizontal parts, the architrave at the bottom, the frieze in the middle and the cornice at the top. Finally, there is the triangular form at the end of the pitched roof, known in the Greek system as the pediment (the more general architectural term for this triangle is the gable). To ensure that they captured the correct divine essences, the Greek architects codified rules of design which spelled out everything from the overall building organization to the smallest detail. Eventually every temple design derived from one of three types of column and beam structures. Each type varied according to the slenderness of its column, the column spacing, and the details of ornamentation, and was named after a location in Greece where the type was supposed to have emerged.

9 Parthenon, Athens, Greece, 447–436 BC, Ictinus and Callicrates

10 Five Orders of Architecture. Left to right: Tuscan, Doric, Ionic, Corinthian, Composite

The Doric came from Doria, the Ionic from Ionia, and the Corinthian from Corinth. The Romans later modified details of these types and added two more to the collection: the Tuscan, named after the Tuscany region of Italy, and the Composite, a combination of the Ionic and Corinthian. We now know these as the Five Orders of Architecture, upon which much subsequent European and American architecture was based [10]. The five were eventually seen as an ordered system, ranging from the most stubby, coarse and plain, to the most slim, refined and decorated. Genders were also attributed to the system. The plainer and ruder orders were considered masculine, appropriate for rough and ready buildings like military barracks, while the more elaborate and refined were considered feminine, appropriate for some temples and important civic buildings. Since educated people in the cultures who regularly employed the Five Orders understood these attributes, architects could provide important clues to the nature of their building by choosing an appropriate Order.

### The Roman developments

The Romans living at the eastern edge of the Greek world eventually acquired a number of the latter's ideas about the individual, society and architecture. In the spirit of democracy they originally established a republican form of government which, centuries later, inspired Thomas Jefferson and the other founding fathers to develop a similar idea for the United States. As we have seen, the Romans also appropriated and added to the Greek architectural Orders. However, where the Greeks had used the Orders to create proper structural frames, the Romans increasingly applied them as mere surface decoration on the other ancient system of construction, the load-bearing masonry wall. They became masters of wall construction, expanding dramatically the repertoire of architectural forms that can be built with this system. From the Egyptians, probably, they learned how to carry the massive weight of a load-bearing wall over an opening with an arch. Although arches can take a variety of shapes, the Romans continued the ancient preference for simple geometry and employed arches shaped as perfect semi-circles. These later became a hallmark of their style, and therefore provide one of the key ways in which we can identify styles derived from the Romans. The Roman addition of the arch to the Classical architectural language created two basic types by which we can classify many traditional buildings: trabeated, or using columns and beams, and arcuated, or using arches.

The Romans developed a number of new structural and spatial variations on the arch idea, spinning it about its center to form a dome, continuing it along its length to form a barrel vault, and intersecting two barrel vaults to form a groin vault [11]. The Romans linked their various architectural forms together according to the venerable geometrical rules we have already seen in earlier civilizations, like bi-axial symmetry, crossing axes and modular proportions. These geometrical rules, the semi-circular arch, the vault and dome, and the Orders of architecture, eventually comprised what we now call the Classical language of architecture. The Romans used this language to build structures and interior spaces unprecedented in the ancient world for their scale and grandeur [12]. And when Europeans periodically attempted to revive the social and political glories of Rome over the next two millennia, they also astutely revived the language of its architecture, eventually establishing the Classical language as a key component of the Western heritage.

The Roman Republic eventually gave way to the autocratic rule of the Roman Empire, and to militaristic expansion around the Mediterranean Sea and up into northern Europe. To control the locals, the Romans built colonial towns as military and administrative centers. A number of European cities, including London, were founded this way. The Romans continued what we have now seen as a common tendency in the ancient civilizations to lay out new towns according to precise geometries. They typically set out an orthogonal grid of squares, aligned with the cardinal points. A major north-south and an east-west street intersected at the center of the town, forming a great cross-axis around which were gathered the major public buildings. These two major streets passed through gateways in the defensive town wall, and then continued on as roads to the next colonial outpost [13]. The roads themselves followed dead straight lines wherever possible, suddenly bending to take a new alignment only when natural obstacles prevented a more direct route. The Romans also divided the territory surrounding the towns into a great grid of squares measuring 728 meters (2400 feet) per side, and containing 100 landholdings. Traces of the Roman grids can still be found in many European street and road alignments. America later used a similar gridded system for many of its new towns, as well as to divide the lands west of the Appalachians.

### The Middle Ages

In the third century AD, the Roman Empire began to unravel, while two centuries later it collapsed altogether. This temporarily brought to an end the unusual social and philosophical experiment initiated by the Greeks. During the ensuing Middle Ages, the European cultures returned to the more common world pattern of chiefdoms or monarchies, of specialized priesthoods, and of the individual giving way to the shared. The Classical concept of the autonomous individual gradually faded away, as people looked primarily to religions and political authorities for direction on what to think and do. Cities were abandoned in favor of sustenance farming in the countryside, while the production of large buildings in the Roman Classical mode eventually declined. Lost, too, was a Classical distinction between the architect who conceived of the building form, and the builder who constructed the building according to the architect's plans. Increasingly in the Middle Ages, design and construction

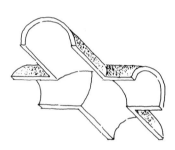

11 Elements of Roman Classicism. Above: arch; barrel vault; groin vault. Below: arch; apse; dome.

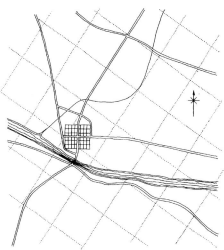

12 Basilica of Constantine, Rome, Italy, AD 307–12

13 Roman colony of Florentia (Florence), Florence, Italy, 59 BC

were taken over by the same person. The bulk of buildings consisted of simple vernacular forms adapted to local geographical conditions and available building supplies. In wooded areas, for example, the ancient frame and cover idea evolved into a characteristically medieval form known as half-timbering. Typically, the medieval carpenters constructed a frame of large timbers connected together with mortise and tenon joints, and then infilled the frame with wattle and daub or with brickwork called nogging [14]. The medieval masons constructed in brick or stone when wood was less readily available. Roofs also gradually adapted to local conditions. When the Romans colonized much of northern Europe, they brought with them the shallow pitched roofs originally adapted to the dry Mediterranean climate. But as the Roman influence faded away, most medieval builders more sensibly built steeply pitched roofs to help shed their damper and snowier weather. The medieval carpenters eventually developed elaborate framing systems for supporting these large roofs. Roof coverings varied according to local availability of materials, which might be thatch, clay tiles, or wooden shingles. Each region of Europe gradually acquired its own distinctive character, based on localized building traditions and materials.

14 Half-timbered cottage, Weobly, England, c. 1500

15 Old St Peter's, Rome, Italy, AD 320–30

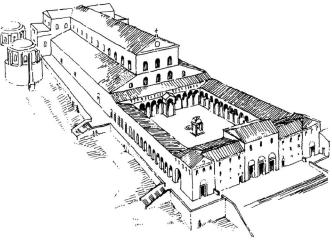

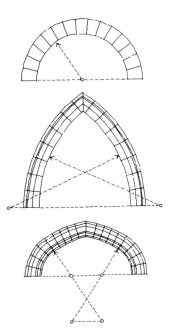

16 Maria Laach, Germany,
1093–1156

17 Diagram of Gothic
construction, thirteenth century

18 Roman, Gothic and
Tudor arches

This period invented a new building type significant in the subsequent history of European and American architecture, the Christian church. As the Christian Church rose to fill the political and spiritual vacuum caused by the collapse of the Roman Empire, it wished to distance itself from the pagan religions and hence the pagan temples of

the ancient world. The Church authorities eventually appropriated the old Roman basilicas, or law courts, for their new church form. As we see here in Old St Peter's in Rome, the basilica form comprised a high central nave lighted by clerestory windows in the upper wall, and flanked by lower aisles on either side [15]. Unlike the ancient temples in the Old World and New, where the priesthood typically performed their rituals before an outdoor audience gathered around the temple, in the Christian Church the audience stood or sat within the nave, watching the priesthood perform their duties before an altar located at one end. The first Christian basilicas retained not only the nave and aisle idea, but also the other elements characteristic of the Roman style, including shallow roofs and sunny courtyards, or atria. However, as memories of the Roman Empire faded away in the ensuing six centuries so, too, did the use of distinctly Classical architectural elements like the Five Orders.

At first during Charlemagne's reign in the eighth century, and then more completely after the millennium, the Europeans attempted to revive their earlier levels of cultural attainment. In the eleventh century trade began again, the cities revitalized, and Europeans began to rediscover their ancient heritage. Throughout the next five centuries, the Europeans constructed a civilization based partly in their still dominant Christian culture, and partly in a revival of ancient Greek and Roman concepts. Throughout this period, we witness the gradual rediscovery of the concept of the autonomous individual, the revival of interest in sensory nature for art and science, and a rediscovery of the ancient Classical language of architecture.

The fusion of Christian and Classical ideas shows in the first great church building program after the millennium. In a style known as the Romanesque, the medieval builders revived the Roman ideas of the basilica, the round-headed arches, and the symmetrically disposed basic geometrical elements like squares, octagons and circles. But in a medieval society still preoccupied with the otherworldly and with divine salvation, these Roman architectural ideas were transformed into something more appropriately spiritual by dramatically attenuating the entire building vertically [16]. This new style abandoned the horizontal repose of the original Classical language in favor of forms that emphatically pointed to the heavens. Like the ancient mounds, pyramids and stylized earthworks in the Old World and New, the Romanesque style mediated between humans and the divine and, as a useful by-product, asserted on the skyline the authority and importance of the Church.

Just a few centuries before the European invasion of the Americas, the medieval masons evolved the Romanesque style into the Gothic. In essence they abandoned the load-bearing wall construction at the heart of the Roman and Romanesque traditions, turning instead to the other ancient constructional idea, the structural frame. A series of columns, or piers, run down the length of the nave and along the sides of the aisles, establishing a structural frame and the limits of the space to be enclosed [17]. Instead of spanning between the piers with beams, as we have commonly seen in the frames of the ancient world, the Gothic masons ran thin ribs up from a pier, across the space, and then down to a pier on the other side. The lacy network of ribs formed the frame of a vault, the interstices of which were filled with non-load-bearing masonry. The spaces below the vaults were typically left as open as possible, often filled with expansive windows of stained glass to cast ethereal light into the building. To support the upper reaches of this thin structural frame without blocking the expansive glass openings, the Gothic designers invented the flying buttresses seen in figure 17. They also abandoned the Roman semi-circular arch struck from one point in favor of a distinctive pointed arch struck from two [18]. The pointed arch solved a technical problem of how to build a groin vault over a bay whose width and length are of different dimensions (that is, over a bay not perfectly square). If the two sides of a bay are different lengths, then by the rules of geometry the semi-circular arches constructed upon them would be of different diameters; and this meant that they could not meet levelly at the crown of the vault. In contrast, pointed vaults can be made narrower or wider at their bases while still keeping their apexes at the same level. This ability to vault gracefully over a non-square bay allowed the Gothic designers to pull the structural bays closer together down the length of the nave without narrowing the nave itself, creating a staccato effect of soaring piers reaching to heaven uninterrupted by horizontal lines. They reinforced the soaring effect of the vaults with numerous devices including pointed spires and pinnacles [19]. These great churches daringly pressed the structural possibilities of stone to the extreme in order to serve the Christian outlook of the age. And as we will see later in the book, the Gothic church formed another cultural icon like the Greek temples to which subsequent cultures in Europe and America returned time and again.

The revival of cities after the millennium led to a variety of town designs. Some new towns were rigidly laid out according to the old Roman grid system, while others softened or bent their grids to accommodate local geographical conditions like curving rivers or hilltops. Yet other towns developed by widening an existing roadway or a crossroads to form a marketplace, and then built houses in ribbon developments along the roads. Existing towns built on an old Roman grid still showed hints of the grid, but over centuries of destruction and reconstruction the street layouts usually altered to what we now typically think of as a medieval street pattern. Streets curved to follow the lay of the land, or to avoid obstacles; they might abruptly change direction altogether after someone constructed a building directly on the old street line [20]. This haphazard growth harks back to the casual arrangements of archaic cultures like Çatal Hüyük, where no strong central authority imposed a plan onto the town. Both the Roman grid and the medieval street pattern eventually found their way to the Americas.

One other idea developed in the Middle Ages eventually shaped the early development of the Americas, namely the feudal system of land ownership and control. Feudalism had evolved during the Middle Ages as a method for building social and economic interdependencies, and for managing the land. A lord who owned vast tracts of land leased sections of it to vassals, who in return promised to provide services to the lord like supplying knights for military actions. The vassals did not then own the land; they merely received what the peasants on the land produced and took responsibility for its management. The peasants received physical protection and the right to work a small piece of land for their own sustenance, in exchange for which they had to work some of the land for the vassal (or lord of the manor), and pay an annual rent in farm produce. Meadows and pastures were held in common, upon which all could graze their animals. Aspects of this system of land ownership were initially carried over to the Americas, as we will see later.

The layout of the manor farmstead itself also later entered into the American architectural vocabulary. Due to limited trade and the reduced production of goods in the few remaining towns during much of the Middle Ages, each farmstead became in effect a small self-contained village. The manor house, usually a fortified dwelling or even castle, protected the village and provided accommodation for the lord of the manor and his family. Around the manor house clustered various farm outbuildings, gardens, cottages for the peasants, and perhaps a small church and a mill. Although the peasants received a house, a means of sustenance, and physical protection, they

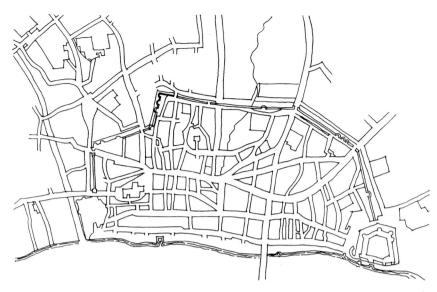

**19** Notre Dame, Paris, France, 1163–1250

**20** Plan of medieval London, England, *c.* fourteenth century

paid a fairly high price. They were legally bound to the land and could not leave without the lord's permission and the payment of a fee. This idea of a self-contained economic entity, managed by the lord of the manor living in a grand house and worked by a bound servant class, eventually transformed into the Virginia plantation system and the grand southern plantation house.

So in their long cultural history, the Europeans had developed two broad and often fundamentally different outlooks. The Classical heritage of Greece and Rome stressed individual perceptions and rights, and a rationally intellectual and sensory interest in the physical world. The medieval heritage contrarily stressed hierarchical social relations and a spiritual and emotional interest in the divine. Each age developed architectural ideas commensurate with its prevailing outlook and social conditions. In later centuries, Europeans and Americans looking back on this dual heritage found inspiration in one or the other for ideas and values that suited their own outlook. Those who valued the individual and the rational looked back with admiration to the Classical world, for example, while those who preferred social unity and a more emotional or spiritual response to things preferred the medieval. The Classical and the Gothic styles provided the two cultural icons between which much subsequent European and American culture and architecture vacillated.

## Civilizations in the New World

Like Europe before and after the interlude of the Greek and Roman experiment, the New World continued to develop civilizations based on the more common world pattern of chiefdoms or monarchies, of specialized priesthoods, and of the individual giving way to the shared. We will find a number of civilizations rising and falling, each adapting the ancient ideas to its particular geographical region. The remainder of this chapter will examine these Native American civilizations in turn, introducing at the same time the regions of North America which provide the backdrop to all subsequent architectural production on the continent.

## Mesoamerica

Although Central America strictly speaking is beyond the geographical scope of this book, it is worth discussing one more stage in its cultural and architectural development, the city and civilization of Teotihuacán. This city is important to our story for several reasons. It was the largest and most significant city in the Americas in its day, it refined and codified many of the social and architectural trends that we have so far examined, and it probably prodded its neighbors in North and Central America into higher levels of civilization.

About the time the Athenians defeated the Persians at Marathon, in the fifth century BC, the Olmec civilization waned. In its place rose first the Zapotecs in the Mexican highlands, and, after 150 BC, the Teotihuacáns near present day Mexico City. This period saw dramatic population increases, and a migration from small villages into the burgeoning city centers. By AD 100, the city of Teotihuacán had grown to well over 60,000 people, or 80 per cent of its region's entire population. By AD 650, at the height of its influence, it might have housed as many as 200,000 people. London at the same time was a tenth as large.

Teotihuacán continued and refined the Olmec architectural ideas. Much like the ancient Roman colonial towns with which this New World city was contemporary, Teotihuacán was planned orthogonally and divided roughly into quadrants by crossing central axes [21]. The city aligned with an extinct volcano 15 degrees east of north, whose springs provided a major source of water. For three miles along the north-south axis ran a broad avenue, now known as the 'Street of the Dead', gently stepping up terraces towards this natural object of veneration. To the east of the central avenue stood a flat-topped pyramid 210 feet high and 650 feet square at its base, terraced in four stages, and capped with a temple of wood and thatch. Stone facing slabs covered over a million cubic yards of earth. The priests devoted this pyramid to the sun god, and, with its 15 degrees north of west orientation, it aligned exactly with the setting sun on the June 21 zenith. A pyramid half the size and probably dedicated to the moon goddess stood at the north end of the avenue.

More than 20 other temple complexes, a marketplace, and possibly a palace, also lined the avenue, while residential neighborhoods spread out on the same orthogonal grid. This concern for geometrical order extended into the city's suburbs as well: after AD 100, the peasants living in the countryside around the city were resettled into

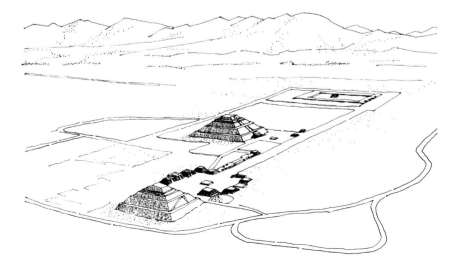

21 Teotihuacán, Mexico,
100 BC–eighth century AD

planned villages designed according to standardized layouts. Deeply embedded in the very layout of this city, then, we find a fusion of the natural and human domains. Its design acknowledges the important natural phenomena of water, sun and the monthly cycles that marked the seasons, while at the same time it expresses human control through geometry.

We must be content to note, before leaving this region for good, that Teotihuacán gave a number of these cultural and architectural ideas to their Mayan neighbors to the east, probably through trade and possibly through political domination. The Mayan civilization rose around AD 300, and fell into decline after AD 800, just after Teotihuacán itself finally collapsed. Subsequent civilization in Mesoamerica culminated in the Aztecs, who lasted less than 150 years before they were defeated by the invading Spanish in 1520. Their main city of Tenochtitlán, later taken over and renamed Mexico City by the Spanish, followed ideas similar to those in Teotihuacán. A grand and orthogonally arranged ceremonial plaza, marked by several large pyramid temples, stood in the center of residential neighborhoods comprised of flat-topped courtyard houses.

### The Southwest

These Mexican ideas about agriculture, complex social organizations and architecture gradually spread northward into what is the present day southwestern United States. Vast lakes and coniferous forests once covered the area of Utah, Nevada, Arizona and New Mexico. At the beginning of the Holocene era the lakes dried up, leaving only the Great Salt Lake in Utah and an arid desert region covered in scrubs, low piñon pines and, further south, cactus. Archaic groups struggled hard to find sustenance in this region, adding to their hunting and gathering a small supplement of maize acquired from Mexico.

Around 300 BC, Mexican immigrants moved into what is now southern Arizona and established a village at Snaketown. In one stroke they introduced the twin ideas of agriculture as the main source of sustenance and the village life that goes with it. Known as the Hohokam culture, they built extensive irrigation systems in the arid landscape for their maize, beans and squash, and continued to hunt and gather wild foods in the archaic fashion. Reviving the Siberian architectural precedent, they built shallow pit houses with sloping walls and flat roofs, constructed of wooden poles and grass. The well-insulated pit houses helpfully moderated the extreme daily temperature swings in this region. Around AD 550, further Mesoamerican contact encouraged the Hohokams to build those symbols of Mexican urbanity, platform mounds and courts for a sacred ball-game.

The Hohokam ideas spread to their neighbors, eventually spurring the Anasazi living to the northeast to develop the most urban culture and architecture in the Southwest before European contact. Originally hunter/gatherers, the Anasazi lived in the four corners region where the boundaries of present day Colorado, Utah, New Mexico and Arizona intersect. Deep, precipitous canyons score this high and semi-arid plateau, in some places to a depth of 600 feet. The later Spanish explorers called the distinctive flat-topped land forms *mesas*, or tables. Countless open-faced caves in the canyon walls provided temporary homes for early stone age hunters, and later for the Anasazi.

The Anasazi experimented with agriculture two millennia ago, around the birth of Jesus. After AD 450, they made it their primary means of sustenance. Now with significant fields to tend, they settled in permanent villages on the mesa tops and in

25 Taos Pueblo, Taos,
New Mexico, sixteenth
century and later

the Anasazi had no wheeled vehicles, to integrate the wider community they constructed a system of roads 30 feet wide radiating out from Chaco Canyon into the
hinterlands. Running dead straight on accurately surveyed lines – sometimes right
over cliffs accessible only by carved handholds – and then suddenly bending to take
a new straight course, they reached for 65 miles to the outlying villages. This echoes
the Roman road system, although on a much smaller scale.

After AD 1130, serious difficulties apparently confronted the Anasazi. A fifty-
year drought threatened their agricultural base at the same time as the population
increased. Furthermore, the trade route with Mexico might have moved elsewhere,
and warlike nomads – perhaps the ancestors of the Utes and Paiutes – might have
threatened the villages. For whatever reasons, the Chacoan system collapsed around
AD 1150 and the great pueblos there were abandoned. Further north, in what is now
the Mesa Verde National Park in southern Colorado, the Anasazi began building
their masonry pueblos within the protective open-faced caves of the canyon walls
[23]. Tall towers stood next to the underground kivas, perhaps to let lookouts warn
the men within of approaching danger. The largest cliff dwellings contained almost
200 rooms stacked up to four stories, while many smaller settlements holding one or
two families dotted the region's canyon walls. Altogether, 500 to 1000 cliff dwellings
housed 7000 people in this area at its peak in the mid-thirteenth century. By the
end of the century, these pueblos were also abandoned. The Anasazi moved south
and southeast to become, most probably, the ancestors of the Native Americans still
living in the region. The Navajo hogans [24] show the influence of the ancient pit
houses, while the pueblos like the one still inhabited at Taos, New Mexico [25],
clearly reflect the Anasazi's urban heritage.

### Woodland civilizations

Seven hundred years after the demise of the nascent civilization at Poverty Point,
more complex civilizations rose again in the regions surrounding the Mississippi,
Missouri and Ohio river valleys. Just as the Olmec influence was drawing to a close
in Mexico, around 500 BC, villagers of the Adena culture in the central Ohio valley
revived the Poverty Point mound building tradition. Some kind of societal ranking

system had clearly emerged. Under the direction of some loose central authority, the Adenas periodically gathered from scattered villages in order to bury noted individuals in elaborate ceremonies. They built a mortuary house at the base of the mound, sometimes burned it down with the body inside, and then mounded earth over it. Three to five hundred mounds have been found; the largest, at Grave Creek Mound in West Virginia, rose 70 feet high and spread 240 feet in diameter.

The Adenas also built large earthen sculptures. Some works formed large enclosures shaped as circles, squares or pentagons, which probably served as settings for ritual ceremonies. Burial mounds often stood inside and outside these sacred enclosures. The largest and most remarkable Adena earthwork formed a giant serpent 1254 feet long and 4 to 5 feet high [26]. As with the earlier earthwork tradition at Poverty Point, these designs are apparent only from above, and must have been directed to the celestial spirits who were presumed to control natural events. The Adenas probably lived in houses similar to those at the Koster settlement 5000 years before. Wattle and daub, or perhaps sheets of tree bark, covered a wooden frame [27].

Around 100 BC, the Adena culture transformed into the Hopewell culture, possibly through an influx of outsiders. They lived in villages of no more than several hundred, in frame and cover houses like the Adenas. The Hopewellians continued mound building on a larger scale. A complex of circles, a square and an octagon near present day Newark, Ohio, covered four square miles [28]. The Hopewell beliefs spread throughout a wide region, bringing together disparate cultures to form a pan-American religion from Missouri to West Virginia and from Minnesota to Mississippi. Perhaps on the basis of this shared religion the Hopewellians formed an extensive trade network ranging from Yellowstone Park, 1500 miles to the west, to

**26** Serpent Mound, Locust Grove, Ohio, 900–1200, Adena Culture

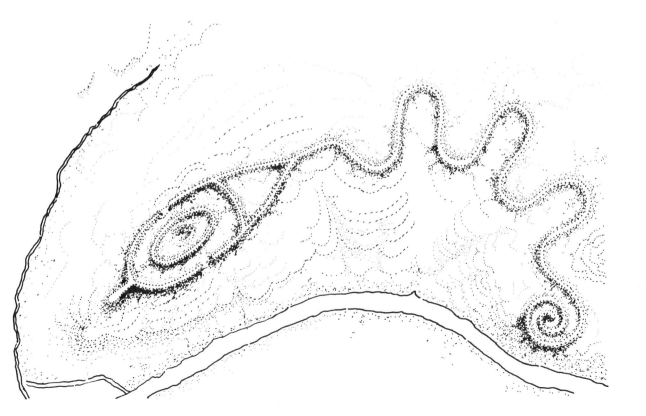

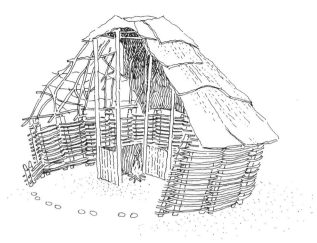

**27** Adena Culture house,
900–1200

Florida, 1000 miles to the south. Hopewellian burial mounds have been found near Kansas City, in the northeastern plains of the Dakotas and in southern Manitoba. The entire culture finally collapsed around AD 400, perhaps because of climate changes, uncontrolled population growth, increased warfare, or a disruption of their redistribution system.

The eighth century AD witnessed significant changes in the American social, political and architectural scenery. The Teotihuacán and Mayan civilizations were in decline, and the Anasazi had begun to develop their new pueblo forms and the more complex social arrangements that went with them. In the same period, the most complex and extensive Native North American civilization of all emerged in the valleys of the Mississippi and its tributaries. Known, appropriately, as the Mississippian culture, these people built on the traditions of the Hopewellians, perhaps borrowed some ideas from the Mexicans, and eventually shaped the social and architectural

**28** Newark Earthworks,
Newark, Ohio, 300 BC–AD 700,
Hopewell Culture

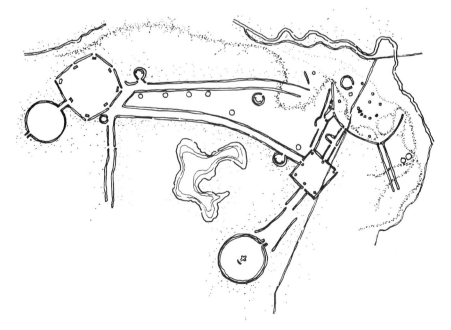

landscape of North America from the Great Plains to the eastern seaboard. It was the Mississippian civilization and its derivatives that the Europeans first encountered when they entered North America in the sixteenth century.

The new civilization depended more thoroughly on agriculture. The Mississippians grew maize, squash and later beans, in the river flood plains, and they dedicated their religious system mainly to ensuring good crops. A sun god served as the chief source of religious devotion, just as in ancient Egypt and in the civilizations of Mesoamerica. Increased food supplies, we now know as a common pattern, led to population growth; and population growth demanded more complex social arrangements. A strong social hierarchy emerged. A central chief with absolute powers controlled regional chiefs, who in turn managed their local scattered villages and farmsteads. Through this system, Mississippian control eventually spread from Georgia to Oklahoma, and from the Gulf of Mexico to Wisconsin. Throughout the region, a rigid social hierarchy ranked everyone in a number of levels from aristocracy down to commoner, although prowess in warfare could elevate one's position. The Mississippian civilization consequently suffered from endemic warfare.

Just as in the Mesoamerican civilizations, central chiefs and their entourages took up residence in a central town. Cahokia, near present day East St Louis, Illinois, became the capital of the new empire [29]. It stood at the strategically important confluence of the Mississippi, Missouri and Illinois rivers, and controlled the entire inland river network. At its peak around AD 1100, Cahokia possibly housed 40,000 people in six square miles. And just as in the Mesoamerican civilizations, a large rectangular platform pyramid served as the religious and administrative focus not only for the settlement, but for the entire culture. Now known as Monks Mound, it was the largest of all North American earthworks. The pyramid stepped up four asymmetrical terraces to 100 feet, about the height of an eight- or nine-story building, while its greatest length at the base measured three and a third American football fields, or a thousand feet. A temple or a royal residence capped the pyramid. This structure, probably a traditional Woodland timber frame with a wattle and daub infill, may have stood 50 feet tall and extended 100 feet in its longest direction. As many as 120 smaller pyramids were grouped around six major plazas in the town. A stout wooden palisade guarded the central pyramid and ceremonial district, while another defended the town's northern perimeter. Large pyramids also stood at the centers of the regional towns, serving a similar purpose for the regional chiefs. Like

29 Cahokia, near East St Louis, Illinois, c. 1150

the Cahokian temple, Mississippian houses continued the Woodland tradition of frame-and-infill, and might have been roofed with thatch [30, *upper left*].

The Mississippian civilization had reached levels of social complexity and political control almost comparable to those of the Olmecs and Teotihuacáns. It conceivably could have evolved into an even greater empire like that of the Aztecs or Incas. But it was not to be. Perhaps for the same reasons that ruined the earlier Hopewell culture – warfare, climatological changes, loss of control over the redistribution system – Cahokia itself eventually declined in influence after AD 1250, and the entire system disappeared by AD 1500. Lest anyone doubt its significance at the time, however, it is worth remembering that Cahokia as a major political and cultural power lasted at least twice as long than the entire life, so far, of the United States.

Mississippian ideas carried on in subsequent Native American cultures and architecture throughout the East and Midwest. The Natchez of the lower Mississippi river continued the culture most completely. When the French encountered them in the seventeenth century, they were still organized socially and politically according to the Mississippian traditions, and they were still building mounds. Elsewhere, the influences diminished according to distance and time. Many continued the pottery and art traditions, others retained vestiges of the social structure, almost all retained and elaborated the Woodland architectural ideas.

Many tribes throughout the Woodland region developed variations on the prehistoric idea of the tent. Many of them had to move their villages periodically, either because they still took advantage of seasonal food supplies, or because they simply used

*clockwise from left]* **30** Woodlands house construction, Seminole chickee, Iroquois longhouse village, Winnebago wigwam

up the resources surrounding the existing village. Wattle and daub was obviously too brittle and heavy to move, so they developed various portable coverings for their frames. An assemblage of mats woven from bulrushes and cattails provided one of the most effective coverings. These were light, easily rolled up, weatherproof, and woven in such a way as to trap insulating dead air. Long sheets of bark stripped off the tree trunks were also used, although these were heavier and less flexible. Grass was often bundled together and tied to the frame, much like thatch.

The shape and arrangement of the frame itself varied from area to area. Throughout the South, and down into the Florida peninsula, tribes like the Seminoles had to moderate the oppressively humid climate. Within the usual frame they constructed a flat platform raised off the ground, allowing cooling breezes to circulate all around the inhabitants. These were known as chickees [30, *upper right*]. A number of other tribes, including the Winnebagos living near present day Chicago, constructed a dome-shaped frame, known as a wigwam [30, *lower left*]. Like the ancient Roman domes, they created this form by erecting a number of arched frames around a circular plan. Further north, tribes living in the colder climate of northern New England and the subarctic belt of Canada built a conical frame also known as the wigwam. The conical form offered more resistance to fierce winds in this area, since it employed the most structurally stable form of all, the triangle.

The Iroquois in present New York State, and the Huron in the Great Lakes area, developed an impressive version of the frame and cover idea, known as the longhouse [30, *lower right*]. The Iroquois were matriarchal, reflecting the importance of agriculture and the women's responsibility for it, and they lived in groups of families related through the female line. To accommodate the extended family under one roof, they simply stretched the usual wooden frame to whatever required length. Some of the largest houses approached 200 feet. A fourteenth-century longhouse at Howlett Hill, near present day Syracuse, New York, was 334 feet long, more than the length of an American football field. Since the Iroquois men continued the Mississippian preoccupation with warfare by raiding neighboring tribes, they prudently surrounded their villages of longhouses with defensive wooden palisades. In time, the Iroquois developed a confederacy of tribes in the northeast region so skilled in warfare that it remained a significant military force until the late eighteenth century.

**Civilizations on the Great Plains**

Thanks to Hollywood, the most familiar Native American cultures and architectural forms are those of the Great Plains. At their height in the eighteenth and nineteenth centuries, these were the cultures of war-bonneted, consummate horse-riders following the bison, and living in mobile villages of brightly painted tipis.

The Plains certainly provided a landscape worthy of these swashbuckling nomads. Covering over three-quarters of a million miles between the Mississippi and the Rockies, this semi-arid and largely treeless prairie stretches as far as the eye can see in all directions. Long grass covers the eastern part, but as the Plains gradually climb in altitude to the west, the flora changes to short grass and desert scrub. Only an occasional wooded river bottom or a rock outcropping provides some visual relief. The early white pioneers who traversed this landscape through the winter blizzards and the sweltering summers ominously referred to it as the Great American Desert. Despite its forbidding appearance, however, the prairie supported extensive game and wild foodstuffs. Most spectacular of all were the vast bison herds who may

31 Bird's eye view of Mandan
village, 1800 miles above St Louis,
1837–39, George Catlin

have numbered over fifty million at their peak, before they were almost exterminated by white hunters in the nineteenth century. Until the Spanish reintroduced the
horse to the American continents in the seventeenth century, the early Plains
dwellers had to hunt the bison on foot. They followed the herds, and then devised
rock fences on the top of nearby cliffs through which they could funnel the bison to
their deaths. Like their Clovis ancestors, these big game hunters probably lived in
portable tents.

After 250 BC, the groups roaming the eastern edge of the prairie acquired cultural and agricultural ideas from their Woodland neighbors. Hopewellian burial
mounds, we have already seen, have been discovered along the eastern plains from
Manitoba to Kansas City. The eastern Plains groups also began to cultivate crops and
settle in semi-permanent villages. Around AD 900, village farmers migrated out of
the eastern woodlands – perhaps to escape Mississippian control – and also settled
on the eastern edge of the prairie from the Dakotas to Texas. Later they expanded
deeper into the prairie, up the Missouri River. They grew maize in various river
bottoms, and built multi-family lodges on the bluffs.

These eastern Plains villagers, including the Pawnee, the Arikara and the
Mandans, built versions of the prehistoric Siberian subterranean pit house [31]. A stout
structure of wood, at first rectangular, later circular, supported a heavy covering of

32 Crow camp on the Little
Bighorn River, Montana

earth and sod. This thick blanket of natural insulation moderated the intense summer sun and the windy, bitterly cold winters. The largest were 90 feet in diameter. Typically, the earthlodges were grouped around a central circular plaza and defended by natural bluffs or palisades. A Mandan village near present day Bismarck, North Dakota, contained 130 houses. The house shapes, and their arrangements in the village, often conformed to important cultural, religious and even astronomical symbolism. The dome of the roof stood as a metaphor for the dome of the sky; the circle stood for a shared community in which every voice was heard. Like many other early cultures, they took special interest in celestial movements and patterns. In the Bighorn Mountains in Wyoming, Plains dwellers laid out a series of lines and stone markers forming a circle 70 feet in diameter, and aligned with important stars and solar solstices.

The arrival of the horse in the seventeenth century, and the arrival of the rifle from white traders a century later, transformed the Plains cultures. Horses and guns so improved their hunting successes that they could rely on the bison entirely for their sustenance. A number of groups, including the Dakota Sioux and the Cheyenne, abandoned their farms and villages altogether. Some like the Arikara abandoned the matrilineal tradition of the farmers and returned to the patrilineal tradition of the hunters.

Back in the ancient tradition of big game hunting again, they had to follow the herds and live in portable shelters. The horse's ability to carry heavy loads, however, allowed them to develop houses more elaborate than their ancestors could ever have imagined. Perhaps combining the prehistoric Siberian mammoth skin tent with the northeastern conical wigwam (brought to the Plains by the Cree around 1600), they designed the most familiar of all Native American structures, the tipi [32]. This was an elegant and functional structure. A lightweight frame of lodgepoles lashed together at the top provided a strong triangulated armature. Around this wrapped a windproof and waterproof skin of sewn bison hides both lightweight and durable. Inside, furs draped from the frame trapped insulating dead air and retained the heat of a central fire. The top of the cone shape stood off center from the base in order to brace the short side of the cone against the prevailing wind, while windflaps could be adjusted to draw the fire whichever direction the wind blew. The tipis were as snug in the cold winters as the massive earthlodges. In the summer, the skin could be lifted up to admit cooling summer breezes. When it was time to move, the entire assembly could be dismantled in minutes and packed on a travois, a triangular frame dragged behind a horse. Tipis were usually arranged in a large circle when the temporary village formed up, again reflecting the values of an egalitarian society and the circle by which this was symbolized.

### Civilizations along the Pacific coast

The final civilizations that we will explore arose along the Pacific coast, from California through Oregon and Washington to Canada (the geographical scope of this book precludes discussing the equally interesting Eskimo culture even further north). These Pacific coast civilizations developed without aid of significant agriculture, because they enjoyed remarkable natural resources on the coast and along the rivers that could support dense populations. With secure food supplies close at hand, the populations grew and settled in villages.

The unusually wide variety of ecological zones in California supported an equally wide variety of Native American cultures and architectural forms. The northern end of the state shares in the rainy, temperate climate of Oregon, but as one proceeds further south the land becomes dryer and hotter. The latitude of present day Los Angeles is about level with Damascus in the Middle East; arid deserts like the Mojave and Death Valley adjoin Nevada, Arizona and Mexico. The coastlines enjoy mainly balmy weather, while the inland valley running down the center of the state wilts under intense sun. And in contrast to the tropical palm trees in southern California, giant sequoia redwood trees grow in the alpine ecology of the east central Sierra Nevada mountains. A myriad of architectural forms were adapted to these regions, although most of them we have already seen in a similar form elsewhere: earth-roofed pit houses, Woodland frame-and-infill structures covered in grass, conical wigwams covered in redwood bark, and so on.

More interesting for our architectural story are the cultures in the Pacific Northwest. These emerged around AD 1, and had matured by AD 1000. The settlers in this region inhabited one of the most spectacular natural settings in North America. A coastal range of mountains climbs out of the sea along present day British Columbia, Washington and Oregon, forcing ocean storms to dump over 80 inches of rainfall a year onto numerous islands and a dense mainland rainforest. This is one of the wettest regions in the world. Cedar, spruce and hemlock trees, among others, still grow to considerable heights. Plentiful food supplies, including salmon in the rivers, and sea mammals and fish in the ocean, supported a dense population in relative ease. Surpluses were easily acquired. They could fish intensively during certain periods, and then store supplies to last the entire year. The resulting leisure time meant they were able to devote creative energy to matters beyond simple survival, including the development of elaborate ceremonies, art and architecture.

Surpluses, as we have now seen a number of times before, also led to ranking in society. A chief took responsibility for storing and then redistributing food to the population, and then personally accumulated privileges and wealth for his trouble. According to their own ranking in society, other families inherited land use rights, certain roles, and names and crests by which they might be readily identified. The redistribution system, so important to archaic cultures living with more marginal resources, largely transformed into a symbolic ceremony for the wealthy Northwest

groups. Known as potlatches, these ceremonies involved families and even entire tribes competing with each other to give away enormous quantities of gifts. Those who received the bounty, in turn, gave it away at the next potlatch.

Their villages and houses supported and expressed these cultural ideas. Several hundred people lived in the largest villages, sometimes spread over several acres and defended with palisades or natural landforms against attack by other tribes. The

33 Haida House, Queen Charlotte Islands, Canada

house forms varied along the coast; some tribes housed each extended family in a separate dwelling, others housed the entire tribe in one structure. Captain Cook, on landing near present day Seattle in 1792, discovered 600 people living in a single building a fifth of a mile long. The northwestern tribes invested their houses with great symbolic meaning. Many gave their houses proper names, as if they were living things. Aristocratic families living in single houses proudly broadcast their social standing by painting their crest along the entire front façade. Social rank in the longhouses was indicated by proximity to the center, where the chief and his entourage lived. In some settlements, ornately carved totem poles stood either in front of or attached to the houses. These told a story through monsters and animals of the world's mythical origins, or noted the life of a great deceased chief. Potlatch ceremonies usually took place in front of the houses, or within large central spaces in houses of high prestige.

The houses were constructed on the same principle of the frame and cover that we have observed elsewhere [33]. Posts were driven or buried at intervals into the ground, to support horizontal beams spanning across the space. With huge trees readily available, however, this system took on gigantic proportions. Columns were sometimes five feet thick and twenty feet high, while a single beam log might span over sixty feet. The usual coverings we have seen in other Native American constructions, like mats, bark, bundled grass, or wattle and daub, would not have survived the relentless rainfall in this region. The Northwest builders substituted instead great planks of wood, usually cedar, split from living or fallen trees. These planks were unimaginably large by today's standards, sometimes approaching four feet wide, three inches thick and over 40 feet long. The rain also influenced the roof shapes and material. Flat mud roofs like those of the Anasazi would have leaked uncontrollably. The Northwest builders sloped their roofs to help shed water, sometimes as a gable with a high central ridge beam sloping to two sides, sometimes as a mono or shed pitch sloping to one side only. Cedar planks on the roof overlapped like shingles. Although many of the houses were simply lashed together, the Haida culture in Canada developed sophisticated joinery systems commonly found in Europe or Japan, like the mortise and tenon.

These Northwest houses look so much like European or Japanese forms and methods of construction that some have doubted whether they were entirely indigenously developed. The Northwestern art and architecture, the argument has gone, owe a great deal to the metal tools and fasteners, later even sawn boards, that the Native Americans acquired through trade with the Europeans and European-Americans. Although the damp climate has rotted away most archeological evidence that could establish an origin much before European contact, recent digs in Canada have discovered traces of rectangular houses and plank construction possibly 5000 years old. It is not difficult to see how the ancient system of frame and cover, together with the availability of large trees and the challenges of intense rainfall, could have naturally evolved into these remarkable wooden structures.

These, then, were the accomplishments of the European and Native American civilizations on the eve of their confrontation in the late fifteenth century. Facing the same cataclysmic changes in world climate at the beginning of the Holocene era, and yet separated from each other entirely after their initial common culture, they independently invented all of the essential components of civilization from agriculture to complex political systems. They also independently invented the same architectural types and constructions systems, from temples and marketplaces to tenoned structural frames and gabled roof forms. One can view these parallel cultural developments either as astonishing coincidences, or as evidence of some universal human characteristics. Given a similar wiring in the human brain, and given similar problems to solve as humans everywhere adapted to the new conditions, similar social and cultural institutions were bound to emerge. Nor should it surprise us that the New and Old Worlds developed related architectural forms. Given similar human activities in need of shelter and support, given a similar palette of natural building materials, and given the universal properties of water, thermal movement and gravity in the physical world, designers everywhere were more likely than not to develop similar architectural ideas. It was mainly the Greek experiment with the concept of the individual that eventually led the two worlds down different cultural and architectural paths. In the next chapter we will see how these differences led to violent clashes – and ultimately to the overthrow of the Native American civilizations – when the Europeans entered the American continents.

# 2

# CULTURES TRANSFORMED AND TRANSPLANTED

## 1500–1650

WHEN the Europeans invaded the American continents at the end of the fifteenth century, they were also struggling with a momentous upheaval in their own civilization. We have already seen how, after the millennium, the Europeans began to fuse their Christian outlook with tentative revivals of the ancient

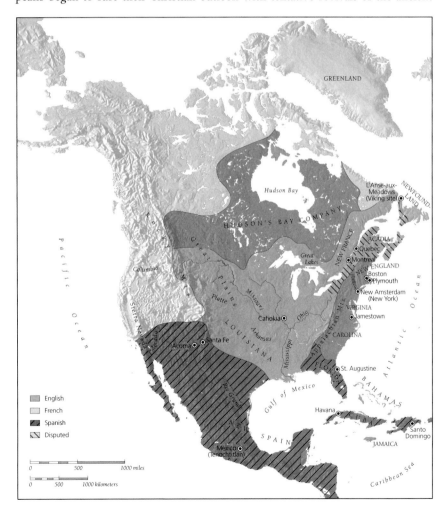

34 European powers in North and Central America, *c.* 1682

Greek and Roman concepts. In the fifteenth century the Italian humanists explicitly rejected this casual accommodation of the ancient and the medieval, insisting instead on a complete and untainted return to the ancient ideas. They conceived of their cultural revolution as a Renaissance, a rebirth of ancient civilization, after the dark shadow of the medieval world. By the end of the fifteenth century, the Italians had revived many of the components of the ancient world view, including the concept of the individual, the importance of realistic art and natural science, and the principles and images of the Classical language of architecture. Around the same time as the Spanish conquistadors plundered their way through Central and North America, Leonardo da Vinci and Raphael were painting realistic images to rival those of the ancient world, Copernicus was rethinking the conception of the universe, and Brunelleschi and Alberti had designed the first buildings in over a thousand years to use the Classical language of architecture undistorted by medieval preoccupations. These revolutionary ideas eventually marked the end of the medieval world and the beginning of our modern age.

However, this transformation did not occur overnight. Europeans further from the Italian center of the Renaissance initially remained committed to their medieval views and architectural traditions. Even as the broader Renaissance spirit began to sweep across northern and western Europe in the sixteenth century, many builders in each country still preferred their locally adapted medieval traditions to what they saw as an inappropriate and foreign Italian style. When the Renaissance spirit finally proved irresistible, they began to apply freely interpreted Classical detailing to their usual medieval forms, in effect creating hybrids of the two traditions. Only in the last half of the sixteenth and the first half of the seventeenth century did most European countries begin to abandon their medieval ideas in favor of a purer Classical expression.

Most of the American colonies were founded in the sixteenth and early seventeenth centuries, exactly in the transitional period between the medieval and the Renaissance. The main colonizing countries of Spain, France, The Netherlands and England were struggling to integrate or reconcile their traditional medieval ideas with the newer Italian notions just as they were establishing beachheads in the new land. As one might expect, these cultural and architectural struggles eventually spilled over into the colonies. However, the first Europeans in America lagged behind their home country brethren in this transition. The first settlers fought to survive in a lonely and sometimes hostile land, and so they built as quickly as possible those architectural ideas with which they were most familiar. Since they were not professional architects or builders, they were not particularly aware of – or interested in – the new stylistic fashions sweeping up from Italy. They built what still comprised the vast bulk of architecture in the colonizing countries, the medieval. Interestingly, then, the medieval ideas and traditions enjoyed one last flowering in America just as they were beginning to die away in Europe. Only later, after the colonists had established a more comfortable standard of living, did they begin to import the hybrid styles. The full blown Classical language did not gain entry into the colonies until the very end of the seventeenth century, well over half a century after its complete acceptance in the northern European countries.

The history of architecture in the first American colonies is therefore a story of European cultures transforming from the medieval to the Renaissance world view, and then transplanting their evolving cultural and architectural ideas into their colonies. This chapter will examine the transitional period itself, when the northern European countries were still experimenting with combinations of the medieval and the Classical, and when the first ideas carried over to the New World consisted first of the medieval and then of the hybrids. The next chapter will take up the story when northern Europe and then the American colonies fully embraced the Renaissance outlook and its accompanying Classical language of architecture.

## The Renaissance in Europe

### The new outlook

Although the ancient Greek and Roman ideas had slowly re-emerged in European culture from the millennium onwards, the Italian humanists in the fifteenth century shifted this revival into higher gear by explicitly rejecting the lingering medieval outlook and embracing the Classical ideals and attitudes in their purest forms. They fully reinstated the cornerstone of the ancient outlook, the concept of the autonomous individual, and insisted again on thinking and reasoning for oneself independently of outside authorities like the Church or inherited traditions. From this followed a number of new developments. First, it helped spur a protest movement within the Church itself, which eventually led to the Protestants splitting away from the Roman Catholic Church in the first decades of the sixteenth century. Reformation is too gentle a term to describe the religious and social upheaval brought about by this schism in the long dominant authority of Europe. The Protestants and Catholics fought bitterly until the middle of the seventeenth century, encouraging many of the first migrations to the Americas.

Second, the renewed emphasis on individuals thinking and experiencing for themselves led to an intensified interest in the appearance and structure of physical nature, where the medieval outlook had long concentrated on the divine. Art returned fully to capturing sensory images as accurately as possible, while the natural sciences blossomed in this period as thinkers like Galileo, Copernicus and Kepler attempted to uncover nature's underlying structure. Many architects, we will see below, also tried to base their forms on what they believed were the underlying principles of nature rather than on the essence of the divine.

Third, the new emphasis on the individual developed into a cult of personal genius. Many Renaissance thinkers and artists claimed that they possessed special gifts and insights, possibly given to them by God, which allowed them to sense, think and create more completely than others less gifted. Unlike their counterparts in the Middle Ages, many Renaissance artists and architects boasted of their abilities, and sought personal fame for their accomplishments. Some like Michelangelo even experienced spiritual anguish as they vainly struggled to fulfill their personal potential. At various times in later centuries this blossomed into a cult of artistic innovation and personal expression unique to the European and American cultures.

The feudal system of land use and control also faded away during the Renaissance. The revival of a monetary economy allowed the nobility to buy the services of armed men, rather than having to rely on the old feudal system of interdependent obligations. The nobility began to turn their landholdings into cash by enclosing the common lands, and by renting or selling parcels to individuals. The process, although gradual, provoked a number of violent but ultimately unsuccessful revolts by the peasants who could not afford to buy the fields they had tilled for generations, but who were now denied access to the old common land. Here we have the new

Western conception of the land as an economic commodity to be bought and sold. This was one of the Western ideas most foreign to the Native Americans when the two cultures met, because the latter still conceived of the land as something collectively shared and managed for the good of all present and future generations. This new idea of individual land ownership also eventually contributed to more visual variety and even clutter in the future cities and suburbs of Europe and America, when many individuals owning small pieces of land built according to their own fancies and without regard to their neighbors.

The Italian aristocracy invented a new idea in this period which subtly worked to change Western architecture from the Renaissance onwards. To regain what they believed were the higher standards of civilization in the ancient world, they established a code of gentility. The new values stressed refinement in all manners of speech, posture, clothing and behavior. Coarseness was to be avoided at all costs, since civility, urbanity and gentility were the marks of true gentlemen and ladies. Appearances understandably counted for everything in an aristocratic culture that, by this time, had largely lost its original medieval function. With nothing of substance to occupy oneself while lounging idly at court, it was essential to be seen embracing the correct fashions and manners, and equally important to see how these were embraced by others in one's social circle.

At first, the code of gentility helped popularize the Classical language of architecture, because that ancient language expressed the highest standards of civilization with which the aristocracy wished to be associated. As we will see in the next chapter, it also began to change the layout of houses in order to provide settings more suitable for the display of one's gentility. And perhaps most significantly of all, the concept of gentility eventually encouraged a rapid pace of stylistic change in post-Renaissance Western societies. At first this seems like a paradox. The code of gentility stresses the adherence to clearly defined rules of behavior and taste and discourages personal expression outside the rules, and so would seem to exert a stabilizing influence on taste. However, the code of gentility was also used as a means of exclusion. Those who knew and used the rules were accepted into a particular social circle, while those who did not were excluded. The inherent snobbishness of the system encouraged tastemakers to change the rules regularly, because if the rules were too static, eventually everyone would learn them and the social distinctions could not be maintained. In this system, the greater the popularity of a given architectural style, the greater was the compulsion for the tastemakers to find a new and therefore exclusive style. The code of gentility, together with the new Western emphasis on personal creativity and innovation, helped encourage a rapid cycle of stylistic stability and change from this point on.

In the Renaissance rose the middle class, standing between the aristocracy and the peasantry, and comprised of successful merchants, lawyers and the lower orders of the old feudal system. Eventually we will witness the emergence of a distinctive middle-class taste and outlook, but not yet. For the next several centuries, the middle classes mainly deferred to aristocratic taste, attempting to recreate for themselves as much of the aristocratic lifestyle as they could afford on their more meager means. Many bought land, and mimicked on a reduced scale the architectural fashions of the great aristocratic houses. They also acquired from their social mentors the code of gentility and the changes in social behavior and house design which accompanied it. In this way, high architectural fashions designed for the aristocracy began to percolate down into the vast bulk of more modest houses that, for centuries, had simply followed vernacular traditions.

### The return of Classicism

Along with the revival of classical attitudes and philosophies came a wholesale revival of the Classical language of architecture. The Italians had long lived in the midst of Roman ruins, and were generally aware of this other architectural tradition. Once the Renaissance thinkers urged a complete return to the glories of the ancient world, it was only a matter of time before the Italian architects abandoned Gothic and medieval forms altogether in favor of the ancients' architectural language. No one had accurately spoken this language for over a thousand years, of course, and so the Renaissance architects needed to reconstruct its grammar and vocabulary. For this they turned to careful measurements of Roman ruins, and to a close study of the only architecture book to survive from antiquity, Vitruvius' *The Ten Books on Architecture*. Filippo Brunelleschi's Pazzi Chapel in Santa Croce, Florence [35] demonstrates how clearly the Renaissance architects shifted from the medieval to the Classical. The horizontals are stressed over the verticals, bringing the viewer's eye away from the heavens and firmly back to the earth. Compared to the nervously compressed elements of the Gothic, the Pazzi Chapel leaves plenty of room around each element and consequently exudes an aura of calm and repose. It revived as accurately as possible the specific elements of the Roman language, including bilateral symmetries, the semi-circular arch, a triangular pediment over the door and a version of the Corinthian Order. All of the details are subservient to the geometrical order of the building.

Given the general Renaissance desire to reject traditions and to see and think for oneself, how did the Renaissance architects justify throwing out one architectural tradition only to replace it with another? According to Leon Battista Alberti, good architecture captures an underlying, timeless beauty in nature. Unfortunately, the long medieval night blunted the ability of contemporary artists and architects to see these ideal beauties for themselves. Until they regain this sensibility and learn to design properly for themselves, they will have to copy the Roman architectural

35 Pazzi Chapel, Santa Croce,
Florence, Italy, 1440–61,
Filippo Brunelleschi

forms which already perfectly embody the timeless essences. Although ingenious, this reconciliation still left the Renaissance pulling in two architectural directions. The new emphasis on personal creativity would not tolerate working out variations on the inventions of others, while the emphasis on the timeless beauties in ancient work would not allow architects to stray very far from the architectural norms for fear of losing their embodied inner beauties. Alberti's idea both reflected and further encouraged the rapid cycle of stylistic stability and change discussed earlier.

The Renaissance theorists developed another troublesome polarity still embedded in Western cultures today. They acquired from Vitruvius a distinction between theory, which is the knowledge of the principles behind an art, and practice, which is the actual production of the art. From this they developed a concept of the architect as a scholar. The architect studies the Classical language, seeks the underlying essences in nature, and invents new forms based on his learning. Mere builders then follow his instructions to construct the building itself. This entirely overthrew the medieval conception of the master builder who both designed and built, whose theory informed construction as equally as his construction informed his theory. The Renaissance conception increasingly divorced the architect from the technical realities of construction, and divorced the builder from thoughtful design. From the Renaissance on, we have an image of the architect as a professional gentleman and artist, and an image of the builder as a working-class technician.

### Mannerism, the hybrids and the return to order

In the first decades of the sixteenth century, just as Renaissance Classicism was poised to sweep out of Italy over the rest of Europe, the language began to distort. Perhaps because of the religious and spiritual upheavals of the Reformation, or perhaps because the next generation of architects was simply looking for new expressions, the calm harmonies of the Renaissance architects transformed into something more frantic. Michelangelo's Laurentian Library stairway in Florence reveals the new mood [36]. Compared to the calm, horizontal repose of the Pazzi Chapel of the previous generation, Michelangelo crammed his elements nervously together, leaving no room for them to breathe. The bottom of the stairway almost crashes into the opposite wall, while the paired columns subvert the structural logic of the Classical columns by implying that one alone cannot carry the full load. We now call this style Mannerism, denoting an agitated, highly personal, and inventively mannered use of the shared Classical language.

It was this mannered version of Classicism that first made its way into northern and western Europe after mid-century, and in some cases eventually to America. Mannerism's visual density and complexity appealed to artists and architects outside Italy who had long appreciated similar visual qualities in the Gothic tradition. They did not see an entirely new system of design, but rather a new set of stylistic elements with which they could freshen up their existing medieval traditions. In the colonizing countries of Spain, France, the Low Countries and England, designers acquired a taste for what they called the 'new fashion' of mannered Classical elements freely piled up and applied as surface decoration to traditional medieval forms. They typically encrusted every surface of these hybrid designs with attached columns, pediments, scrolls, cartouches and writhing straps seemingly cut out of leather. Several influential books of the period, including ones by Hans Vredeman de Vries and Wendel Dietterlin, spread these mannered ideas throughout Europe. We will see in the following sections how each of the colonizing countries developed its own variation on the theme.

36 Laurentian Library, Florence,
Italy, 1524, Michelangelo

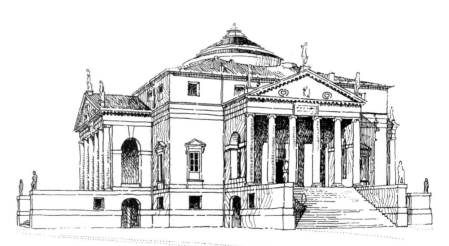

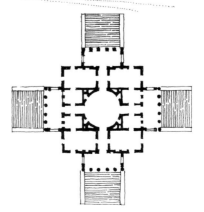

37 Villa Rotonda, Vicenza, Italy,
finished 1569, Andrea Palladio

Just as the rest of Europe began to embrace and elaborate the mannered versions of Classicism, the Italians regained their composure and returned to stressing the language's underlying logic, simplicity and order. In the 1540s, the Catholic Church fought back against the Protestant Reformation with a militant Counter-Reformation of their own, demanding faithful adherence to the principles and practice of the Catholic Orthodoxy. In the same way, after 1550 a number of Italian theorists and architects including Sebastiano Serlio, Giacomo da Vignola and Andrea Palladio attempted to establish what they claimed were the objective rules of the Classical language. Unlike Alberti, who had offered the Classical Orders as convenient shortcuts for discovering universal beauties, and unlike Michelangelo, who freely distorted the Classical elements and syntax for visual effect, this new generation wished to establish the Orders as an absolute and final regulation from which one could not deviate. From this point on, the Orders acquired an air of authority bordering on that of the Scriptures. Palladio's own design for the Villa Rotonda at Vicenza summed up the renewed interest in Classicism as an orderly system, with its resolute symmetries, its rational juxtapositions of a circle, cruciform and square, and its elements like windows generously spaced in plain surfaces [37]. In later centuries in a number of countries, this building was held up as the archetypal example of Classicism in its purest and most rational form. How this influenced Europe and then America will have to wait until the next chapter, because the designers outside Italy lagged well behind the cultural leaders of this age.

## The colonization of the Americas

When Christopher Columbus landed on a Caribbean island in 1492, he was searching for a western sea route to Oriental spices. The Europeans were not immediately seeking new land for its own sake, and for two more centuries, explorers continued in vain to seek a water passage to the Pacific through this annoying land barrier. However, when Columbus reported finding gold on one of his trips, the Europeans soon rushed to exploit the unexpected new resource.

Although up to the Renaissance the Native Americans and the Europeans had developed many ideas in common, at the time of the invasion their paths had clearly diverted. The Europeans had developed a higher level of technology, including alphabetic languages, wheeled vehicles, deep ocean-going ships, extensive iron technology and guns. European art and science now focused on the sensory world rather than on divinities. Architecture in Europe periodically came to be seen as a matter of personal expression, rather than as the result of gradually evolving traditions. On the demise of feudalism, Europe now regarded land as a commodity owned by individuals, not as a shared resource. And after the religious upheavals of the Reformation and Counter-Reformation, the Europeans had acquired an evangelical desire to convert others to their own beliefs. Therefore, when the Europeans first landed on American soil, they dismissed as barbaric the Native American cultures and architectural traditions they found. We might regret now that the two did not seek some accommodation, acquiring the best of what each had to offer. But it was not to be. The first Europeans arriving on the shores of America made it perfectly clear that their civilization would become the new order.

At first Portugal and Spain convinced the Pope to divide between the two of them all lands in the New World. For a time, these two countries took advantage of their favored position without interference from their European rivals. However, as conflicts mounted among European states during the Reformation and Counter-Reformation, other countries like France, England, Holland, Germany and Sweden saw no reason to obey the Pope's edict. The political and religious rivalries in Europe during one of its most tumultuous periods eventually spilled over to America. Countries actively sought to thwart each other's efforts at exploiting the new land, each conspiring to seize as much territory as possible in the name of its own king or queen.

Different countries tried different strategies. Some, like Spain, sent small groups of adventurers, priests, and colonial administrators to manage the native populations and to extract natural resources. Others, like England and Holland, sent permanent settlers to farmstead and to build communities. In North America, the latter strategy proved the most successful, and the British employed this strategy most successfully of all. By 1700, the British population in North America numbered about a quarter of a million, the French 20,000, and the Spanish north of the Rio Grande could be counted in the hundreds. The British eventually controlled North America by sheer weight of numbers. Although the British architectural traditions therefore came to dominate the ensuing development of the continent, each of the earlier rivals contributed interesting architectural ideas during its sojourn in the new land. In the following sections we will examine each one in turn.

### Spain and its colonies

The Spanish in the sixteenth century ascended to their highest level of political power in Europe either before or since. Through various deaths, births and marriages, the Spanish Habsburg dynasty took control of Spain, the Low Countries, Austria, Burgundy, Bohemia, Hungary, and the various dukedoms of northern and southern Italy. Charles V, and later his son Philip II, believed that God had given the Habsburgs control of this vast land in order to keep the peace and to defend their subjects from all enemies. For the staunchly Catholic Spanish, enemies meant not only economic rivals like France and England, but also the heretic Protestants throughout Europe.

The Spanish began to blend their traditional medieval forms with mannered Renaissance motifs after the beginning of the sixteenth century, as we see here in the University at Alcalá de Henares [38]. If we look closely, we see familiar Classical elements like the columns, the triangular pediments over doors and windows, and a classical balustrade along the cornice. But they are used without regard for the language's underlying logic. The columns are coupled, the entablatures are broken and the window details break into the horizontal bandings. More in the spirit of the Gothic, the pilasters on either side of the taller central pavilion stack up to stress the vertical, while the horizontal entablatures are virtually suppressed. Although most Spanish builders and architects continued to use either medieval or hybrid ideas through most of this period, around the middle of the century the court architects began to employ the Classical language correctly. Charles's Palace in Granada, and his son Philip's Escorial near Madrid, followed the language's clear geometrical order and used the correct syntax for combining accurately revived details [39]. The sheer scale and ruthlessly blank façades of the Escorial rivaled the palaces of the ancient world for expressing the political power and wealth contained within.

Christopher Columbus sailed on behalf of the Spanish crown, and his discovery of gold lured other Spanish adventurers to the New World in search of fortune for themselves and the Spanish king. At first they overran the West Indies, killing or enslaving the Native Americans they found there. When the native slaves died digging for gold, the Spanish continued the work with black African slaves they bought from the Portuguese. Here began the importation of slaves that later profoundly and tragically shaped American social and economic life.

On the mainland of Central America itself, Hernán Cortés led a small band of 1500 conquistadors in a two-year military campaign against the Aztecs. At first, the hugely outnumbered Spaniards made little headway against the crack Aztec troops, despite the former's superior European military technology of horses, metal armor and swords. Then an infected Spanish soldier brought smallpox from Cuba to the Mexican coast. The Aztecs had no immunity to this disease. Once the defenders were decimated, their capital city of Tenochtitlán fell in 1521. Other European diseases, measles and typhus, soon joined smallpox to sweep through South and Central America, killing off an estimated 39 million Native Americans in less than 50 years, or 90 per cent of the pre-European population.

The Spaniards then turned to the North. Ponce de León and Pánfilo de Narváez explored the coasts of Florida and what are now the Gulf of Mexico states. Hernando de Soto then raided his way through the farms and towns of the Mississippian chiefdoms, in futile quest of a great inland city like Tenochtitlán. In 1541–42, Francisco de Coronado led an army from Mexico through the Southwest as far as Kansas, in search of seven legendary cities of gold. He found only the relatively poor pueblo towns in New Mexico. The slim pickings discouraged further expeditions, but these first adventures established Spain's claim to the southern parts of the present day United States.

Colonization eventually replaced expeditionary plunder. The Spanish established a colonial government headed by the king and administered locally by viceroys and bureaucrats. Into what was now called New Spain they imported a version of the medieval European feudal system. The king gave a relatively few Spaniards silver mines or huge tracts of land for ranches and farms (*haciendas*), together with rights to large numbers of Native Americans who were bound to work at token wages. In

**38** University, Alcalá de Henares, Spain, 1537–53, Rodrigo Gil de Hontañón

**39** Escorial Palace, near Madrid, Spain, 1562–82, Juan Bautista de Toledo and Juan de Herrera

return, the new mine owners and landowners paid substantial taxes to the Spanish crown. Vast sums poured into Spain, further fueling the Habsburgs' continuing political and religious wars in Europe.

As part of his defense of Catholicism, Charles V established the Roman Church in the colony, and sent armies of priests to convert the Native Americans. The king and the priests saw an opportunity in America to establish a unified Catholic domain untainted by the Reformation. The Church in New Spain consequently worked to convert the Native Americans peacefully, and to protect them from the worst excesses of economic exploitation. To help assimilate the Native Americans into the imposed culture, many Spanish priests learned the Native Americans' languages, studied their cultures, and attempted to explain the virtues of Catholicism in familiar terms. They established missions to provide settled communities where local native groups could learn Christianity for their souls, and farming techniques for their physical sustenance. The Spanish also built forts, or *presidios*, to defend against the hostile groups who resisted the missionaries. They vigorously destroyed all physical evidence of earlier 'heathen' religions or cultures wherever possible.

The Spanish decided to resettle the mostly rural Native American population into towns, where they could be controlled more effectively. Although their first settlements in the Antilles grew haphazardly in the medieval fashion, when the Spanish settled the mainland of Mexico they decided to impose an orderly pattern. A systematic approach to town planning would encourage rapid and orderly resettlement, and it would remind the native population of the political authority to which they now had to submit. The Spanish planners looked for ideas in the medieval new towns based on orthogonal geometry, in the Renaissance theories of rational town planning, and in the rational layouts of the great Mexican cities they had overrun. In 1573 they issued the 'Laws of the Indies' to codify earlier practices and to provide minute guidance in selecting sites and planning towns. The new Mexican settlements were to be laid out on a grid with a plaza in the center, much in the spirit of the ceremonial plaza at Tenochtitlán. The plaza would have *portales*, or arcades, around its perimeter for the convenience of the merchants who would set up shop there in the traditional Spanish fashion. The church and other public buildings were to stand within or close to the plaza. For the new Mexico City, they laid out the new plaza directly over the ceremonial plaza of Tenochtitlán itself, taking over the old palace and constructing a cathedral on top of one of the pyramids. In one stroke they obliterated the old way of life and appropriated its traditional symbols of authority for the new government.

The Native Americans were strictly segregated from the Spanish, in separate towns or in separate residential districts. The Native Americans continued to live in courtyard houses or single room houses arranged around courtyards, constructed in wattle and daub, adobe, or sometimes stone. For their own accommodations and for the public buildings, the Spanish naturally attempted to re-create the architectural traditions of their European homeland. They, too, constructed courtyard houses, a familiar and ancient Mediterranean type quite appropriate for the similar hot climate in the new land. The first religious buildings followed the medieval model of the Catholic monastery, with a longitudinal church focused on an altar at one end, a walled courtyard, and simple accommodations for the friars [40]. Since the buildings were laid out by Spanish clerics who were not professional architects, and were constructed with native labor unfamiliar with the European traditions, they necessarily had to be simplified. The usual basilica idea often reduced to a long box without aisles, sometimes roofed over with a flat timber roof, other times with a Romanesque barrel vault, and occasionally

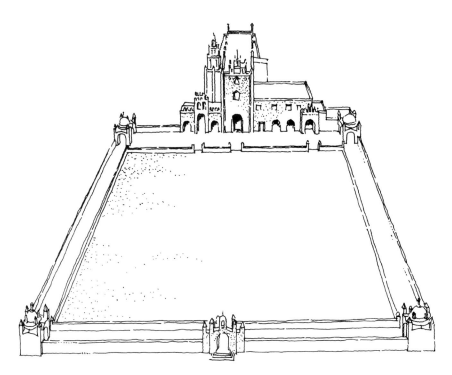

40 Church and atrio complex,
Atlatláuhcan, Mexico, 1570s

with a few Gothic rib vaults. The missionaries used the exterior courtyard, or *atrio*, as a ceremonial space in which large groups of former Aztecs could gather and watch the Catholic mass performed in front of a small attached chapel. This unorthodox idea had no precedent in the Catholic tradition, and was astutely invented in the New World to provide an easier transition to Christianity for the Native Americans who were used to observing religious ceremonies in front of outdoor temples.

After the middle of the sixteenth century, as the Counter-Reformation gained strength back in Europe, a more orthodox hierarchy of Church officials took charge of Mexican religious affairs, and banned these informal building arrangements in favor of more traditional church designs. New churches and cathedrals were built in the main cities, designed more like contemporary European models. Some were styled with the hybrid fusion of medieval and Classical still popular in Spain, while eventually Classical ideas made their way to the Mexican colony. At this point the geographical scope of this book unfortunately prevents further discussion of developments south of the Rio Grande. It was important to understand the origins and development of the early Spanish ideas at the center of its new American colony, because the subsequent story of Spanish settlement further north is largely a story of outposts at the frontier attempting to emulate patterns and styles back in the Mexican centers of culture.

North America lay at the fringes of the Spanish American colony through most of the sixteenth century. In 1565 the Spanish government established the first permanent European settlement in North America at Fort Augustine, in Florida; and by the end of the century it had established missions throughout Arizona and New Mexico. Isolated missions, presidios and haciendas remained the only forms of Spanish settlement in North America during this period. Away from the centers of Spanish civilization, and without benefit of Spanish architects or builders, the local friars and soldiers had to improvise the construction of the new missions as best they could.

CULTURES TRANSFORMED
AND TRANSPLANTED

41 Palace of the Governors,
Santa Fe, New Mexico, 1610–14

More than their brethren further south, the Spanish at the northern outposts fused their traditional conceptions of architecture with those they found in the local Native American settlements. There are several possible reasons for this sensitivity to local conditions. First, by accident of geography, the Spanish missionaries happened to encounter in Arizona and New Mexico the pueblo cultures that already possessed sophisticated building skills and a strong tradition of urban settlement. The missions could be constructed with Native American labor and ideas, using materials locally available and employing construction techniques familiar to the work crews. Second, the Spanish in the outposts were few in number and usually single men who may have felt less need for familiar domestic surroundings. Third, the priests possibly wanted to make the new way of life as familiar and as palatable as possible so as to encourage peaceful conversions.

We can see the beginnings of what we now commonly call a Southwestern style in the Palace of the Governors, Santa Fe, New Mexico [41]. The surviving building formed one side of a fortified enclosure 800 feet long by 400 feet wide. The walls were constructed of sun-dried adobe bricks cast in Spanish molds. Although the Native Americans had not previously used molds, they were of course familiar with adobe and with load-bearing wall construction. For centuries the pueblo dwellers had either plastered the outsides of stone masonry walls with adobe, or had laid up wet bricks of adobe and then smoothed the surface with an outer coat. Both the pueblo dwellers and the Spanish understood the insulating advantages of heavy masonry walls in hot climates. In the tradition of the Anasazi and their descendants, the roof of the Palace was formed by laying beams (called *vigas* by the Spanish) across the tops of the walls. The ends of the *vigas* projected beyond the wall surface to ensure that they would not pull free from the wall; a short parapet completed the wall and further anchored the *vigas*. Layers of smaller poles and brush covered with earth completed the flat roof.

Although the colonnaded porches (*portales*) had no precedent in southwestern Native American traditions, they were an ancient and familiar component of much Mediterranean and southern European architecture. In the hot Mediterranean climate, the covered walkway protected numerous outdoor activities from the sun. This architectural form now served the same useful purpose in the southwestern deserts. From the Moors the Spanish acquired what has become another characteristic piece of

42 Mission of Acoma
and San Estevan, Acoma,
New Mexico, *c.* 1629–42

the Southwestern style, the carved brackets (*zapatas*) that served as capitals between the columns and the beams.

   This fusion of Native American and Spanish ideas also shows in the mission architecture. In the mission at Acoma, New Mexico, a church dedicated to San Estevan stands beside a cloistered monastery in the usual fashion of medieval European monastic structures [42]. The church form itself follows the normal Catholic tradition of a long nave with an altar at the end. Like Romanesque and Gothic cathedrals, towers stand on either side of the main door to lift the eye heavenwards. As in the Palace of the Governors, however, this European form is constructed in the *viga* and adobe system. Like many masonry structures throughout the world, the walls are thicker at the base than at the top, giving an appearance of a slope or taper. Known as a battered wall, this taper sensibly provides a wide foundation at the base, which carries all of the weight of the wall above, and a thinner top to ease the weight on the wall below.

   These rudimentary structures on the outposts of the Spanish colony were necessarily basic in form and fairly crude in execution. Later, in the eighteenth century, as the Spanish settlements in North America grew larger and more prosperous, the buildings acquired more sophisticated construction systems and more elaborate decorative detailing based on Spanish fashions in Europe. Yet as we will see in later chapters, this initial fusion of Spanish and Native American architectural ideas laid the foundations for a Southwestern style that reappeared time and again in America's architectural history.

### France and its colonies

Early in the sixteenth century, Francis I consolidated power in what is roughly present day France, and established an absolutist state with a strong army. The new French kingdom provided the only effective counterbalance to Spain, thereby ensuring clashes throughout the century. Francis was also a patron of the arts. His enthusiasm for Italian Renaissance fashions led to invitations to Italian architects to work in France. And under the influence of the Italians, French Gothic buildings constructed in this period began to acquire Classical detailing.

   Francis's own Château de Chambord shows the new style [43]. The plan itself is medieval in origin, with a square keep (fortified castle) flanked by defensive round

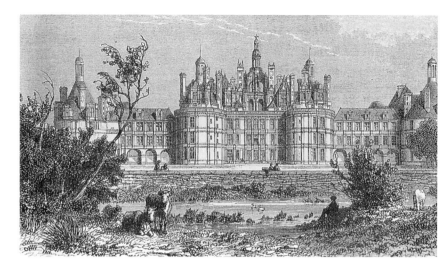

43 Château de Chambord,
Chambord, France, c. 1519–50,
Domenico da Cortona

towers at the center of the composition. A lower range of buildings encircles the keep and a central courtyard, and is itself finished at the corners by great round towers. Large unprotected windows on the outside of this defensive form, however, betray the reality that these forms were no longer needed to defend against attacks and sieges. The castle form had become mainly a symbolic reminder of the monarch's power and authority. The fantastic roofscape, with its steep roof pitches and vertically attenuated dormers, turrets and chimneys, shows the continuing French preoccupation with northern European medieval forms. A prominent roof remained a favorite French device even when more thoroughly Classical ideas were embraced. Only when we look closely at the building do we see the triangular pediments, the Ionic pilasters and the entablatures of Classicism. Although Classicism triumphed completely in France in the next century, these half-Gothic, half-Classical châteaux inspired a number of American mansions in the late nineteenth and early twentieth centuries.

The French explored the Atlantic coast of North America in the first half of the sixteenth century, but a failed settlement on the St Lawrence River in 1541, and a protracted civil war back home, discouraged further French interest in the area until the beginning of the seventeenth century. Samuel de Champlain finally founded Quebec in 1608, establishing a French claim to what is now Canada. Although the French crown wanted to solidify the claim with settlers, a number of factors worked against many French moving to America. The climate in Canada was fierce and the soil poor, so farming proved difficult. The French colonial government imposed restrictive feudal rules, and had to submit to tight control from France. Also, only those French who were religiously and politically orthodox were allowed to emigrate. In the end, relatively few French bothered. A few missionaries attempted to convert the local Native Americans to Catholicism, while fur traders traveled down the Mississippi River valley to barter European goods for valuable skins like beaver. Most of these French befriended the locals, lived in their villages, and sometimes intermarried.

The French sporadically constructed permanent fur trading posts along the Mississippi from Canada to the Gulf of Mexico, establishing a French claim to the entire interior of North America. Drawing their building materials from the surrounding forests, they constructed half-timber buildings of closely spaced vertical wooden members, filling the spaces between with grass and clay or stones and clay. At first, they set the members in the ground like fenceposts, but probably problems

with rot encouraged them to modify this method and set the timbers on a masonry foundation capped with a wooden sill. The French typically wrapped these frames with stucco or clapboards to provide more weather protection. The earliest French buildings continued the northern European medieval tradition of steep roofs, which still made sense for the harsh and wet climates into which the French transplanted the idea. Probably in response to the greater humidity they found in the New World, however, they developed the idea of a *galerie*, or surrounding colonnade. Like the Spanish *portales*, this intermediate space between inside and outside conveniently provided an outdoor room cooled by breezes yet protected from rain and sun. The French trader's house now known as Cahokia Courthouse shows the system, although this particular building dates from the next century [44]. In the next chapter, we will see how the large roof and the surrounding *galerie* shaped the French plantation houses when the French began settling the southern end of the Mississippi River in the next century.

44 Cahokia Courthouse, Cahokia, Illinois, 1737

### The Netherlands and its colonies

Spain, we have seen earlier, controlled the Low Countries as part of its greater European empire during the first part of the sixteenth century. At mid-century, the higher nobility in The Netherlands formed a league under William of Orange to protect their traditional privileges. While the southern provinces remained Catholic and affirmed their allegiance to the Spanish king, the northern provinces embraced Protestant Calvinism, fought a successful war of independence, and established the Republic of the United Netherlands in 1609. The Dutch Republic rapidly rose to a position of considerable economic power in Europe. Thanks to a number of factors, including its central location on the trade routes of northern Europe, its fleets of newly developed and more efficient freighter ships, and the astute business sense of its mercantile classes, Amsterdam eventually became the financial and trade center of Western Europe in the seventeenth century. As the first independent country dominated by the merchant classes, and as the first country fully committed to Protestantism, it also became the center of experiments to find new artistic and architectural expressions for the new views. A number of their ideas spread to England and America.

To understand the Dutch experiments, we must first note how the Catholics had reacted architecturally to the Reformation and Counter-Reformation. After the initial expression of angst and stress that we saw in Mannerism, the Catholic Church fought back with renewed vigor and a plan to seduce the faithful and the wavering with sumptuous buildings and extravagant public spaces that proclaimed the glory of God. The new idea first shows in St Peter's in Rome, which had undergone numerous design changes and modifications by some of Italy's greatest architects from the beginning of the sixteenth century onwards. By 1630, the Pope possessed a grand church with a Mannerist core and exuberant decorations like Bernini's baldacchino [45]. Complex spatial arrangements obscure the underlying geometry of the building, while cleverly hidden windows mysteriously bounce light off rich, gilded surfaces. The viewer is encouraged to respond to this building more emotionally than intellectually, sensing the presence of great forces which cannot be fully understood. St Peter's still uses the rational, Classical language of form, but it speaks a florid, emotion-filled dialect. This is the beginning of a Baroque style that, as we will see in the next chapter, was carried to even greater extremes in the latter half of the seventeenth century.

The Protestants could not abide these theatrical trickeries. Their new religious views led to a rejection of ostentatious decoration, and eventually to a new form of church architecture altogether. The Protestants opposed the Catholic notion that the priesthood stands as intermediary between God and individual. God speaks directly to individuals through his written Word, the Bible. Since no priesthood should reinterpret or misinterpret this vital message, all individuals must study and understand God's word for themselves. In this sense, the laity is the priesthood. However, to help individuals think more carefully about the Bible, a lay preacher or pastor in most Protestant sects offers sermons on Biblical passages and themes. So in contrast to the Catholic Church, where individuals passively observe rituals performed by the priesthood, the Protestant Church urges individuals actively to participate in the discussion of the Bible led by the preacher.

A new church form emerged to accommodate this new religious conception. The long, linear nave of the Catholic church was abandoned in favor of a more centralized auditorium space, where everyone could gather around the preacher to hear his sermon. The pulpit, with a sounding board overhead to help carry the preacher's voice to all corners of the church, replaced the altar as the focus of the congregation. Like auditoria or theaters, second-floor galleries sometimes provided additional seating close to the pulpit. The Nieuwe Kerk, in Haarlem, shows the new arrangement without galleries [46]. Protestant churches around the world developed numerous variations on this theme, but the basic philosophical intention always remained the same.

Unlike the opulent Baroque Catholic churches, the new Protestant buildings were often severely plain. The severity stems partly from a rejection of Catholicism's preoccupation with worldly riches, partly from a desire to reduce religion to its bare essentials, and partly from religious doctrine. Protestantism stressed the weak and sinful nature of humankind. Individuals, according to Lutheranism and Calvinism, cannot even achieve grace through their own actions. Only God can determine who will be saved, and this decision is already made at birth before the individual has a chance to demonstrate virtue or sinfulness. Yet even though personal actions have no influence on the eventual outcome, individuals must show their respect to God for his grace and mercy. Furthermore, in a number of sects, only those predestined for salvation may join the Church or help govern its affairs. Since the outward sign of salvation is an inner peace and a lack of selfishness or greed, the Protestants

45  St Peter's, Rome, Italy,
1506–1626, Bramante, Raphael,
Sangallo, Michelangelo,
Maderno *et al.*

46  The Nieuwe Kerk, Haarlem,
The Netherlands, 1645–49

therefore attempted to lead a life of exemplary decorum, unstained by sinful behavior, excessive playfulness, or ostentatious displays of wealth. To help their weaker brethren, they implemented numerous laws prohibiting disrespectful activities like card-playing, drinking and even theater-going. This dour attitude naturally carried over to their building designs.

The Dutch had long lived in towns with medieval street patterns. Their new republican form of government, run without a strong central authority, did not encourage them to impose rational grids on further development. Indeed, the priority of the individual in the Dutch world view shows in their tendency to turn the gables of their houses towards the street front, separately identifying each house in the row. Each gained further distinction through its particular decorative scheme on the gable end. Favorite treatments included steps, and alternating convex and concave curves capped with a small triangular pediment. The Dutch roofs were still steeply pitched in the normal northern European medieval tradition. With limited access to wood or stone, the Dutch preferred to build their structures in brick.

As Holland's economic power grew, it also sought a foothold in the New World. In 1609, a year after Champlain founded Quebec for the French, Henry Hudson discovered the river later named after himself and claimed the region for the Dutch. They built New Amsterdam at the mouth of the river beginning in 1624, and then other trading posts on the Delaware and Connecticut Rivers. The Dutch, like the French, saw the New World mainly as a source of raw materials like fur, fish, timber and crops. They welcomed settlers, but like the French they did not offer attractive conditions for mass migration. A feudal system of patroonships gave large tracts of land to landlords, who then allowed tenant farmers to work the land. Tenant farmers in the Old World apparently found little inducement to trade continents for the same economic arrangement, and the Dutch settlements grew slowly. Eventually, the relatively sparse Dutch settlers could not resist the encroaching British. In 1664 the Dutch peacefully surrendered all of New Netherland to the British, and New Amsterdam became New York.

The Netherlanders transplanted their architectural traditions to their short-lived colony. Although the planners of New Amsterdam originally laid out a gridiron plan for the town, the settlers let the town grow of its own accord, following the contours of the land. The houses turned their stepped gable ends towards the street, just as in Amsterdam [47]. For these town houses the settlers continued to build in the normal Dutch tradition of brick, even though plentiful supplies of timber were now available. In rural areas, however, they substituted stone for brick. Many of the rural Dutch settlers had emigrated from Flanders, a region of present day Belgium and northern France where rural houses were typically built in stone, and so they probably brought this tradition with them. The rural Dutch settlers also occasionally tried building in the favored English tradition of half timbered frames covered in shingles or clapboards, particularly in areas close to British settlements.

By the middle of the eighteenth century, rural Dutch houses had acquired their most distinctive feature of all, roofs with gambrel shapes, flared eaves, or both [48]. The gambrel shape provided more inhabitable space in the attic, and while the English experimented with a similar roof shape about this time, the idea became popularly identified with the Dutch colonial in the nineteenth- and twentieth-century revivals of the style. The flared eaves may have derived from a tradition in Flanders or France of kicking out the roof to protect an easily damaged plastered wall below, although the same protection is not required on a masonry or wooden building. The flare did provide a convenient covering for the porches which increasingly appeared on

Dutch colonial houses. Like the Spanish *portale* and the French *galerie*, this offered a sheltered outdoor space part way between the private realm of the house inside and the public realm of the world outside. The porch in all of its stylistic manifestations increasingly entered into the American architectural legacy.

### England and its colonies

England was the last to emerge as an economic and political power in sixteenth-century Europe. Isolated by the English Channel, the English had lived at the fringes of continental European civilization from the Roman period on. After the French Normans successfully invaded the old Anglo-Saxon kingdom in 1066, and brought with them French manners and customs that eventually fused with the homegrown ones, no other foreign force ever successfully invaded again. In their isolation behind their natural defense, the English developed ideas and institutions that diverged from continental notions as much as they paralleled them. Throughout the rest of this history, we will see how the British often followed their own independent course in matters cultural and architectural.

The British emerged from a hundred years of unsettling change towards the end of the fifteenth century, when the Italian Renaissance was well under way. They had struggled through the Black Death, a slow collapse of the feudal system, an economic depression, a hundred-year war with France, and disputes over the crown. Their fortunes then rose under the secure leadership of the Tudors, first Henry VII and then his son Henry VIII. At the height of the Reformation, the younger Henry rejected the control of the Catholic Church and established his own independent Church of England. Protestant in name yet practically indistinguishable in its liturgy from the Catholicism it replaced, the Anglican Church happily continued to use traditional Catholic church designs and needed no new building type like that which the Dutch had developed.

Towards the end of the sixteenth century, in the reign of Henry's daughter Elizabeth I, English society and architecture began to change even more fundamentally under the influence of the encroaching Renaissance ideas. The middle class rose in power and prestige. As feudalism waned, the common lands throughout the country were largely enclosed and transferred into individual ownership. Classical details began to appear on English medieval architectural forms. In Robert Smythson's design for Wollaton Hall, for example, we find a building whose massing is still based on

**47** Stadt Huys (City Hall), New Amsterdam (New York), New York, 1641–42

**48** House, Hackensack, New Jersey, 1732

49 Wollaton Hall, Nottinghamshire, England, 1580–85, Robert Smythson

medieval ideas, in this case a castle with a central hall and defensive corner towers [49]. But like the French châteaux, the large windows belie the defensive image and reveal the castle form as merely a symbol of power. And like the French buildings, the outside of this medieval idea is now decorated with Classical details like paired pilasters, niches, and entablatures.

Grand Elizabethan houses like this stand at the end of a dying medieval world, and at the beginning of a full-blown Classical revival in the seventeenth century. Historians in the nineteenth and twentieth centuries who valued Classicism as an ideal perfection therefore saw these buildings as imperfect gropings towards a later, more correct expression. More sympathetically, we might say that their designers found a new language of form through which they could reinterpret their long-standing medieval traditions. Smythson's contemporary Shakespeare did no less when he told stories meaningful to his English audiences through the fresh device of Julius Caesar's life, yet we do not think of Shakespeare as imperfectly groping towards Cicero.

Half-timbered construction for more modest houses carried on through the Elizabethan age. Towards the last quarter of the sixteenth century, however, extensive foresting for houses and ships without provision for replanting had begun to thin out the once endless English forests. The price of wood rose to match the cost of brick and stone. Builders of smaller houses jumped at the chance to construct in masonry, because it offered both more durability and a closer affinity to the great masonry houses of the aristocracy. By the end of the century, masonry became the dominant means of construction for most buildings in England. In the same period, the use of fireplaces to funnel smoke from internal fires passed down from the great houses into the vernacular. The characteristic image of small English village houses constructed in masonry and displaying prominent chimneys began to emerge in this period.

Although the Englishman John Cabot explored the coast of North America in 1497, the English made no further efforts to exploit the new continent for most of the next century. In the last quarter of the sixteenth century, first Humphrey Gilbert, and later his half-brother Sir Walter Raleigh, convinced Queen Elizabeth to grant charters for English colonies in North America. They argued that colonists could use the local natives to exploit the raw materials (just like the Spanish strategy), and that they could conveniently raid Spanish shipping from a North American base. After Gilbert's two colonizing efforts failed, Raleigh added to his arguments the idea that they might try to build a more permanent settlement with larger numbers of English emigrants. He founded a town on Roanoke Island in 1585, but when a supply ship returned in 1590 the colonists had mysteriously disappeared. All that remained was the name Raleigh had given to the region: Virginia, in honor of Elizabeth the Virgin Queen.

The next serious effort to found a colony eventually established the settlement pattern for much of the southeastern United States. In 1606, a number of English gentlemen, merchants and nobles formed the Virginia Company, a private joint-stock company, to finance two colonies in North America. They offered to pay for the passage of settlers who would work for seven years for the company, after which the settlers would be free to make their own fortunes. King James I granted one charter to the London investors to settle the area of present day Virginia, and another charter to the Plymouth investors to settle the area of present day New England. The Plymouth settlement lasted only one winter. The Virginia group, however, successfully founded Jamestown in 1607.

At first, the English investors hoped that their Jamestown settlers would find either gold or a passage to the Orient or both; when both quests proved futile, they decided to build a more mundane crop economy. They settled on tobacco, a native plant that the Native Americans had introduced to the Spanish, who in turn had popularized smoking in Europe. Tobacco proved to be enduringly lucrative. To entice more settlers, the Virginia Company agreed to give land away for free, in return for a small cash rent each year in perpetuity. A few wealthy investors thus acquired huge tracts of land. They employed tenant farmers to work the land in their name, trading the cost of passage for seven years servitude. This re-created a version of the European feudal system of land ownership, where numbers of farmers were bound to work one man's large landholding. At first, the tenant farmers were Englishmen who were free to leave or to acquire their own landholdings at the end of their indentured period; towards the end of the seventeenth century, though, the land-holders turned increasingly to using black slaves for their labor.

Here is the beginning of the plantation system of the American South, and the culture that goes with it. Like the manor house in medieval Europe, the plantation owner's house became the center of a small community of farm buildings and housing for the workers. The plantation settlements in Virginia were largely self-sufficient and substituted for towns. Towns were not needed in this system. Plantation owners simply exported their crop on one ship, and received new supplies on another. The extensive tide-waters and river inlets even allowed the ships to sail right up to docks near each plantation, thus avoiding the need for the usual intermediary port around which towns typically grow. Without towns, the plantation houses eventually became the centers of social life for the landowners, and the principal means of expressing their wealth and status.

The great plantation houses, however, were still in the future. The first Virginians had to concentrate their energies and resources on establishing the farming system, clearing the land and building the infrastructure of farm buildings. For their first houses they constructed traditional, medieval, English half-timbered wooden dwellings. The eastern woodlands obviously provided a ready source of this building material, so the imported tradition and local circumstance went hand in hand. Perhaps as many as a third or a half of the Virginian population continued to live in simple wooden houses for the remainder of the seventeenth century. Unfortunately, nothing other than the foundations remains today of these early Virginian houses, due to the damp climate's tendency to rot wood.

The American houses were organized like their counterparts in England. At the time of the first American settlements, English houses had evolved out of medieval roots into a new generic form. In the early medieval period, the houses of the English aristocracy centered on the large hall. Here the family and the retainers ate, entertained, and often slept. The long side of the hall was always oriented to the front of the house, so that one entered the hall from the long side at one end [50, a]. A screen of columns or a low partition – the 'screens passage' – typically formed a vestibule at the end of the hall, providing a transitional space between the entry and the hall, and often a support for a minstrel's gallery above. Later in the evolution of the house, an increasing number of rooms was added to this nucleus. Private chambers for the family, private chambers for guests, cooking and storage areas all clustered around the hall in various configurations.

Smaller English houses also centered on the hall, and provided at least some rudimentary form of a screens passage. The smallest houses possessed this one room only. Bedrooms, kitchen, living room and dining room were all rolled into one. At the next level of complexity, a parlor joined the hall. The parlor provided an additional room for the entertainment of visitors, although it might also contain a bed in a two-room house. The parlor was added onto the hall in two different configurations. The first arrangement placed the parlor on the other side of the screens passage, with fireplaces for each room at the ends of the building [50, b]. This in effect created two rooms divided by a corridor. The other arrangement placed the fireplaces in the center of the house, essentially filling up the screens passage with a massive masonry core [50, c]. As the house grew larger, ancillary rooms were grouped around either of these cores in various arrangements. At the next level of complexity beyond a two-room house, a second floor typically contained two bedchambers aligned with the two rooms below.

The early Virginians built mainly one-, two- and four-room houses. They favored the parlor-passage-hall arrangement, perhaps because they emigrated from a part of England that used this type, or perhaps because it worked well with the humid climate. With doors or windows thrown open at either end of the passage, cooling breezes could waft through the center of the house. Southern houses used this plan type well into the nineteenth century.

Those who could afford it soon aspired to construct more substantial houses that expressed their status as the lords of the manor in the new land. They naturally emulated the image of small manor houses in England, with brick construction, steep roofs and prominent chimneys. The Adam Thoroughgood House, in Princess Anne County, is probably the oldest surviving example [51]. Adam Thoroughgood himself was one of the first examples of the self-made man so valued in the American outlook. He arrived in Virginia as an indentured servant. Only a year after completing his service he was elected to the local representative assembly, and he began to build his personal estate that eventually amounted to over 5000 acres. He expressed his new status with a house that was practically indistinguishable from many small houses in England at the time. This is a version of the parlor-passage-hall house, with the passage merged into the hall and partly filled with a staircase to the second floor opposite the door. The chimneys exposed at the ends of the building conveniently provide an opportunity for some shape-making that gives the house an expressive medieval character.

The charter of the Virginia Company required the colonists to establish the Church of England as their official religion. Soon after the colonists arrived, they

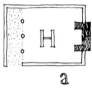

a

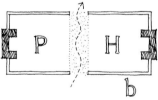

b

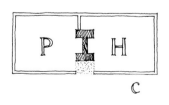

c

50 Evolution of the English house plan. H=Hall, P=Parlor. a, Hall with screens passage; b, Hall and parlor with central passage; c, Hall and parlor with central chimney

built wooden shelters for church services. By the end of the seventeenth century, they had constructed over fifty small churches in the colony, mostly in wood. The absence of towns meant that these churches were built in rural locations on crossroads or near rivers for the convenience of nearby plantations. Like the early wooden houses, none of the early wooden churches survived.

When time and resources permitted, the Virginians undertook the construction of more durable, and more dignified, churches. They copied the designs, as one might expect, of small English parish churches. The 1632 Newport parish church in Isle of Wight County, now known as St Luke's, is the oldest surviving Virginian church and a good example of the type [52]. Like the Anglican churches in England, St Luke's is based on the traditional linear nave taken over from Catholicism. The chancel with its sacred altar and communion table stands at one end, separated from the congregation with a traditional medieval rood screen, or partition, and a chancel rail. As in the English parish churches, there is no architectural acknowledgment of the Protestant revolution in liturgy here. Following the common English precedent, the roof of St Luke's is constructed with exposed medieval trusses. Outside, the building mimics the Gothic style of numerous English parish churches, with its steep roof, dominant vertical tower, exposed buttresses, pointed window arches, and brick construction. The crude triangular pediment over the main door and the semi-circular arches in the tower betray a later re-working and completion in the Classical spirit.

Although individuals in the colony amassed land and fortunes, the financial profits that returned to the original investors in England were so poor that the Virginia Company eventually declared bankruptcy. In 1624 the English government stepped in and established a royal governor for the colony under the supervision of a bureaucracy back in England. With its large estates in the hands of a few individuals, its aspiration to build a manor house lifestyle, its preference for the rural over the urban, and its firm embrace of the Anglican Church, Virginia remained the most English of all the American colonies.

The second colony to succeed in America, in New England, took an entirely different direction. The initial motivation for its settlement was more religious than financial. A number of Protestants in England were not content with the limited reforms undertaken by the Anglican Church. They wanted to 'purify' the Church as thoroughly as the Lutherans and Calvinists had achieved on the continent. Even

51 Adam Thoroughgood House, Princess Anne County, Virginia, 1636–40

52 St Luke's, Smithfield, Isle of Wight County, Virginia, 1632

more extreme than these Puritans were the Separatists, mostly from the working classes, who wished to break from the Anglican Church altogether. Neither group made much headway in England at the beginning of the seventeenth century. The Anglican Church hierarchy was not inclined to reform, and the crown did not appreciate dissension from the official state religion. A group of Separatists, after a period of persecution, left to settle in Holland in 1608. A decade later, afraid of losing their cultural identity to the Dutch, they decided to found a settlement in America where they could freely practice their religion. One hundred and two of these pilgrims arrived in the fall of 1620 at Cape Cod in New England, and named their settlement Plymouth after the English town from which they had embarked. Poorly equipped and ill-prepared for the coming winter in the harsh New England climate, they survived through help from the Native Americans, hard work and religious fervor.

When Charles I ascended the English throne in 1625 and began a battle for control against Parliament, he allied with Anglican church leaders who were keen to suppress Puritanism. As the chances for reform receded further, the Puritans eventually decided that they, too, would have to emigrate. They intended to establish a model Church and state in the new land that would support their religious beliefs, and that might inspire reforms back home. Since the Puritans came from a wide range of social classes including nobles and merchants, they were able to orchestrate their move carefully. They bought into and soon controlled a commercial company, later renamed the Massachusetts Bay Company, that won a charter from the king to settle north of Plymouth. Best of all, they won the right to govern their territory locally, without interference from England or the Anglican Church authorities. In 1630, a score of well-provisioned ships carried over 1000 settlers to Massachusetts Bay; by the early 1640s over 20,000 English people had settled in the Puritan Commonwealth in the Massachusetts area.

Unlike the other European settlers in America, including even the English in Virginia, the New England settlers came mainly to find new homes in the new land. They did not emigrate to make personal fortunes, or to extract resources for the home country, or to convert the Native Americans. They brought families, and attempted to build a utopian community of true believers free from external coercion. Their special motivations, and their Puritan beliefs, eventually created a special settlement pattern for the New England area.

At first, the Massachusetts Bay Company hoped to establish a plantation system like that in Virginia. However, the rocky soil and long winters discouraged agriculture on this scale, while their Puritan concept of a community of individuals equal before God precluded placing control of the land in a few hands. The Company switched instead to a system of small, freehold farms and small communities. Typically, a group of settlers received from the legislature of the Puritan Commonwealth a parcel of land, which they then divided by mutual agreement into individual freehold farms. At the center of the new settlement they set aside a village green to be shared by all, upon which they built a public meetinghouse (which we will discuss below), a house for the parson, and perhaps a school. Much of the remaining land was left undivided to anticipate future growth. This common land was freely available to all members of the community for pasturage, much like the common land in the European feudal system. However, the original proprietors of the village retained the right to subdivide the common lands further, as new settlers moved in.

The New Englanders grouped their houses around the village green and along the approach roads, clustered together for mutual protection. They followed no grid. The buildings simply followed the contours of the land in the usual medieval

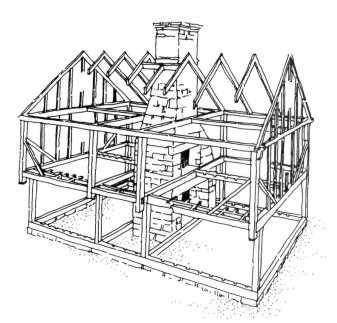

53 Gleason House, Farmington,
Connecticut, c. 1650–60

European fashion. Like the first Virginian houses, these were also based on the
venerable English medieval half-timbered tradition [53]. Large timbers were connected with mortise and tenon joints, while wattle and daub or rough bricks inter-
spersed with smaller vertical studs filled in the frame. In the normal medieval pattern,
second-floor walls often jettied over the ground floor, and steep roofs sometimes
jettied over the entire building. Horizontal clapboard siding wrapped around the
outside of the frame to provide further insulation and weatherproofing. Although it
was once thought that this skin originated in America to accommodate the greater
climate extremes in New England, the clapboard idea can be found in a number of
East Anglian houses that predate the American settlements.

As in Virginia, the first New Englanders built mainly one-, two- and four-room
versions of the English plan types. They favored the plan with a massive chimney
in the center of the house, perhaps because they were most familiar with this type
in England, and perhaps because it worked more effectively with their colder climate [50, c]. Most of the heat from a fireplace comes not from the fire itself, but from
heating the surrounding masonry which then radiates warmth into the rooms. When
chimneys are placed at the ends of the house, as in the South, much of the heat
wastefully radiates into the outside air. A chimney at the center of the house more
usefully radiates all of its heat into adjacent rooms.

Parson Joseph Capen's house, in Topsfield, Massachusetts, is a typical example
of a New England four-room house [54]. One enters at roughly the center of the long
side, into the vestige of what would have been the old screens passage. A stair to the
upper rooms, and a massive fireplace beyond, immediately turns the visitor either
right into the hall, or left into the parlor [55]. Here the hall served as the kitchen
and family room, while the parlor was mainly reserved for entertaining guests. In
the spirit of Puritan decorum, the interior is sparsely decorated, although the low
exposed beam ceiling and the massive warming fireplace must have provided a sense
of cozy security on a cold winter's day [56]. On the outside, the house is equally
expressionless. The clapboards conceal the half-timbering that had given medieval
English houses their visual richness, while the lack of chimneys on the outer ends

CULTURES TRANSFORMED
AND TRANSPLANTED

54 Parson Joseph Capen House,
Topsfield, Massachusetts, 1683

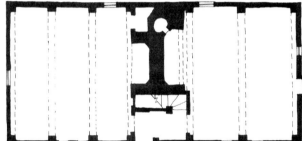

55 Parson Joseph Capen
House plan

56 Parson Joseph Capen
House interior

57 Old Ship Meetinghouse,
Hingham, Massachusetts,
1681 and later

provides no opportunity to enrich the building visually there, either. Only the jettied projections at the second floor and roof levels, and the decoratively carved wooden drops or 'pendills' at the corners, offer some visual interest to what is otherwise a fairly plain box. This understated architectural image was entirely appropriate to the Puritan view of the world.

When rooms were added to this basic shape in New England, either as later additions or as part of a larger house from the beginning, they were often attached as a shed to the back of the house. The characteristic 'salt-box' form resulted when the roof on the main body of the house aligned exactly with the roof of the shed. This became one of the most enduring images of early American colonial architecture.

The meetinghouse mentioned earlier served as the cultural and religious center of the New England village. Unlike the Virginian settlements, the Puritan communities were locally self-governing both politically and religiously. The Virginian plantation owners sent representatives to their colonial capital to make secular laws, and they accepted the regulations of the Anglican Church from England for religious matters. The Puritans, on the other hand, held town meetings to help determine secular laws. And, as Congregationalists, they locally determined their own religious affairs without interference from some distant hierarchy of Church authorities that they had found so distasteful in Catholicism and Anglicanism. The meetinghouse served as the central place where they could gather regularly for town meetings and for religious services.

For the architectural form of the meetinghouse they largely appropriated the Dutch Protestant church layout. The Old Ship Meetinghouse, in Hingham, Massachusetts, shows the idea [57]. Like the Dutch churches, this building abandoned the long linear nave of the Catholic and Anglican churches in favor of a more centralized assembly hall. Originally it was almost square in plan, with a prominent

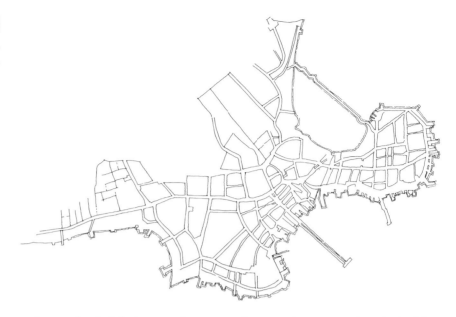

**58** Plan of Boston,
Massachusetts, 1722

pulpit on the slightly longer side opposite the entry door. Even when the building
was subsequently lengthened in the eighteenth century, the pulpit was again placed
on the longer side. This location not only provided more opportunity for townsfolk
to gather closely to the speaker, but it also symbolically distanced the building
from the Catholic and Anglican idea of an altar at the end of the church. The building takes its name from the exposed wooden truss system in the roof. The massive
timbers and curved struts reminded this shipbuilding town of their stock in trade,
although the roof is derived from medieval traditions.

The New England town, with its cozy houses picturesquely clustered around
the village green, its tradition of local town meeting governance, its close-knit community of people who knew each other and who largely shared the same values,
and its fusion of the secular and the religious, set the prototype for small town
life in America. Many later towns in the country aspired to a similar quality of life.
Unfortunately, as we will see in the next chapter, the conditions which made this
New England system possible began to break down as early as the beginning of the
eighteenth century. Americans nonetheless continued to romanticize the small town
life that the Puritans had first established, even more so as the country became
increasingly urbanized in the nineteenth and twentieth centuries.

Larger towns were not long in coming to New England. The huge numbers
of settlers and families demanded more trade goods than were required in the more
sparsely settled southern plantations. Just as in a number of the Native American and
the European civilizations, towns grew up to serve the trade at the strategic crossroads.
In New England, the crossroads were the seaports. Ships most efficiently carried goods
between the colonies and England, and between the colonies themselves. Unlike the
rivers and tidewaters in the South offering innumerable places for ships to dock, the
rocky and stormy northern shores demanded protected ports at the few good natural
harbors. Here grew the towns like Salem and Boston. Continuing the medieval traditions of the home country, these New England towns were not consciously planned
according to a rational grid. Their streets followed the contours of the land, bent to
avoid obstacles and grew informally as local circumstances dictated [58]. The Puritan
aversion to central authority would not have been inclined to do otherwise.

62  Jaén Cathedral façade,
Jaén, Spain, 1667—86,
Eufrasio Lopez de Rojas

63  Queen's House, Greenwich,
England, 1616—35, Inigo Jones

interest in patterning and decoration that originated in the Middle Ages under the influence of Islam. These Baroque elements soon made their way into Mexico and, after the turn of the eighteenth century, into the American missions.

### The English Baroque synthesis

The English Baroque style can usefully be seen as standing somewhere between the Italian and French extremes. Compared to the Italians, the Protestant and Puritan influence on English culture urged more restraint on exuberant expression. Compared to the French, the English showed less interest in abstract logic for its own sake. The new mood for compromise and accommodation in English society and politics after the Restoration of the monarchy found expression in an architectural style that sought a moderating balance between these two.

The stylistic road to this English Baroque synthesis paralleled the English culture's transition from the political dogmatism of the first half of the century to the spirit of greater compromise in the second. In the reign of James I at the beginning of the century, Inigo Jones imported a full-blown and historically correct Classicism into England, promoting its virtues over the quasi-Classical, quasi-Gothic amalgamations of the previous century. Jones had traveled through Italy, studying ancient Classical works and particularly the projects of Palladio. The strict controlling order of Palladian Classicism must certainly have appealed to King James, who sought absolute power for the monarchy and wrote books on the divine right of kings. He appointed Jones the Surveyor to the King, and gave him a number of choice architectural commissions. Jones's design for the Queen's House at Greenwich clearly illustrates how he strictly and soberly followed the Classical rules of design in the Palladian manner [63]. Plain rectilinear boxes straddle a public road, and gain their architectural interest entirely through carefully planned proportions, a slightly projected middle bay, and historically accurate details. No medieval traditions like prominent roofs or chimneys intrude on the purity of the Classical form. When Charles I gained the throne and inherited from his father the concept of an absolute monarchy, Jones continued to build for the king and court a number of equally controlled buildings in this correct Classical style.

Jones's rationally austere Palladianism did not last long in an England increasingly hostile to dogmatic extremes. Outside the court, most buildings continued to be designed and constructed by master masons in what Sir John Summerson has called the Artisan Mannerist style, variations on Italian and Low Countries mannerism of the previous century. And as resistance to Charles's absolutist plans erupted into Civil War at mid-century, even those who admired Jones's Classicism wished to temper its dogmatic adherence to rationally correct models.

Out of this new mood for moderation emerged one of the most pervasive English building types of all, the rectangular, hipped roof Classical house. Although this style is popularly known as Georgian, after the dynastic period in the next century in which it widely proliferated throughout Britain and America, William Pierson, Jr has pointed out that its main characteristics were developed over half a century before George I ascended to the throne. We will follow his suggestion, and call this the small English Baroque house to avoid confusing it with styles that actually emerged in George's time. These were the houses that rapidly filled the American British colonies in the eighteenth century. The new house type was first developed by Sir Roger Pratt for his own house Coleshill, in Berkshire [64]. At first glance, Pratt faithfully adhered to the Palladian ideals favored by Inigo Jones. He began with a symmetrical and strictly

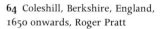

64 Coleshill, Berkshire, England,
1650 onwards, Roger Pratt

rectangular free-standing block, abandoning the traditional asymmetrical screens passage arrangement and the picturesque aggregations of forms long favored for English houses. In what he called a 'double pile' design, he arranged two rows of main reception rooms on either side of a corridor running down the center of the long axis. On the shorter axis he placed a large entry stair hall and parlor on the exact symmetrical center [65]. From Jones he also borrowed the quoins at the corners, the slightly projecting cornerstones alternating narrow and wide at each course (although quoins long predated Jones as well). Onto this formal arrangement, however, Pratt superimposed a number of distinctly non-Palladian and even medieval features, including a prominent hipped roof, dormer windows and dominant chimneys. These effectively moderated the severe rationality of the Italian Renaissance models, giving the Classicism a traditional English flavor. Reversing the emphasis of the earlier hybrids, however, here the Classical order and control dominates the medieval touches.

Pratt's new house offered more than updated styling. His use of Classicism, and his placement of a grand stair hall at the entry and a prominent parlor behind, reflected a new way of life for the English aristocracy and later for the middle classes who copied them. We saw in the last chapter how the Italian Renaissance aristocrats had developed a concept of gentility, the code of behavior which stressed refined manners of speech, posture, clothing and behavior. The English aristocracy acquired this code at the beginning of the seventeenth century as part of their enthusiasm for Renaissance notions. It was essential in the code of gentility to be seen embracing the correct fashions and manners, we will recall, and equally important to see how these were embraced by others in one's social circle. The design of one's house became an essential component in the performance of these rituals. Here one could entertain other equally refined people, showing off one's own taste, and allowing them to show off their own. The use of the Classical language naturally expressed an adherence to the highest standards of refined civilization as defined by the Renaissance, while the arrangement of the house itself changed to provide a more appropriate stage for playing out the rites of gentility. In the old English screens passage house, guests were limited to the hall and the parlor. Only the occupants of the house could retire to the upper rooms, by way of an unobtrusive stairway. In the new genteel house, guests were entertained in reception rooms on both floors, the upper chambers providing a

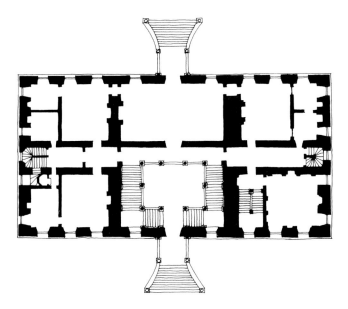

65 Coleshill plan

more intimate setting for teas or soirées. The stairway acquired an important new significance as the public processional route between the two floors.

The new influence of gentility extended to the design and use of the parlor. Although the parlor in the old medieval house was used to entertain guests, it also doubled this function with other, more mundane, family activities. Now the parlor in the new genteel house was devoted entirely to entertaining guests. It received the most lavish decoration, housed the most prized personal possessions, and functioned mainly to display to the world the taste and refinement of the house owner. The old whitewashed wooden beams in the earlier medieval tradition were now regarded with the same distaste as that shown for rough homespun woolen britches, and were covered with a false plastered ceiling decorated with Classical details.

In the latter half of the seventeenth century, the ideas in Pratt's Coleshill passed down into the British middle classes. We saw in the last chapter how the merchants, bankers, professionals and small landed gentry accumulated a larger proportion of the country's wealth in the reign of Elizabeth. This trend accelerated in the seventeenth century, creating a class of wealthy people proud of their accomplishments and seeking some way to express their new status. They not unnaturally turned to the aristocracy for ideas about how to live with and to exhibit greater wealth. Pratt's double pile design became the ideal model for a new house of higher stature. Enough aristocratic houses had used the idea to make it fashionably desirable, while its basic form could be reduced in scale to suit the more limited resources of the upper middle class.

Mompasson House in Salisbury typifies how the double pile idea transformed into the small English Baroque house [66]. One free-standing and rectangular block completely contains the house. Like the rational Palladian model from which Coleshill itself was derived, the building is precisely symmetrical on the outside, with the entry at the exact center of the long side. In the Classical tradition of repose, horizontal lines dominate over vertical with a string course between the first and second floors, and with a Classical cornice under the slightly projecting roof. Classical details appear again at the front door. In Mompasson House, the broken pediment over the door betrays the prevailing Baroque tastes of the time, since this detail was long employed by high fashion Baroque architects who preferred the visually complex over the pure.

66 Mompasson House,
Salisbury, England, 1701

The English deviation from this otherwise Classical ideal shows in the prominent hipped roof and in the large chimneys on the end walls. Also English is a new invention of about 1660, the sash window. This offered practical advantages over the traditional medieval casement window in that air flow could be regulated more carefully, and it offered aesthetic advantages for Classicists in that the bold geometrical pattern of the sash bars reinforced the pervasive sense of geometry controlling the entire design. These windows now march regularly across the façade, to which are aligned dormer windows in the roof. Although both Coleshill and Mompasson House are constructed in stone in keeping with the Classical ideal, many small English Baroque houses more economically reverted to the earlier English tradition of building in brick with stone details. Sometimes the corners were constructed with stone quoins like those in Coleshill, other times the idea of the quoin was simply expressed through a contrasting color of brick at the corners. This popular new middle-class house form was ready for export by the end of the seventeenth century.

The other characteristic building form of British colonial America, the spired Classical church, was also developed in England soon after the Restoration of the monarchy. The new mood for compromise and accommodation set the tone, the massive reconstruction required after the Great Fire of London in 1666 gave the opportunity, and Sir Christopher Wren developed the ideas. Wren came to architecture without training at age 30, having first made his name as a distinguished astronomer. In 1669 with only a few buildings to his credit, he was named Surveyor General of the King's Works and given responsibility for rebuilding St Paul's Cathedral as well as 52 new churches for the City of London. In this task Wren was forced to find a compromise between apparently mutually exclusive demands. On the one side, as a scientist and geometer he was attracted to the systematic clarity of Classicism, but, on the other hand, the clergy and London populace expected to rebuild their churches in the familiar Gothic tradition.

Wren ingeniously combined both. He employed historically correct elements of the Classical language, including the five Orders, semicircular arches and triangular pediments. He also rationally organized his designs with circles, rectangles and squares

inventively superimposed in three dimensions. However, he piled these Classical elements up into distinctly Gothic-feeling towers and spires, using the same method of composition as we saw in the towers at San Carlo alle Quattro Fontane and Jaén Cathedral. Rather than follow the compositional rules of Classicism dogmatically, Wren transformed the Classical elements into basic building blocks that he could then freely combine into complex compositions without undue regard for their normal usage. Each church tower was given its own unique character while drawing upon the same simple repertoire of forms [67]. Wren's towers are unique in the history of the Baroque for the exceptional heights to which he piled his Classical elements, giving his buildings the most Gothic flavor of all.

For the interiors of the City churches, Wren abandoned the traditional linear nave of the Anglican church and took up instead the Dutch Protestant idea of a centralized auditoria dominated by a pulpit. Over the centralized spaces Wren deployed a number of ingenious variations on Classical vaults and domes. He found little joy in the sparse finishings of the Dutch Protestant churches, preferring instead to infuse his spaces with the richer decorations and more dramatic spatial effects of the Catholic Baroque churches. With this skilled blending of opposites – Gothic and Classical, Protestant and Catholic, rational and emotional – Wren managed to find a satisfying balance in the conflicting tendencies of the age that suited the new English outlook.

Wren inspired an English Baroque movement in the next generation of architects. Most notable were Nicholas Hawksmoor, who worked in Wren's office for 20 years, and Sir John Vanbrugh, a professional playwright and self-trained gentleman architect. Together and singly they evolved Wren's style into something bolder and more abstract. As seen here in Seaton Delaval by Vanbrugh [68], the new style conceived of architecture – even more than had Wren – as a dramatic massing of large three-dimensional sculptural shapes. Classical details like the paired columns are abstracted almost beyond recognition, reading more as pure cylinders in the composition. Vanbrugh and Hawksmoor often left large masonry surfaces unadorned in order to stress the visual power of a massive wall in the raw. This style presciently anticipated the revolutionary forms of Ledoux and Boullée (which we will examine in the next chapter) by more than three-quarters of a century.

### The Baroque in British America

The American colonies stood at the fringes of these developments in Europe. At first, the varying fortunes of the combatants at mid-century mainly affected immigration to and from the colonies. The English Civil War and the Puritan Commonwealth temporarily stemmed the exodus of Puritans to America. With their brethren in control in the colonizing country, some even returned to England. In the other direction, many Protestants left France when Louis XIV restricted their religious freedom by revoking the Edict of Nantes in 1685. Migration still overwhelmingly flowed to the New World, dramatically boosting the population of the British colonies from 50,000 in 1650 to 251,000 in 1700.

In this period, British America continued to follow many of its traditional medieval patterns of land ownership and building design. When new colonies were founded in the Restoration period, for example, they still adhered to the feudal concept of land ownership and control. A proprietor received a charter from the king to found a colony, took responsibility for its governance, and then granted leaseholds to individual settlers who paid an annual rent. When the Dutch gave up New Holland

67 St Mary-le-Bow, Cheapside, London, England, 1670–77, Christopher Wren

68 Seaton Delaval,
Northumberland, England,
1721, John Vanbrugh

in 1664, the Duke of York (later James II) personally gained control of the colony now known as New York. New Jersey, the Carolinas and Pennsylvania followed a similar pattern.

In the latter half of the century, however, a number of factors conspired to push the British American colonies away from its medieval traditions and more closely towards the newer European models of culture, land ownership and architectural fashion. To begin with, life had become more settled for the American colonists towards the end of the century. With matters of sheer survival out of the way, and with more leisure time and money at their disposal, they could turn their attentions more fully to the finer aspects of culture. Now if they had been left entirely to their own devices, much like the first New England townspeople, they might have eventually developed their own indigenous conceptions of higher culture. But for better or worse, larger geo-political concerns drew them more closely to the contemporary English ideas. After the Restoration of Charles II, the British government began to rationalize the relationship between the colonies and the colonizing country. Its motivation was to organize and consolidate its growing empire, and to maximize its economic assets. It conceived of a system whereby the colonies supplied cheap raw materials to the home country, and then purchased at higher prices the goods manufactured with these materials.

To encourage this relationship, the crown gradually revoked each colony's old proprietary charter and declared it under royal control. The king then appointed a royal governor to work with the local representative government on his behalf. Where once the colonies were free enterprise affairs and had remained fairly auto-nomous of the colonizing country, now they were political entities within the larger British Empire. The crown further passed a number of Navigation Acts in the last half of the seventeenth century which prohibited trade between the British colonies and any countries other than England in a number of essential commodities and manufactured goods. It also prohibited the manufacture of many goods in the colonies, insisting that they be purchased from the home country.

Although the colonies increasingly chafed at these economic restrictions and political control, these policies inevitably drew the British colonies more fully into the sphere of contemporary English culture. In an age when one could travel more efficiently by water than by land, the American seaports eventually maintained closer contact with London than did many provincial English towns. And since many of the colonists' goods were manufactured in England, they were highly aware of – even dependent upon – changing English aesthetic fashions. The Americans began to emulate more explicitly the values, cultural mores, and aesthetic ideals of the colonizing country. In this period we find a more strongly delineated social hierarchy, with wealthy plantation owners and merchants at the top, black slaves at the bottom, and a range of professionals, artisans and small farmers in between. In the last decades of the seventeenth century, the upper social ranks in America began to embrace the European concept of gentility. Just like their peers in England, the well-to-do aspired to display their station in life by maintaining the appropriate codes of dress, speech and behavior. Inevitably, we will see later, they also acquired a taste for the small English Baroque house with which their English counterparts expressed their membership in the genteel classes.

Unlike the English class structure, however, the more fluid American society offered greater opportunities for upward mobility. Hard work more than accidents of birth determined the level to which one might rise. Americans at all levels consequently aspired to a higher social standing than the one they currently enjoyed, in the reasonable expectation that they might well achieve it. This pervasive sense of upward mobility rapidly hastened the spread of genteel ideas down into the lower ranks of American society, as each social group mimicked the behaviors of those immediately above it. By the beginning of the nineteenth century, even those in the humblest homesteads at the frontiers of America eventually sought respectability through refined tea parties and good manners. So pervasive was the call of gentility that even the lowliest of houses eventually set aside a large proportion of the house as a parlor, used only for rare visits from esteemed guests like the local preacher. At all levels of society, the medieval vernacular traditions that had once served the colonies so well now seemed as coarse as wiping one's mouth on one's sleeve.

Before examining the new Baroque buildings that entered America at the end of the seventeenth century, we should briefly note how the influence of contemporary British values and ideals eventually changed the pattern of land control and use in the colonies. When the crown replaced the old proprietors with royal governors, they essentially removed the feudal conception of private estates charging annual rents to tenants. Increasingly the colonies turned to the more modern conception of land held in absolute title that could be freely bought and sold as a commodity. This eventually helped dismantle the original system of town development in New England. The common lands disappeared as more settlers moved in. And rather than give away land for new towns, as was the custom in the seventeenth century, the colonial governments auctioned land to people often more interested in investments than in establishing a new community. Settlers now preferred to scatter their houses further apart, each on a contiguous piece of land, rather than to cluster their houses around the meetinghouse and to scatter their individual landholdings as before. The feudal conceptions of land and community eventually disappeared altogether.

The new towns established in this period began to show the influence of European Classical ideas. Rather than let towns grow haphazardly, as Boston continued to do, the new towns were laid out on rational grids. New Haven, Connecticut, was designed in 1638 as a square divided into nine equal parts with the central square as

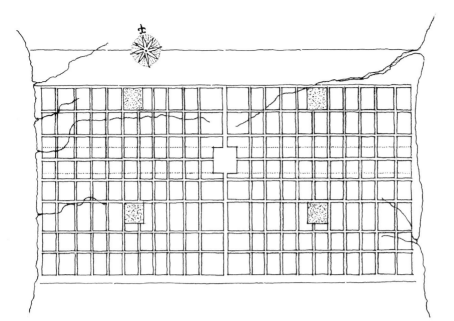

**69** Plan of Philadelphia,
Pennsylvania, 1682, laid out by
Thomas Holme with instructions
from William Penn

the town common. Philadelphia, Pennsylvania, was laid out in 1682 as a rectangle
divided into four quadrants, each given a public square and the whole given a major
public square at the intersection of the main east-west and north-south streets [**69**].
This plan largely duplicates the ancient Roman colonial town plans. Pennsylvania's
proprietor, William Penn, stipulated broad streets and widely spaced individual houses
so that fire and disease could not sweep as easily through his town as they had through
densely packed London. Penn's proposal abandoned the continuous row of houses
along streets that had characterized most urban developments throughout history.
This concept of detached houses lined up on a gridiron street plan points the way to
what would eventually become the ubiquitous scheme for new towns in America.

    In the last decades of the seventeenth century, as a result of the cultural changes
we have just discussed, the first Baroque versions of Classical buildings began to appear
in the British colonies. One of the first might have been the Foster-Hutchinson House
in Boston, around 1688, although it is not clear if its characteristically Baroque
features date from later remodeling. More certain is the royal College of William and
Mary, constructed in Jamestown, Virginia, in 1695 [**70**]. As an institution under the
purview of the British crown, the design might well have originated in the office of
the King's Surveyor, Sir Christopher Wren. Some records claim this distinction, while
the design certainly owes much to Wren's Baroque style. In particular, it mimics
Wren's Royal Hospital in Chelsea of 1682, borrowing a long rectangular masonry
block subdivided by repetitive bays of sash windows with dormer windows above.
Both buildings mark the symmetrical center with the main door, a cupola, and the
triangular pediment of a Classical temple front. The pediment is built too steeply to
accord with the Classical rules, although this may have resulted from a local builder
modifying the general plans sent from the home country.

    When Jamestown burned in 1698, the village around the College of William and
Mary was renamed Williamsburg and redesigned as the new capital city. The design
for the Governor's Palace largely followed the style of the small English Baroque
house [**71**]. The basic elements are here, including the simple masonry block perfectly

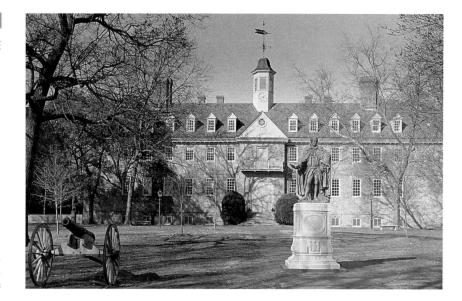

**70** College of William and Mary, Williamsburg, Virginia, 1695–1702

bifurcated by the entrance on the long side, the prominent hipped roof and chimney stacks, the regular rhythm of sash windows, and the horizontal string course and Classical cornice. It varies from the norm mainly in the steeper roof, in the balustrade

**71** Governor's Palace, Williamsburg, Virginia, begun 1706, destroyed 1781, rebuilt 1932

around a flat platform at the top, in the absence of obvious Classical details around the front door, and in a capping cupola inspired by Coleshill but usually omitted in the smaller middle-class version. This quickly became the new standard against which the Virginian planters and later other Americans measured their own homes.

The Virginian plantation house Westover remains one of the most elegant examples of the small English Baroque house in the South [72]. Built in 1730–34 by a successful second-generation planter William Byrd II, it joins the steep roof of the Governor's House with a main body of the house closer to the English norm. The split and scrolled pediment over the door betrays a Baroque taste, just like Mompasson House. In keeping with the requirements of the new code of gentility, a prominent Classical stairway hall fills the center of the building [73]. Notice, however, that the absolute symmetry in the façade does not carry through into the stairway hall, which is offset from the central axis [74]. Maintaining the symmetry of the façade required balancing a window into the hall with a window into a reception room. Outward appearance no longer directly matches the inner functions, as in the earlier medieval tradition of the screens passage house. This disparity between the symmetrical outside and the

72 Westover, Charles City County, Virginia, 1730–34, William Byrd II and Richard Taliaferro

73 Westover, entry hall

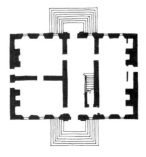

74 Westover, plan

asymmetrical inside often offends modern critics, although there are so many examples like this in the history of Classical architecture before and after that it seems to worry the critics more than it did the architects who employed the language.

The small English Baroque house form also made its way into the northern colonies, eventually obscuring the regional variations of the previous century and providing far more visual uniformity to the colonies as a whole. In order to adopt the new style, the northerners had to change their building traditions more thoroughly than had the southerners. We saw in the last chapter how northern houses placed the chimney in the center of the house in order to radiate heat from the chimney into the surrounding rooms. Unfortunately, this placed a mass of masonry in the very location where the new fashion wished to locate the central stairway hall. The northerners dutifully moved their fireplaces to the end walls as the southern colonists had always done, even though the new location made less sense for the northern climate. The inefficiency of this arrangement was moderated, to a certain extent, by improvements in fireplace designs in the eighteenth century. Smaller firebox openings drew less air from the room up the chimney, while sometimes ducts were designed to transmit more heat from the chimney into the room. Benjamin Franklin's cast iron stove, perfected in 1742, burned fuel even more efficiently and gradually found its way into colonial homes through the remainder of the century. But however more efficient these innovations proved to be, they would have been more efficient still at the center of the house.

Many northern colonists still preferred to build in wood, even though the new aesthetic derived from the masonry construction of Classicism. Some answered this dilemma by clothing the frame with wide wooden boards chamfered on the edges to look like masonry joints. Others used narrower clapboards in the traditional manner, perhaps consoling themselves with the thought that from a distance the boards look like rows of bricks. They constructed false quoins by applying thin wooden boards to the wall as decorations. To simulate the texture and color of stone, many northern colonists painted their wooden buildings in muted earth colors with sand mixed into

75 Wentworth-Gardner House, Portsmouth, New Hampshire, 1760

76 Williams House, Old Deerfield,
Massachusetts, 1706–7 and 1756

the paint. The much admired earth tones of colonial America derive from a clever
effort to disguise wood as stone.

The Wentworth-Gardner House, in Portsmouth, New Hampshire, is a good
example of the northern small English Baroque house [75]. It closely follows the
new ideal, with its hipped roof, dormer windows, sash windows, central doorway
with a Baroque scrolled pediment over and corner quoins. Here the appearance of
masonry is simulated by wide chamfered boards. Williams House, in Old Deerfield,
Massachusetts, shows how the new style permeated down in the social ranks and out
to what was the frontier in the eighteenth century [76]. Originally constructed in
1706 as a typical seventeenth-century New England house with a framed overhang
and a central chimney, this house was remodeled in the new fashion in 1756. Now
absolute symmetry controls the front façade, and crudely executed Classical details
decorate the front door and window heads on what might otherwise be mistaken
for the earlier medieval form.

High fashion English Baroque ideas finally appeared in the colonial churches
built in the first decades of the eighteenth century. The declaration of Massachusetts
as a royal colony in 1691 eventually led to the establishment of Anglican parishes in
the heartland of Puritanism. The Anglicans obviously eschewed the Puritan meetinghouse, and chose instead to build in the style of Wren's by now well-established and
familiar City churches. Christ Church, or Old North, built in Boston in 1723 shows
the new type. Its design followed Wren's basic idea and combined stylistic ideas from
several of his own designs. On the outside, a tall rectangular tower derived from
one Wren church and a capping spire derived from another stands in front of the
rectangular box enclosing the auditorium [77]. Brick is used in preference to the
wood of the traditional Puritan meetinghouses, in large part to emulate the masonry
construction of the London originals. The inside follows the arrangement of Wren's
St James, Piccadilly, with side galleries supported on columns which, in turn, support a longitudinal plaster vault and several transversal vaults. Only thinner details
and more subdued decorations distinguish this design from something that Wren
might have done.

**77** Christ Church (Old North), Boston, Massachusetts, 1723, William Price

**78** Old State House (Independence Hall), Philadelphia, Pennsylvania, 1731, Andrew Hamilton

These two new styles, the small English Baroque house and the Wrenian church, were combined in the design for one of the first large secular public buildings, the Old State House or Independence Hall in Philadelphia. A Wrenian tower sits on top of a Baroque house base, looking either like a greatly overgrown cupola or a church spire displaced from its usual position at the short end of the building [78]. Long revered as the site of the signing of the Declaration of Independence, its symbolic importance and widespread exposure has done much to create the modern popular image of colonial American architecture.

## The Post-Baroque 1700–50

Just as the American colonies took up the Baroque ideas at the turn of the century, the style began to change in Europe. Each country emphatically redirected its architectural emphasis, usually in reaction to whatever had dominated its culture in the previous half-century. In opposition to the dramatic inventiveness of Wren, Hawksmoor and Vanbrugh, the English eventually returned to a more austere and correct Classicism known as Anglo Palladianism (see figure 79). In opposition to the bold and rationally assertive Versailles, the French developed a more delicate and refined style known as Rococo (see figure 88). And in reaction to the relatively reserved forms of the Escorial and the Spanish Baroque, the new generation of Spanish designers developed a riotous system of surface decoration known as Churrigueresque (see figure 91).

What caused these changes in architectural direction? First of all, the Baroque style had largely grown out of the social and political conflicts of the previous century. By the first decades of the eighteenth century, a number of these tensions and conflicts had moderated. The religious passions ignited by the Reformation and Counter-Reformation were now largely spent. Neither monarchs nor the churches would attempt again to impose a religious unity onto Europe. Internal politics were also less volatile, once more stable governments had emerged from the civil wars of the mid-seventeenth century. Only England and France were left as the main European rivals on the decline of the Dutch and Spanish empires. After a series of wars between the two concluded with an English victory and the Treaty of Utrecht in 1713, Europe experienced unprecedented peace and prosperity until mid-century. And although the philosophical conundrums still remained, like those between science and faith and sense and reason, the general easing of tensions in this period allowed architects to retreat from the great clash of opposites.

The new French and English styles, although quite different in many ways, shared a common feeling of decorum, repose and refinement. Both abandoned the brash assertiveness of the Baroque. We can attribute much of this new architectural sensitivity to a change in the code of gentility in this period. In a time of increased prosperity and more stable social conditions, gentility blossomed into a cult of Polite Society. Extremes were frowned upon, rules of behavior and taste proliferated, and refinement, delicacy and decorum were valued above all. The English stressed decorum. They established the same absolute rules of taste for buildings that they applied to manners and speech. The French stressed the delicacy of taste, and reveled in the sensuous pleasures of light and airy decorations. Nothing was so aggressive that it would offend the delicate palate. Like the French, the Spanish largely abandoned the austere rationalism of their Baroque and turned increased attention to sensuous surface decoration. In what appeared like a release of long pent-up pressure, the Spanish quickly developed one of the most extreme expressions ever of writhing decoration overcoming rational form. For the remainder of this chapter, we will examine in turn each of these developments together with its colonial manifestation.

### England and its colonies

England enjoyed unprecedented social stability through the first half of the eighteenth century, under the guidance first of Queen Anne and then George I of Hanover. Curiously, the former's name was later given to styles of furniture and architecture invented well after her death, while the latter's name was given to styles invented over a half a century before his reign. In this period, more power devolved down the social ranks and more personal freedoms were gained, eventually earning England the admiration and envy of social reformers in other countries. England also became an undisputed world power. Its armies defeated those of Louis XIV at the beginning of the century, while its powerful navy increasingly dominated international trade. Its population and wealth rose dramatically.

Before the final flowering of the English Baroque in Hawksmoor and Vanbrugh could cross the Atlantic or filter further down into the buildings of the middle classes, the aristocratic tastemakers in England abruptly stopped its development and redirected the efforts of most English architects in the 1720s and 1730s. Now known as the Anglo Palladians, the leaders of this movement bitterly attacked the exuberant late Baroque style, plumping instead for the more austere Classical tradition of Palladio and its English variant, Inigo Jones.

Why the sudden and dramatic shift? Besides the general changes in European culture mentioned above, the fate of this style also got caught up in partisan British politics. When James II seemed determined to restore Catholicism and rebuild an absolutist monarchy after the Restoration in the previous century, a political party with Puritan sympathies emerged to oppose what they perceived as an evil trinity of Catholicism, James's Stuart dynasty, and absolutism. Known as the Whigs, they intermittently swapped control of Parliament with their rivals the Tories, until the

Stuart dynasty finished on Queen Anne's death in 1714. The Whigs swept into power when George I assumed the crown, receiving a number of new powers from a German king unfamiliar with English customs. An oligarchy of a few powerful Whig families subsequently dominated the British government until mid-century. They wished to distinguish themselves from anything remotely Stuart, Catholic or absolutist. The Baroque, they thought, was the distasteful architecture of all three.

The Whigs sought a new national architectural style free from these unpleasant associations. They found it in the architecture of Palladio and Jones. In hindsight this choice is somewhat ironic, since this austere version of Classicism was a favorite both of James I, the founder of the Stuart dynasty, and of Louis XIV, the most absolutist king of all. Nonetheless, the Whigs argued for its virtues on grounds of its objective truth and freedom from individual fancy. The style certainly suited the 'age of taste', because it is a learned style with clear rules. While one might freely indulge in the Baroque style with a limited understanding of the Classical rules, amateur and uninformed dabbling in Palladianism quickly shows up one's ignorance.

A number of architecture books were published in this period to inform and disseminate the new style. The gentlemen-scholars who wished to learn the new taste and manners could select from a number of expensive, large format books with beautiful illustrations. Colen Campbell brought out five volumes of *Vitruvius Britannicus* from 1715 to 1725, showing his favorite examples of British Classical architecture. Giacomo Leoni introduced an English translation in 1715 of Palladio's own 1570 book, *Quattro Libri dell' Architettura*, renamed as *The Architecture of A. Palladio*. William Kent, one of the foremost architects of the Palladian movement, stressed the English heritage of the idea with his 1727 *Designs of Inigo Jones*. The carpenters and masons who wished to emulate the new taste could select from a number of more prosaic handbooks, including William Salmon's *Palladio Londinensis* of 1734, Batty Langley's *The City and Country Builder's and Workman's Treasury of Designs* in eleven editions from 1740 to 1808, Langley's *The Builder's Jewel* of 1741, as well as numerous other titles by authors like William Halfpenny and Robert Morris. These popular guidebooks rapidly hastened the dissemination of the new rules throughout England and America.

Lord Burlington's own design for his Chiswick House outside London showed the new ideal [79]. Modeled after Palladio's Villa Rotonda (see figure 37), the building abandoned the movement and drama of the Baroque in favor of the more static repose of the Renaissance. The individual parts are clearly separated and distinct,

**79** Chiswick House, Chiswick, England, begun 1725, Lord Burlington

not fused together. Precisely rational cubic forms replace the more sensual curves, ovals and ellipses of the earlier style. Perhaps most importantly, an historically correct Classical temple front dominates the front façade, reminding the viewer of the essential basis of the language, and illustrating like a schoolmaster how to speak the language clearly and without mannered distortion.

These ideas eventually passed to America at mid-century. The British colonies by this time had grown and matured into a substantial and complex culture. Yet more immigrants had poured into the colonies in the eighteenth century, now from a number of Western European countries as well as Britain. By 1763 the population of the British colonies had grown to 2,250,000, almost nine times the population at the turn of the century. This more diverse immigrant group brought an almost bewildering variety of sects and religions. America had become a melting pot of nationalities and religions with a surprising degree of tolerance for each other. Some non-English groups, like the Germans who settled in Pennsylvania, vigorously retained their own cultural and architectural traditions. Most immigrants, however, adapted to the prevailing British culture. The Native Americans had been pushed off their land and had retreated to the west, leaving the seaboard settlements to develop their version of English culture unopposed. The American cities grew so dramatically that by the middle of the eighteenth century, the largest ones like Philadelphia were more populous than most cities in England.

Once the Baroque ideas had overthrown the earlier medieval traditions in America, subsequent English fashions like Anglo Palladianism passed more easily into these now thoroughly British colonies. A good example of the new style can be seen in the Miles Brewton House, in Charleston, South Carolina [80], which went directly to the source of the style and mimicked a plate out of Palladio's own book. The brick walls give a more lively texture to the building than the purest Palladians in England would have preferred, and the wide-framed sash windows pushed out to the surface of the wall in the Baroque manner fails to achieve the sharply cut flavor of the recessed windows in numerous Anglo Palladian schemes back in the home country; but the two-story temple front emphatically proclaims a return to pure, unadulterated Classicism.

The Redwood Library, in Newport, Rhode Island, expressed the Palladian ideal even more dramatically [81]. The building's designer, Peter Harrison, is generally

80 Miles Brewton House, Charleston, South Carolina, 1765–69

81 Redwood Library, Newport, Rhode Island, 1749–50, Peter Harrison

82 St Martin-in-the-Fields, London, England, 1721–26, James Gibbs

83 St Michael's Church, Charleston, South Carolina, 1752–61

recognized as America's first serious and most talented gentleman architect. Harrison was born in Yorkshire, England, and came to America in 1739 when he was 23. Although he designed a number of significant buildings in the new land, he undertook this work mainly as a hobby and usually without any payment other than an occasional token gift. He supported himself first as a sea captain, and later as a merchant. Harrison's method of design exemplified that of gentlemen architects back in England. He collected an extensive library of architecture books, and then constructed his designs out of various plans, elevations and details in his books that caught his fancy or seemed appropriate for the project at hand. His talent lay in creatively synthesizing the parts into a meaningful and consistent composition. In an age of taste, originality was neither valued nor sought.

The Redwood Library, his first design, copied an elevation in a plate from Palladio and details from a number of other books. In true Palladian fashion, the historically correct temple front dominates the façade. Harrison understood more than the designer of the Miles Brewton House that the new style depended upon crisp masonry detailing, even though his library was to be built in wood. In the northern fashion, he simulated stone with wide wooden boards chamfered on the edges, and with sand mixed into masonry colored paint. Here the effect is carried through more thoroughly by simulating masonry keystones and voussoirs over the openings, and by recessing the window frames into the wall.

Far more influential in eighteenth-century America than this correct

Palladianism, however, was the style of James Gibbs. A Tory Catholic Scot, Gibbs studied under the great Italian Baroque architect Carlo Fontana in Rome at the beginning of the eighteenth century. On returning to England at the height of Vanbrugh and Hawksmoor's influence, Gibbs sought to blend his Italian Baroque ideas with elements of Wren. He built St Mary-le-Strand in London in this new style just before the Whigs swept into power and dismissed him from his Surveyorship to the church building commission in London. After his Whig rival Colen Campbell published hostile comments about his Italian master and his London church design in *Vitruvius Britannicus*, Gibbs sensed the direction of the political winds and refrained from using the Italian ideas again.

Gibbs astutely developed instead a fusion of Wren and Palladio. At first glance, his St Martin-in-the-Fields looks like a typical Wrenian church [82]. A rectangular box contains the church auditorium, down the length of which runs a colonnade of Classical columns supporting the usual side galleries and a longitudinal vault in the ceiling above. On the outside, the church tower follows the Wrenian language of Classical elements freely composed. The relationship of the tower to the auditorium box, however, shows a new invention inspired by Palladianism. Wren and his pupil Hawksmoor had always built the tower in front of the box, in the Gothic fashion. Gibbs built his tower *inside* the box at the west end, so that it emerged out of the church roof. This allowed him to build a dominant Classical temple front across the main façade of the building in the Palladian manner. The new arrangement so cleverly fused the familiar tradition with the new taste that it became the prototype for many subsequent Anglican churches in the next century. When the colonists eventually saw the design in Gibbs's own *Book of Architecture* (1728), they also widely copied the idea. Here, then, is the origin of the typical colonial American church with a prominent spire and a Classical temple front. St Michael's Church in Charleston, South Carolina, is a good early example [83].

Gibbs's equally influential house designs also blended Palladianism with Wrenian Baroque. One of the plates in his *A Book of Architecture* shows the new idea [84]. Like the typical small English Baroque house, this building contains the main house functions within a rectangular block that is organized symmetrically and capped with a hip roof. But where the usual English Baroque façade emphasized the central entry with little more than a pediment at the head of the door and perhaps some pilasters on its sides, here Gibbs has proposed a greatly enlarged projection for the middle third of the building with a pediment over the entire projection, not just the central door.

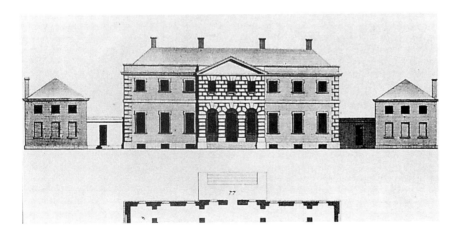

**84** Design for a house, 1728, James Gibbs

**85** Mount Airy, Richmond County, Virginia, 1758–62, John Ariss

In scale and spirit, although not in detail, it brings the Palladian temple front to the house. Less Palladian and more Baroque are the projected quoins at the corners of the house, and the heavy rustication on the central pavilion. Palladians would have objected that these obscure the underlying cubic forms, while Wren would have admired how they enliven the surfaces in the Baroque fashion. Palladians would certainly have approved of Gibbs's unrelenting symmetry in his plans, and of the way he treated outbuildings as absolutely distinct volumes linked back to the main central block with linear or curved corridors.

Like his church design, Gibbs's blend of the old tradition and the new taste in his

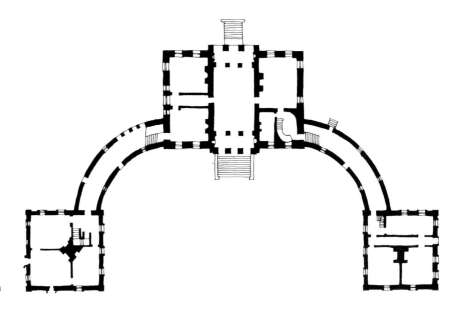

**86** Mount Airy, plan

87 Vassall (Longfellow) House,
Cambridge, Massachusetts, 1759

house designs appealed to the colonists from north to south. They had already taken up the basic English Baroque house form, and the Gibbs fashion required only relatively minor stylistic changes to that basic idea. Mount Airy, in Virginia, is a good example in the South. It virtually reproduced the Gibbs façade discussed above, even to the point of mimicking the different tonal values of Gibbs's drawing with different colored stones [85]. Its plan with outbuildings came from another Gibbs plate [86]. This plan type proved popular in the South, because it organized the multifarious buildings and functions of the plantation farm into one coherent composition.

The Vassall (Longfellow) House in Cambridge, Massachusetts, is a good example of the new Gibbs style in the North. Here the characteristic mark of the style, the pedimented central pavilion, gains emphatic expression with pilasters on either side [87]. These appear again at the corners of the house, giving the entire composition a strong unity through repetition, and showing a continuing Baroque preference for decorative elaboration as opposed to Palladian purity. Also Baroque in feeling are the broken entablatures over the tops of the pilasters, and the way in which elements like windows and cornices crowd each other.

### France and its colonies

The demise of the Baroque culture and style in the first decades of the eighteenth century took a different direction in France. On the death of Louis XIV in 1715, the absolutist system of government that had ruled French life and had dominated European culture for half a century fell into decline. The French nobility, long resigned to the role of powerless courtiers, successfully reasserted a number of their ancient prerogatives against a weaker Louis XV. Although the French aristocracy moderated the control of the monarchy, neither could fully regain its earlier powers because these were based on feudal obligations and responsibilities that no longer existed. As in England, power flowed increasingly to the landed gentry and to an upper middle class populated by the merchants and bankers who were building the country's wealth.

The revived fortunes of the aristocracy combined with the new fortunes of the upper middle classes to create a new Rococo style. After Louis XIV's death, the aristocrats abandoned Versailles with a vengeance and returned to Paris. Together

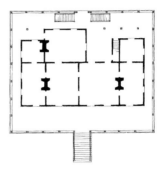

88 Hôtel de Soubise, Paris, France, 1732, Boffrand and Natoire

89 Parlange, New Roads, Louisiana, 1750

90 Parlange, plan

with the upper middle classes, they replaced the social life of the court with a new one based in the salons of private homes. As before, the concept of gentility and taste governed their behavior. And, as before, the architectural setting provided the stage upon which they would see and be seen displaying the proper fashions, behavior and speech. In the salons, however, the emphasis was now on delicacy of taste, and on a rarefied refinement. The sensual overtook the rational. The Hôtel de Soubise, in Paris, exemplifies the new style [88]. The light and airy proportions lend a sense of grace and refinement to the room. Although the decorations are quite animated, they are less overbearing or aggressive than those in the Baroque fashion. Indeed, the decorations are now little more than a thinly applied veneer, not the bold sculptural elements of the Baroque. The writhing decorative surface blends walls and ceilings into each other indeterminately, obscuring the underlying geometry of the building in a way that the previous generation of French rationalists would have found capricious and distasteful. For the aristocrats and aspiring aristocrats, the style represented a refreshing lightness and gaiety after the years of serious rationality in Louis' court.

Of course, the poor French fur traders and missionaries in America had little use for the high French fashions, either Baroque or Rococo. In this period, the French continued to lay claim to the two major river routes into the heartland of the American continent, the St Lawrence and the Mississippi rivers. Quebec, founded in 1608, controlled the northern approach, while new settlements at Biloxi (1699), Mobile (1702), and New Orleans (1727) controlled the Mississippi delta. The French also planted a number of forts and trading posts in between, including St Louis (1764) near the strategically important site of the old Native American capital city of Cahokia. New France still failed to attract large numbers of settlers. By the middle of the eighteenth century, its total population is estimated at no more than 60,000.

For their simple building needs the French continued mainly to use their timber and infill system, sometimes leaving the wood bare, sometimes covering it with plaster. In the wet, humid climate of the Mississippi River, particularly in what is now present day Louisiana, wood rot rapidly destroyed these buildings. The prison in New Orleans, built in 1730, was the first major public building to be constructed in brick. A plain brick Ursuline convent in New Orleans, constructed in 1745 to replace an original wooden structure, remains the only surviving public building from the original French settlement.

Of more lasting influence on the subsequent history of American architecture was the French plantation house design. Parlange, the oldest surviving plantation house in Louisiana, shows the type [89]. Similar in form to the Cahokia courthouse that we examined in the last chapter (although it is not clear which preceded the other), Parlange protects itself from the hot sun and heavy rains in Louisiana with a large, steeply pitched hip roof. The house itself nestles well back from the outer edge of the roof, forming a colonnaded *galerie* around all four sides of the structure. This arrangement not only protects the windows from direct sun and the walls from driving rain, but it also provides a useful space partly indoors and partly out that is both dry and cooled by breezes. This space was particularly valued in the exceptionally humid climate of the lower Mississippi River. The main living areas are lifted off the damp ground, just like the Native American chickees that had earlier evolved in response to this climate. At Parlange the designer learned the lessons about rot, and placed the wooden superstructure on a brick foundation. The plan betrays a more casual arrangement than the Classically symmetrical outer appearance would lead us to expect [90]. However, the arrangement does provide a room at the center of the house that is open on two sides, allowing for effective cross-ventilation before the invention of air conditioning. This house form was so well adapted to its climate that it spread throughout the region and remained the preferred house type well into the next century.

War between France and Britain erupted again in 1740. The War of the Austrian Succession, known as King George's War in the colonies, ended in an uneasy truce eight years later. France determined then to strengthen its hold on its American claims, in preparation for the next war. It built more forts along the western edge of the British colonies, and mobilized the Native Americans against the British settlers at the frontier. The British hastily formed an uneasy alliance with the Iroquois tribes in defense. The ensuing Seven Years' War, known as the French and Indian Wars in the colonies, concluded with an English victory in 1763. The terms of the Peace of Paris gave all of the French land in America east of the Mississippi to the British, and all of the land west of the Mississippi to the Spanish. Spain also gave Florida to the British. The Native Americans, no longer organized or supplied by the French, could not put up an effective defense against the British and gradually retreated beyond the Appalachian mountains. The frontier was now open for rapid British expansion into the American interior. Direct French influence on American architecture had finished. Ironically, high fashion French ideas would appear in America through more indirect means at the end of the century and beyond, when Americans became infatuated with the culture of their comrades in their shared and successful fight against the British.

### Spain and its colonies

We have seen how Spain embraced the principles and practices of the Italian Renaissance at the height of its power in the sixteenth century. After the rebellions

**91** Hospicio de San Fernando, Madrid, Spain, 1722, Pedro de Ribera

**92** San Jose y San Miguel de Aguayo, San Antonio, Texas, c. 1730, sculptor Pedro Huizar

and wars in the middle of the seventeenth century that marked the beginning of the end of Spanish world power, Spanish architects rebelled against their austere Classical heritage as represented in the Escorial and developed energetic versions of the Baroque. At the end of the seventeenth century, the Spanish architects retreated even further from the Classical ideal. They developed a strikingly elaborate style of decoration known as Churrigueresque, after the Churriguera family of architects that invented and popularized the new fashion. Typically, the sensually rich ornament in this style overwhelms the rational order of the building. Although comprised of vaguely Classical motifs like entablatures, capitals and arches, each decoration repeats itself like folds of a cloth until everything swirls together over the surfaces. The old Spanish interest in pattern and ornament, along with revived decorations from sixteenth-century European Mannerism, contributed to this new style. These designers may have also found inspiration in the elaborate decorative systems of the ancient Native American civilizations, with which the Spanish were well familiar through their colonies.

The Spanish architects often attached this rich decoration to the exteriors of buildings, particularly as an elaborate surround to a main entry or doorway. The Hospicio de San Fernando, in Madrid, offers an example [**91**]. Here a complex aggregation of sculptures in niches, pieces of entablatures, broken arches, pediments, and pilasters with inverted tapers are intricately bound together with carved draperies and garlands of flowers. The entire ensemble contrasts markedly to the plain wall on which it sits. It bears so little relationship to the building's underlying conceptual order that its omission would not change the building form in the slightest. Modern critics have therefore often objected to this kind of applied ornament as superfluous or even deceitful, although someone less concerned with intellectual clarity will obviously enjoy this riotous appeal to the senses and emotions.

The new style spread rapidly in the New World in the eighteenth century, first to the major churches in Mexico, and then to the mission churches at the frontier. In the first decades of the century, the missionaries pushed further east into North America, establishing a number of missions in present day Texas. The most significant ones gathered around San Antonio. As before, few Spanish settlers entered the region. By the time of the American Revolution later in the century, the entire Spanish population north of the Rio Grande could probably still be counted in the hundreds.

In Texas the missionaries encountered opportunities quite different from those in New Mexico. The Native Americans in Texas were not part of the pueblo culture, and therefore offered fewer building traditions or construction skills that could be applied to Western architectural ideas. The Texas missions consequently had to import Mexican or Spanish artisans for the design and construction of their buildings, using the Native Americans for basic labor only. As one might expect, the Texas churches correspond more closely to prevailing Mexican and Spanish fashions than did the mission buildings in the pueblo regions.

San Jose y San Miguel de Aguayo, in San Antonio, embodies the imported Baroque and Churrigueresque ideas [92]. A simple church with a nave and no aisles, San Jose was constructed in rough masonry plastered over. The local Native Americans offered no skills in adobe construction, and so the Spanish or Mexican artisans in charge of the project reverted to their more familiar constructional system. There is evidence that the entire church was once covered with a web of red, blue and yellow painted quatre-foil and floral patterns. San Jose boasts two Baroque towers on either side of the front entry. The church remains unfinished; the one tower never received its upper story, while the sculptures on the upper story of the other tower were never completed. The bold curvilinear shapes on the upper story give only tantalizing hints of the ornaments that were meant to be carved into them. The surround of the main entry gives a clearer idea of the ornamental scheme. Like the entry to the Hospicio in Madrid, the surround is encrusted with sculptures, garlands, Baroque scrolls, brackets, and Classical elements like entablatures and pilasters. Here the Churrigueresque fashion for elaborate decoration came full circle. It was partly inspired by the Native American traditions in the first place, developed in Spain, and then brought back to the New World transformed.

In this chapter we have explored the astonishing transformation of European and American architecture brought on by the conflicts in European culture during the seventeenth century. We ended on a note of stability and calm, as the first half of the eighteenth century settled into the now familiar patterns of Post-Baroque gentility and taste. But this was just the calm before the real storm. In the next chapter we will see how social, political and philosophical revolutions in the second half of the eighteenth century overthrew the old order altogether, ushered in the foundations of our modern world, and created entirely new attitudes to architecture and its production.

# 4

# THE AGE OF REVOLUTION
## 1763–1820

**93** Early 1820s, showing extent of settlement

THE AMERICAN Revolution against Great Britain represented a fundamental turning point in American history. It marked a rejection of colonial rule and the beginning of a new nation, the United States. Americans are rightly proud of this event. The social and political events leading up to the first armed resistance at Lexington and Concord belong to common American folklore, including the hated Stamp Tax, the Boston Tea Party and the Declaration of Independence.

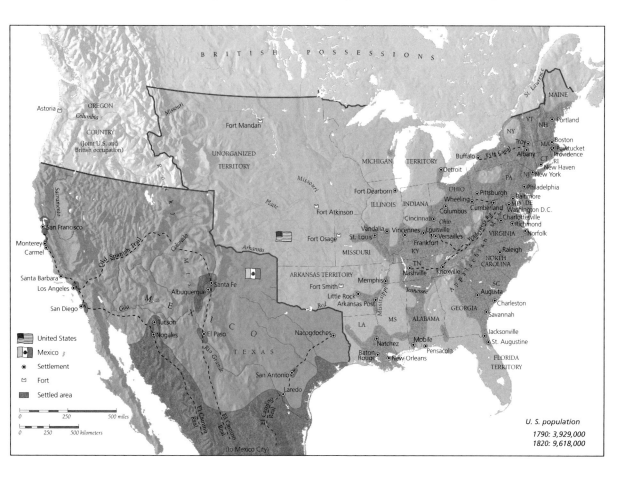

U. S. population
*1790: 3,929,000*
*1820: 9,618,000*

Less well known, however, is that the American Revolution was part of a much broader revolution in European culture in the last half of the eighteenth century. Revolutionary movements in politics, philosophy and architecture fundamentally reoriented the Europeans' most basic assumptions about themselves and their culture. The philosophical movement called the Enlightenment radically questioned common assumptions including the nature of human behavior, the justifications for political power and monarchies, the nature of historical development, and even the suitability of reason itself. At the same time, a Romantic Rebellion in the arts fundamentally challenged the aesthetic assumptions that had dominated Western culture since the Renaissance, celebrating instead aesthetic qualities that were quite diametrically opposed to Classicism's underlying rationalism. This period broke the hegemony of the Classical tradition, eventually leading to the proliferation of architectural styles for which the ensuing nineteenth century is well known. Other countries and colonies joined the United States in their own political revolutions, including the French Revolution and the liberation movements in Central and South America that formed thirteen nations by 1826. As if this were not enough upheaval, this period also saw the beginning of the Industrial Revolution, whose ultimate impact on Western civilization rivals the Agricultural Revolution ten millennia before.

This period marks the end of a 300-year European world view that began in the Renaissance. The new world view it ushers in is recognizably modern. That is, many of the ideas developed in the last half of the eighteenth century still underlie and animate many of the concepts and beliefs that we accept and even hold dear today. Furthermore, many of the problems that resulted from the new world view continue to plague modern society and architecture. We can consequently identify with the ideas, conflicts and personalities in this period more easily than with those in the Renaissance or even the Baroque periods. This chapter explores the ideas behind this cultural revolution, and the architectural concepts and forms that attended it.

## The Enlightenment in Europe

The key to understanding society and architecture in this revolutionary period lies in the philosophical concepts of the Enlightenment. Building on the successes of the natural sciences in the previous century, a number of European thinkers after 1750 believed they could equally apply reason and the scientific method to human and cultural issues. Once they discovered in human affairs underlying principles and laws like those the natural scientists had found in nature, they hoped they could direct and control culture for the benefit of all. They optimistically believed that this understanding and control would lead to continuous improvement and progress towards greater perfection. Once achieved, such a world could indeed be called enlightened.

This attitude led to a radical rethinking of traditional social institutions. Just because humans had long lived with institutions like monarchies was not a justification in itself for the institutions' continuation. The Enlightenment philosophers sought rational reasons for every institution, and argued for their overthrow if they could not find any. Following the model of the natural philosophers, they typically sought these reasons in nature itself. There is a natural order to human affairs and relationships, they insisted, that they could discover by looking back to the origins of human cultures. In the pure and original state of human society they would discover how humans once lived in harmony with the natural order, unconstrained by later artificial social conventions. From this view followed concepts like the Natural Rights of Man that were built into the American Declaration of Independence. From this also followed a general dissatisfaction with existing political structures that encouraged the revolutions of the period.

**Classicism reconsidered**

This search for first principles also led to the first radical critique of Classicism. Carlo Lodoli, a Franciscan monk who was not an architect, rejected every prevailing architectural convention as artificial and contrived. He proposed in their place only two guiding principles. First, base architectural forms on a definite function, and derive them from the strictest necessity. Second, buildings should conform to the nature of materials. By the first principle, he rejected most architectural ornament as functionally unnecessary. By the second principle, he rejected the entire Classical language on the grounds that it artificially transformed into stone what was originally a timber constructional system. He offered as more suitable models Stonehenge and the monuments of ancient Egypt.

The Abbé Marc-Antoine Laugier contrarily defended Classicism, using the common Enlightenment strategy of looking back to historical origins. He speculated that the first ever building must have comprised four tree trunks naturally growing to form a rectangle in plan [94]. The first architect placed tree branches over these trunk-columns to form beams and a simple gable roof. From this beginning derived the Greek temple with its columns, beams, gable roof and triangular pediments. Arches, vaults, broken entablatures, curvy walls and all of the other non-temple elements that had entered the Classical language over the centuries clearly deviated from this original source. The closer architects approximate the rational construction and form of the Greek temples, according to Laugier, the closer their buildings stand to the true principles of nature.

The French visionary architect Étienne-Louis Boullée carried the search for the basic principles of architecture in another direction. In the spirit of Lodoli, he stripped the ornament from Classicism to reveal the raw underlying geometrical forms. He further abstracted from these shapes the basic geometrical elements of cubes, cylinders and spheres. His imaginary Cenotaph for Sir Isaac Newton, drawn at an impossibly fantastic scale, shows both the Enlightenment admiration for one of the geniuses of the natural sciences, as well as the quest for fundamental architectural principles carried to an extreme unprecedented in Western architecture [95]. Along with a number of other Enlightenment French architects including his contemporary Claude-Nicolas Ledoux, Boullée recognized that forms stripped of their traditional details not only lost some of their original meanings, but also could be reshaped to express new meanings. They developed a concept called *architecture parlante*, in which architectural forms were meant to express the purpose of character of the building. Ledoux, for example, designed a house for a cooper designed like a giant barrel.

Lodoli, Laugier, Ledoux and Boullée forcefully expressed what many architects in the eighteenth century deeply felt. Architecture had somehow lost its direction. Under the influence of the Renaissance and Baroque, shapes and forms had crept into the Classical language that had no rational basis or historical foundation. Although they showed little enthusiasm for the extremes of these three theorists, many eighteenth-century architects did wish to find more solid roots for their familiar Classical tradition. A number consequently sought the historical origins of Classicism in the first Classical buildings themselves. In this period, architects traveled to ancient ruins to excavate, measure and reconstruct the original monuments. This was the beginning of the science of archeology. Roman ruins were the first to be explored, since they were more familiar to the West and were more easily accessible. In 1738, excavations began in the ruined Roman town of Herculaneum; ten years later, Pompeii was discovered and studied.

As the century wore on, explorers became more adventurous and wandered further afield. In the 1750s Robert Wood traveled to Syria and published drawings of the Roman buildings he found there. In 1764 Robert Adam, about whom we will hear more later in the chapter, published drawings he made of Diocletian's Palace at Spalato on the coast of present day Croatia. These studies, as we will see, uncovered a number of ideas once commonly used by the Romans that were ignored or overlooked by the Renaissance. These studies also clarified the rules of the Classical language as it was originally used. The effect of the new archaeology on eighteenth-century architects must have been like hearing an articulate speaker of formal English for the first time, after growing up speaking a limited regional dialect. The purified buildings that derived from these archeological studies are commonly called Neoclassical, to distinguish them from the earlier and more florid Baroque use of the Classical language.

The more they learned about Roman culture at its source, the greater the Enlightenment thinkers held it in high esteem. Particularly in France, where pressure was building against the absolutist monarchy, Rome was admired for its Republican form of government in which the citizenry (although narrowly defined) elected their leaders. The heroism and simplicity of the sturdy citizen farmers in the Roman Republic also appealed to the revolutionaries who wished to overthrow the excesses of the French court. They avidly read Roman literature, and quoted extensively from Cicero. Thomas Jefferson acquired this enthusiasm for Roman culture while he was the ambassador to France in the 1780s. His admiration for the Republican system of government, and his taste for Roman architecture, as we will see below, both followed from this exposure.

Until the 1750s, Greek architecture was not well known in Europe. Only the Greek temple at Paestum, in Italy, offered a hint of the style close to home. Greece itself had long been controlled by an Ottoman Empire hostile to Europe and so travel

**94** 'Primitive Hut', 1753, Marc-Antoine Laugier

**95** Cenotaph for Sir Isaac Newton, 1784, Étienne-Louis Boullée

there was hazardous. But as the Enlightenment thinkers dug more deeply into the origins of Classicism, they began to recognize that its true sources lay in Greece, not Rome. James Stuart and Nicholas Revett boldly undertook a journey to Athens in 1751, and published the extensive drawings of their excavations in *The Antiquities of Athens* in 1762. Two years later, Johann Joachim Winckelmann published a highly influential book, *History of Ancient Art*, in which he clarified the differences between Roman and Greek sculpture and argued for the virtues of the latter. Armed with this new justification and more like it, architects who sought to base their designs on the true origins of Classicism rejected the Roman version outright, and turned enthusiastically to the Greek. Others defended the Roman version against the new pretender. The Enlightenment's radical critique of institutions ultimately fractured the Classical language into competing camps, just as the Reformation had fractured the Catholic Church two and a half centuries earlier.

### The Romantic movement

Even though the various proponents in this debate disagreed about the proper source of Classicism, they did not challenge the Classical idea itself. However, another broad intellectual and artistic movement in this period wished to overthrow Classicism altogether. Known as Romanticism, or sometimes the Romantic Rebellion, this movement objected to everything that the Renaissance and Baroque world view held dear. The Romantics saw the Renaissance as a time when individuals were divorced from each other, from nature and from their own culture. The Romantics wished to heal these ruptures and to bring these various components back into harmony. The key point of divergence between the Enlightenment philosophers and the Romantics centered on their respective views of reason and rationality. However radically the Enlightenment philosophers critiqued human institutions, they still accepted without question the primacy of human reason. This was their essential tool for rethinking and remaking society. But even this came under attack by the Romantics.

Jean Jacques Rousseau spearheaded the Romantic assault on reason with a radical rethinking of human nature. Renaissance and Baroque thinkers had long valued reason, he pointed out, because they believed that reason set humans apart from beasts and primitives. The degree to which individuals cultivated their powers of reason was the degree to which they achieved their full potential as humans. Rousseau turned this assumption upside down, using the common Enlightenment strategy of looking back to the origins of culture. If we regard humans in their natural state, he argued, we find that they relied on intuitions and feelings, not reason. Their natural feelings provided reliable guides to good behavior, and even supplied more reliable knowledge about the world than did reason itself. In its natural state, furthermore, each human mind grows in its own personal direction. Unfortunately, the invention of civilization and reason constrained individuals' natural urges and intuitions, and led to hateful and angry passions. The 'noble savage' living in the grace of nature and uncorrupted by society is therefore to be preferred to the modern rationalist.

Rousseau's new conception of the individual provided philosophical justification for two essential components of Romanticism in the arts. First, he attacked the long-standing belief in the uniformity of human minds. For the Classicists to believe that everyone perceives the same objective beauty in objects, they had to assume that all minds are wired similarly, or have infused within them an understanding of the same timeless forms. Rousseau raised the possibility that each mind might perceive a different beauty according to its own unique personality. Second, by elevating intuitions and emotions to a status above reason and rationality, he justified the sensual and emotional side of art and architecture that had often been practiced but never explained.

The new emphasis on emotion led the Romantics to judge the aesthetic qualities of objects in a new way. The Classicists always coolly and rationally judged the beauty of objects according to whether they possessed desired rational properties like good proportion, symmetry and visual balance. The quality of beauty for them elicited a pleasurable feeling of order and controlled delight. The Romantics, in contrast, abandoned reasoned judgments in favor of emotional, intuitive reactions to things. The stronger the emotional response an object elicited, the more value it held. The two views led to quite different attitudes about nature itself. The Classicists regarded untamed nature with some distaste, since it possessed none of the valued properties of order or rationality. The Romantics contrarily reveled in the dangers of untamed nature, particularly seeking out those frightening places like jagged abysses and thundering waterfalls that most excited the emotions. This view found expression in a new fashion of landscape design known as the picturesque. As seen here in Capability Brown's design for the gardens of Stourhead House in Wiltshire, England, the Renaissance and Baroque geometries that found their fullest expression at Versailles are utterly abandoned [96]. The landscape is arranged to appear as if no human hand touched it. Nature is to be admired in its raw state, not artificially controlled.

Classicism and Romanticism similarly diverged on the qualities to admire in manufactured objects like buildings. Where Classicism's emphasis on intellectual clarity valued orderly and complete forms, symmetries, and smooth, manufactured surfaces, Romanticism's emphasis on sensory thrill contrarily valued irregular and incomplete forms, asymmetries and rough, organic surfaces. Giovanni Battista Piranesi expressed these new qualities in a number of extraordinary and influential engravings of imaginary prison interiors [97]. The visual effect of these drawings could not be further removed from the Classical ideal. Forceful asymmetries sweep the eye around the rough and incomplete elements in the picture, never allowing a point of rest or repose. Elements far in the background hint of spaces extending without rational limit into the distance. Given this interest in raw nature rather than in the rational products of human intellect, the Romantics also attacked the Classical idea of art and architecture as the composition of parts. They began to conceive of art as resulting from an inner artistic urge, a vital force much like that which drives nature itself. Just as an acorn organically grows into an oak, the work of art organically and spontaneously grows of its own accord from within the artist.

Given these aesthetic preferences and philosophical ideals, it is not surprising that the Romantics rediscovered the Middle Ages. The visual qualities they admired were to be found in abundance in medieval and Gothic buildings, with their picturesque skylines, dramatic massing, asymmetries and richly complex details. Along with this renewed appreciation of the medieval aesthetic sensibility, the Romantics began to see in the medieval culture all of the values that they missed in their own contemporary society. They perceived the Middle Ages as a time when individuals were part of an organic cultural whole, free from the alienation and artificiality of the Renaissance and Baroque. In the design and construction of Gothic cathedrals in particular, the Romantics saw an ideal world where individual artisans willingly submitted their work to the requirements of the larger project, and where the building arose out of the spiritual and emotional unity of the entire culture.

96 Stourhead House gardens,
Wiltshire, England,
mid-eighteenth century,
Lancelot 'Capability' Brown

97 Carceri, 1751,
Giovanni Battista Piranesi

This admiration for medieval culture and architecture eventually led the Romantics to revive Gothic architectural forms and decorative motifs. Architects throughout the Baroque including Sir Christopher Wren had built in Gothic on occasion, usually for additions to traditionally medieval projects like churches or universities. With the rise of Romanticism after 1750, however, architects began to explore the possibilities of the Gothic for a wider range of building types and for new construction. At first, they simply substituted fanciful Gothic details for Classical ones. Later, they began to employ the medieval language more fully and correctly. Horace Walpole's design for his own country retreat at Strawberry Hill near Twickenham, England, offered one of the first and most influential examples of a full-scale Gothic revival.

If emotions are used to perceive objects, the Romantics realized, then emotions must also play an important role in creating objects. They conceived of an inner vital force within the artist or architect that generates artistic ideas, just as the vital force of nature causes trees to grow or bear fruit. Those artists who possess a stronger inner vital force than others we call artistic geniuses. This special and profound quality cannot be learned. One is either born with the gift, in which case no learning is needed, or one is born without it, in which case no learning can cause it to appear. From this period we get the modern conception of the genius artist or architect who possesses special talents, and who strives to express deeply felt inner emotions. Originality of expression in this view is more important than conformity to prevailing norms.

These new Romantic ideas fundamentally challenged the conception of the architect we saw in Peter Harrison and the other gentlemen architects of the eighteenth century, who rationally and dispassionately composed elements out of pattern books without ever seeking to express their own personalities in the design. Inadvertently, the new conception even challenged one of the most basic values of Romanticism itself. We have already seen how the Romantics valued the Middle Ages precisely because individual artisans willingly submitted their own creative urges to the greater good of the larger society; but now the concept of the autonomous genius argued for the priority of the individual over cultural convention. This paradox plagued the Romantic view well into the twentieth century.

What was once a unity – the universal language of Classicism – was now a trinity of Greek, Roman and Gothic. At first, the proponents of each view offered various reasons why their chosen language should replace the others as the one correct and universal language of architecture. Eventually, though, new philosophical developments swept away the belief in one universal language and ushered in many more stylistic variations than these. Here begins the Battle of the Styles that characterized all of the nineteenth century and most of the twentieth.

The transition from one architectural language to many was reinforced by a new conception of history that emerged in the latter half of the eighteenth century. Since antiquity, Western culture believed that history follows a rational and inexorable plan. The Greeks developed a theory of recurring cycles, the Christians proposed a continuous progression from a definite beginning to a final end in the Day of Judgment, and the Renaissance humanists conceived of culture as beginning in the ancient world, flagging in the Middle Ages, and then reviving in their own period. In all of these views, individuals exerted little control over the grand plan that history followed. But as the eighteenth-century thinkers focused more attention on the individual, they began to conceive of history as the sum total of individual decisions and actions. If a particular individual – like Alexander the Great – did not happen to appear at a particular time with his own particular personality traits, then history might have taken a very different turn. The thinkers in this period began to see history as a series of compartments, each with its own intrinsic character. The Middle Ages was not a decline in culture, it was simply another period with its own cast of individual players and its own equally valid outlook. For the first time, historical periods were valued in their own terms, not as an incomplete stage to something after, or as an inferior version of something that came before.

From the new conception of history came the idea of artistic and architectural style. The Classicists had long conceived of their architectural language as the one correct and timeless approach, either handed to them by a divinity or based in objective properties of nature. But as the Enlightenment and Romantic thinkers focused attention on the special characteristics of individual cultures and historical periods, they began to see that each possessed its own unique aesthetic taste, and therefore its own forms of artistic and architectural expression. In the spirit of the new conception of history, these were not considered inferior versions of some universal taste, but rather as valid expressions in their own right. The word 'style' was developed in this period to denote the particular aesthetic manner of a given culture or historical period.

The concept of style obviously left architects in a dilemma. Just as the Reformation forced Europeans to choose their own religion after centuries of belief in one idea, the new concept of style forced architects self-consciously to choose their style. In his *Architecture in Britain 1530–1830*, Sir John Summerson has pointed out that three approaches can and did follow from this stylistic dilemma: the archeological, the eclectic and the modern. In the archeological approach, one looks to the past and revives wholesale a style that seems appropriate for a present design problem. We have already seen this with the revivals of Greek, Roman and Gothic. At the end of the eighteenth century, architects even began to explore what were called the exotic styles, including Chinese and Indian traditions. At first, each style was used indiscriminately for many different functions. A Greek temple could be a house, a university or a hospital. Later, as more styles flooded into the architects' consciousness, this period developed a theory of associationalism where particular historical styles stood for particular functions. Egyptian forms should be used for mausoleums and cemeteries, Gothic for Christian churches, and so on. This archeological approach dominated architectural thinking in the last half of the eighteenth century.

In the nineteenth and twentieth centuries, as we will see in later chapters, the modern and the eclectic approaches rose to join the archeological in popularity. The modern approach developed when architects realized the full implications of the idea that each historical age had its own particular architectural expression. Why, then, would the contemporary world not have its own particular style? Many nineteenth-century architects tried, and most failed, to invent a uniquely modern style that caught on. Only in the twentieth century did this attempt succeed. More popular in the nineteenth century was the eclectic approach. The eclectics combined the archeological and the modern, by selectively picking and choosing elements from a number of historical styles, and then combining these elements into new and unprecedented compositions. Modernists in the twentieth century disparaged both the eclectic and the archeological approaches because they failed to find a new style appropriate for the new age that was emerging. However, Summerson points out that the modern approach is as irrational as the archeological. Where the archeological approach betrays an irrational quest for a golden age gone by, the modern approach equally betrays an irrational idealization of the future. Only the eclectic approach refuses to romanticize the past or the future. The remainder of this book shows how most European and American architectural production from this point to the present responded in some way to the invention of this idea of style.

# Revolutions

This radical rethinking of traditional ideas eventually culminated in revolutions and wars in Europe and America in the last quarter of the eighteenth century and the first quarter of the next. It is important to note that the intellectual and architectural revolutions we have just examined preceded the political ones, giving lie to the sometimes popular idea that architecture simply responds to prevailing social and economic conditions. Although each revolution had its own particular predisposing causes, the late eighteenth-century mood of radical criticism certainly encouraged events to take more extreme courses than they might have done in times more deferential to authority and tradition.

## The American Revolution

The Americans were the first to revolt against traditional authority. George III gained the British throne in 1760, and managed to rule for 60 years through one of the most tumultuous periods in modern European history. Although he remained popular with his British subjects, his reputation with the American colonists quickly plummeted soon after the conclusion of the Seven Years' War (French and Indian Wars in the colonies) in 1763. The causes of discontent are familiar in American folklore. Britain levied taxes against the colonists to help pay for their defense against the French and the Native Americans during the war, and for their defense against continuing Native American attacks at the frontier afterwards. While the reason for the tax might have been bearable, the colonists objected to the lack of representation in the British Parliament that levied the tax. The colonists further chafed at the continuing restrictions on trade with other nations. In the spirit of the Enlightenment, the colonial thinkers began to look in vain for logical and natural reasons why the British monarchy should continue to govern them, and found a number of reasons why it should not. Civil disobedience and a boycott of British goods escalated into armed confrontation as George and his ministers grossly underestimated the strength of American feeling. The British government attempted to smash resistance to British rule rather than answer the causes of discontent. The two sides joined battle in 1775 and called a truce eight years later with the establishment of a new and independent nation.

Although George mismanaged the conflict and eventually lost the colonies, his actions mainly precipitated what was bound to happen sooner or later. The colonies were doubling in population every 25 years. At that rate, Benjamin Franklin pointed out at mid-century, the number of colonists would exceed the number of British within a hundred years. The population reached two million in 1770 and a little under four million in 1790. At the time of the Revolution, most colonists were born in America and had never set eyes on the homeland. Feeling even less allegiance to Britain were the many other ethnic groups in the colonies that had migrated from other cultures altogether. The sailing time of six weeks between England and America further weakened the control of the homeland over the colonies, particularly at a time when the nascent Industrial Revolution was quickening the pace of social change. The American colonies were bound to strike off on their own.

Without some help, a disparate collection of semi-autonomous colonies without a standing army could offer little resistance to one of Europe's most powerful countries. The colonies astutely formed an alliance with England's greatest enemy, the French. This alliance not only helped secure a favorable outcome to the Revolution, but it also injected a new set of cultural ideas and fashions into the colonies that, until now, had faithfully followed mainly English traditions. Although English fashions remained the dominant influence on American taste well into the twentieth century, from this point on high French fashions periodically find their way into the American culture.

The Americans knew what they were fighting against. They were less clear about what to put in its place at the successful conclusion of the Revolution. The Americans were wary of a central government, since they had long considered themselves citizens of individual colonies and had no experience of a central government other than the distant and detested one they had just overthrown. Through the influence of the Enlightenment philosophers, they became infatuated with the idea of the Roman Republic in which the local citizenry controlled its own affairs. However, as the Romans themselves discovered, a republic cannot effectively govern a widely dispersed population because the seat of government is physically too remote from its constituents to remain responsive to their wishes. The Americans conceived instead of a loose federation of republican states, each comprised of a former colony.

The relative balance of power between the states and the central government immediately became – and remains – one of the most contentious issues in American culture. An early experiment with a weak and powerless central government failed to protect individual states from each other or from various hostilities by foreign powers. In 1787 a Constitutional Convention developed a system of a stronger central government with numerous checks and balances on power. This new system, once ratified by the states, established the United States of America.

Even with this system in place, two almost diametrically opposed visions of the American ideal emerged in the first decades of the new country. These two visions continue to frame a debate about the central core of the American ideal up to the present. Thomas Jefferson, looking to the rural character of his native Virginia, conceived of the new United States as a collection of sturdy gentlemen farmers. These farmers live close to nature and the soil, and determine their own fate through local democratic control. Cities are to be avoided if possible, while minimal power should be delegated to the central federal government. To advance this vision he helped form the Republican Party. Alexander Hamilton, in contrast, saw the strength and future of the new country in commerce and industry. These activities are supported in cities. He argued for a strong central government that could promote and regulate this activity, and fight against other commercial rivals in international trade. He helped form the Federalist party to advance his conception. Under the benign supervision of the first president George Washington, Hamilton as Secretary of the Treasury managed to promote his conception over Jefferson's in the early days of the new nation.

In the hindsight of history, we might say that Jefferson looked back to a fast disappearing agrarian world, while Hamilton looked forward to the new industrial world just appearing on the world stage. However, Jefferson's image derived from powerful Romantic ideas of individuals living in harmony with nature and flourishing under minimal social control. His vision animated much of subsequent American culture, particularly when it began to suffer the pains of urbanization and industrialization. Frank Lloyd Wright's ideas about houses and town planning in the twentieth century, as we will see in a later chapter, derived in large part from Jefferson's Romanticism.

## Architecture for the new nation

One might have expected, after this revolutionary break with the home country, that the Americans would equally overthrow their English architectural traditions. After all, English architecture stood as a constant reminder of the culture they had rejected. For just this reason, Thomas Jefferson proposed to replace the English architectural ideas with others more suitable for the new Republic. However, most Americans after the revolution did not follow Jefferson in this notion. They continued to build according to the fashions of England and sometimes other European cultures well into the twentieth century. This did not simply represent an habitual continuation of existing traditions, because as Europe's fashions changed so did the Americans mostly follow. Despite the Americans' stirring declaration of independence from Europe in matters political, they humbly acquiesced in matters of fashion and taste to what they must have seen as a more sophisticated social and visual culture across the ocean. This puzzling sense of inferiority towards European culture and taste continues even today in consumer product marketing campaigns that promote 'Eurostyle' or European sophistication. The Americans might have reveled in the Rousseauian idea that they stood closer to nature and were less tainted by artificial European civilization. Instead, they usually chose to acquire as much of that civilization as possible.

The most popular architectural style in America after the revolution has been called the Federalist style. This name may have derived from the members of Hamilton's Federalist party in Boston who promoted the style, or more generally from the new period that followed on the Constitution's strengthening of a central federal government. It mostly mimicked the styles of two rival English architects who dominated English taste from 1760 to 1790, Robert Adam and Sir William Chambers. The work of these two architects was fairly traditional, in that it mainly evolved from the earlier Renaissance/Baroque/Palladian ideas of the previous generation, and did not fully embrace the revolutions in architectural theories and taste that we have so far examined. This fact alone may well account for the popularity of these two in England and America during the first half of this revolutionary period. They did, however, add ideas noticeably different from the earlier tradition.

Robert Adam was the same who had studied the ruins of Diocletian's Palace at Spalato. There he discovered in the original Roman structures new ideas that had been overlooked by the mainstream of Classical architects from the Renaissance on. Most importantly, he uncovered in the Roman baths a method of planning rooms which combined a rich variety of oval, circular and rectangular spaces within an overall simple box. Where a circular room adjoined a rectangular one, the Romans made up the difference between the two spaces with a thickened wall sculpted to each shape. Adam found archeological justification for the very shapes that Laugier had rejected as artificial and arbitrary inventions. Adam used this Roman method to plan houses with an unprecedented variety of room shapes [98]. This planning principle became one of the key characteristics of his own architectural style, and of the Federalist style in America that copied it.

The other lesson Adam learned from his study of Roman domestic architecture was its characteristic system of rich surface decoration and pattern, of which Roman floor and wall mosaics are most familiar today. He translated this idea into a highly personal version of decoration that was both astringent and elegant [99]. This became another characteristic mark of the Adam and the Federalist style. On the outside of his buildings, Adam continued the Anglo Palladian tradition of simple, box-like forms

and prominent temple fronts. To this he added a few subtle ideas in the detailing. As if to signal in advance the oval rooms beyond, he sometimes placed a semi-oval fan-light over the front door. In another favorite device much copied by the Federalists, he often set a Palladian window into a larger arched recess.

The house Woodlands, in Philadelphia, is a good example of the Federalist style modeled after Adam's ideas [100]. Not strikingly different in massing from the popular Gibbsian house style of the previous generation, the front façade presents a straightforward rectangular box capped with a hipped roof. Here the temple front stands free of the wall, whereas in the Gibbs version it was usually attached. Typical of the Adam and Federalist style, the columns themselves are more slender and more widely spaced than was common a generation before. The Adam semi-elliptical fan-light window over the main door, and the Palladian window within the larger arched recess, also subtly betray the new style. Only on the inside does the full effect of the new style become clear. Following Adam, the plan is comprised of rectangles, ovals, semi-circular apses and squares linked together with sculpted walls [101]. The oval rooms at the back dramatically burst out of their rectangular confinement, providing a surprising visual contrast to the austere rectangular front.

Adam's oval and circular room shapes gave rise to another dramatic invention characteristic of his style. A staircase placed into such a room sweeps up and around in a helix, providing an exhilarating sense of a stair floating in space. Woodlawn in Fairfax County, Virginia, shows the effect [102]. Adam's decorative system was so intensely personal and original that his style is one of the few to be named after an individual, and so few Federalist houses in America attained the same degree of decorative control and expression which we find in his own works. Closest to his style, although more restrained in its expression and wall coverage, was the work of the American sculptor Samuel McIntire.

William Chambers also traveled and studied various architectural styles first-hand, including French, Italian and even Chinese. In the spirit of the Enlightenment, he wrote a *Treatise on Civil Architecture* in 1759 which attempted to abstract from these various styles certain principles of architecture lying behind them all. He built in a number of styles himself, including a Chinese Pagoda at Kew Gardens outside London. Mostly, however, he favored a Neoclassical style derived from the Anglo

100 Woodlands, Philadelphia,
Pennsylvania, 1788–89

Palladians earlier in the century. His most important design was for Somerset House on the bank of the Thames in London [103]. The largest English public building since Wren's grand Baroque project at Greenwich a century earlier, Somerset House was planned to bring a number of government offices and learned societies together under one roof. Chambers used his preferred Neoclassical style for this public government building, no doubt noting how the style suited the dignified character of the building type. For the center of the water-front façade, he took up a standard Classical motif that we have already seen in Palladio's Villa Rotonda, Burlington's Chiswick House and a number of churches: a pediment and a projecting colonnade stand in front of a central rotunda capped with a dome.

101 Woodlands, plan

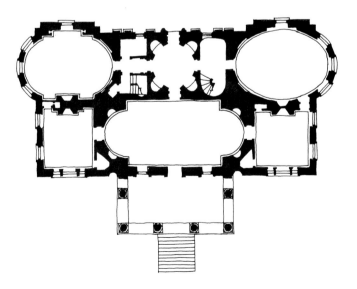

102 Woodlawn, Fairfax County,
Virginia, 1799, William Thornton

The central compositional arrangement of Somerset House exerted considerable influence on subsequent American architecture. The American architect Charles Bulfinch saw the design during his Grand Tour of European architecture in 1785–87. On his return, he was given the commission to design the new Massachusetts State House in Boston. Until now, as we have seen, the few public government buildings in America modeled themselves after English Baroque ideas. These comprised either enlarged English Baroque house forms or, in the case of Independence Hall in Philadelphia, a house form with an attached English Baroque church steeple. Bulfinch rejected this earlier Baroque tradition in favor of the idea he had seen in Somerset House. Chambers' building, after all, represented the latest and most sophisticated idea about government buildings in one of the premier capitals of Europe. Bulfinch simply attached the central motif of Somerset House to a box which sported Adam's Palladian windows within an arched recess [104]. Many subsequent State Capitol buildings took up the motif of the dome and temple front in preference to the earlier Baroque ideas. In the minds of most Americans, this motif is now largely synonymous with a government building.

103 Somerset House,
London, England, 1776–80,
Sir William Chambers

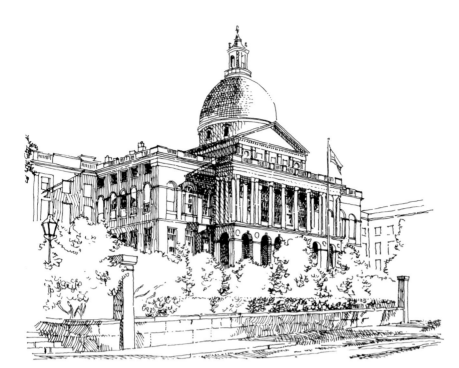

104 Massachusetts State House,
Boston, Massachusetts, 1795–97,
Charles Bulfinch

The post-revolutionary preference for conservative architectural forms carried into the design of the new federal capital city and government buildings. To appease regional concerns about the location of the new national center, George Washington selected a site halfway between the north and south on the Potomac River. He asked one of his aides during the Revolution, the French engineer Pierre Charles L'Enfant, to draw up a plan for the new city of Washington in the District of Columbia [105]. L'Enfant turned to Baroque town planning concepts as he would have seen at Versailles. He arranged the entire city around the two important branches of the new government. One high point he identified as the site for a president's house, and another he selected for the house of Congress, later called the Capitol. Like nearby Williamsburg, he connected the two with axes crossing at right angles. The axis west from the Capitol to the river (now known as the Mall) was to be lined with government buildings, while the axis south from the president's house would remain a grand lawn and garden. A rectangular grid of streets for the remainder of the city aligned with this cruciform plan. So the two centers of government could watch each other, L'Enfant provided a diagonal street now known as Pennsylvania Avenue directly connecting the two hilltops. To this diagonal he aligned a number of other diagonal streets, intersecting at various nodes throughout the city and creating a web-like pattern just like in the garden at Versailles. L'Enfant's plan provided a grand Baroque framework for a new capital city, much more French than English, and based on ideas that were last fashionable in Europe over a hundred years earlier.

At Thomas Jefferson's suggestion, a national competition was arranged in 1792 to solicit designs for the President's House and the house of Congress. The Irish immigrant architect James Hoban proposed a traditional English country house design for the President's House, largely based on Gibbs, which quickly won over its rivals. It was mostly completed to this design except for the interiors by 1814. Unfortunately, the competition turned up no satisfactory designs for the Capitol building. As

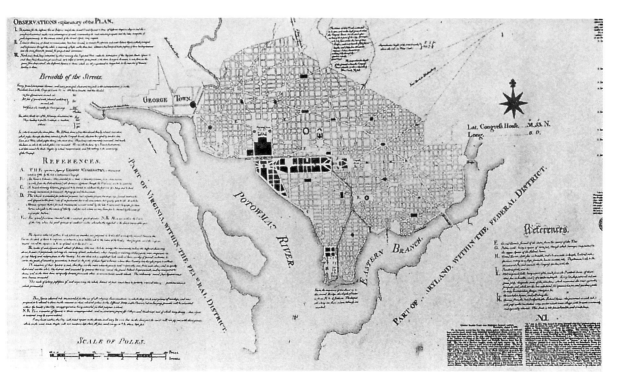

105 Plan of Washington, DC,
1791, Charles Pierre L'Enfant

106 United States Capitol,
Washington, DC, 1792,
William Thornton

several commentators have noted, the American builders and amateur architects had little experience with monumental public buildings and could not conceive of forms beyond grandiose country houses. After the competition closed, the amateur Dr William Thornton received permission to submit a design whose grander scale and stature immediately placed it above its competitors in the eyes of Washington, Jefferson and the Commissioners of Federal Buildings. Although Thornton had no practical knowledge of construction, he derived his design from the usual eighteenth-century architecture books. At the center he placed a Palladian temple front and low dome over a central rotunda [106]. Each of the two chambers of government received its own wing on either side of the center, clearly expressed in the usual Palladian manner as discrete blocks. These were linked back to the center with recessed connecting forms, appropriately throwing most of the visual attention onto the center and the two ends.

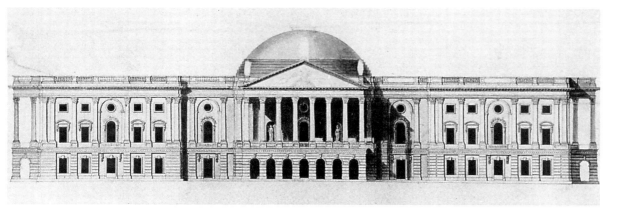

The form symbolically expressed the structure of the government housed within, although it could have been designed anywhere in England from the 1720s on.

With no practical experience, Thornton could not supervise the construction of his own design. A number of architects were subsequently hired to undertake the project over the next forty years, many of whom wished to impose their own ideas onto his scheme. This and the technical complexities of such a large building slowed construction. By 1814 only the two wings without a center were completed. The story of this building and the President's House continues later in the chapter, when stylistic interests changed early in the nineteenth century. The important idea to keep in mind at this point is the conservative origins of the country's first and most important major public buildings. Revolutionary zeal in politics did not convert to revolutionary zeal in architecture at the symbolic and political center of the new republic.

Only Thomas Jefferson saw a connection between politics and architecture in this period. He began his career as an amateur gentleman architect before the revolution in a conventional manner, employing ideas similar to ones we have already examined. He discovered Palladio through books and through discussions with other amateur architects during his college days at William and Mary. For his own house at Monticello in Virginia, he derived a plan from a plate in Robert Morris's *Select Architecture*, and an elevation from a plate in Palladio. Construction began in 1771 on a fairly conventional Palladian house with large two-story porticos on either end of the central block, and flanking service wings. The only remarkable characteristics of this design were the octagonal elements in the plan that he took from Morris's plate, and the unprecedented decision to build on the top of a hill, rather than in the valleys as was the custom with previous Virginian mansions. Letters Jefferson wrote to friends about the glorious views from the hilltop of unconstrained nature reveal a Romantic motivation for the selection of this site. Work proceeded until 1782, when Jefferson had to concentrate his attentions fully on helping to construct the new nation.

Jefferson's favorable disposition towards chaste Palladian forms led him to criticize the English Baroque buildings that dominated the American scene. In his view these were aberrations from the Classical ideal as expressed in Palladio. After the Revolution, this objection to British traditions on visual grounds increasingly translated into an objection on cultural grounds. Why, he wondered, would the new American nation not find its own style of architecture independent of its British colonial heritage? His search for new architectural ideas and forms began in 1784, when he moved to Paris to take up his new post as Minister to the Court of France. There he encountered the French Neoclassical movement in full force. He learned of the Enlightenment philosophers' admiration for the Roman Republic, and the notion that Roman Republic architecture best expresses that ideal political arrangement. He also learned of Laugier's call to return architecture to basic structural principles as seen in the Classical temple form. He toured southern France, and saw there for the first time an authentic Roman temple, the Maison Carrée in Nîmes. Jefferson was overwhelmed by the clarity and purity of the form, and by its positive association with valued political concepts. This, he realized, should be the new style for his new country. His views were confirmed by a brief visit to England, whose architecture he later described as the 'most wretched stile I ever saw'.

Jefferson soon found an opportunity to translate the new ideal into a practical reality. Before leaving for Europe, he helped convince his fellow Virginians to move

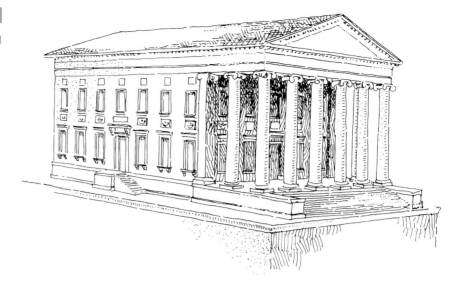

**107** Virginia State Capitol
(model), Richmond, Virginia,
1785–89, Thomas Jefferson

their capital city from Williamsburg to Richmond further west. This move served symbolically to sever the link with the old center of British colonial rule, and it acknowledged the state's westward expanding population. While in France, Jefferson was asked to obtain designs for the new capitol building. Seizing his chance to influence American architecture, he designed it himself with the advice of C.L.A. Clérisseau, one of the leading proponents of Neoclassicism. His design attempted to recreate the Maison Carrée as much as functional necessity would allow [**107**]. Only the windows for a second floor betray a foreign set of functions within the Classical temple form. This was the first post-revolutionary American building utterly to reject British architectural traditions. Even more significantly, it was the first building in America and Europe to follow fully the precepts of Laugier in modeling itself after a literal temple form. Small temples had been constructed as Romantic follies in European gardens after 1750, but this was the first time since antiquity that a pure temple form housed a fully functioning building. Jefferson anticipated by twenty years and more what later became a common architectural desire in Europe and America to recreate authentic Classical temple forms for a variety of functional purposes.

### The French Revolution and its aftermath

By the end of the eighteenth century, not even the most progressive European architects had carried the Enlightenment concepts to the radical conclusion we saw in Jefferson's Virginia State Capitol. The most adventurous still designed buildings with Renaissance/Baroque/Palladian massing and compositional elements, although stripped down and simplified in detail. Indeed, it is sometimes difficult to discern the differences between many of the Neoclassical buildings of this period and the Anglo Palladian buildings of three-quarters of a century earlier.

European architecture, and later American architecture, took a more radical turn after the French Revolution. The French rejection of their monarchy in the last decade of the eighteenth century eventually turned much of Europe upside down.

The Napoleonic Wars that followed on the heels of the revolution profoundly upset Europe's social and political structures, while Napoleon himself adapted a more extreme version of Neoclassicism as a symbol of his empire. Architects in Europe either followed his lead, or developed different but equally radical architectural forms.

France spent heavily to support the American Revolution, exacerbating a financial crisis back home. In 1789 Louis XVI was forced to call an assembly of the aristocracy, the clergy and the commoners to help find additional funds. The commoners cleverly gained voting control of the assembly and began a revolt against both king and aristocracy. They abolished the last legal vestiges of feudalism, spelled out the rights of man in keeping with Enlightenment ideals, and established a constitution with a virtually powerless monarchy. France was well on its way to a bloodless revolution, until Austria, Prussia and later England tried to take advantage of France's political instability and declared war. Chaos followed. The French monarchy was abolished altogether, a Republic was established, a civil war broke out between royalists and republicans, and the king was beheaded. Even the most ardent admirers of the French Revolution in America and other European countries recoiled in horror at the Reign of Terror in 1793–94 accompanying the civil war.

Here began one of the most dramatic events in modern European history, the age of Napoleon. Only the briefest of details need be spelled out here, to set the background for the architectural ideas which emerged in this period. Napoleon was France's most successful general in the war against the European aggressors. As one part of his campaign he invaded Egypt, where he also took scholars to study the remains of the ancient civilization. Although the British soon drove him out, the new knowledge of Egypt quickly entered into high European fashion, leading to an Egyptian style of furniture and interior decoration that was particularly identified with Napoleon himself. On his return to Paris, he maneuvered himself into control of the new Republic, first as a Consul answerable to the legislative body and, after 1804, as Emperor Napoleon I with absolute personal powers. He carried the war deep into Europe, sometimes adding territory directly to France, sometimes indirectly controlling territory, and usually forging a new national spirit among groups who fought against him. The idea that nations ought to be formed out of groups with a common culture and language, rather than out of dynastic arrangements, strengthened in Europe in this period.

Napoleon saw himself carrying the French Enlightenment ideals of 'liberté, égalité, fraternité' to the rest of Europe. He consequently took on the cultural and architectural trappings of the Roman Republic that had earlier fascinated the French philosophers. The painting of his coronation as Emperor portrays him in a Roman laurel-wreath crown. He also directed his architects to construct archeologically correct Roman buildings in Paris. These included the Arc de Triomphe du Carrousel modeled after the Arch of Septimus Severus, a copy of Trajan's Column in the Place Vendôme, and the Madeleine or Temple of Glory accurately modeled on its exterior after a typical Roman temple. The latter put in Europe what Jefferson had put in America twenty years before. However, there was now a twist to the idea. Napoleon appropriated the symbols of ancient Rome to stand for his imperial reign, whereas before they stood for a democratic republic. This must have caused some consternation for those who believed he had betrayed the lofty Enlightenment ideals of the French Revolution. Did the Roman architectural language now stand for democracy or imperialism? This debate continued well into the twentieth century, between those who saw Classicism as an expression of democracy and those who saw it as the architecture of oppression.

**Revolutionary architecture in Britain and America**

This revolutionary period at the turn of the century also eventually goaded a number of British architects into developing more extreme versions of Romantic and Neoclassical ideas than they had so far attempted. The most original work, and the work that exerted the most influence on American architecture, came from Sir John Soane. Soane's work largely defies categorization. He used Greek and Roman architectural elements almost interchangeably, seeing no strong philosophical reason to favor one over the other. Some of his forms are recognizably Classical, while others are entirely original expressions in no known style. He was an eclectic, in Summerson's terms, but he possessed such a powerful ability to synthesize and transform his selected architectural elements that his work became much more than a sum of the parts.

His Bank of England project shows the most significant components of his new architectural approach [108]. Nowhere in this particular room do we find the usual Classical elements like columns and entablatures. Only thin incisions in the wall vaguely remind us of pilasters. Lodoli's prohibition against ornament is here carried to an unprecedented extreme. Even the dome and arches are not what they seem. Traditional Classical domes rest on what are called pendentives, separate triangular

**108** Bank of England, London, England, 1788–1823, Sir John Soane

elements that fill up the corner space between the round base of the dome and the square room beneath. From his master George Dance, Soane acquired the idea of a pendentive dome, where the pendentive flows smoothly into the dome itself. Rather than sitting solidly on heavy columns or buttresses, the lower points of the pendentive dome seem to rest solely on the knife edges of each buttress. The effect is more like a balloon floating away than a heavy weight bearing down. Further enhancing this almost magical effect, Soane sliced off the top of the dome to admit a mysterious light through a clerestory lantern above. The building is both Classical and Romantic, in the sense that the rational and geometrical are fused with the picturesque and sensual. A similar attitude of radical reductionism informed the exteriors of his buildings, often reducing the various components to their most severely plain geometrical expression.

Soane's ideas came to America through Benjamin Henry Latrobe. The son of a school headmaster in Yorkshire and an American mother, Latrobe studied architecture with the British architect Samuel Pepys Cockerell and set up his own practice in London in 1791. There he came into contact with Soane's new Neoclassical ideas. Four years later he declared bankruptcy and emigrated to America for a fresh start. Latrobe became America's first professional architect, fully trained in engineering and architecture, and making his living solely from fees. Indeed, with some difficulty he introduced the European idea that the architect should be paid a percentage of the building costs. A number of his commissions drew upon his engineering expertise, including designs for canals, waterworks and dockyards. As he learned to move in the circles of America's cultural and political leaders including Washington and Jefferson, he also received important commissions for major public buildings and churches.

The Roman Catholic Baltimore Cathedral remains one of his most notable buildings, and clearly shows his debt to Soane and Neoclassicism. Like Wren's St Paul's in London, Latrobe superimposed a circular dome onto a traditional cruciform plan [109]. Like St Paul's, the domed central space sits over both nave and aisles, fusing together the component spatial parts. In the treatment of the interior spaces and surfaces, however, the building owes more to Soane and Neoclassicism than to Wren [110]. Unlike St Paul's, the central rotunda becomes the main space, much like the

109 Baltimore Cathedral, Baltimore, Maryland, 1804–18, Benjamin Latrobe

110 Baltimore Cathedral, interior

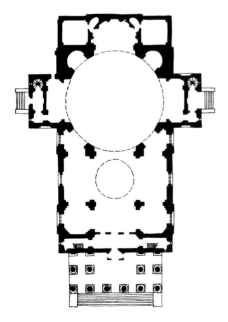

111 Baltimore Cathedral, exterior

112 Christ Church, Washington,
DC, 1808, Benjamin Latrobe

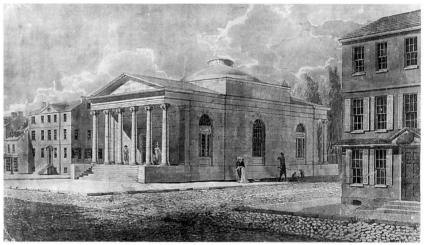

113 Bank of Pennsylvania,
Philadelphia, Pennsylvania,
1798–1800, Benjamin Latrobe

domed spaces in Soane's Bank of England or even like the circular Pantheon in ancient Rome. In the spirit of Soane's pendentive domes, Latrobe flows the circle of the dome into the circular walls below, stressing at one moment the geometrically independent elements, and at the next moment their intimate connection. The Classical details are reduced to a minimum in the Neoclassical spirit. Incisions in the wall, barely projecting cornices, and the occasional thickened corner merely hint at traditional Classical elements. The same radical reductionism shapes the exterior [111]. The projecting Ionic portico two bays deep reminds us of the Classical temple origins of the language, while the rest of the building reduces mainly to simple geometrical elements distinguished from each other by thin incisions or slight projections. Only the faintest of cornices and a change of materials hints at a capping entablature. Unlike the now pervasive Gibbsian tradition of a single spire behind the temple front, here Latrobe returned to the twin towers of Gothic cathedrals and Baroque churches. Perhaps he wished to distinguish this Catholic cathedral from the now standard Protestant church form in America.

Thomas Jefferson in his design for the Virginia State Capitol, as we have seen, enthusiastically committed to one particular style on aesthetic and political grounds. Latrobe, like Soane, contrarily accepted the Enlightenment concept of a multitude of equally valid styles and chose one or another as convenient. He did not even relate his styles to particular functions. He used Gothic for the house Sedgeley in Philadelphia (built in 1799, this was the first Gothic revival house in America), and Gothic for the Christ Church in Washington, DC [112]. He even submitted two designs for Baltimore cathedral, one in Gothic and one in the Neoclassical style that was built. For the Bank of Pennsylvania built in 1798–1800 he employed the first Greek Ionic order in America [113]. In the latter building, he juxtaposed a Roman domed rotunda with a Greek temple whose details derived from the north portico of the Erechtheum at Athens. With this astonishing array and synthesis of styles, Latrobe introduced to America the Enlightenment concept of architectural eclecticism. As America's most prominent architect at the beginning of the nineteenth century, he also gave the concept an intellectual and aesthetic respectability that encouraged it to flourish throughout much of the century.

Although Thomas Jefferson never wavered from his unabiding admiration for Roman Classicism, around the turn of the century he shifted away from his early archae-ological correctness towards a more eclectic use of the language. In 1796 he dismantled most of his earlier Palladian Monticello and began again with a new conception. The building as it stands today blends so many ideas that, like Soane's work, it largely defies historians' efforts to categorize it as a particular style [114]. The central com-positional device of a shallow dome and a portico front derives from Palladio and even the Anglo Palladianism of Lord Burlington's Chiswick House. However, from con-temporary French Neoclassical practice Jefferson acquired the idea of building a single story house in the manner of Roman Republic villas. Numerous sophisticated and subtle adjustments to the form, including chamfered corners, a slightly recessed wall behind the portico, and ingenious separations of public and private spaces within, mark the transformation from Jefferson as an amateur copier of pattern books, to Jefferson as a mature designer with original conceptions of space and form [115].

Jefferson applied his new skills and eclectic approach to his design for the Uni-versity of Virginia. In Europe at the beginning of the nineteenth century, educators like Wilhelm von Humboldt had attempted to reform the universities and bring them more in line with Enlightenment ideals. Where universities had long been associated with religious education and the transmission of the classics, now the reformers wished to base higher education more on scientific research and on the pursuit of ideas wher-ever reason might lead. The University of Berlin was founded in the first decade of the century with this program in mind. In 1816, after years of negotiations, Jefferson convinced his fellow Virginians to found a similar university near Monticello. No theology would be taught. Rather, the sciences, agriculture and the classics would carry equal weight in the new curriculum.

For the new campus, Jefferson conceived of an 'academical village'. He wished to avoid the traditional English university cloister dominated by the chapel and turned inward against the world. He equally wished to avoid the unplanned growth of buildings at other American university campuses like Harvard, where the casual and irregular arrangement of buildings was not conducive to the rational pursuit of knowledge. Jefferson designed instead a symmetrically organized, highly rational and outward looking building complex [116]. At one end of a central lawn stood the library and lecture rooms, dominating the composition just as the chapel dominated the traditional English university cloister. He modeled the central building after the Pantheon in ancient Rome, with a temple portico standing before a domed circular

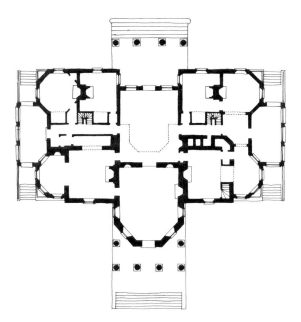

114 Monticello, Albemarle County, Virginia, after its 1796–1809 remodel, Thomas Jefferson

115 Monticello, plan

form. On either side of the central lawn he arranged a row of dormitories for the students, interrupted periodically by larger pavilions for the professors. Each pavilion employed a different version of the Roman Classical orders, so that the instructor in architecture could refer to them for ideal architectural prototypes. By placing students and faculty in close proximity to each other, Jefferson hoped to encourage meaningful conversations between them. Colonnades linked the dormitories and pavilions back

116 University of Virginia,
Charlottesville, Virginia,
1823–27, Thomas Jefferson

to the main building, while an additional row of dormitories faced each inner row across smaller gardens. The end of the central lawn opposite the library opened up to views of the mountains beyond, focusing the academic community's attentions at one moment on the repository of human knowledge, and at the next moment on raw nature unadorned. The building linked both the Enlightenment and Romantic ideals.

The federal buildings took new shape in this eclectic period. After Jefferson's election as President of the United States in 1800, Benjamin Latrobe gained the position of Surveyor of the Public Buildings and undertook a number of revisions of the President's House and the original Capitol. He added the now familiar colonnaded portico to the entrance of the President's House, for example, updating the original English Baroque design and contributing a more monumental character to the building. Work ceased during the war of 1812, the unfortunate conflict which resulted in part from the British policy of searching American ships bound for Napoleonic Europe, and in part from suspicions that the British were stirring up Native American resistance on the Northwestern frontier. The British stormed Washington, DC, in 1814 and ignominiously burned the President's House and the Capitol. After the war, first Latrobe and then Bulfinch undertook necessary repairs and reconstruction. The President's House was painted white to disguise the charred masonry, from which derived the now familiar title White House. In rebuilding the Capitol, Latrobe was politically obliged to

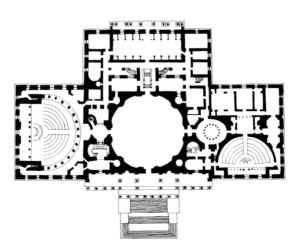

117 United States Capitol,
Washington, DC, 1793–1829,
Thornton, Latrobe, Bulfinch,
plan in 1829

118 American Orders of Architecture, Washington, DC, c. 1815, Benjamin Latrobe

119 United States Capitol, Washington, DC, 1793–1829, Thornton, Latrobe, Bulfinch, exterior in 1829

retain Thornton's original design for the exterior, although he extensively remodeled the interiors and submitted a design for the still incomplete center. His interiors included complex asymmetries within an overall symmetrical plan [117], Soanian Neoclassical treatments, and a wide variety of Greek Orders. For the north wing he ingeniously invented two new architectural Orders appropriate for America. The capital of one sprouted the flowers and leaves of the tobacco plant, while the other bundled together ears of corn [118]. Although these were greatly admired by the members of Congress, they did not subsequently enter into the common American architectural vocabulary. Bulfinch took over the Capitol work in 1817 and completed the work largely to Latrobe's design in 1827, changing mainly the height of Latrobe's proposed dome at the Congress's request [119]. A British military incursion brought a Baroque building into the mainstream of contemporary Neoclassical thinking.

### The end of the Spanish Empire

Spain and Portugal, already well beyond their days of glory and power, sank even further during the Napoleonic Wars. Even when the allies defeated Napoleon and banished him to the Island of Elba in 1814, Spain and Portugal could not manage their own internal affairs, much less the affairs of their colonies. Inspired by the Enlightenment and emboldened by the success of the American Revolution, the Spanish and Portuguese colonists rose in revolt between 1808 and 1826 and created thirteen new nations in Central and South America. Mexico gained its independence in 1821 and took possession of the former Spanish land in much of central America and the present day southwestern United States, including Texas, Colorado, Utah, New Mexico, Arizona, Nevada and California.

One of the last important acts of the Spanish Empire before it fell, at least in terms of United States history, was to extend the mission system into California. From 1769 onwards, Father Junípero Serra established most of the 21 missions that eventually dotted the coast from San Diego to San Francisco. Unlike the Pueblo dwellers in present day New Mexico and Arizona, as we have seen, the California Native Americans did not develop masonry construction systems. Father Serra therefore drew nothing from the indigenous architectural traditions, and instead imported his architectural ideas from Mexico. Some of the missions he and his padres designed themselves, others he turned over to Mexican masons brought up to undertake the construction. The Native Americans provided basic labor.

The architectural style of the California missions remained fairly simple and utilitarian. The attached churches, as usual, were given the most elaborate treatment. San Carlos de Borromeo, in the administrative center of the California mission system at Carmel, shows how the California buildings largely continued the Baroque traditions of the previous century [120]. The bold massing, the piled up geometries of the towers and the lack of archeologically correct Classical details show no hint of the revolutions in architecture discussed earlier in this chapter. Only in one of the last missions to be built, at Santa Barbara in 1815–20, do we see evidence of the Neoclassical fashion [121]. Here the lines of the building are more horizontal, the surfaces are more plain, and the tell-tale Classical columns and pediment are more historically correct. A number of Californian architects at the end of the nineteenth century, as a later chapter will show, regarded the mission buildings with the utmost reverence. They attempted to create a 'mission style' based on these forms, although we will see how that style in the end bore little relationship to Father Serra's original buildings.

120 San Carlos de Borromeo, Carmel, California, 1793–97, Manuel Estevan Ruiz

121 Santa Barbara Mission, Santa Barbara, California, 1815–20

## Western expansion and its architecture

The relentless migration to the West continued in this period, as people sought new opportunities and land just beyond the last settlement. In the North, Americans broke through the barrier of the Appalachian Mountains into the Ohio valley, and in the South moved into the areas of present day states Alabama and Mississippi. By 1800 nearly a million people lived between the Appalachians and the Mississippi River. Soon after the successful conclusion of the revolution, and after initial quarrels about who controlled the new territories and settlements, the original states agreed to hold the western land collectively. They further agreed to divide it into territories that could be admitted as new states into the Union, once each had gained sufficient population.

American migration was blocked at the Mississippi River, since the fast waning Spanish Empire still owned the lands beyond. However, as part of Napoleon's remaking of Europe's political landscape, he announced in 1800 that France had taken possession of most of Spain's North American lands. In greater need of cash for his European wars than of a distant colonial region that he could not defend, Napoleon agreed to sell the territory to the United States for 15 million dollars in 1803. The Louisiana Purchase added 828,000 square miles to America, stretching from the mouth of the Mississippi to the Rocky Mountains. By 1821, 11 new states had joined the Union, whose borders now extended from the eastern seaboard to the west side of much of the Mississippi River, and from the St Lawrence River to the top of the Florida panhandle (Spain finally ceded Florida to the United States in 1819, and it became a state in 1845).

Those who migrated west usually sought a better life than was available to them where they originated. To carve a new home out of what they regarded as an untamed and hostile wilderness required self-sufficient independence, incredible perseverance and the mutual support of neighbors. These qualities are still regarded by many as the core American virtues, and the frontier is regarded as the forge where these qualities were hammered into shape. The late nineteenth-century American historian Frederick Jackson Turner even credited most of the differences between European and American culture to the American frontier experience.

However, carving out new homes at the frontier came at a price. First of all, while the white and sometimes black settlers regarded the frontier as a westward moving boundary between triumphant civilization and untamed wilderness, the Native Americans contrarily saw this boundary as the leading edge of an invading and foreign culture. The Native Americans were pushed off the land yet again, often through the instrument of dubious treaties that were as quickly broken as they were signed.

Second, the struggles to build in the wilderness created a pervasive attitude among the Americans that nature should be submitted to human control and order. The eighteenth-century Romantic ideal of living in harmony with nature – usually espoused by philosophers living in the comforts of the city or on well-established farms – did not find a receptive audience at the frontier. The desire to control nature found a spectacular expression in the Cartesian grid that was imposed onto the lands between the Ohio and Mississippi Rivers in 1785. A Congress in desperate need of funds after the revolution wished to sell off the public lands as expediently as possible. It decreed that the land be surveyed into townships six miles square aligned on the cardinal points. Each township was then divided into 36 lots, later called sections, a mile square each. The grid was subsequently imposed upon most of the land to the Pacific, marching inflexibly and inexorably over plains, mountains, rivers and lakes. Town layouts, county lines, state boundaries and often roads in two-thirds of the present day United States reflect this system. Just like the ancient Anasazi and Roman road systems, highways in the West often run dead straight for miles over hill and dale, and then suddenly turn ninety degrees at the corner of a section line [122]. Although the imposition of this grid is partly explained by planning expediency, it also revives the practice we saw in the ancient world and at Versailles of asserting human control through geometry.

As part of the conquering mentality, the American settlers at the frontier did not see nature as something to be nurtured and gradually developed over generations. Many settlers stayed in one place until the soil depleted or the natural resources were extracted, and then moved on to the next frontier. This attitude contributed to a uniquely American concept of physical mobility that accompanied its already well-established social mobility. New opportunities always beckoned over the next horizon, and many Americans answered their call. America, particularly in the West, consequently never developed to the same degree the European sense of connection to the land, or the tradition of generations rooted to one place.

**122** Aerial view of western plains

At the beginning of the nineteenth century, the frontier had not yet reached the western edge of the great deciduous forest that still covered much of the eastern United States. Like the Native Americans who had adapted to the woodlands for millennia, the first European settlers in new territory relied extensively upon woodland products for their construction materials. But rather than building time-consuming and technically difficult wooden frames, as in the early colonial architecture, the settlers in urgent need of quick shelter at the frontier turned instead to the log cabin [123]. This system of piling up horizontal logs notched and interconnected at the corners, as already seen, was first developed in prehistoric northern Europe. It remained a popular constructional system in Scandinavia and north central Europe up to the present period, and was carried to America by the Swedes sometime in the seventeenth century. Although the log cabin is profligate in its use of material, the trees were free for the cutting. The system required little constructional skill and no tools other than an ax.

Once the frontier settlements were established, their occupants devoted more time and energy to more substantial structures. One might have expected that they would have developed some new architectural forms in response to their new surroundings and social realities. After all, they were fiercely independent and self-reliant, they often expressed disdain for conventional life back east, and they were highly dependent upon local materials. Despite these factors, the settlers at the frontier humbly acquiesced to the architectural fashions back East, just as most of the eastern seaboard acquiesced to European fashions further east still. Even the concept

**123** Crittenden House, Versailles, Kentucky, late eighteenth century

of gentility, originally invented for the aristocracy idling their time in European palaces, found its way out to the frontier. The western settlers reproduced as best they could the social conventions and architectural forms from whichever eastern region they left. Without benefit of architects at the frontier, they were helped in this regard by a number of builders' handbooks published by Asher Benjamin, who had worked in Bulfinch's office. In 1797 he produced the first such book in America, the *Country Builder's Assistant*, with plates of Gibbsian and Federalist elevations and plans. He followed this with *The American Builder's Companion* (1806 and subsequent editions to 1827), *The Rudiments of Architecture* (1814), and a host of others published beyond the period covered in this chapter. These books were carried to all reaches of the frontier, and provided practical advice and detailed drawings so that settlers could reproduce the architectural fashions back East.

All of these factors at the frontier conspired to prevent new communities at the frontier from establishing their own special characters or unique sense of place. The ubiquitous western grid did not allow a town to adapt to its special landscape or geographical features, the transient population never stayed in a place long enough to understand and adapt to the special conditions, and the architectural styles imported from back East gave every town largely the same look. There would be no highly identifiable Venice, Paris or Heidelburg, or even Boston in western America.

## The Industrial Revolution

To cap off all of the dramatic events in this period, the Industrial Revolution emerged in the latter half of the eighteenth century to rival the Agricultural Revolution for its impact on Western civilization. Much of world history from this point on reflects the consequences – both good and bad – of industrialization in the Old and New Worlds. The processes and ideas that attended industrialization still largely drive our modern culture today.

Industrialization did not suddenly spring up without precedent. Since prehistoric times, individuals had invented ingenious tools for manufacturing material goods. The ancient world had developed a number of key processes, including metallurgy, spinning and weaving, and harnessing natural energy through mechanical devices like windmills and waterwheels. However, all of these inventions and devices were used on a small scale, and mainly to assist hand skills. In the latter half of the eighteenth century, a number of factors pushed this slowly evolving technology dramatically forward. First of all, the burgeoning natural sciences discovered important principles upon which later industrialization would depend, including Lavoisier's discovery of the chemical nature of combustion. Second, the Enlightenment desire to improve the human condition, and to achieve a perfect world, drove many inventors to devise new processes and machines that could aid human labor or enhance the material world. Third, the population boomed after mid-century. The population of England doubled from 1750 to 1820, while the population of America more than quadrupled in the same period, reaching 9.6 million people. These rapidly swelling numbers needed more houses, clothing and food than the traditional methods of manufacturing and agriculture could provide.

England first led the world in industrializing technology. Among other factors, it already possessed a surplus of capital from its dominance of world trade, it sat on reserves of coal that could be used for manufacturing iron after the invention of the coking process early in the century, and it provided a congenial intellectual setting for the scientists and tinkerers who rapidly invented new mechanical devices after mid-century. James Watt perfected the steam engine in 1769 and patented a steam locomotive in 1784, while Richard Arkwright invented the water-powered spinning frame in 1769. These and other inventions vastly improved productivity, poured more money into the country, and allowed England to dominate the world economically and politically through much of the nineteenth century. Although other countries worked hard to catch up, England maintained its overwhelming lead well to the end of the nineteenth century. For example, in 1870 England produced 30 per cent of all the world's manufactured goods, and controlled as much world trade as France, Germany and the United States combined.

America's industrialization began at the end of the eighteenth century. The ink was hardly dry on the new Constitution, as has already been seen, when Alexander Hamilton pressed to base the new country on industrialization and trade. Early American efforts to build textile machines were greatly enhanced when Samuel Slater emigrated from England with intimate knowledge of the latest technological ideas. With American partners, he helped set up the first successful textile mill in America at Pawtucket, Rhode Island, in 1790. Many other factories quickly followed in the New England region. Eli Whitney, for example, developed the important industrial concept of interchangeable parts at his firearms factory near New Haven, Connecticut. The first industries chose New England partly because of its plentiful water power, partly because of its ready supply of labor in the towns, and partly because of its well-established commerce and banking. Industry spread northwest from New England into, for example, Pittsburgh in western Pennsylvania which opened its first iron rolling mill in 1811.

Like a microcosm of the English phenomenon, money and power increasingly flowed to the North as the Industrial Revolution accelerated, exacerbating the regional differences between it and the still largely agricultural and rural South. The South was not left untouched by the new mechanization, however. In 1793 Eli Whitney invented a cotton gin that efficiently separated seeds from the cotton plant. Cotton

124 Mills, New Lanark, Scotland, 1785, David Dale and Richard Arkwright

125 Old Slater Mill, Pawtucket, Rhode Island, 1793, Samuel Slater

joined tobacco as a staple and highly profitable crop for the South, the former eventually providing over half of the United States' exports after 1815.

The first factory buildings in England evolved from earlier utilitarian building traditions, particularly those that had housed pre-industrial manufacturing. One important precedent was a Royal Dockyard building form long used by the Royal Navy for laying up ropes. By the nature of the manufacturing process within, these buildings were lengthy and thin. The early factory designers saw several advantages in a long and narrow building form. First, power was transmitted from the waterwheel to the individual machines by a series of shafts, pulleys and belts. A single shaft down the length of a building could efficiently supply a number of machines lined up in a row. Second, before the invention of efficient artificial lighting, thin buildings allowed the entire interior to be illuminated from side windows alone. The early factory designers stacked up as many as four or five floors of machinery, thereby gaining more floor space on a given plot of land, and keeping the drive shafts as close to the waterwheel as possible. The resulting building form – long, thin, four or five stories tall, and externally perforated with rows upon rows of large windows – became the archetypal factory for England and later America through most of the nineteenth century [124]. Even when steam engines took over from waterwheels, the basic design requirements remained the same.

Samuel Slater's second mill at Pawtucket shows its English factory heritage in the long, thin multi-story building and the rows of windows [125]. Here the building attains a domestic feeling, with a short wing breaking up the linearity of the main block, with a cupola taken from the English Baroque house tradition, and with materials and a roof shape that could be found in any number of colonial houses in the New England area. Like many of the early English factories, the Old Slater Mill blended into its surroundings, answering well the contemporary Romantic ideal of harmony and integration. The worst excesses of the Industrial Revolution were clearly yet to come.

# 5

# CULTURE REALIGNED

## 1820–65

AFTER the defeat of Napoleon in 1814, a number of European heads of state and negotiators formed the Congress of Vienna to discuss how Europe might be patched together after the upheavals of the previous decades. They attempted to turn back the clock on the Enlightenment and its revolutionary events, by restoring the monarchies that Napoleon had overthrown, and by carving up territories among themselves. However, the revolutionary ideas unleashed in the previous genera-tion could not be suppressed. European and American culture had fundamentally

126 United States in 1861

Settled area

Original manufacturing belt

– – Main roads & trails

⊙ Town

⊠ Fort

0    250    500 miles

0    250    500 kilometers

*U. S. population*
*1820:  9,618,000*
*1865: 35,701,000*

127 'The Architect's Dream',
1840, Thomas Cole

realigned. The history of the nineteenth century in these countries is largely the history of how Western civilization explored the implications of, and adapted to, the realities of its new world view.

Architecture in this post-revolutionary period also explored the implications of the new ideas that had been developed in the last half of the eighteenth century. The concept of style was now fully embedded in the architects' consciousnesses. They were fully aware of a number of competing styles, and had to develop reasons for choosing among them. In this period, we find more elaborate justifications than ever before for using a particular style. Of the three possible approaches that follow from the concept of style – Summerson's archeological, eclectic and modern – the nineteenth century mostly followed the first two. The Roman, Greek and Gothic revivals of the previous century carried into this period, to which were added other historical styles like Egyptian, Romanesque, Italian Renaissance and Italian vernacular. Sometimes these styles were revived with as much historical accuracy as possible, sometimes they were modified or adapted in the spirit of eclecticism.

Up to the middle of the eighteenth century, as has been seen, one style mainly followed sequentially on another. From this point on, the multiple styles run roughly in parallel, with one or another occasionally rising to prominence. Thomas Cole's painting of 1840, *The Architect's Dream*, sums up the architectural view of the first half of the nineteenth century with its Greek and Gothic forms featuring equally in the architect's imaginings [127]. These styles and their predisposing causes so overlap that it proves inconvenient and even misleading to discuss them in sequential subsections like Greek Revival, Gothic Revival, and so on. Rather, we will examine the broad cultural forces working in this period, and then examine how the various styles answered the desires and requirements of the time.

Two major and interrelated forces shaped culture and architecture in this period. First, following from Napoleon, Europe and America experienced rising nationalism coupled with an emerging political liberalism. That is, individuals wished to exert more control over their own personal destinies by grouping together with others sharing their own culture and language, and by gaining more rights to choose leaders who would look after their own interests. Second, the Industrial Revolution rapidly accelerated in this period, leading not only to new construction technologies, but also to profound and sometimes violent social changes, including a Romantic rebellion in the arts. This chapter will explain these two forces in turn, and investigate how they influenced the architecture of this most complex period.

## The architecture of nationalism and political liberalism

Napoleon's militaristic adventures in the first decades of the nineteenth century, as we saw in the last chapter, stirred up nationalistic feelings throughout Europe. Before his campaigns, the boundaries and political control of European countries were still determined as much by dynastic relationships and accidents of history as by groups sharing a common language and culture. A Spanish king could own Belgium, or a German king could take the throne of England. When Napoleon exported the French Revolution and overthrew monarchies, he raised the possibility in many Europeans' minds that cultural groups might control their own destiny. They did not give up on this dream even when the Congress of Vienna restored the old monarchies. The first half of the nineteenth century saw a series of revolts, repressions, and uneasy peaces as one national group after another sought independence from the old dynastic order.

Indirectly, the Napoleonic Wars also generated a new sense of nationalism in America. The war of 1812 that followed the British blockade of Napoleonic Europe generated a bitter anti-British feeling, and an intense desire to extricate America from European politics. In his Annual Address of 1823, President James Monroe asserted what is now known as the Monroe Doctrine. From now on, he proclaimed, the United States will no longer tolerate any European interference or colonization on the American continents. In turn, America will not involve itself in European affairs. America emphatically determined to follow its own destiny independently of Europe. This second declaration of independence from Europe gave America a second opportunity to follow Jefferson's advice and find its own architectural direction, but again it was not to be. America largely continued to follow European tastes and fashions.

### The Greek Revival

One of the most important nationalistic movements at the beginning of the nineteenth century, in terms of its influence on the culture and architecture of Europe and America, was the Greek War of Independence. Having lived for centuries under the control of the Turkish Ottoman Empire, in 1822 the Greeks declared their independence and fought for eight brutal years to a successful conclusion. This war naturally stirred up strong feelings of sympathy among Europeans and Americans, who regarded Greece as the homeland of Western civilization. The English Romantic poet Lord Byron kept the Greek revolution before the eyes of the Europeans, and the Greek style of architecture that had first tentatively revived in the Enlightenment enjoyed a resurgence throughout Europe in this period.

To the untrained eye, the revived Greek style looks very much like the Roman Classicism that has so far dominated our history. Both originate in temple forms, with colonnades and pedimented gable roofs on a simple rectangular plan. Even to the trained eye, the differences between the Roman and Greek versions of the Ionic and Corinthian Orders are sometimes difficult to spot at a distance. However, many of the Greek Revival buildings in this period are readily identifiable by their use of

the Greek Doric Order, historically the earliest and least refined Greek system. Its columns are much shorter and thicker, stand closer together, exhibit greater entasis or curvature along their lengths, and spring directly out of the floor platform without bases. The overall effect is one of greater heaviness and primitive power. In this spirit, the basic architectural elements out of which the Greek Revival buildings are composed remain simple and rationally pure. No Baroque flourishes, sinuous curves, or broken pediments find their way into the Greek Revival. In the broadest terms, we can see the Greek Revival as a logical continuation of the Anglo Palladian movement a century earlier, and of the Enlightenment desire to reduce everything to its simplest and purest form.

Although the Greek War of Independence bolstered a Greek Revival, it did not create it. In England particularly, the Greek style can be found weaving in and out of fashion from the late eighteenth century onwards. Sir John Soane had used Greek ideas as early as 1778, while Lord Elgin thrilled young English artists and critics by 'liberating' the sculptures in the friezes and pediments of the Parthenon and bringing them back to London between 1806 and 1812. After 1806, Thomas Hope, William Wilkins and Sir Robert Smirke, among others, began to rely more heavily on accurate revivals of Greek designs. However, as the Greek War of Independence progressed, the Greek Revival in architecture greatly expanded both in numbers and in scale. In the early 1820s, for example, Smirke wrapped an archeologically correct Greek Ionic Order around his massive British Museum in London, the German architect Karl Friedrich Schinkel based his national Altes Museum in Berlin on an Ionic stoa [128], while Thomas Hamilton designed the richly eclectic High School in Edinburgh around a Greek Doric temple [129]. Numerous other Greek Revival churches, houses, and public buildings joined these throughout Europe, some accurately following archeological precedents, others more freely working within the general idiom.

Americans also caught the Greek fever in the 1820s. They saw a clear parallel between the Greek fight for independence from the Turks and their own fight for independence from the British. As the first modern democratic republic, they also felt a close affinity to the original home of democracy. Greece, they suddenly realized, could become a model for their own young country. In this period, new settlements were given Greek names like Syracuse, Troy, Olympia and Athens, while college professors and school teachers spread the good word about the virtues and lofty ideals of Greek civilization. Political rallies raised money from all levels of society to aid the Greek cause at its source.

**129** High School,
Edinburgh, Scotland,
1825–, Thomas Hamilton

This enthusiasm for Greece inevitably sparked a pervasive Greek Revival in architecture throughout America in the 1820s. Benjamin Latrobe had already laid the groundwork with a Greek portico on the Bank of Pennsylvania of 1798–1800, and later with a Doric Order at the entrance to the Philadelphia Water Works of 1801. Latrobe's own students Robert Mills and William Strickland embraced the Greek idea even more completely. For the Treasury Building in Washington, DC, for example, Mills restated the idea in Smirke's British Museum and Schinkel's Altes Museum by running a giant Greek Ionic colonnade along the street front [**130**]. Strickland's Second Bank of the United States, in Philadelphia, literally recreated the Parthenon in Athens [**131**]. The Parthenon had become the shining symbol of Greece in its struggle for independence, as the result of an unfortunate accident in 1687 when an attacking Venetian army lobbed a shell into a Turkish powder magazine stored in the temple. The badly damaged building subsequently stood silhouetted against the skyline of Athens as a stark reminder of the tragedy that had befallen the Greek civilization. Strickland's reconstruction of the Parthenon on American soil served

**130** Treasury Building,
Washington, DC, 1836–42,
Robert Mills

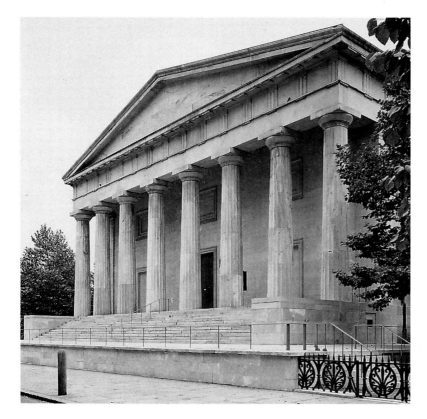

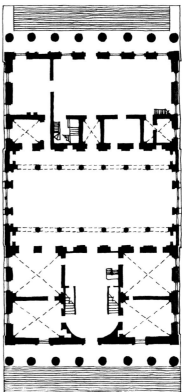

131 Second Bank of the United States, Philadelphia, Pennsylvania, 1818–24, William Strickland

132 Second Bank of the United States, plan

not only to acknowledge the glory of ancient Greece, but also implicitly to suggest that the torchholders of democracy now resided in America.

Like Jefferson's reproduction of a Roman temple at the Virginia State Capitol, Strickland's design drew a clear connection between architecture and the society it represents. And like Jefferson's design, Strickland's polemical statement caused

133 Second Bank of the United States, interior

difficulties when it came to placing modern functions in an ancient temple form. He had to accommodate a wider variety of activities than the simple Greek religious ceremonies for which the temple form was originally designed [132]. Strickland consequently inserted a Roman barrel vault and arches within the temple form, to create a grand banking room [133]. Modernists in the twentieth century disapproved of buildings like this, on the grounds that the outside of a building should closely express its inside or at least be consistent with it. However, consistency between the inside and outside did not concern many architects before the twentieth century, who saw instead a virtue in letting the outside of a building speak to an audience in the outside world, and then letting the inside speak to a different audience within.

This time around, the idea that architecture expresses social ideals caught on like wildfire. Americans in every region and at all social levels wished to associate themselves with the new style and the ideals for which it stood. For the larger commissions and the houses of the upper classes, the steadily growing numbers of professional architects accommodated this demand with a variety of Greek inspired buildings. One of the most influential Greek Revivalists was Thomas Ustick Walter, who worked for a time in Strickland's office, and who managed to fit a number of building types from houses to colleges into historically correct Greek temples. Another important proponent of the Greek Revival was the first large commercial architectural firm of Town and Davis. Ithiel Town contributed to the partnership a rational understanding of building form and construction technology. He investigated the use of iron, and invented a popular wooden truss bridge system. His younger partner Alexander Jackson Davis originally trained as an artist, became the most accomplished watercolorist of his day, and conceived of architecture as a scenic stage set for human activities. As his own career developed, as will be seen, Davis emerged as one of the most significant architects of the nineteenth century by spearheading a number of influential architectural movements. Town and Davis fitted a number of different building types within an archeologically correct temple form, and also explored what a Greek house interior might look like.

Few of the Greek Revivalists were content merely to reproduce archeologically correct Greek temples for every project. They also explored the eclectic possibilities of the Greek language. The Town and Davis design for the Indiana State Capitol in Indianapolis tried to render in Greek the now commonly accepted idea that state houses must be marked with a dome or tower. They somewhat incongruously juxtaposed a Greek temple base with a drum, dome and lantern derived from Wren's St Paul's Cathedral in London. William Strickland more consistently carried off the same idea for his Tennessee State Capitol in Nashville, Tennessee [134]. Here he turned the temple form sideways, unusually entering through a colonnade on the side rather than from the pedimented end. He based his tower on the ancient Choragic Monument of Lysicrates in Athens. Alexander Parris used the same precedent to transform the usual Gibbsian church of the previous century into the more fashionable Greek for his Unitarian Church in Quincy, Massachusetts [135]. Although a number of designers attempted to shoehorn houses into a pure temple shape, a more popular use of the language added wings to the temple body as in the Elias Brown House, in Old Mystic, Connecticut [136].

The Greek idea spread to the southern plantation houses where, as we have seen, free-standing colonnades were long employed for climate control in this region. Updating the plantation house in the new style required little more than constructing the columns and entablatures with more accurate Greek proportions and details. The Shadows-on-the-Teche in New Iberia, Louisiana, shows a Greek Doric frieze with

**134** Tennessee State Capitol, Nashville, Tennessee, 1845–59, William Strickland

**135** Unitarian Church, Quincy, Massachusetts, 1828, Alexander Parris

traditional metopes and triglyphs [**137**]. Its heavy, closely spaced, and freely inter-preted Doric columns support the entablature as well as the traditional second-floor *galerie* taken over from the earlier French tradition. With the fusion of these two ideas we get the familiar ante-bellum southern plantation house.

Political liberalism joined the rising nationalism of this period. Just as groups wished to overthrow foreign rulers who were not part of their own culture, less privileged social classes wished to throw off the control of their ruling elite where their own interests were not being satisfied. In 1830 revolutions broke out in France, Italy, Belgium and the Rhineland. The elected legislative Chamber in France invited Louis-Philippe, a distant cousin of the deposed monarch, to establish a new monarchy. England narrowly averted a revolution itself between 1830 and 1832 by undertaking legislative reforms. The political stability of England was reinforced when Queen Victoria gained the throne in 1837 and ruled benignly for 64 years.

**136** Elias Brown House, Old Mystic, Connecticut, 1835

137 Shadows-on-the-Teche,
New Iberia, Louisiana, 1834

America asserted its political liberalism through the ballot box. Andrew Jackson won the presidential election in 1828, ushering in what has been called the era of the common man. He himself rose from poverty to wealth, won fame fighting in the War of 1812, and became the first president not descended from a wealthy and established American family. Jackson consequently positioned himself against the old ruling elite in Virginia and Boston, while his supporters described the election as nothing less than a contest between democracy and aristocracy. He championed the vast middle class of small farmers, small tradespeople and city laborers, and extended the voting franchise to non-property holders. Jackson redefined the heart of the new nation as this humble but energetic class, at the same time building a sense of national unity among them that served to stabilize the country as it rapidly expanded west.

The extended franchise renewed enthusiasm for democracy in a larger portion of American society, fueling an enthusiasm for the Greek Revival even among those of modest means. Jackson's common Americans could not afford the services of an architect, and so turned instead to a number of builders' books published in this period. Asher Benjamin, the originator of builders' handbooks in America mentioned in the last chapter, added titles to his list in this period, including *The Practical House Carpenter* (1830), *The Builder's Guide* (1839), and *Elements of Architecture* (1843). In later editions of his books he replaced plates of older styles with the new Greek fashion. Equally influential were the books from Minard Lafever, *The Modern Builder's Guide* (1833 and subsequent editions to 1855), and *The Beauties of Modern Architecture* (1835 to 1855). Lafever illustrated Greek details, plans and elevations, with a special emphasis on how the Greek fashion could be built in wood with relatively unskilled workers. The small house in Wellington vicinity, Ohio, shows how the Greek idea appeared even in the most modest of houses [138]. A heavy entablature wraps partly around the building, apparently carried on thin applied pilasters at the corners. An equally heavy entablature and thin pilasters surround the front door. The weight of these details, and the severity of their ornament, clearly refer to the Greek Doric Order.

**138** House, Wellington vicinity, Ohio, mid-nineteenth century

The obvious wooden clapboard siding, however, reminds us that only a thin veneer creates the illusion.

### The medieval reconsidered

Nationalism, the force that gave rise to the Greek Revival, also encouraged a nascent revival of medieval styles in the same period. In the 1820s, a number of English writers 'discovered' the Middle Ages, and began romantically to identify that period as a high point in English civilization. Sir Walter Scott set a number of novels including *Ivanhoe* in the Middle Ages, thrilling his readers with detailed accounts of medieval life. Others began to look afresh at the Gothic buildings throughout England. John Britton, for example, surveyed English cathedrals and published his findings in several books. Perhaps because the Gothic style had died out latest of all in England, or perhaps because there were so many fine examples of Gothic spread throughout the country, the English began to see Gothic as a particularly English style. In this age of nationalism, the connection was sufficiently strong to drive a Gothic revival. The same architects who led the Greek Revival movement consequently turned their hands to Gothic, including Smirke, Wilkins and Cockerell.

The English were not alone in claiming the style. In France, Victor Hugo set his 1831 novel *The Hunchback of Notre Dame* in the famous Parisian Gothic cathedral, and helped inspire a French enthusiasm for what they believed to be their national style. Eugène Viollet-le-Duc, working for the Commission for the Conservation of Historic Monuments, did much to restore French Gothic buildings and further popularize the style. Likewise, the Germans looked back to their former glorious days under the ruler Charlemagne and later in the Holy Roman Empire, and championed the medieval as the best expression of their new nationalism. These early German civilizations of course built in the Romanesque style, not the historically later Gothic, and so the early nineteenth-century German architects enthusiastically revived a version of the Romanesque they called the *Rundbogenstil*, or rounded arch style. The Germans did not ignore the Gothic, either, since they still possessed a number of fine Gothic cathedrals from a later period in their history. Karl Friedrich Schinkel designed as happily in the Gothic and Romanesque as in the Greek and Neoclassical.

Nationalism helped revive these medieval styles of Gothic and Romanesque, but they also drew considerable sustenance from another important source early in the nineteenth century, a Romantic reaction to the Industrial Revolution. We must therefore continue the story of these medieval revivals after first exploring this other important cultural development.

## The Industrial Revolution

We left the last chapter with a bucolic view of industrialization at the beginning of the nineteenth century. The lingering optimism of the Enlightenment led people to believe that the new technologies would provide greater material comfort for greater numbers, while the factories themselves blended romantically into the peaceful countryside. For those not born into the wealth and privilege of the upper classes, the Industrial Revolution initially offered a further advantage of possible social advancement. Changing the economic base from agriculture to industry shifted power further away from the landed aristocracy and towards the middle class who built, financed and ran the machines. A similar shift of power took place in America. The new factory owners and skilled artisans increasingly joined the New England merchants and Jeffersonian gentleman farmers in wealth and power.

The shift of power down the social scale brought with it a change in matters of artistic and architectural taste. The aristocracy, as has been seen in previous chapters, had long set fashions that the lower classes earnestly attempted to mimic to the best of their financial abilities. To a great extent, this mimicry continued into this period. In one direction, those who rose in social standing immediately surrounded themselves with the trappings of the upper class to which they aspired. In the other direction, upper-class tastes and values continued to percolate further down into the lower orders. However, in this period the sheer weight of numbers who took on the upper-class ideas inevitably transmuted them according to values more appropriate to their own class and standard of living. In the past, historians have sometimes referred to a coarsening of taste in the Victorian period. Viewed more sympathetically, we might see this as a recognition at last that the concepts of gentility, refinement and delicacy – so important in the courtly occupations of the aristocracy – made less sense in the rough and ready world further down the social scale.

The typical Victorian domestic interior is a case in point [**139**]. Nothing has been condemned more completely from the twentieth century than the plush interiors of the Victorian middle classes. The ornately decorated mirror and fireplace mantle, the florid fabrics and carpets, the bric-à-brac and chandelier, the curvaceous furniture, all offended the delicate sensibilities of critics who preferred more chaste environments like the Neoclassical or the modern. We can now see these interiors as expressing a newly achieved standard of living, and as fulfilling a desire to surround oneself with conspicuous evidence of recently won comfort. Only those who were once poor and are now better off can fully appreciate the luxury of owning objects like bric-à-brac that have no functional value, and that therefore clearly proclaim a level of wealth beyond mere survival.

### Revolt and utopia

Although the factory owners and financiers clearly benefited from the rapidly accelerating Industrial Revolution, many others further down the social scale did not. Material conditions dramatically worsened for those who actually worked the

139 Colonel Robert J. Milligan
House, Saratoga Springs,
New York, 1853

machines. Workers crowded into the cities where the factories were located, finding
accommodation only in densely packed, overpriced, and often filthy and airless tenements. In the factory system of mass production, workers mindlessly repeated the
same sub-task over and over throughout a fourteen-hour day, never able to take an
artisan's pride in the completion of a piece. Children were drawn into the factories
despite the physical danger there, because they were cheap and could not effectively
complain. Alcoholism and other diseases of social stress were consequently rife. As
a visual symbol of the depressed state into which society had sunk, the smoke from
coal-fired power plants coated the cities in grime. Jefferson's worst fears about cities
and industrialization had come true.

These conditions engendered a rising class-consciousness and a solidification of
class structures. In the early days of nationalism and political liberalism, the workers
and factory owners fought together to overthrow monarchies or to reform parlia-
ments. The factory owners initially convinced the workers that all of their interests
would be served by putting the factory owners in positions of power. But as the gulf
in the standard of living widened between these two groups, each side began to see
itself as inherently different. Social mobility from the working class to the upper class
became more difficult. Each side began to look out for its own interests, which they
increasingly saw as a matter of mortal competition. Inevitably, these changes led to
strife and a general reaction against the Industrial Revolution. Between 1811 and 1816
the Luddites moved through the midlands and the north of England destroying
industrial machinery. In 1848 all of Europe erupted into revolution, as much to do
with class as with nationalistic conflicts. During this revolutionary year Karl Marx
issued his Communist Manifesto and a call to the workers of the world to throw
off their chains of oppression. Although most of the revolutions failed to achieve
their goals, they effectively killed off the lingering optimism of the Enlightenment.
Orderly progress towards material and social perfection no longer seemed easily

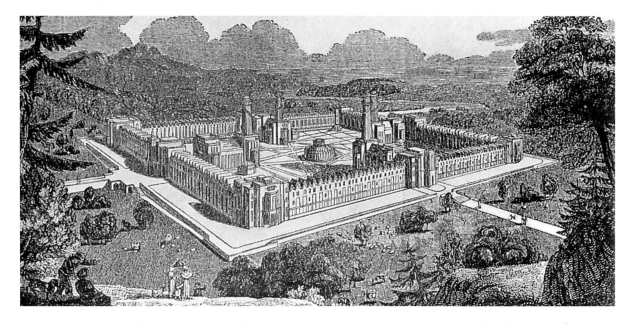

attainable, while the hidden costs of industrialization began to outweigh its benefits in the minds of many.

140 New Harmony, Indiana, 1825, Stedman Whitwell

Some thinkers in this period saw political revolution as too extreme and reform as ineffective. They proposed instead to redesign society altogether, and to establish new modes of working and living based on more equitable social arrangements. They hoped to establish model utopian communities where these ideas would be implemented, expecting that all of society would follow their lead once the obvious virtues of the new arrangements were recognized. Usually these schemes rejected the individualism that was held responsible for the excesses of the Industrial Revolution, and embraced instead varying degrees of collectivism. Charles-Edmond Fourier and Count Henri de Saint-Simon proposed such experiments in France, while the Welsh industrialist Robert Owen pursued these ideas in England and America.

Owen developed the idea that individuals would achieve their potential more fully in a collective society than in the traditional family. He aimed to establish self-supporting Villages of Cooperation of about a thousand people each, where everyone would live and work together for the common good. In pursuit of this end, in 1825 he purchased the town of New Harmony, Indiana, recently vacated by a religious commune. The design for his new town shows a rectangular block enclosing a central courtyard, much like a traditional English university cloister. Entrances into the four sides lead to factories standing within the cloister, which in turn face a symbolically important central common building across an open green. The living quarters that comprised the rigidly rectangular outer block were shaped like individual houses, giving visual expression to the idea of many individuals living together in harmony [140]. Unfortunately, Owen's building was never constructed, because dissension among the participants quickly tore the community apart. Owen's other experimental community, in Queenwood, Hampshire, in England, met the same fate.

### Romanticism

Owen's project betrays a Romantic desire to return to a golden age past, when life was perceived to be more harmonious and when it was thought people lived in cooperation rather than in competition. Indeed, it was part of a larger Romantic movement that swept through Europe and America in the first half of the nineteenth century in reaction to the Industrial Revolution. The more industry worked like a corrosive acid on traditional society, poisoning people against each other and against nature, the more the eighteenth-century Romantic themes of harmony and integration appealed to this period. European writers including Lord Byron, Percy Bysshe Shelley, John Keats, Samuel Coleridge, William Wordsworth and Victor Hugo, and American writers including Ralph Waldo Emerson, Henry Thoreau, Nathanial Hawthorne and Margaret Fuller, all restated the major Romantic themes we saw in the last chapter. The modern world has gone astray, individuals must learn to live again in harmony with nature and with each other, and intuitions provide a more reliable guide to goodness and knowledge than do reason or empirical science. Interestingly, the old paradox in the Romantic idea also resurfaced in the early nineteenth century, as many thinkers stressed the priority of the individual personality over the coercion of shared society. Thoreau's *Essay on Civil Disobedience*, for example, insisted on the right to follow one's personal conscience even when it collides with democratically determined legislation.

To these ideas nineteenth-century Romanticism added a new concept that exerted considerable influence on architectural thinking well into the twentieth century. The German Idealist philosophers, including Friedrich Wilhelm Joseph von Schelling and Georg Friedrich Wilhelm Hegel, followed the usual Romantic program and wished to heal the dualities between humans and nature, and reason and intuition. To this end they developed a concept of the 'spirit of the age'. They conceived of a universal and absolute Spirit that creates the physical world, and then exerts a coercive influence over everything in the physical world including individuals and their cultures. All human inventions, including art and architecture, are therefore merely the outward physical expression of the absolute Spirit. Furthermore, the Spirit progresses through various stages of development and therefore causes humans and their cultures to pass through similar stages. According to the German Idealists, this explains the existence of artistic and architectural styles. The Spirit evolves into a new stage of its development, and manifests a new form of artistic and architectural expression in which all artists and architects in the period inevitably participate. This conception attacked the Enlightenment idea that artists or architects can personally choose from a number of equally valid styles. It drew an explicit connection between the prevailing spirit of a culture and the artistic style that the culture must produce. Particularly in the twentieth century, this led architectural theorists and historians to praise or condemn architectural styles according to whether they properly expressed the prevailing spirit of the age. In the early nineteenth century, we will see presently, it became a tool for justifying the Gothic.

### The Gothic Revival

We saw earlier how strong nationalistic feelings encouraged various European groups to look back to the Middle Ages as high points in their own cultural histories. We can now remind ourselves that the Romantics in the last half of the eighteenth century also looked back to the Middle Ages as an ideal period when their valued harmonies once prevailed, and that they tentatively revived the Gothic style because of its association with that period. For the same reasons the Romantics in the nineteenth century followed the same course. They wished increasingly to revive the harmonious Middle Ages and the architecture that goes with it. Supported both by nationalism and Romanticism, the medieval revivals began to supplant the Greek Revival and to dominate architectural production in the middle third of the nineteenth century.

Augustus Charles Pugin and his son Augustus Welby Northmore Pugin gave the general Romantic predilection for the Gothic even greater force and authority. Compelled to flee to England from the French Revolution, the Pugins were not favorably disposed to any Enlightenment ideas. As a devout Christian who converted to Roman Catholicism in 1835, the son also looked on with despair as Christian virtues and spirituality seemed to disappear under the weight of the Industrial Revolution. Like the Romantics generally, the Pugins saw the Middle Ages as the perfect antidote to the mess of the present period. They consequently championed the architecture of the Middle Ages through a number of books. The father wrote *Specimens of Gothic Architecture* in 1821, and began *Examples of Gothic Architecture* which the son finished after his death and published in 1838. The younger Pugin published *Contrasts* in 1836, a year after his religious conversion, in which he contrasted the glories of the Christian Gothic to the debased qualities of pagan styles like the Classical. *The True Principles of Pointed or Christian Architecture* of 1841 further advanced the cause of the Gothic by emphasizing its clear relationship between structure and form.

These books helped create a serious Gothic Revival in England and America in the second third of the century for two main reasons. First, they offered drawings of medieval structures so clear and accurate that they could be – and were – used as pattern books for a style less well known to architects than the Classical. Second, the younger Pugin offered persuasive philosophical justifications for the style that gave more substantial reasons to choose it than mere whim. One main justification derived from the German Idealist connection between culture and architectural expression. Gothic buildings possess an unparalleled harmony and fitness, Pugin said, because the people who built them were thoroughly immersed in a medieval culture devoted to harmonious values. The right culture leads to the right buildings, and, by implication, rebuilding the artifacts of that culture as thoroughly as possible might help restore the valued culture itself. Pugin insisted on following the medieval models with archeological precision, making no concessions whatsoever to the nineteenth century or to individual creative urges.

His second philosophical justification appropriated Lodoli's functionalist theory from the previous century. Good architecture, Pugin insisted, follows two essential principles: first, nothing should be included in a building that cannot be justified in terms of 'convenience, construction or propriety'; and second, the only ornament permitted should enrich the structure of the building. Pugin valued buildings that 'honestly' express their structure and means of construction, and for that reason he objected to all of the architecture since the Renaissance that hid its structure beneath false plaster ceilings, fake parapets and arbitrarily applied ornaments like Classical details. The style of the Gothic, he pointed out, derives entirely from a clearly expressed structure judiciously ornamented to reinforce the main structural lines.

Pugin's third philosophical justification for the Gothic followed from two broad ideas in the period. The Enlightenment philosophers, we will recall, had established the idea that each culture possesses its own special artistic expressions. The nationalism of the day further argued that each culture has its own special geographical place. Put these two together, and we arrive at the idea that each architectural style should be rooted in its own locale. Speaking with the patriotic enthusiasm of the recent immigrant, Pugin strenuously opposed the prevailing international styles of the Greek and the Italian, on the grounds that they did not emerge from English conditions.

Only the Gothic, he insisted, derived from the English culture and climate. Furthermore, the same ideas that argue for a national style also argue for regional variations on that style. The differences in culture, climate and available materials within different regions of England should result in different versions of the Gothic.

So where once the choice of a style was merely a matter of convenience or appropriate association, now Pugin had made it a matter of cultural correctness. To build in Gothic is to stand for spiritual harmony, patriotism, function and honesty, values as unassailable as motherhood and apple pie. These ideas resonated well in a period noted for its moralistic and nationalistic tone, and helped bolster the Gothic style to which Pugin insisted these ideas inevitably led. However, the ideas about function, about honesty of construction and structure, and about national and regional styles could, with some adjustment, just as easily apply to many other styles. Many subsequent architects who held no particular interest in Gothic itself used a variety of these ideas to justify their own favorite architectural images, in many cases up to the present day.

The Ecclesiological movement in England and America in the second third of the century threw further weight behind the Gothic. These Church reformers objected to the excessive rationalism of the eighteenth-century Anglican Church, which had stripped away most of its ceremonial rituals and architectural richness for fear of looking Catholic. In the face of the crass materialism of the Industrial Revolution, the Ecclesiologists wished to revive a sense of spiritual and emotional richness, both in ceremony and building structure. They naturally rejected all forms of Classical churches and insisted on accurate revivals of the Gothic as the only true Christian style. Most Ecclesiologists even pinpointed the purest form of Gothic as the early Decorated style that developed between 1260 and 1360.

The Gothic Revival received yet further philosophical justification at the middle of the nineteenth century from the widely read and highly influential British architectural critic John Ruskin. In his books, *The Seven Lamps of Architecture* (1849) and *The Stones of Venice* (1851–53), he restated a number of themes from Pugin and carried them further. Like Pugin, he disparaged the state of current British society and architecture, preferring instead the more harmonious Middle Ages and its Gothic expressions. To justify his preference for the Gothic, Ruskin offered a new moral twist. A building form expresses the inner emotional state of its creator, he claimed, and therefore good and beautiful architecture can only result from emotionally stable and morally good people. The Middle Ages were morally healthy, and so by definition its architecture was beautiful. Unfortunately, Ruskin continued, the social divisions and crass materialism of the mid-nineteenth century have created an immoral society out of which no good architecture can ever emerge. Only if we revive the good culture of the Middle Ages will we be able to construct beautiful buildings again. In keeping with this moralizing tone, Ruskin also agreed with Pugin on the value of honestly expressed structure and construction. To this he added the importance of hand craft, through which we gain a glimpse of the artisan's inner spirit. Ruskin objected to any cast and machined work whatsoever, proclaiming it bad and dishonest. These ideas not only supported a Gothic Revival through mid-century, but also gave philosophical justification to a related Arts and Crafts movement in the 1880s, as we will see in a subsequent chapter.

A number of these ideas also found expression in the writings of the American sculptor Horatio Greenough and the American poet and philosopher Ralph Waldo Emerson. Restating the Romantic concept of art as an organic process, they both insisted that art grows naturally from within. The resulting beauty derives from its natural fitness to its purpose. Greenough in particular applied this to architecture, insisting that fitness of purpose meant a frank expression of function and structure. Although neither practiced architecture, their ideas appeared again at the end of the century as part of an architectural theory developed by Louis Sullivan.

Bolstered by these philosophical, functional, moral and religious arguments, the Gothic style in its archeologically correct form flourished in England and America after 1835. In America it supplanted the Greek in the 1840s on the Atlantic seaboard, and in the 1860s further inland. Pugin himself showed the way with his own carefully studied and accurate revivals of traditional forms. His design for St Oswald's in Liverpool, England, authentically abandoned the absolute symmetries of Classical churches and of the earlier 'Gothick' churches that applied medieval details to otherwise symmetrical Classical forms. Here Pugin revived a medieval parish church tradition of entering the building through a small entrance porch on the side, not through a central door at the end of the nave as was the fashion with Classical churches [141]. A small sacristy joined the entrance porch as an appendage on the side to the main church body, neither of which was counterbalanced by equivalent forms on the symmetrically opposite side. Together with the slightly smaller chancel at the end of the nave opposite the spire, all these irregularly placed additional forms recreated the medieval flavor of a building that grew casually over time. An overarching rational order is abandoned in favor of a carefully careless picturesque effect. Although St Oswald's was a Catholic Church, the Anglican Ecclesiologists so admired it that they held it forth as a model for churches of their own denomination.

In America, the Gothic style had floated around in the background from the earliest days of the colonies. From St Luke's church in Virginia onwards, parishes here and there continued to prefer the Gothic over the Classical as the most appropriate setting for Christian religious services. Towards the end of the eighteenth century and into the first quarter of the next, the Gothic style usually meant adding Gothic details like pointed windows, pointed spires or castle battlements to an otherwise typical Wren/Gibbs Classical Baroque church form. Benjamin Latrobe's Christ Church in Washington, DC, is a good example of this inauthentic application of Gothic to Classical (see 112). Town and Davis who helped lead the Greek Revival in this period equally turned their hands to the Gothic. Their early essays also mainly added Gothic details to the Wren/Gibbs church form. As the earnest Gothic Revival gained ground in England in the 1820s, however, Americans began to follow suit with more accurate Gothic buildings.

Churches initially provided the most suitable building type for the new style, particularly those for the Catholic and Episcopalian (Anglican) denominations. Helped along by the Pugins and the Ecclesiologists, these groups were reminded of their close affinity with the traditions of the Middle Ages. America acquired the latest architectural thinking about authentic Gothic largely through Richard Upjohn. A devout Episcopalian trained as a cabinetmaker and carpenter, he emigrated from England to the United States in 1829 and set up practice as an architect with a special interest in church design. His largest and most influential work, Trinity Church in New York City, carefully followed the advice and drawings in the Pugins' books and drew mainly from fourteenth-century prototypes [142]. Reverting to medieval traditions, he abandoned the usual side galleries that had become a tradition of Protestant churches since the Reformation, and based the church design strictly on a Catholic nave and aisle plan. Sailing dangerously close to 'popery' in the eyes of some parishioners, he also insisted on adding a chancel behind the altar in the traditional Catholic fashion. In essence, the Protestant modifications to the traditional Catholic church form were here

141 St Oswald's, Liverpool, England, 1839–42, Augustus Welby Pugin

142 Trinity Church, New York City, 1839–46, Richard Upjohn

abandoned in favor of Gothic authenticity, and as part of a general Ecclesiological desire to bring more traditional ritual back into the Protestant Church. Although the Ecclesiologists emphatically drew a distinction between their English Protestant churches and buildings of Catholic 'Romish' origins, the actual differences between the two were now difficult to detect. Their ideal models in the Middle Ages were, after all, Catholic churches. Pugin would not have approved of the false plaster vaults that the building committee compelled Upjohn to hang from the wooden roof trusses, although his massing and detailing inside and out offered the most authentic Gothic in America to date.

The Catholics, of course, felt quite free to appropriate the Gothic without having to justify its appropriateness. In 1808, rapid population increases encouraged the Pope in Rome to establish a number of new dioceses in America. The one in New York City was raised to an archdiocese in 1850, and its Archbishop immediately set in motion the design and construction of a cathedral dedicated to St Patrick that would rival European cathedrals and stand as a symbol of Catholic authority and power in the new land. The New York architect James Renwick took on the task of designing the first Gothic cathedral in America. Since the Catholics obviously owed no religious or architectural loyalty to England, Renwick turned instead to continental models for inspiration. Both French cathedrals and the German cathedral at Cologne contributed ideas. Alas, partly because of cost and partly for lack of skilled masons, the medieval system of vaulting the nave with stone arches was abandoned in favor of hanging a false plaster vault from a wooden truss. Renwick consequently had to strip off the flying buttresses on the outside, since they were no longer needed to resist the diagonal thrusts of non-existent vaults.

The Gothic idea rapidly spread to other building types after 1830. One of the most enduring uses of the style was for university buildings. Until now, American universities like Harvard and William and Mary were typically housed in Baroque house-like buildings with no special collegiate associations. The traditional English universities at Oxford and Cambridge, on the other hand, were still predominantly housed in their medieval and Gothic cloisters and chapels. Perhaps sensing an opportunity to provide an instant history and a clear reference to venerable English educational traditions, in 1814 James Renwick's father, a professor at Columbia College in New York, proposed rebuilding the College's buildings in the Gothic style. The project was not realized, and so in 1827 Kenyon College in Gambier, Ohio, became the first American college constructed in the Gothic. More influential still was Town and Davis's 1832–37 design for New York University. Although Davis originally offered a Greek solution, the university rejected it in favor of the Gothic scheme proposed by his partners Town and James Dakin. The firm based its design on English Gothic precedents, including King's College Chapel in Cambridge, the Chapel of Henry VII at Westminster in London, and the choir of Oxford Cathedral. Davis subsequently designed other colleges in the Gothic, including the Library and Chapel at the University of Michigan in Ann Arbor. The association between the Middle Ages and the university was so obvious and appropriate that many other colleges and universities subsequently built in varieties of medieval forms well into the twentieth century.

**143** Lyndhurst, Tarrytown, New York, 1838 and 1865–67, Alexander Jackson Davis

Architects in this period, including Davis and Richard Upjohn, also built numerous houses in the Gothic style. Although houses had less obvious associations with the Gothic than churches or universities, there were of course countless European houses built during the Middle Ages in the Gothic and other medieval styles. Once the Gothic Revival reached its stride in the late 1830s and the architects had acquainted themselves more thoroughly with the medieval body of work, it was only a small step to applying these ideas at the domestic scale. Gothic houses particularly appealed to those clients who identified with the broad Romantic movement of the period. One of Davis's clients, for example, visited the English Gothic novelist Sir Walter Scott and then wished to live in a medieval setting.

The Gothic houses marked a dramatic departure from the history of American dwellings that we have so far examined. Whether medieval salt-boxes, Baroque and Federalist hipped boxes, or Greek temple forms, American houses tended to pack all of their functions and spaces into one or a few simple geometrical shapes. The skylines or profiles were relatively unbroken, and clearly separated the building from the sky. Architectural interest came from the pattern of openings in mainly flat walls, and from applied decorations. The new style turned all of this upside down, as we can see here in Davis's design for Lyndhurst in Tarrytown, New York [143]. The architectural interest now comes from a dramatic juxtaposition of varied masses, some stepping forward and others receding back for no apparent reason other than picturesque variety. Some forms stand higher than others which, together with pinnacles and turrets, create a skyline as varied as the plan. Here the skyline reaches up like spread fingers to embrace some sky between building elements, just as the projecting elements in plan embrace the land. These picturesque devices gave visual expression to the Romantic desire to fuse humans with nature. This building and other Gothic ones like it planted a picturesque seed in American architecture that sprouted into a number of subsequent offshoots, including Queen Anne, Arts and Crafts, Frank Lloyd Wright and many modern American houses today. We will examine these in subsequent chapters.

Like the Greek Revival, the Gothic Revival ideas eventually passed down into the vernacular. Churches and houses of modest size and often without benefit of an architect took up the Gothic throughout America, in some regions up to 1880. In this case, the diffusion was actively helped along by Gothic Revival architects themselves, some of whom undertook modest commissions, and some of whom actively attempted to spread the style more broadly through books. Alexander Jackson Davis wrote *Rural Residences* in 1837 partly to showcase his work, but partly to explore how the Gothic ideals could be realized at a more modest level. Inspired by English books like Robinson's *Rural Architecture* of 1823, Davis drew a distinction between villas for the wealthy, and cottages for the middle and artisan classes. To show how the latter could benefit from the virtues of the Gothic, he illustrated his design for a gatehouse that would later redirect the designs of subsequent modest American houses [144]. Here the small size of the structure precluded the elaborate projections and recessions of forms in the larger Gothic structures like Lyndhurst. Davis developed instead a simple and symmetrical cruciform plan, entered on axis through a gable-fronted projection. The 'Gothic' was then applied to this almost Classical shape in the form of a steep medieval roof broadly overhanging the walls, medieval drip moldings over the windows, projecting porches and bay windows, clustered chimney stacks, and elaborately pierced bargeboards. Battens covered the joints of wall boarding vertically aligned, frankly expressing the wooden structure and giving the entire building the desired Gothic vertical emphasis.

**144** Gatehouse, Blithewood,
Barrytown, New York, 1836,
Alexander Jackson Davis

Davis's new idea was given further philosophical justification and disseminated more widely through a friendship and alliance he formed with a young landscape architect and architectural critic, Andrew Jackson Downing. Downing revived the Romantic and Jeffersonian conception of living in harmony with the land, and wrote several books to explain how landscapes and buildings could be designed together. Davis provided Downing with a number of the house designs for his 1841 *Treatise on the Theory and Practice of Landscape Gardening, Adapted to North America*. Downing further elaborated the theories that justified the new style in his 1842 *Cottage Residences, Rural Architecture and Landscape Gardening*, and his 1850 *The Architecture of Country Houses*. Restating themes we have already seen in Pugin and Ruskin, he related architecture to the character of the people who live in it. A rational, well-organized person, for example, should prefer the Classical as the most suitable architectural expression of that particular way of life. However, he went on, most Americans are individuals of imagination, not bounded by rationality. Their variety of characters and bold energy demands the picturesque architecture of the Gothic. Furthermore, the image of a battlemented castle expresses personal ambition, even among those who have not yet achieved wealth. Restating Pugin, he also insisted on honesty of structural expression. Wood should not be disguised to look like stone. Rather, it should be used according to its own inherent properties, as in Davis's board and batten cladding system.

Where earlier the Americans embraced the Greek Revival because it represented the ideals of their shared democracy, now they were to embrace the Gothic Revival because it represented the independent spirit of individuals. Perhaps flattered by the portrait Downing presented of the American spirit, and now armed with books filled with specific examples of how to build in the new Gothic style, homeowners of modest means throughout the country demanded versions of Davis's rustic cottage. The Neff Cottage in Gambier, Ohio, is a good example [145]. Rich, picturesque variety is achieved through relatively simple means, including a cruciform plan, the steeply pitched and overhanging roof with exposed rafter ends, projecting bay windows and the porch, and Gothic tracery on the bargeboards and balustrades.

145 Neff Cottage, Gambier,
Ohio, *c.* 1845

Note how the porch has begun to extend across more of the front façade. Although we earlier encountered a wide porch across the eighteenth-century Dutch house in New York and New Jersey, and around the French southern plantation houses, the English traditions that have so far dominated American domestic architecture either reduced the porch to a classical portico or eschewed it altogether. The English weather that shaped those traditions was seldom conducive to sitting outside for any extended period. The Gothic Revival reintroduced the porch, at first because it provided an excellent opportunity to provide more visual variety for a modest extra cost. However, its functional value quickly became apparent, providing a cool place to sit on balmy and often humid American summer evenings. It remained a cherished part of the American domestic idiom until well into the twentieth century, even as the style that originally popularized it died away. Note, too, that the tracery details on the Neff Cottage appear thin and flat, as if they were punched out with a cookie cutter. We see here the first visual evidence of a nineteenth-century invention, the powered jigsaw. Where traditional Gothic tracery was tediously and expensively carved by hand in the round, the jigsaw allowed relatively unskilled workers to reproduce at high speed repetitive shapes of great variety. Tools invariably stamp their own character on the works they produce, and here the tool can only cut straight up and down without rounding over the edges. The resulting proliferation of sharply cut wooden tracery gave these American vernacular buildings a distinctive character that is sometimes called Carpenter Gothic.

### Romanesque Revival

The Germans, we have already seen, revived the Romanesque style in the 1830s as part of a nationalistic and Romantic look back to high points in their civilization. We will recall from a previous chapter that the original Romanesque style vertically stretched the ancient Roman Classical language, in keeping with that period's religious preoccupations. The major characteristics of the original style are therefore the round-headed arches and simple geometrical forms of Classicism, together with thinly attenuated shapes that reach into the sky. The Gothic of course evolved from this general scheme, and so from afar it is sometimes difficult to spot the differences between the two, particularly when the distinguishing flying buttresses are omitted from the Gothic. Sometimes only the shapes of the window heads, either semi-circular or pointed, definitively identify a building one way or another. To make identifying matters worse, sometimes the nineteenth-century Romanesque Revival architects stressed the horizontal to the point where it is difficult to distinguish their buildings from a straight Classical Revival.

In the 1840s, while the Gothic Revival was still going strong, some American architects began to take notice of the contemporary German Romanesque Revival. They saw several important virtues in the style. First, the simpler forms and decorative system of the Romanesque might prove more economical to build than the Gothic. For the same reason, American masons who were struggling with the complexities of the Gothic might find this style more suited to their level of skill. Second, some of the Protestants who felt that the Gothic was too closely allied to the Catholic Church claimed that this style was less tainted with popery. This view required a creative reinterpretation of history, of course, because the Romanesque style was built for the Catholics as well. Finally, some claimed that since the style was less flamboyant than the Gothic, it was probably more suited to the austere republican spirit of America.

Richard Upjohn, the same architect who had popularized Gothic churches in America according to Ecclesiological doctrine, designed in 1844–46 America's first Romanesque building, the Church of the Pilgrims in Brooklyn, New York. Other architects including James Renwick, Henry Austin and Leopold Eidlitz, subsequently turned to the style. Typical in their schemes were round-headed openings, tall towers, and what are called arcaded corbel tables, a row of small arches supporting a slightly projecting wall or molding above. The most familiar Romanesque Revival building from this period is Renwick's Smithsonian Institution on the Mall in Washington, DC [146]. Here we can see the style applied in a picturesque manner, with asymmetrically

146 Smithsonian Institution, Washington, DC, 1848–49, James Renwick, Jr

arranged masses and towers. The tell-tale characteristics of the style reveal themselves in the round-headed openings, and in the arched corbel tables particularly noticeable on the gable ends of the two main blocks. Numerous churches, public buildings, railway stations and even houses were built in the Romanesque style in the period leading up to the Civil War. After the war, as we will see in the next chapter, Henry Hobson Richardson evolved the Romanesque into a more personal – and at the same time more popular – style that swept across the nation.

### Technological revolution

We have so far examined the social consequences of the Industrial Revolution, and their effects on the architects' stylistic choices in the first half of the nineteenth century. In the long run, however, the Industrial Revolution exerted a far greater influence on architecture through the invention of new building materials and construction processes. The changes were profound and unprecedented, eventually transforming the shapes, sizes and outward appearances of buildings throughout the industrialized world.

From the earliest civilizations to the beginning of the nineteenth century, the materials and technology available to pre-industrial cultures placed outer limitations on the size and appearance of buildings, no matter what their style. The widths of buildings were restricted by the need to illuminate the interiors with natural light from windows, and by the structural limitations of the traditional building materials wood and masonry. Although trusses and interior columns were sometimes used to expand the limits, most floors and roofs built in wood fitted the lengths of timbers that could be harvested. Masonry vaults eventually reached a maximum span determined by the tensile and crushing properties of the material itself. The heights of buildings were restricted to the number of floors that individuals could regularly walk up, at most four or five. The masonry walls themselves eventually reached a maximum upper limit, determined by their need to thicken at the base as they gained in height. The walls for tall masonry buildings became so thick that they began to eat up a significant percentage of the floor area on the ground. Even the sizes of openings in outer walls were limited by traditional building materials. Load-bearing masonry walls transmit their loads through the mass of the wall, in which each opening is a weakness. Stone beams or even arches can only span an opening so far before they are overcome by the weight of the wall above. Larger openings were possible in wooden frame and infill buildings, although the cost and limited size of glass, and the heat loss through windows, usually precluded opening up walls more than in masonry.

As a result of these structural and material limitations, all buildings in history to this point fell within a broad but ultimately limited spectrum of texture, mass, scale and proportion of solid to opening. At one extreme stood the lowly medieval half-timbered house, at the other the grand Gothic and Baroque cathedrals. Yet despite the differences, the similarities of construction and material were sufficient that pre-industrial towns and cities possessed a remarkable visual uniformity by twentieth-century standards. We see this yet today in older parts of European cities like Venice, Rome, Paris and London, and in the older parts of American cities along the eastern seaboard like Boston.

New technologies invented in the Industrial Revolution removed the traditional limitations on buildings, and ultimately transformed their size and general visual texture. The Scottish inventor William Murdock developed a gas lighting system at the very beginning of the nineteenth century that revolutionized the lighting of public streets and the insides of buildings. By 1835 New York, Baltimore and Philadelphia operated gas lighting companies. By 1860, natural gas lighted industrial and commercial buildings, and the homes of the well-to-do, in the major cities throughout the country. Even those without access to natural gas were able to light their interiors with whale oil lamps perfected around 1830. With the invention of reliable artificial lighting, buildings were no longer limited in width by the need for natural light. Rudimentary steam heating and air cooling systems were also developed in the period before the Civil War, the latter eventually removing the traditional need for cross-ventilation and therefore the last technical justification for constructing relatively thin buildings in hot or humid climates.

Equally revolutionary was the development of iron as a building material. The English perfected the reliable and cheap production of iron in the last half of the eighteenth century, thereby providing the essential raw material for the tools of the Industrial Revolution like steam boilers, railroad tracks and heavy industrial machinery. The material gradually improved throughout the nineteenth century. The earliest version was cast iron, which is stronger than wood or stone in resisting compression, but unfortunately suffers from brittleness and weakness in resisting tension. In the 1820s the English perfected a method of rolling iron, called wrought iron, that improved the material's tensile properties. The final step of reducing the carbon content and thereby further improving the malleability led to the introduction of steel towards the end of the century.

It was the strength of iron, as we will see in a minute, that allowed buildings to grow much larger. However, the first extensive uses of iron in building construction took advantage of another of its properties, the ease with which it could be cast into molds. Where a traditional stonemason laboriously carved each architectural element one after another, the iron foundry carved an element only once and then reproduced it by the hundreds as quickly as it could pour the metal. The cost of architectural detail suddenly plummeted.

At first architects used the new material as an economical substitute for traditional materials. In 1830, for example, John Haviland covered the face of a bank in Pottsville, Pennsylvania, with flat cast iron plates painted to resemble stone. Thomas Ustick Walter built the new Capitol building dome in cast iron, to mimic the wood and stone original at St Paul's in London. Even many of the decorated lintels over nineteenth-century windows and doors are cast iron replicas of stone carvings. By the middle of the century, innovative ironworkers like James Bogardus and Daniel Badger had developed the ability to cast entire façades that looked like the stone originals. The architect John P. Gaynor, for example, used Badger's foundry to build the Haughwout Building department store in New York as a cast iron reproduction of an Italian Renaissance palazzo [147]. Here the Renaissance style of repetitive bays aesthetically justified the technological convenience and economy of casting all the bays from one mold. By the middle of the century, iron foundries offered extensive catalogues of pre-manufactured architectural elements, from lintels and street lights to entire store façades. Cast iron store fronts lined the main streets of America in the decade leading up to the Civil War.

A number of architects in this period began to object to iron masquerading as other materials, citing the now common Puginian argument that this was a dishonest use of the material. Interestingly, they failed to level the same charge at their stone Classical buildings, which evolved from original wooden temples. Nonetheless, a number of architects and iron foundries began to explore new design possibilities for the new material. The strength of iron allowed designers to reduce dramatically

147 E. F. Haughwout Store,
New York City, 1857,
John P. Gaynor

148 Short-Moran House,
New Orleans, Louisiana, 1859,
Henry Howard

the thickness of forms, leading sometimes to astringently thin straps and pipes, and sometimes to sinewy and interlacing webs. The most spectacular results of the new design idea were the lace-like iron galleries which particularly found favor in New Orleans [148]. Eventually cast and wrought iron elements showed up as frankly expressed fixtures and fittings inside and out buildings throughout America.

Architects and builders were not long in seeing the structural possibilities of iron. Iron columns could be made thinner than wooden ones carrying the same load or, conversely, carry a heavier load at the same size. Iron beams could span much further than traditional materials. The English began to substitute iron members for wood in the last quarter of the eighteenth century, while William Strickland appears to have used the first iron columns in America, for a Philadelphia theater in 1822. Throughout the first half of the century, builders and architects retained masonry load-bearing walls for the exteriors of their buildings, employing iron for the internal columns and beams only. This is easy to understand, because at first they were simply substituting iron for the wooden parts of traditional buildings. The most spectacular of these hybrid buildings was Henri Labrouste's Bibliothèque Ste-Geneviève in Paris, where he inserted into an Italian Renaissance masonry shell two soaring iron barrel vaults [149]. The cast iron store front buildings took the next step towards an all iron building structure, although these iron walls still functioned like a load-bearing wall system. That is, the façade itself still had to carry its own weight all the way to the ground.

The key to building higher structures lay in the ancient principle of the frame and infill, of which we have already seen so many wooden examples. In a multi-story frame system, the walls at each floor no longer bear down upon each other and therefore no longer accumulate thickness further down the building. Rather, the weight of the wall at each floor is carried to the frame, which in turn carries the load down to the ground. Obviously the frame itself accumulates a greater load the taller the building, and so it must provide sufficient strength either through greater thickness or through stronger materials. Wooden frames reach a practical limit of five stories or so, as seen in the multi-story Japanese pagodas. Iron and later steel, on the other hand, possess sufficient strength to build frames over a hundred stories tall without becoming unduly thick at the base.

The concept of the iron frame was finally realized at mid-century by the Englishmen Decimus Burton and Joseph Paxton, first in garden conservatory designs and then in Paxton's Crystal Palace for the Great Exposition of 1851 in London [150]. The latter building was prefabricated in iron, bolted together on the site, and then covered with large panels of sheet glass that had just become available. The new technology allowed Paxton and his team to construct in just nine months what was then the world's largest building, 408 feet wide and 1848 feet long. St Peter's in Rome, in comparison, is 450 feet wide at its greatest point and 700 feet long. Demonstrating the vertical possibilities of the system, in 1856 James Bogardus put up a nine-story all iron frame shot tower for the McCullough Shot and Lead Company, into which brick walls were inserted at each level. The structural technology was now available for tall buildings, although it would not be exploited until well after the Civil War. The other practical limit on the height of buildings, the number of stories people could climb, was also removed at mid-century. Following on earlier experiments with hoists for freight, Elisha Otis perfected a steam-driven passenger elevator that was installed for the first time in a public structure in 1857, in the Haughwout Building. Now it would be as easy to reach the hundredth floor as the first.

At first architects and builders saw a further advantage in iron that it did not burn in fires. Unfortunately, in high heat it loses its shape and bends, usually leading to a collapse of the structure. A wooden structure comprised of thick members is in fact more likely to survive a fire than an iron one, because the outer surface of the wood chars and then protects the middle. Densely packed European cities were therefore wary of cast iron façades; the London fire code of 1844 even prohibited them. Americans happily built them until disastrous urban fires in Boston and Chicago in the early

149 Bibliothèque Ste-Geneviève, Paris, France, 1838–50, Henri Labrouste

150 Crystal Palace (after relocation), London, England, 1850–51, Joseph Paxton

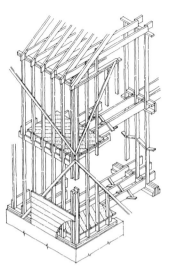

**151** Balloon-framing system using
machine-made lumber and nails

1870s revealed this fatal flaw. To fireproof iron structural frames, builders later in the nineteenth century typically wrapped the frame with a skin of masonry, effectively hiding the frame within the wall. From the outside it is often impossible to tell if these buildings are iron frame or more traditional masonry load-bearing structures.

The construction of wooden buildings was also revolutionized in this period. Wooden structures up to the first third of the nineteenth century were still built in the medieval manner, with large hewn members widely spaced apart and joined together with mortise and tenon joints. The method was time-consuming, required skilled craftsmen, and depended upon a ready supply of large timbers. In the 1830s, Chicago builders invented an alternative method called the balloon frame [151]. Drawing upon two recent developments, machine-sawn dimensional lumber and machine-made nails, the balloon system employed many small timbers closely spaced and rapidly fastened together. Now relatively unskilled labor could build frames in a fraction of the time previously required. The balloon system became the ubiquitous framing system for American houses by the middle of the century, and remains the principle behind the platform system universally used in American construction today. (The balloon system used vertical studs several stories tall, while the platform system evolved in response to a shortage of long timbers and uses studs only as tall as each floor.) From the outside, it is often impossible to tell if a house is half-timbered or balloon-framed. However, the latter system imposes less geometrical constraint on the shapes of forms that can be constructed, and no doubt helped encourage the spread of the varied and picturesque forms that we have examined in this chapter.

An improved national transportation system also helped shape architecture in this period. First the water canal system, then the steamboats on the Mississippi River, and finally the railroads tied great eastern seaports and small frontier towns together into a vast network by 1860. Goods and people could move cheaply and reliably from region to region. This inevitably began to exert a unifying influence on architectural production. Where once designers and builders in a particular region were mostly limited to constructional materials locally at hand, now they could avail themselves of supplies throughout the country. The spread of the cast iron store fronts, for example, depended upon moving materials from the iron mines to the foundries, and from the foundries to widely dispersed local communities. Quarries shipped their local stone to opposite ends of the country, while timber producing areas shipped lumber to prairie regions. Styles fashionable at one end of the country could move rapidly to the other end. This easy access to goods and ideas certainly opened up more possibilities for architects and builders throughout the country, but it also served to remove an indigenous flavor from the architecture in any given region. The Romantic desire in this period to fuse buildings with the land increasingly could not resist the spread of architectural ideas generally suited to all regions but in close harmony with none.

## Other revivals

### The rediscovery of Italy

As much as the Greek and medieval revivals wished to turn their backs on the Italians and the Classical language of ancient Rome that had dominated since the Renaissance, Latin ideas and values still ran deep in Western civilization. Indeed, we have just seen how the buildings of the Romanesque Revival begin to turn into Classical buildings when the horizontals dominate over the verticals. Europe and America 'rediscovered' Italy and its architecture in this period, after only the short-est of interludes. A younger generation of British and American architects who grew up in a period dominated by picturesque styles, and for whom the last true Roman Classical buildings of the eighteenth century were distant history, looked afresh at the Roman style and obviously admired its logical clarity. Sir Charles Barry in England, who also designed in the Greek and Gothic styles, resurrected the fifteenth-century palazzo designs of the Italian Renaissance. First in his Traveller's Club of 1829–32, and then in his Reform Club of 1836–40, he fitted all of the spaces and functions into one simple rectilinear block [152]. Following the Renaissance precedent he placed the main reception rooms on the second floor, marked on the exterior by the largest and most elaborately decorated windows. The roof in each case is hidden behind a parapet dominated by a projecting Classical cornice, so as to suppress further any non-rectilinear forms. These buildings picked up the strand of Palladianism and Neoclassicism from the previous century.

Besides appealing to the intellect after so much picturesque design, this Renais-sance Revival offered further advantages to the architects. It was more economical to build than the complex picturesque forms where every twist and turn in the wall plane cost extra money. Furthermore, the simple block form was more suited to urban sites than the piled up forms we have so far examined. The former could maximize the space available on a restricted site, and could build directly up to adjacent buildings and to the street line. Finally, since the palazzo design is comprised of an indeterminate number of equal bays, it can be expanded lengthwise as a building is enlarged without harming the design (see figure 147). The Greek temple form, in contrast, is a finite shape that cannot be enlarged without adding additional blocks that destroy its purity. Whiffen and Koeper relate contemporary comments that identified the Greek style with a society foreign to our own, representing an antagonistic religion and an obsolete government. Better suited to modern society is the familiar and common architectural language of the Western heritage, the Roman Classicism of the Italian Renaissance.

American architects took up the new style in the 1840s and 1850s. One of the first was John Notman's Athenaeum of Philadelphia in 1845–47, a club similar to those for which Barry first proposed the idea [153]. Here the large windows and balcony express the usual palazzo formula of placing the main rooms on the second floor, while the roof hides behind the parapet and projecting cornice. The style quickly expanded to other building types. As Supervising Architect of the Office of Construction in the 1850s, Ammi B. Young designed a number of new federal post offices and customs houses in palazzo-like blocks with dominant cornices. Urban houses, most con-spicuously along Fifth Avenue in New York City, also took up the form.

The revival of Classicism was given additional impetus by the French national school of architecture, the Ecole des Beaux-Arts. Evolved from the old Royal Academies founded in the reign of Louis XIV and reorganized by Louis XVIII in 1819, this school based its entire teaching program on a rational interpretation of French and Italian Classicism. It stressed the logical planning of rooms based on axial arrangements, and insisted on close adherence to the Classical rules of structure and decoration. Although it was conservative in nature, it taught architecture more formally and systematically than the apprenticeship system that still prevailed in England and in America. Some of these ideas came to the United States through Richard Morris Hunt, who was the first American to attend the Ecole. Upon his return to New York in 1855 he established a teaching studio, or atelier, based on the Ecole model. This

152 Travellers' Club, London, England, 1829–31, Charles Barry

153 Athenaeum of Philadelphia, Philadelphia, Pennsylvania, 1845–47, John Notman

provided not only the first systematic architectural education in America, but also introduced rational Beaux-Arts theories to a number of young architects who provided leadership in the next generation. These included George Post, William Robert Ware, Henry Van Brunt and Frank Furness.

Perhaps inevitably, the revival of Renaissance Classicism soon led to a revival of the Baroque versions of the style. Most influential was the New Louvre, a project undertaken by Napoleon III as part of his grandiose scheme to make Paris a fitting capital for his new empire [154]. The new building added ministries, a library and stables to the old French kings' Parisian palace, the Louvre. To convey a properly palatial air to the new structure, the architects Visconti and his successor Lefuel explicitly drew upon various architectural traditions associated with the rise of the French nation under Francis I and Louis XIV. In the transitional period between the medieval and the Renaissance in Francis I's sixteenth-century France, we will recall, the French combined picturesquely steep medieval roofs with more rational Classical bases. François Mansart modified those roofs in the seventeenth century by chopping off their tops and adding a much flatter capping roof pitch. The resulting mansard or gambrel roof enjoyed intermittent popularity throughout the subsequent history of French architecture, appearing again in the New Louvre as prominent caps to the rationally symmetrical central and end pavilions. This building also recalls the projecting bays that we saw in Louis XIV's Baroque palace at Versailles, here layered onto the pavilions to enliven the surfaces. The overall effect of this building is a sumptuous richness controlled through its underlying Classical geometry. This building defined what came to be known as the Second Empire style. It subsequently exerted

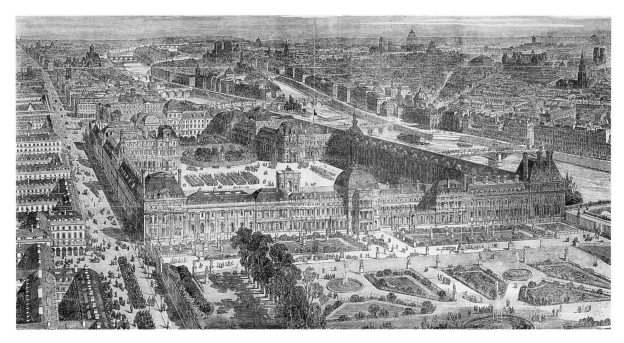

considerable influence on architectural thinking in the English-speaking world, first in Britain and then after the Civil War in America. We will examine the American examples in the next chapter.

Before the Civil War, the Baroque version of Roman Classicism found its most famous expression in the United States Capitol, remodeled by Thomas Ustick Walter at mid-century. The rapid addition of states to the Union meant that the Congress no longer fitted into its original building. Walter had to lengthen the structure dramatically, which meant that the original dome now looked too small for the composition. He solved this by capping the project with a close copy of Sir Christopher Wren's dome for St Paul's Cathedral in London, which was itself derived from Italian Renaissance precedents [155]. Now the dome is so large in comparison to the low,

154 New Louvre, Paris, France, 1852–57, Ludovico Tullio Joachim Visconti and Hector Martin Lefuel

155 United States Capitol, Washington, DC, after additions of 1855–65, Thomas Ustick Walter

horizontal body of the building below that the two flanking wings of the Senate and the House of Representatives are clearly visually subservient to a central unifying idea, more so than in the earlier version.

Architects of the period who were still interested in the picturesque also found new sources of inspiration in Italy. At the very beginning of the century, the English architect John Nash discovered the picturesque qualities of vernacular farmhouses in the Italian countryside. These were typically asymmetrically organized, often arranged around squat, square towers. In keeping with the Mediterranean climate, the roofs were flatter than in northern Europe, and often projected over the walls rather than hiding behind parapets. These indigenous buildings were as desirably picturesque as the Gothic, but they offered several advantages over the latter. First of all, like the Renaissance Revival buildings, they were more simply decorated and therefore cheaper and easier to build. Second, they avoided the overtly medieval overtones of the Gothic. William Pierson, Jr points out that a number of wealthy and aggressively pragmatic Americans in this period found little to value in the mysteries and fantasies of the Middle Ages. The Romantic philosophies did not touch them, but they nonetheless admired the aggressive forms of the picturesque as a suitable expression of their own values. The Italian vernacular offered these qualities with the additional advantage of referring vaguely to the respectably formal Italian Classicism. Alexander Jackson Davis developed some designs along these lines, and his friend Downing subsequently popularized what has been variously called the Italian villa style, the Tuscan style and the Italianate style.

Henry Austin's Morse-Libby House in Portland, Maine, is a good example of the idea [156]. Here an L-shaped plan wraps around a tower, forming picturesque arrangements of asymmetrical shapes. The roofs are shallow and project well beyond the wall. Bay windows and the porch add further visual variety. So far, except for the shallow roof pitch, this could describe any number of Gothic Revival houses as popularized by Davis and Downing. Only in the detailing does the new style assert itself. Classical elements like the segmental and triangular window crowns, the Ionic columns, the semi-circular arches in the tower, and the corner quoins stylistically fuse the Classical with the Gothic. Not seen in this building, but most typical of the Italianate style, are large brackets under the overhanging eaves that appear to support the roof (see figure 148 for an example). It was the prolific Davis, again, who first placed this subsequently pervasive element into the American architectural idiom. By the 1860s the Italianate fusion of the Gothic and the Classical proved so popular that it overtook the earlier Gothic Revival in many parts of the country. We will see further variations on the style in the next chapter.

### Exotic revivals

The Greek and Gothic, and to a lesser extent the Romanesque and Italianate, dominated architecture in the first half of the nineteenth century largely because they were popularly perceived as expressing deeply felt values of the period like nationalism, democracy, personal ambition and spiritual harmony. However, the Enlightenment concept of style opened up the floodgates for a number of other styles which also poured into Europe and America in this period, including Egyptian, Oriental, Elizabethan Revival and Swiss Chateau. Most of these tapped shallower or less commonly held emotions, and so never gained the same popularity as the mainstream styles. Nonetheless, they did provide some interesting projects in Europe and America.

Most popular of all the exotic styles was the Egyptian. We have already seen how Napoleon took an entourage of scientists and artists to Egypt during his military campaign there in 1798. Although the English soon forced them out, the French returned with a new appreciation of the ancient Egyptian Empire that fueled a limited Egyptian Revival in architecture and even more so in furniture design. The style usually involved massive and closely spaced Egyptian columns, readily identifiable by their simulation of reeds bound together and deformed under weight at the top. Sphinxes, obelisks and the bottom-heavy forms of massive masonry construction also made their way into the revival's vocabulary.

Egyptian forms were so foreign to the cultural values and functions of Western Europe and America that the architects who employed the style had to search cleverly for appropriate associations. Joseph Bonomi, Jr, for example, saw a connection between Egypt and cotton when he chose the style in 1842 for the Temple Mill flax spinning factory in Leeds, England. Had it been built, readers in Benjamin Latrobe's Egyptian design for the Library of Congress in 1808 might have been reminded of the importance of writing and scribes in the early civilization. The Medical College of Virginia in Richmond used the style to conjure up the traditional view of Egypt as the cradle of medicine. Funerary and cemetery buildings, like Henry Austin's 1845 gate to the Grove Street Cemetery in New Haven, Connecticut, found the most obvious connection to the style of the pharaohs. The use of the style for other building types probably drew less on these functional associations and more on the massive and foreboding nature of the style. A number of prisons, for example, like John Haviland's New York City Halls of Justice and House of Detention, popularly and ominously known as the Tombs, sent a clear and sober message about the dire consequences of falling afoul of the law [157]. Architects including Alexander Jackson Davis also built houses in the Egyptian style, usually by adding Egyptian columns to an otherwise Greek Revival house form. Obviously few clients appreciated the funerary or foreboding qualities of the style for houses, because few were built.

Architects perhaps more appropriately took up the Egyptian style for symbolic monuments, where massiveness and a striking image were more important than housing functions. We saw in the last chapter that Napoleon erected an Egyptian

156 Morse-Libby House, Portland, Maine, 1859–63, Henry Austin

157 New York City Halls of Justice and House of Detention (The Tombs), New York City, 1835–38, John Haviland

**158** Washington Monument, Washington, DC, 1833–34, Robert Mills

obelisk in Paris to relate his empire to the ancient one. In 1877, at the height of their empire, the English obtained an ancient Egyptian obelisk, now known as Cleopatra's Needle, to sit in the center of London on the banks of the Thames. The Americans as yet had no empire, but they dutifully turned to the obelisk for their first monuments. In 1825 an Egyptian obelisk was built to mark the Revolutionary War battle of Bunker Hill in Charlestown, Massachusetts. Robert Mills won a competition in 1833 for a monument to George Washington in the nation's capital with a gigantic Egyptian obelisk sitting on a Greek Doric base. Completed in 1884 after long delays and without its Greek base, it stands at the center of the Mall on axis with the Capitol building and the White House [158]. Topped out at 555 feet, it quickly became one of the most familiar monuments in America, even though the associations to ancient Egypt remain obscure for most viewers. Does it mark the empire of America, or link America to the origins of civilization? Indeed, the associational possibilities of this style were so tenuous and even trite that it never seriously caught on for more than a few novelty buildings.

## Manifest destiny and the settlement of the West

The population of the United States more than tripled in the forty years between 1820 and 1860. We have seen how many of these people entered the industrial labor force in the cities. Many, however, sought their opportunities in the apparently limitless land to the west. At first, further expansion was blocked by the edge of what came to be known as the Great American Desert, the vast treeless plain starting about a third of the way into Kansas and rolling for five hundred miles to the foot of the Rocky Mountains. This area was blessed with far less than the 20 inches of annual rain required for unirrigated crops, and so it did not hold out any hope of agricultural development. The United States happily gave this land to the Native Americans in perpetuity.

Some Americans looked for room further south. They took up an offer by Mexico in the 1820s to settle its northeastern province of Texas, agreeing to live under Mexican jurisdiction. Relations soured for a number of reasons, and in 1836 the Americans in the region fought and won a war of independence from Mexico. The mission church San Antonio de Valero, or the Alamo, provided the setting for an important battle in this revolution. Annexation as a state was delayed until 1845 over complex concerns about how it would influence the balance of slave and free states in the Union. Meanwhile, American fur trappers and later missionaries periodically brought back reports of lush lands beyond the Great Desert and the Rocky Mountains, in the Willamette Valley of Oregon. In the late 1830s and early 1840s wagon trains of intrepid emigrants bravely decided to chance the 2000-mile journey over the Oregon Trail to the Pacific Northwest. Although the romance of this journey has sometimes been overstated in American folklore, it was nonetheless an astonishing migration. It gives compelling evidence of the urge in American culture at this time to seek a better life in greener pastures west.

Other Americans looked for additional opportunities beyond the Rockies in this period. The Mormons, a religious group whose views alienated them from a number of communities back East, finally decided to move their entire culture out West beyond the jurisdiction of the United States. They found an isolated and forlorn place in Mexican territory at the edge of the great Utah desert, established Salt Lake City in 1847, and built farms in the desert watered by spring runoffs from the mountains.

Yet others left the Oregon Trail just north of Salt Lake City to join the California Trail leading down to the present day area of San Francisco. Although this was still Mexican territory, internal disputes in Mexico had destroyed the mission system there, leaving no organized authority. The Americans were attracted to the agricultural and ranching possibilities that had already provided a comfortable living for the Mexicans in the area, while the natural harbors of present day San Francisco and San Diego offered tantalizing possibilities for trade with the Far East.

As Americans established footholds in the western lands, they began to think that they might eventually possess the entire continent. A New York editor in 1845 proclaimed that the United States had a 'manifest destiny' to spread its experiment of liberty and federated self-government to the rest of North America. His call was quickly taken up by the press and the politicians, even though vast Mexican territories still stood in the way of this dream. On a pretext of straightening up the southern boundary of Texas, President James Polk prodded Mexico into war in 1846. At the conclusion of hostilities in 1848, America took possession of all the Mexican lands north of the present day border between the two countries, for a payment of 15 million dollars. This added a half a million square miles to the United States, gave it seaports to the Pacific, and also brought under its jurisdiction the established Hispanic Mexican and Native American populations of California and New Mexico.

The discovery of gold in California in 1848 attracted hopeful miners from around the world. Instant towns grew up around the mines, while San Francisco flourished as the center of trade. California's population reached 100,000 by the time it became a state just two years later, the same year Paxton built the Crystal Palace in London. In 1858, the discovery of gold in the region around present day Denver and in Montana spurred a gold rush to the middle of the continent. New towns sprung up throughout the Rocky Mountains, attracting not only miners but merchants, farmers, artisans and others who provided services and supported these towns' development. Farmers developed techniques for retaining the spring runoffs from the mountains and growing crops in the prairie. Suddenly these settlers wanted the lands that the United States government only a few years earlier had given to the Native Americans in perpetuity.

We saw in the last chapter how settlers at the frontier throughout America's history mainly brought with them the architectural traditions of their previous homes further east. The same pattern continued in these new settlements in the Rocky Mountains and beyond. Although the Native American and Mexican settlers in California and the Southwest had already adapted architectural forms to this special climate, like pit houses, courtyards and massive adobe walls, the new settlers were frankly chauvinistic about the virtues of their own predominately Anglo-Saxon culture. They disparaged the local cultures including the architectural traditions, opting instead to import architectural fashions from back East.

Most of the new towns in the West laid down a gridiron plan, just like the new towns at earlier frontiers in American history. The Mormons established unusually wide streets in Salt Lake City that were broad enough to turn around a cart and oxen team. San Francisco rashly plopped its grid onto exceptionally hilly terrain, inadvertently creating its now familiar precipitous streets and picturesque setting. Denver originally aligned its grid on a north-east axis to abut an adjacent river, but then realized the error of its ways and aligned subsequent suburbs on a rigidly north-south axis in keeping with the western national grid.

The buildings in the new Western towns followed the architectural styles back East with some delay, given their remoteness. Greek Revival, Gothic Revival and

159 House, Breckenridge, Colorado, mid-nineteenth century

160 Last Chance Gulch, Helena, Montana, 1865

Italianate predominated in this period, with some cast iron Renaissance Revival store fronts in the larger towns. Sometimes architectural elements and even complete buildings were shipped around Cape Horn; more often buildings were put up by local builders using pattern books or relying on vague memories of buildings seen back East. A small house in the mountain mining town of Breckenridge, Colorado, reduced the Greek Revival to its minimal essence, with a symmetrical gable front, little pediments over the doors and windows, and wood whitewashed to resemble Classical stone [159]. The Gothic Revival Surgeon's Quarters in The Dalles, Oregon, was taken from a plate in Downing's *The Architecture of Country Houses*. The Western builders did make an original contribution to America's architectural heritage, however, in the false front stores of the frontier towns. These were later rendered familiar world-wide by countless Hollywood westerns [160]. Here Greek Revival or Italianate façades only a few inches thick stand in front of rude cabins, thereby lending instant urbanity and civilization to these rough and ready towns.

We have seen in this chapter how European and American culture dramatically realigned itself after the revolutionary developments of the Enlightenment. Not only were a number of architectural styles elaborated and given plausible philosophical justification, but also the technological foundations were laid for even more dramatic architectural developments to come. America expanded to its present day borders in this period, and began to fill this vast new territory with the cultural and architectural products of its eastern civilization. However, all of these developments gradually ground to a halt in America after 1857. A severe economic depression led to extensive bankruptcies and unemployment, and a cessation of construction. After heightened conflict and violence between North and South over the problem of slavery, the southern states ceded from the Union in 1861 and established the Confederate States of America. The Civil War that followed remains one of the greatest tragedies in American history, setting family members against each other and eventually laying much of the South to ruin. The emancipation of the black slaves on the conclusion of the war in 1865 provides the bright note in this otherwise sorry affair. The culture in which architects operated after the war, as we will see, proved to be quite different from the one we have just examined.

period, including those of J. Pierpont Morgan in banking, Andrew Carnegie in steel, and John D. Rockefeller in oil. The industrialists' fabulous wealth bought the power to direct national social and economic policies. This new plutocracy buried the Jacksonian ideal of democracy for the common man that had fueled the American imagination only a few decades earlier. Those who personally benefited from industrialization not surprisingly developed a brash confidence, asserted an unbounded faith in progress, and enthusiastically embraced technology.

The leaders of this new order developed what was later called the Gospel of Wealth. Their main motivation was to accumulate capital and the power that attended it. They found justification for their views in the theory of Social Darwinism expounded by Herbert Spencer in England and William Graham Sumner in the United States. According to this adaptation of Charles Darwin's theory of natural selection, human progress results from the survival of the fittest. Competitive economic struggle weeds out the weak and enables a natural aristocracy of leaders to rise to the top. Slums and poverty are unfortunate by-products of this competition, proponents of this view conceded, but efforts to help the weak are ultimately misguided. This emphasis on personal gain at the expense of others led to extensive corruption in the Grant administration after the war, and to the Northern carpetbaggers exploiting a devastated South. The Gospel of Wealth also transformed the social values which particularly influence architecture. Whereas the pre-industrial culture based on the values of the landed aristocracy had stressed gentility, decorum and beauty, the new culture based on the values of the industrialists stressed personal assertiveness, function and value for money. Architects in the post-war era had to sell their design ideas as much on function and practicality as on matters of taste.

Terms like the Age of Enterprise that have been applied to this period suggest that everyone happily joined in, and benefited from, this new order. There were many who did not. Gross exploitations of labor by management, and in America of farmers by railroads and banks, led to considerable unrest throughout this period. Workers formed trade unions to protect themselves, and occasionally rose up in strikes that were sometimes violently put down. Farmers who had watched crop prices decline from the mid-century on also agitated for reforms. The socialist movement that began in the European riots of 1848 continued well into the twentieth century both in Europe and America. Its proponents rejected the laissez-faire model, called for collective ownership of industries, and agitated for a welfare state that would offer greater benefits for those who had lost much and gained little in the new industrial world.

Those with the money commissioned the buildings. Given their assertive outlook, they sought an exuberant architectural expression to match. They found it in two appropriately brash architectural styles that dominated America and Europe in the third quarter of the nineteenth century: the French Second Empire Classicism of Napoleon III that was briefly introduced in the last chapter, and a High Victorian Gothic developed in England. Although this period occasionally experimented with exotics like the Saracenic or Moorish style, the high fashion architects at mid-century mainly settled on the two streams of the Classical and the medieval as the most supple or appropriate bases from which to explore new variations. When the differences between the two were most sharply drawn, they respectively represented the rational and the picturesque. However, in this expansive and unrestrained age after mid-century, even the Classical tended towards a more picturesque or Baroque expression.

Both of these styles played fast and loose with the historical traditions from which they derived. In Summerson's terms, the architects at this time were less interested in archeologically correct revivals than in creative eclecticism. Many fully appreciated how rapidly nineteenth-century society had changed, and how the architectural challenges they faced were quite different from those faced by an ancient Greek architect or a medieval master mason. They did not think they could simply apply old architectural solutions to their new design problems. Many therefore sought a new style appropriate for the modern nineteenth century. However, these architects were not willing to abandon old ideas altogether. Architectural forms unrelated to previous traditions would lose all meaning and would not be able to communicate to society at large. So architects attempted to formulate a new style by creatively assembling parts from a traditional style, retaining just enough of the latter's spirit and detail to remind the viewer of the new building's historical ancestry.

In keeping with the assertive nationalism of the entire nineteenth century, many architects at mid-century continued to seek a national style. Each country possesses its own character, they claimed, that should find an appropriate expression in its architecture. Sometimes this meant playing variations on styles that had clearly originated in the country, other times it meant playing variations on styles that the architect thought captured the spirit of the country. Following this line of thinking, some American architects began to question the degree to which architecture in the New World can follow European traditions, given their different cultures and climates. Although all of the American styles developed in this period still derive from European sources, we find particularly after 1870 an increasing willingness to adapt those sources to American conditions.

The Second Empire style, we will recall from the last chapter, emerged in the 1850s following on Visconti and Lefuel's design for the New Louvre in Paris (see figure 154). This building revived and elaborated French Renaissance and Baroque ideas including symmetrical and axial planning, prominent pavilions at the center and ends, mansard roofs, richly carved decorations, and projecting bays of columns layered onto the outer walls. This opulent image clearly fit the bill for many in the mid-nineteenth century. It represented a grandiose monarchy whose ostentatious display of wealth others envied. It stood prominently at the center of an urbane and sophisticated Paris that had become the cultural and artistic center of Europe during Napoleon III's reign. In addition, an era that valued both the expressive and the practical clearly enjoyed the New Louvre's fusion of rich ornamentation and rational planning. The Second Empire style rapidly spread through Europe and America in the 1860s and 1870s, its way paved in America and Britain by a few earlier experiments with elements of what was called at the time the Louis XIV style. Since the entire Louvre complex housed a variety of governmental office, residences and cultural facilities, the style was not identified with a particular function. It was easily appropriated for a variety of building types including even train stations.

Alfred B. Mullett, the supervising architect for the federal government after the Civil War, popularized the style in the United States by using it for numerous federal buildings across the country. His State, War and Navy Building, now the Executive Office Building, shows his interpretation of the Louvre idea [162]. The building is symmetrically and axially organized with central and end pavilions marked by mansard roofs. The emphatically horizontal lines break the façade into piled up layers like a wedding cake, while the multiple layers of projecting bays over the central pavilions enrich the walls and seem to reach out to the street. Compared to a government building of the previous century like the Massachusetts State House, this new style is more brazen than refined, more muscular than delicate. So many post-war government buildings and post offices followed this new style that it became the standard image for public buildings across the land. For many, the style came to symbolize the contemporaneous Grant administration, and in some cases local government corruption.

The Second Empire Style was also used extensively for houses. Some designers closely followed the symmetrical planning of the Louvre, and applied mansard roofs and projecting central pavilions to rigidly symmetrical boxes. Others applied the stylistic trappings to the Second Empire's cousin related by Classicism, the picturesque Italianate of the previous decades. The Hubbell House, now the Governor's Mansion in Des Moines, Iowa, offers one of the most flamboyant examples of the second approach [163]. On first appearance, this house and others like it could pass for versions of the Italianate. Both styles seek picturesque effects with asymmetrical massing and dramatic towers, and they both employ variations on Classical detailing including the distinctive Italianate brackets at the eave lines. The Second Empire variation on this theme mainly appears in the mansard roofs which, over time, took a number of different shapes including straight, concave, convex and even S-curves. Proponents of the new style noted as one of its virtues that the inhabitable mansard roof could provide an additional floor of usable space, or reduce the overall height of the building while maintaining the same floor area.

The other dominant high fashion architectural style in the third quarter of the nineteenth century, the High Victorian Gothic, first appeared in England about the same time the Second Empire style appeared in France. This style evolved out of the English Gothic revival of Pugin and the Ecclesiologists that we examined in the last chapter. However, the new generation including William Butterfield, George Edmund Street, Edward Buckton Lamb and Alfred Waterhouse was less dogmatic than the earlier Gothicists. They no longer conceived of the Gothic as intimately tied to its earlier religious and moralistic underpinnings, nor did they accept the arguments for a national style with regional variations. Thus freed from the narrowly confined precepts of Pugin and his followers, they began to use the style more eclectically. Rather than continuing to build archeologically correct variations on English fourteenth-century models, they selected from a wider range of Gothic styles, periods

**162** State, War and Navy Building (Executive Office Building), Washington, DC, 1871–77, Alfred B. Mullett

**163** Hubbell House, Des Moines, Iowa, 1867–69, William W. Boyington

and regions, and creatively combined these elements according to more subjective judgments and tastes than Pugin would have accepted.

These more eclectic Gothicists particularly turned to the early period of French Gothic for its aggressive forms, and to the Italian Gothic in Venice and Tuscany for its use of polychromy. The latter describes a method of creating patterns in a wall surface through contrasting colors of brick or stone. John Ruskin offered some of the philosophical justification for these new sources. We will recall from the last chapter that, like Pugin, he stressed the need for structural and constructional honesty. The polychromy he found in medieval Venetian structures like the Doge's Palace satisfied this requirement, because the color was built integrally into the wall fabric rather than applied afterwards. He also praised the powerful massing of French Gothic in comparison to what he called the mean and insubstantial English traditions. Although Ruskin did not recommend the Italian styles for northern countries, the new English Gothicists saw the virtues of these other Gothic traditions for an industrialized and assertive mid-nineteenth-century Britain. Bold massing and the strident coloring of polychromy would help a building stand up against its often grimy industrial back-drop, while providing a more assertive picturesque effect.

The enthusiasm for French Gothic also came in part from the publications of Eugène Viollet-le-Duc, the French Gothicist briefly mentioned in the last chapter. Viollet-le-Duc undertook extensive studies of French Romanesque and Gothic build-ings in preparation for the restorations of ancient buildings throughout France for which he was responsible. His *Dictionnaire raisonné de l'architecture française du Xe au XVIe siècle* (1854–68), and his *Entretiens sur l'architecture* (1863, 1872), not only portrayed the beauties of these French buildings, but also set out a theory of struc-tural rationalism that he had formulated while studying the buildings in detail. While Pugin and Ruskin had already noted in general how Gothic buildings express their structure, Viollet-le-Duc spelled this out more exactly. He recognized that the Gothic structures act like a frame, where the loads are carried along the ribs of the vaults and down thin piers supported only by the flying buttresses. The walls between the piers, often filled with stained glass, provide no structural support to the system and serve merely as infills to keep out the weather. He noted a similar principle in the traditional medieval frame and infill wooden structures. Viollet-le-Duc followed Pugin and Ruskin in appreciating how these medieval traditions frankly expressed their structural realities, and in asserting that the style derived entirely from the structure. However, where Pugin was content simply to reproduce the existing Gothic images, Viollet-le-Duc recognized that the rational expression of structure might lead to other forms of architecture besides archeologically correct Gothic. He himself experimented with ideas of cast iron and glass fused with masonry structures. Although Viollet-le-Duc was widely read in Europe and in America in the 1870s and 1880s, most architects responded more to the Gothic images than to the theory of a new form of architecture. Only towards the end of the century did a number of innovative architects including Louis Sullivan, Frank Lloyd Wright and Bernard Maybeck explore his suggestion.

The earlier Gothic Revival had restricted the style to religiously oriented build-ings like churches, hospitals and schools. The new Gothicists applied their ideas to these building types as well. However, they had cut the style loose from its earlier religious moorings, and so felt free to use their new eclectic versions for many addi-tional building types including train stations, hotels and other commercial structures. They could easily appeal to historical precedent for this widened use of the style, because the Middle Ages had of course employed the medieval building traditions for

164 Town Hall,
Manchester, England, 1869,
Alfred Waterhouse

all of its structures. No building sums up the image of High Victorian Gothic more completely than Alfred Waterhouse's Town Hall in Manchester, England [164]. Here the assertive verticals of the Gothic tradition mark an important civic building on the skyline, while its bold forms proclaim the brash self-assurance of the age.

A good example of the style in the United States can be found in Memorial Hall at Harvard University [165]. The partnership of William Robert Ware and Henry Van Brunt had to accommodate a dining hall, an auditorium and a memorial hall to honor the Harvard graduates fallen in the Civil War. Both architects had worked in Richard Morris Hunt's Beaux-Arts atelier, and so in keeping with the French precepts they sought a rational expression in plan and massing of the building's programmatic requirements. They placed the memorial hall under a tall tower, and adjoined on either side a long refectory dining hall and a semi-circular auditorium. They then elaborated this basic idea in a High Victorian Gothic direction, with exposed roof trusses and a variety of colored bricks, stones and roof slates for the requisite expressions of structural honesty and polychromy.

The overall image of Memorial Hall strikingly highlights a problem that plagued much of nineteenth-century architecture, an increasingly tenuous relationship between meaning and form. The eclectic approach hoped to retain commonly understood meanings by playing variations on commonly understood historical traditions. In this case the meaning backfired. Even though the form of Memorial Hall logically derived from a rational analysis of the unusual collection of functions within, the building inescapably and unintentionally looks like a Gothic cathedral with a long nave, a tower at the crossing of the cruciform, and a semi-circular apse. Of course, Ware and Van Brunt were not the first to fall into this trap of unintended meaning; Greek Revival banks that look like Greek religious temples, or Egyptian Revival houses that look like Egyptian funerary monuments, suffered from the same problem. As the century progressed, architects increasingly tripped over this problem of meaning as they attached traditional forms to an even wider range of new building types

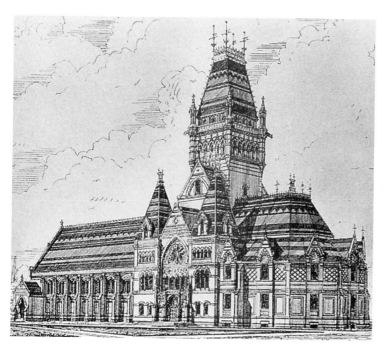

165 Memorial Hall, Cambridge, Massachusetts, 1870–78, Ware & Van Brunt

166 Provident Life and Trust Company, Philadelphia, Pennsylvania, 1876–79, Frank Furness

including massive factories and tall commercial buildings. This erosion of commonly understood meanings, we will see later, eventually encouraged the rise of a modern style that claimed no traditional meanings whatsoever.

Frank Furness showed how architecture could move in this direction with his unprecedented and highly personal architectural experiments beginning in the 1870s. Until Furness, even the most avid eclectics and romantics had worked within the broad framework of existing styles. Their most original compositions could still be recognized as deriving from a traditional idea, and were usually accompanied by philosophical or functional arguments to justify the deviation from the norm. In contrast, Furness essayed buildings that veered markedly away from any standard idiom, and then celebrated their individuality. In his Provident Life and Trust Company of 1879, we find the most extraordinary composition of vaguely familiar architectural elements unconventionally employed [166]. A massive canopy cut with a Gothic arch balances precariously on squashed columns, which are in turn supported by abstracted brackets. Other squashed columns at the ground floor level struggle to carry the apparent weight of the massive granite wall and a pseudo-shingled roof that lies trapped between the canopy and the wall. This is a mannerism of the kind we saw in Michelangelo's Laurentian Library, although here the base language is not so clear. Furness drew a number of ideas from Ruskin about ornament and about pleasuring the senses, and from the French architects Henri Labrouste and Viollet-le-Duc about bold geometrical and structural expression. However, this unprecedented emphasis on personal expression over adherence to more self-evident traditions must also have derived in part from the climate of extreme laissez-faire individualism in the United States after the war. No new architectural style emerged from so personal a vision, although Furness's employee Louis Sullivan later praised his originality and vitality as did numerous later Modernists and historians. Here we see the beginnings of what later became an important part of one strand of Modernism, the emphasis on individuality and free expression at the expense of tradition.

The tradition of American Gothic Revival houses that we examined in the last chapter easily evolved into something more assertive under the influence of High Victorian Gothic concepts after mid-century. Those earlier ideas mixed with Ruskin's ideas about frankly expressed structure, bold forms, and carefully crafted detail, while Viollet-le-Duc's publication of the medieval massive wooden frames offered new images of how one might express structure in wood. From these sources and ideas emerged what was later called the Stick Style by Vincent Scully, Jr. Richard Morris Hunt's design for the Griswold House in Newport, Rhode Island, is a good example of the type [167]. As with the older Gothic Revival tradition, this house evokes medieval images with asymmetrical planning, overhanging roofs and even jettied upper floors. However, Hunt departed from the older ideas by abandoning the usual board and batten vertical siding and substituting instead a rich web of external framing meant to simulate medieval half-timbering. This, and the emphatic braces under the jetties and on the porch posts, convey the High Victorian Gothic ideal of bold structural expressionism. Least typical but most expressive of the High Victorian Gothic idea is the William M. Carson House, in Eureka, California [168]. Built for a lumber producer after the style had already declined back east, and probably elaborated to help keep his employees busy during a slow period, the house exemplifies the picturesque ideal of bold and asymmetrical massing, a dominant tower, steep medieval roofs and extensive wooden detailing.

The immediate post-war period also saw the final push to settle the American interior. In the last chapter we saw that immigrants had begun to settle on the fringes of the great Western prairie. After the war, mass production of farm machinery and the development of dry farming techniques made it possible to grow crops on the 'desert' that had been ceded only a few years before to the sovereign Native American nations remaining on the land. As new immigrants rushed to colonize the prairie, the Native Americans fought back in a series of skirmishes and battles that lasted until 1890. Finally defeated and almost exterminated, they were settled on reservations where their own cultures were actively suppressed. Ironically, even as the new immigrants emphatically rejected the Native American cultures, they had

**167** Griswold House, Newport, Rhode Island, 1862–63, Richard Morris Hunt

**168** William M. Carson House, Eureka, California, 1884–85, Samuel and Joseph Newsom

**169** Sod House, on the South Loup, Nebraska, *c.* 1892

to turn to traditional Native American architectural ideas for their first structures on the treeless prairie. Like the earthlodge builders before them, they dug shallow pits into the ground and then piled up walls of cut sod [**169**]. These efficiently employed local materials, and effectively insulated against the prairie's hot summers and cold winters. However, most of the early settlers despised their 'soddy' houses. As soon as they acquired sufficient capital, most imported lumber from forested regions and built poorly insulated balloon-frame versions of whatever style prevailed back East. Occasionally the wealthier homeowners built the Eastern styles in masonry where masonry was called for.

The post-war period also saw a rapid expansion of formal education throughout the country, and the first schools of architecture. The Morrill Act of 1862 gave federal land to the states to provide sites and a financial base for new colleges. After the war these state-supported land grant colleges proliferated, many focusing on practical subject matters like agriculture and engineering. Along with a number of private colleges, a number of these eventually followed the Massachusetts Institute of Technology in establishing programs in architecture. MIT first founded an architecture department in 1864 (although instruction did not begin until 1868) under the direction of William Robert Ware. Obviously satisfied with the Beaux-Arts training he had received in Hunt's atelier, Ware implemented the same system in his new department. Architecture departments or architectural offerings within engineering departments soon followed in other institutions, including the University of Illinois in 1867, Cornell in 1871, Syracuse University in 1873, University of Pennsylvania in 1874, University of Michigan in 1876, and Columbia University in 1880. They all took up the Beaux-Arts teaching agenda, many employing teachers who had studied or taught at the Paris school. Although most American architects continued to train in the venerable apprenticeship system until well into the next century, those who did attend these schools acquired Beaux-Arts ideas like rational planning and historically accurate detailing. As we will see in the next chapter, these ideas helped support more archeologically correct historical revivals in the last decade of the century and beyond. The shift from hands-on training to more academic studies also inevitably split practice from theory, giving emphasis to the latter.

The rise of formal design education accompanied an increasing professionalization of the field from the mid-century on. Richard Upjohn helped found the American Institute of Architects in 1857 to look after their common interests. Lawsuits against clients by Upjohn and later Richard Morris Hunt had established by the 1860s the right of an architect to receive fees based on a percentage of the building construction costs, and to receive fees for preliminary designs even when the structure remained unbuilt. Although anyone could still call himself an architect regardless of training or experience, the eighteenth-century idea of the gentlemen architect working without fee had disappeared. Professionalization also meant specialization. As buildings in this period grew larger and more technologically complex, the architects increasingly handed over responsibility for technical matters to the engineering profession. This split in professional responsibilities worked against the old Gothic Revival ideal of fusing construction and form. It also became increasingly problematical for the architects, because they were now entrusted with the matters of taste and appearance in an age that valued function and practicality. Different architects and movements subsequently developed different responses to this problem, as we will see in the remainder of this book.

## The moderated 1870s

The wild extravagances of the post-war period moderated in America and Europe in the early 1870s, eventually leading to less exuberant forms of architecture. A number of factors converged to change the mood. Most conspicuously, the continuing nationalism that followed on from Napoleon's Empire had rearranged the European map in the 1860s. Italy and Germany finally emerged as unified nations, and the new Germany quickly seized its opportunities. Under the astute direction of Otto von Bismarck, it rapidly built itself into a major industrial and economic power that eventually rivaled the traditional European powers England and France. Bismarck maneuvered the French into war and defeated them in 1871, bringing down the French Second Empire and the ostentations for which it stood. The republican and largely democratic French Third Republic that rose in its place struggled through endless crises and often stood on the verge of collapse. Bismarck's victory marked a turning point in European history as dramatic and ultimately as tragic as the Civil War in America a decade earlier. From this point on, tensions mounted among the increasingly nationalistic and belligerent European superpowers as they endlessly shifted alliances and jockeyed for dominance. Eventually, the intense rivalries escalated out of control and culminated in the disastrous First World War.

Contributing to the less ebullient mood were serious economic problems in the Western world. Agricultural prices steadily declined from the 1870s on, due to intense competition world-wide. This undermined the American farmers as well as the European aristocracy whose wealth was based in the land. The Panic of 1873, one of the periodic business downturns that plagued the new industrial order, brought on a severe economic depression in the United States that lasted to the end of the decade and curtailed much building. The industrialists in this period tired of the cut-throat competition that brought many of them close to ruin. Many consequently moderated their original enthusiasm for laissez-faire individualism. For example, Rockefeller disparaged the wasteful competition of the post-war period, and formed a monopolistic cartel of oil producers to control the market. State governments responded by legislating business practices for the first time, although their initial efforts were largely ineffective. Adding to the restraint of the period, according to Mark Girouard, was a new mood among the children and grandchildren of the men who had made

170 Leyswood, Withyham, Sussex, England, 1868, Richard Norman Shaw

171 New Zealand Chambers, London, England, 1871–72, Richard Norman Shaw

the money in the previous decades. The new generation reacted against the values in which they were raised, and sought a less strident lifestyle. The opulent Second Empire and High Victorian Gothic styles no longer suited the more restrained mood of this period and rapidly fell out of favor except in provincial areas.

Ironically, the first genuinely original American architectural styles appeared in this era of economic depression and cultural retrenchment, not in the previous era of laissez-faire individualism. Several of the new ideas had their roots in English ideas of the late 1860s, when a number of architects including Philip Webb began to search for architectural expressions more appropriate to the new mood. They wished to find a style that would capture the picturesque qualities of the Gothic without Pugin's moralizing tone, and without High Victorian Gothic's abrasive assertiveness. They also wished to develop a picturesque style for cities that could compete with the popular Italianate, whose character they found lumpy. These and the usual Gothic Revival buildings did not often suit dense urban sites, because they were usually derived from free-standing precedents.

The British architect Richard Norman Shaw developed highly influential solutions to these problems. For rural or suburban houses, he revived what came to be known as the Old English style, the vernacular traditions of medieval manors, farmhouses and cottages that he had studied on sketching tours of the English countryside. These traditions were more modest in scale than the Gothic churches and cathedrals that had originally inspired the Gothic Revival, while at the same time they embodied the picturesque qualities still valued in this period. Shaw's design for Leyswood in Sussex skillfully combined into a seductively cozy composition the traditional elements of tile-hanging, half-timbering, horizontal casement windows, mullioned bay windows and prominent chimneys [170]. Although Leyswood was still a grand country house, it asserted the wealth of its owner less stridently than an equivalent High Victorian Gothic structure.

For urban buildings, Shaw turned to the transitional period of English and northern European architecture in the sixteenth and seventeenth centuries. The Elizabethan, Jacobean and Artisan Mannerist buildings of this period, we will recall, freely combined Classical and medieval ideas without unduly following the exact rules or traditions of either. The fusion of the rational and the picturesque easily allowed the transitional designers to stress one or the other according to the context at hand, without losing entirely the opposite characteristics. Shaw saw how this quality worked to great effect in the Artisan Mannerist buildings of seventeenth-century London. These structures efficiently packed together on urban sites while still obtaining picturesque effects with dramatic stepped and ogee gables, projecting bays and highly decorated surfaces. His design for the New Zealand Chambers in London shows how he successfully applied the lesson [171]. Shaw's revival of these transitional ideas unfortunately came to be known as the Queen Anne style, even though the architecture of Queen Anne's early eighteenth-century reign had already completed the transition to the Classical and Baroque.

Shaw's Old English and Queen Anne styles so successfully captured the new mood of the 1870s that many British and American architects quickly took them up. Dissemination of the ideas was helped along by a number of new architectural journals directed at professional architects in Britain and America. These included the *American Architect and Building News*, and the British journals *Building News* and *The Builder*. Inspired by the lavish illustrations and detailed plans, many British and some American architects faithfully followed Shaw's distinction between the two styles. However, most American architects blurred the two under the generic term Queen Anne while taking most of their inspiration from the Old English (thus rendering the name Queen Anne even less appropriate for the American style that followed).

The ambiguity of the name and the multiplicity of sources meant that Queen Anne could become all things to all people. After passing down from the high fashion designers to the common vernacular, it consequently became the dominant style for American houses from 1880 to about 1910, employed for the most lavish and the most modest. However, its flexibility and popularity meant it took so many different forms that its common characteristics are sometimes difficult to detect. Some versions remained faithful to the English masonry and half-timbered originals, but most evolved into something quite un-English while adapting to the American traditions of the balloon frame, the attached porch and applied wooden detailing. These latter versions of the American Queen Anne emerged as the first recognizably distinct American style.

The earliest American Queen Anne house, Henry Hobson Richardson's Watts Sherman House, shows its close affinity to Shaw's Old English style. Its English medieval sources are reflected in its asymmetrical arrangements, steeply cascading roofs, medieval chimney stacks, horizontal bands of windows, half-timbering and shingles simulating the tile-hanging on the walls [172]. Richardson also adapted from Shaw a new idea for internal planning that later became an important characteristic of the new American house styles. From the late seventeenth century on, as we have seen, British and American houses usually connected their main reception rooms through doors to a central entry and stair hall. Shaw continued this tradition, although he began to elaborate the stair hall into a reception room itself, complete with fireplace. Richardson applied this latter idea to a house on a smaller scale by establishing the elaborated stair/reception hall as the main room of the house. Looked at another way, Richardson opened up the wall between the traditional stair hall and parlor, keeping them distinct yet fusing them together [173]. This idea of fusing spaces passed into the American house idiom and eventually culminated in Frank Lloyd Wright's Prairie houses a quarter of a century later.

Later versions of American Queen Anne, like this house in New York, show how far the style evolved from the original English medieval sources [174]. Here a broad and deep porch extended across the front of the house, terminated at one

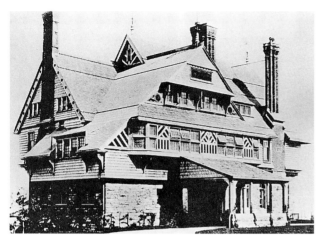

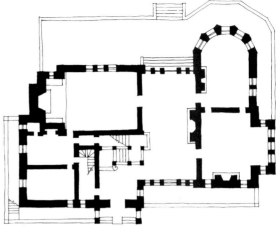

172 W. Watts Sherman House,
Newport, Rhode Island, 1874,
Henry Hobson Richardson

173 W. Watts Sherman House,
plan

end by a short round turret. An upper porch cut into the mass of the house itself. Although these elaborate shapes would have been expensive in masonry, the flexibility of the balloon frame allowed the American Queen Anne designers to mold shapes even on modest houses. The wooden siding smoothed out the surface compared to Shaw's rougher textures of tile-hanging, half-timbering and plasterwork, giving this house in comparison a more delicate and refined feeling. However, Queen Anne designers everywhere abhorred unrelieved surfaces, and so this building layered on machine-made wooden detailing like the sunburst bargeboard, the Italianate brackets under the porch eaves, the latticework at the base of the building and the decorative turned spindles. Although the latter were first suggested by the contemporary furniture of the Englishman Charles Eastlake, they became a characteristic trademark of much American Queen Anne.

174 House, Fleischmanns,
New York, 1895

The popularity of Queen Anne encouraged another American architectural development that ultimately supplanted Queen Anne itself in the first decade of the twentieth century, a Colonial Revival. American architects appreciated that Shaw had been able to draw upon long-forgotten English traditions for his new homey style. They began to realize that America also possessed long-forgotten traditions with similar homey characteristics, the colonial architecture of the seventeenth and eighteenth centuries. These buildings had long fallen out of fashion, and were destroyed indiscriminately throughout the nineteenth century. But beginning in the 1870s, American architects turned their attention to this lost heritage, at first to study it and then to revive it. The Colonial Revival gained considerable momentum after Americans celebrated the Centennial of their Independence in 1876. Nostalgically looking back to their origins from the depths of a demoralizing depression, Americans saw the colonial period as an ideal world when values were clearer, life was simpler, and the world was less crassly materialistic. This inspired a popular enthusiasm for all things colonial that subsequently ebbed and flowed right up to the present. The Colonial Revival became one of the most enduring American architecture styles of all, popular with many architects until Modernism discredited it in the 1950s, and popular with the general public still.

In the first stage of the Colonial Revival, from the Centennial to around the turn of the century, architects mined the new sources as eclectically as every other style we have seen in the post-war period. They typically combined elements from a number of colonial traditions, including the first New England houses with their lean-to additions, the Classical houses derived from Gibbs and Adam, and the Dutch colonial houses with their distinctive gambrel roofs. To these they typically added elements foreign to the originals like full front porches. Architects and builders also freely added Classical details like Palladian windows and columns to buildings quite unclassical in massing [175]. Later Queen Anne buildings also acquired Classical detailing, providing yet one more stylistic variant on that popular theme.

Other Colonial Revival houses, particularly towards the end of the century and beyond, adhered more faithfully to the spirit and detail of the originals. Some of the first fairly accurate examples came from Charles Follen McKim, William Mead and Stanford White who, together with an earlier partner William Bigelow, undertook a walking tour through the coastal towns north of Boston the year after the Centennial. McKim's training at the Ecole des Beaux-Arts had already predisposed him favorably towards the Classical tradition from which the colonial houses were descended, and they all wished to study the existing colonial structures more carefully. The

175  House, Orange, New Jersey, 1880s, Edward Hapgood

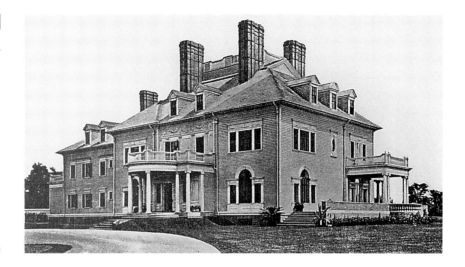

176 H. A. C. Taylor House,
Newport, Rhode Island, 1884–86,
McKim, Mead & White

firm's H. A. C. Taylor House in Newport, Rhode Island, a few years later shows how thoroughly they had learned the lessons [176]. We will see in the next chapter how this initial enthusiasm for the colonial helped inspire the firm to lead a wholesale Classical Revival towards the end of the century.

Out of the Queen Anne and Colonial Revival evolved another uniquely American architectural phenomenon in this period, the Shingle Style. Unlike the first two, the Shingle Style never widely caught on as a popular style. It was mainly developed for the summer 'cottages' of wealthy clients in the Northeast seacoast resort towns, although later examples designed for a wider range of social classes can be found scattered around the country. The architects for these summer houses faced an unusual set of demands. They had to accommodate the wealthy without ostentatiously displaying wealth. These houses were also to be used only two or three months out of the year, and for relatively informal living. The architects who received these commissions, including Richardson, McKim, Mead and White, and William Ralph Emerson, evolved variations on the contemporary Queen Anne and Colonial Revival themes. In keeping with these diverse origins, Shingle Style houses vary from the picturesque to the rational, and from the informal to the formal. Common to them all, however, is the extensive use of wooden shingles as a wall covering. The continuous surface of shingles tended to smooth over the forms, in contrast to the efforts of the Stick Style and the Queen Anne to break surfaces up. When this smooth surface was applied to the picturesque massing of Queen Anne forms, the designer could achieve bold massing without fussy detail. The uninterrupted surface also tended to pull a veil over the building, promising hidden riches within rather than prominently hanging them out as in the earlier picturesque styles. McKim, Mead and White's Isaac Bell House in Newport, Rhode Island, shows one version of the idea [177]. Here we see a massing of forms similar to those of the Queen Anne, with prominent gables, tall chimneys, asymmetrical planning, and a full front porch. But now a continuous surface of shingles sweeps over the walls, relieved only by the colonial sash windows and shutters and minimal moldings. Other Shingle Style houses used even more obvious colonial details like Palladian windows and Classical Orders.

In some of its details and internal planning, the Isaac Bell house also reveals a new influence on American architecture, the Japanese. An authentic Japanese pavilion constructed on the grounds of the 1876 Centennial Exposition in Philadelphia introduced

**177** Isaac Bell House, Newport, Rhode Island, 1881–83, McKim, Mead & White

many Americans to the Oriental architectural tradition of wood frame construction. What they saw resonated well with their continuing enthusiasm for wood construction, and it reinforced the still popular Gothic Revival ideal of art derived from craft. What the Americans also saw in the Japanese pavilion were long horizontal lines, a broadly overhanging hipped roof, latticework, open plans with sliding screens rather than enclosed rooms, and a fusion of the building with the landscape. This fresh look immediately fueled a popular enthusiasm for all things Japanese, while a number of these design ideas began to enter into the American architects' vocabulary. The latticework became a popular element in Queen Anne, as we saw in the house in New York. The Bell House here supports its porch roof on wooden posts turned on a lathe to look like bamboo. Internally, the house wraps its main reception rooms around a central stair hall in the manner of Richardson's Watts Sherman House (White had worked in Richardson's office on that house), only now the adjoining rooms are separated by large sliding doors in the Japanese manner of open planning. This free flow of spaces edged American architecture even further towards Wright's spatial innovations at the end of the century.

Yet one more important American architectural style emerged in this period already rich with innovations. We have already encountered Henry Hobson Richardson as the designer of the first Queen Anne house in America, and as a contributor to the Shingle Style. Of even greater significance, however, was his development of a Romanesque style so striking and influential that it has been called Richardsonian Romanesque in his honor. Richardson studied at Harvard before he attended the Ecole des Beaux-Arts in 1860. He stayed in Paris almost six years, working for the last four years in the office of Théodore Labrouste. In both the academy and the office he learned the French traditions of rational planning and the programmatic expression of form, both of which became essential components of his mature style.

Richardson first turned to the Romanesque for two competition-winning designs in Boston, the Brattle Square Church of 1870 and the Trinity Church of 1872 [**178**]. The selection of the Romanesque was not particularly notable in itself, since the Romanesque had already enjoyed a wide revival throughout Europe and America earlier in the century. Nor was it particularly earthshaking that Richardson turned less to German

178 Trinity Church, Boston, Massachusetts, 1872–77, Henry Hobson Richardson

sources, and more to French, English, and even Syrian and Spanish examples. Most significant and most admired by his contemporaries was the manner in which he employed the style. Compared to Renwick's Romanesque Smithsonian Institution of only a few years earlier (see figure 146), Trinity Church employs bolder and more coherent massing. Richardson drew upon his French training to express the Greek cross plan as a three-dimensional volume comprised of logically distinct parts. A tower clearly stands over the crossing, while smaller abutting forms house the short nave, the transepts, and the combined chancel and apse. The form is muscular in the spirit of the High Victorian Gothic; the latter's influence further shows in the building's use of polychromy. But unlike many High Victorian Gothic buildings, Trinity Church is not as visually complex or as fussy with detail. We are more aware of a crescendo of primitive forms building up to a dramatic tower, the total effect more than the sum of the parts.

Richardson continued to search for bold forms and primitive power in subsequent buildings. His Crane Memorial Library in Quincy, Massachusetts shows several important characteristics of the style he evolved [179]. Here he has reduced

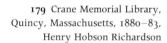

179 Crane Memorial Library, Quincy, Massachusetts, 1880–83, Henry Hobson Richardson

the building massing to a simple box with intersecting gable roofs, in essence turning his back on over a half a century of complicated picturesque forms. The few articulations on the box clearly express internal functions. The large window wall opens onto the reading room, the strong arch marks the entrance, the semi-circular staircase provides access to the offices behind the upper gable, and the high bank of windows provides light to the book stacks behind. To help convey the primitive simplicity, Richardson clothed the form in roughly hewn granite, occasionally interrupted by horizontal brownstone bands that visually tie the various elements together. He enhanced the powerful effect with one of his favorite and most copied elements, the huge Syrian arch that springs from a low base rather than from a line above the door head. We notice the simplified historical ornament less than the powerful forms and the play of the voids against the solids.

Richardson's Marshall Field Wholesale Store in Chicago carried the search for powerful simplicity to an even greater – and widely admired – extreme [180]. Here the internal functions offered no obvious ideas for external massing, because the building consisted mainly of a number of open and undifferentiated loft spaces. Richardson simply stacked up the floors within a rectangular box, relying entirely for architectural interest upon proportion, material, and the pattern of solids and voids on the external façades. In the tradition of the Italian palazzo, he marched a series of identical bays down the sides of the building. But rather than monotonously piling up rows of identical arches on top of each other, Richardson grouped the windows of several floors together behind arches of varying widths. As the arches progress up the height of the building, they increase in number while they decrease in width, finally culminating in rectangular punctuations just under the cornice. Thickened corners, an ever so slightly flared base, a flattened and simplified cornice and the roughly hewn stones provide visual strength. What at first glance appears as a simple and even boring box, turns out with further study to embody power and

180 Marshall Field Wholesale Store, Chicago, Illinois, 1885–87, Henry Hobson Richardson

181 Westminster University, Denver, Colorado, c. 1906, Gregory and White

grace, liveliness and stability, and vague recollections of admired traditions without overt historical associations.

Richardson's bold Romanesque struck a deep chord with many American architects and builders, perhaps because it captured the energy of the earlier High Victorian Gothic and Second Empire styles while avoiding their fussiness and stridency. In this he was the American equal of Richard Norman Shaw. The style rapidly spread throughout the country, employed mainly for public buildings and sometimes for residences. Many of the recently established towns in the prairie and intermountain West turned to Richardsonian Romanesque for their first substantial structures. One can hardly find a Midwestern or Western town without a school, courthouse, or prominent residence housed in a boldly massed, heavily rusticated, and often Syrian arched structure. On the still treeless and intimidating prairie, the powerful Richardsonian forms could stand their ground against the landscape when the idea of harmony with nature had not yet become popular [181]. Richardson's Romanesque style also influenced a number of young British architects, reversing for the first time the flow of ideas from Britain to America. British variations on what was called the American Romanesque style were regularly published in British architecture magazines from the 1880s onward.

## Urbanization and suburbanization

This period saw a dramatic explosion in the number and size of cities. At the end of the American Revolution, less than 4 per cent of the American population lived in towns of 8000 people or more. By 1860 the urban population had grown to about 20 per cent, and by 1900 this figure had doubled. In 1800, only six American cities could claim more than 8000 people; by 1890 this number had climbed to 448, with 26 housing populations greater than 100,000. This rapid urbanization led to the rise of American metropolises in this period, cities of more than half a million residents. Only Rome, Alexandria and Constantinople in the ancient and medieval periods, and London, Paris and Tokyo in the eighteenth century, had achieved this size before. By 1900 America possessed six cities that large, and three were over a million. A number of factors contributed to this urbanization. Industrialization demanded a centralized workforce, not only for the factories, but also for the new office buildings that housed the burgeoning numbers of clerical workers and managers. The declining fortunes of agriculture in this period encouraged a mass migration of farmers from the countryside to the cities in search of work. For the same reason, the immigrants continuing to flow from Europe tended to settle in the cities rather than dispersing into the countryside.

This new urban reality was not easily reconciled with America's traditional conception of itself as primarily rooted in the land. Many intellectuals and social reformers throughout the nineteenth century, including Emerson, Thoreau and Edgar Allan Poe, restated Thomas Jefferson in condemning the cities as cancerous growths. In many regards they were right. The spirit of laissez-faire individualism encouraged growth without planning, and often with few building codes to protect health, welfare and safety. The same spirit sacrificed shared amenities for private development. Chicago, for example, gave up public access to its lakefront so that the railroads could develop the land. In the 1870s most cities had not yet solved the problems of water supply and sewage disposal for their larger populations, continuing to rely on individual wells and privies. The stench was by all accounts quite overwhelming, the diseases like typhus and tuberculosis were rife. Tenement houses thrown up for maximum profit at minimum expense often arranged rooms more than two deep, creating internal rooms with no outside walls for light or ventilation.

The development of streetcar systems in the 1870s provided a way out for those who could afford it. Many families, from the wage-earning working class to the independently wealthy upper classes, deserted the inner cities for the new suburbs that began to ring the urban cores. Although most continued to work in the cities, at night they could escape to their suburban versions of rural country houses and live like country gentlefolk. After 1870 the cities began to form roughly concentric rings with a core of poverty towards the middle and rising levels of affluence further out. At the same time, the conveniences of conducting business next to other businesses led to the rise of the commercial districts at the center of the city. As more businesses crowded into these centers the price of land rose, further encouraging a flight of permanent residents from the middle. Retail shops began to follow the exodus. Shops stretched out in rows along the streetcar routes, and some relocated altogether into the middles of the suburbs. The business centers of some cities like London and Chicago eventually came to be deserted at night, destroying the ancient urban concept of integrally mixing homes, workplaces and shopping.

It is worth noting, by way of comparison, that these changes to cities took place mainly in Great Britain and America, not on the continent. A traveler to continental Europe even today can see that cities like Paris, Rome or Vienna continue to mix a variety of functions throughout the city. There is no 'downtown' Paris as there is a downtown Chicago. People live in apartments above or adjacent to shops and offices, even when different districts specialize in providing particular services. The British and Americans never took as readily to living in apartments, preferring a detached house and garden whenever possible.

Although the first suburbs were small towns already existing at the periphery of the rapidly expanding cities, the burgeoning demand eventually led to the design of new towns. One of the earliest planned suburbs, Llewellyn Park, was developed in 1852–69 on a commuter rail line west of New York City, on the heights of Orange, New Jersey. With advice from Alexander Jackson Davis, the developer Llewellyn Haskell laid out as rural a setting as he could manage. Lots ranged in size from one to twenty acres (a typical post-Second World War suburban lot of 50 by 150 feet comprises about one sixth of an acre). Roads curved to simulate ancient country lanes, while Davis designed most of the first houses in his favored picturesque manner. Richard Norman Shaw designed one of the earliest instant suburbs outside London, at Bedford Park in Turnham Green. Setting the tone for many subsequent suburban developments, he designed a few generic plans for small country houses that could be freely intermixed for visual variety. Although each stood adjacent to its own garden, the economic realities of the development caused him to pack the houses closely together, in many cases by attaching two houses with a party wall (semi-detached in England, duplex in America). The rural ideal for suburban developments also shows in Frederick Law Olmsted and Calvert Vaux's design for the instant town of Riverside, Illinois, outside Chicago [182]. As in Llewellyn Park, the designers curved the streets to simulate country lanes following the natural contours of the land, even though the flat prairie land here offered no obvious contours. Houses were set back from the street and spaced widely apart to attain the requisite country manor image. The idea of picturesque houses standing in informally arranged streets and grounds continues to drive suburban developments even today, because the motivating force of a rural escape from the city remains largely the same.

If cities were not yet something to be celebrated, at least efforts could be made to ameliorate their worst conditions for the burgeoning numbers of city dwellers who stayed. In 1857, New York City revived the seventeenth- and eighteenth-century practice we saw in Boston, Philadelphia, Washington, DC and other cities of setting aside publicly owned land for the common good. Central Park was developed to the design of Olmsted and Vaux, who attempted to bring as natural and as rural a setting as possible into the center of the city. Their meandering paths and irregularly shaped lake reflect the anti-urban mood of the period, a point made particularly clear when one compares it to the distinctly urban and formal City Beautiful projects 35 years later (see figure 192). Olmsted subsequently designed over 30 similar rural parks in cities around the country. To improve living conditions within the tenements themselves, a number of developers experimented with new designs in the 1870s, including doughnut-shaped blocks of flats with a central garden, and courtyards pierced through the middle of row houses to admit more light and air.

In the 1870s, the economic pressures on the commercial urban centers led to the first skyscrapers. As we saw in the last chapter, the technologies required for building to greater heights – the metal structural frame and the power elevator – were already in place by the middle of the nineteenth century. A quarter century later, rising land values and an increasing desire to build for maximum profit led developers to exploit the technology and build dramatically taller. More floors meant more rental income from a given piece of land. Increasing the number of floors was also relatively economical, because intermediate floors cost less per square foot than foundations or roofs. A number of commercial buildings in New York and Chicago after 1870 consequently doubled in height from the traditional maximum of five stories or so. These first tall buildings took advantage of the elevator, but continued to employ traditional construction techniques of external load-bearing masonry walls and often internal metal frames. Even at nine or ten stories they had still not reached the practical limits of load-bearing masonry construction.

More difficult for the architects at the genesis of the new building type was the aesthetic problem. What should these new tall commercial structures look like? Most secular buildings in the history of the West were more horizontal than vertical, and had mainly evolved horizontal stylistic ideas to match. Only the prominent towers of medieval town halls and guild halls offered an obvious visual precedent, since

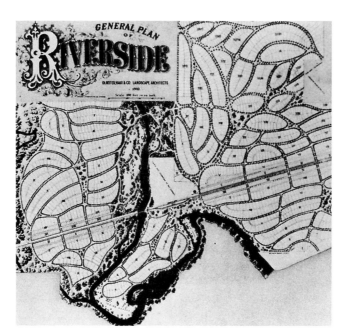

182 Riverside, Illinois, 1868,
Olmsted & Vaux

183 Tribune Building,
New York City, c. 1872,
Richard Morris Hunt

originally they were erected to signal the rise of the merchant classes in the late Middle Ages. For the Tribune Building in New York, Richard Morris Hunt astutely blended this tower idea with the more usual idea of a horizontal commercial structure [183]. In the lower block he followed the traditional Classical tripartite arrangement of a base, a middle and a cap, piling up successive layers of intermediate floors in the middle part to make up the height. Hunt obviously wished to minimize the vertical emphasis of this lower block. He broke it up in the middle with strongly horizontal segmental arches, and treated the entire top floor as a mansard roof to help disguise the building's true height. Celebrating the soaring heights of the new tall buildings would have to wait another decade. Nonetheless, Hunt's formula of a tower rising out of a lower block shaped New York skyscrapers well into the next century.

# 7

# THE AGE OF DIVERSITY
## 1885–1915

THE DECADES spanning the turn of the century saw significant changes in Western culture and architecture. The tensions and upheavals of the post-Enlightenment age had finally stretched to breaking, leading to realignments in a number of spheres. In politics, the intense rivalries of the European superpowers led first to imperialistic empire building around the globe, and then escalated out of control into the First World War. In the social arena, the widening gap between the haves and the have-nots spurred more violent reactions. America in the 1890s suffered

184 United States in 1915

Major industrial areas ca. 1900

0    250    500 miles

0    250    500 kilometers

**Mass Immigration at the Turn of the Century**
The numbers indicate percentages of state populations which were "foreign stock" in 1920, that is, born abroad or with at least one parent born abroad. The country names indicate the origin of each state's largest "foreign stock" immigration.

*U. S. population*
*1885:  56,658,000*
*1915: 100,549,000*

strikes, heightened violence, and even an anarchist movement that seemed to threaten the very foundations of society. Only a concerted reform movement in the first decade of the century headed off disaster. The same pressures in Europe fueled a socialist movement so powerful that many in the First World War suspected the armies would lay down their arms in solidarity with the working classes rather than continue fighting for the capitalists. The Russian army finally did just that, after the Bolshevik Revolution.

Architecture did not escape these tensions. This period is characterized by a burst of ideas, by calls for reforms and revolutions, and by unprecedented hostilities between advocates of different approaches. Never before had so many diverse styles competed for attention at the same time. In this period we find revivals of every imaginable style in complex combinations, including Classicism, Gothic, French Chateau, Tudor, Spanish Colonial, Byzantine, Wrenian Baroque, Scottish Baronial and even Second Empire. At the same time we see the emergence of a number of new styles less obviously connected to historical traditions, including Arts and Crafts, Craftsman, the Chicago School of commercial buildings and Frank Lloyd Wright's Prairie Style. Towards the end of this period, we even find the first Modernist buildings that stridently rejected historical traditions altogether, and that argued for architecture like futurist machines. It is hard to imagine, at first glance, the forces that could engender in the same period both an authentic French Chateau and buildings modeled after steamships. What caused this riot of ideas and styles, and why did the radically different Modernist idea emerge in this particular age? This chapter will explore the complexities of this period.

## Interpreting the period

Most architectural historians looking back from the mid-twentieth century portrayed this period as a fundamental turning point, when the old Enlightenment concept of styles was finally replaced by a Modern approach to architecture more appropriate to the modern industrial world. According to this now common view, the traditionalists after 1885 rallied one more time in a flurry of eclectic revivals that were drawn from wider sources than ever before. At the same time, a number of proto-modernist movements, including the Chicago school, Arts and Crafts, and the Prairie Style, struggled against the prevailing eclectic orthodoxy to give the modern world a more appropriate architectural expression. In the first decades of the twentieth century, this view of history concluded, these proto-modernist movements logically culminated in the first ever Modernist buildings that abandoned traditional styles and ornament altogether. Modernism in this view killed the concept of style by developing a universal method of design that transcended mere appearance and that simply built correctly for the modern world.

With the hindsight of history, however, this now common interpretation seems less satisfactory. First of all, the Modernist approach did not so quickly or thoroughly kill off the traditional styles. Traditional ideas and images, not Modernism, dominated architectural production to the end of the Second World War. Although Modernism finally emerged as the approach of choice in the 1950s, only 25 years later variations on the traditional styles appeared once again as part of a Postmodern movement that eventually eclipsed the Modernist idea. Second, with a more dispassionate view of Modernism afforded us by the passage of time, we can now see that Modernism was itself a loose grouping of styles, not simply a homogeneous approach to correct building. In the history of Modernism we can identify a number of different philosophical viewpoints and distinctive visual types, which we will examine in more detail in the final chapters of the book. Like all other styles before them, the Modernist styles arose, enjoyed their heyday and then declined. So Modernism did not destroy the Enlightenment concept of style as much as it denied its existence while continuing to participate in its basic idea.

The now common interpretation of architectural history particularly distorted the age of Modernism's genesis at the turn of the century. To prove the inevitability of their preferred style, the Modernist historians had to underplay or even disparage the traditional styles in this period. Many classic architectural history books hardly mention the traditional styles once the first Modernist buildings appear. Often the significant commissions of the day were ignored in favor of obscure architectural experiments, leaving subsequent generations of readers with a mistaken impression of the prevalent mood of the period. The Modernist view also had to draw sharp distinctions between the traditional and the Modern in order to stress the conceptual break. Yet as we will see in this chapter and later in the book, many of the Modernist styles took important ideas from the traditional architectural styles and their philosophies. Finally, in a world view that allowed of only Modern or anti-Modern, the Modernist interpretation of history did not know what to do with the Arts and Crafts, Chicago School and Prairie Styles in this period that were neither entirely traditional, nor entirely as Modern as the steel and glass structures of the continental European avant-garde. Many historians therefore viewed these intermediate styles as proto-modern, as stages on the way to pure Modernism. Yet, as we will see later, the philosophical ideas that generated a wooden, hand-crafted Arts and Crafts house differed fundamentally from those that generated a machined steel and glass Modernist factory. The former represented not an imperfect grasping towards the latter, but rather a substantial critique of the ideas that drove the latter.

We will try a different interpretation of the age at the turn of the century. Rather than describing the period as a fundamental turning point in the Western conception of architecture, we will view it instead as broadly continuing along the same architectural path that we have seen since the Enlightenment. That is, we will view it as a period in which a number of architectural styles developed side by side, each attempting to define and to express in its own way the important values and viewpoints of its age. Although the Modernist historians implied that there were only two viewpoints in this period – the retrogressive represented by the traditional and the progressive represented by the modern – there were in fact more viewpoints than ever before. The American and European cultures had reached a number of crossroads regarding their fundamental values and future direction. Capitalism or socialism, machines or handcraft, cities or the rural countryside, empires and colonies or self-determining democracies: all of these questions and more weighed heavily on Western societies at the end of the nineteenth century. The range and diversity of architectural styles in this period represent the range and diversity of views regarding these great issues of the day.

Now in stressing the continuity of the concept of styles in this period, we do not want to underplay or disparage the astonishing architectural inventions that emerged just after the turn of the century. A number of architects in America and Europe actively developed new architectural expressions whose underlying conceptions of space, order and material differed substantially from the ones we have seen so far in the traditional Western styles. These inventions elaborated the vocabulary of architectural ideas available to their successors, and set the tone for most of the architectural production in the three decades following the Second World War. But these were additions to the body of Western styles, not replacements.

In our new interpretation of the age, we will refrain from judging whether one of the architectural styles at the turn of the century was better than the others, or more inevitable. Each attracted numbers of advocates, each offered plausible arguments to support its position. To argue whether the Modernists or the Classicists found the correct interpretation of the age is like arguing whether the Democrats or the Republicans found the right answer to social welfare. The answer depends on one's personal outlook. Far more interesting to us in this history of architecture is to understand the outlooks that each style represented. Why did the Modernists argue against national styles and love the machine? Why did the Arts and Crafts architects dislike the machine and design mainly for suburban and rural sites? Why did the Classicists revive grand Baroque planning for cities in the face of America's historical animosity to urban life? These are the kinds of questions that interest us in our new interpretation, and to which we will now turn.

## Social and architectural complexities

To help unravel the various stylistic movements and their philosophical assumptions, we must first examine the issues and conflicts in this period to which the architects responded. The first great issue involved the value of the machine. The continuing Industrial Revolution spat out new inventions at an astonishing pace. Many of the accouterments of modern life were invented or widely manufactured in the last quarter of the nineteenth and the first decades of the twentieth centuries, including telephones, phonographs, moving pictures, adding machines, typewriters, electric lighting, iron and steam warships, electric streetcars, automobiles, and airplanes. Machines no longer stood isolated in factories, but entered intimately into everyday life and transformed traditional habits. Many people embraced the changes and viewed the machine as the defining characteristic of the age, while others saw a darker side to the transformations and looked back nostalgically to the pre-industrial past. Although we have seen both of these attitudes throughout the nineteenth century, by the turn of the century the battle lines seemed to have hardened, drawing out more assertive proponents of the extremes. The Modernists and Arts and Crafts architects, as we will see, substantially split on this issue.

Conflicts between the social classes also caused much disruption in this period, attracting different architectural responses. American big business grew ever more powerful, as trusts continued to consolidate smaller companies into vast holdings with immense power. The wealthy beneficiaries of industrialization began to flaunt their position and power. Liveried servants, aristocratic mansions and extravagant entertaining (one famous costume ball at the Waldorf Hotel in New York cost almost $370,000 to stage) contributed to what Thorstein Velden in the *Theory of the Leisure Class* (1899) called 'conspicuous consumption'. At the same time (and perhaps partly because of these extravagances) those less fortunate agitated more aggressively for their own interests. Many formed the great socialist political parties in Europe in the last third of the century, and sought change through political action and reform. A few joined anarchist movements that they hoped would bring about change through revolution. In America, the working classes mostly pinned their hopes on the labor unions. They lobbied for collective protections and periodically engaged business in bloody confrontations over lockouts and strikes. The mid-1880s saw several particularly violent clashes, including an anarchist bomb thrown in a demonstration in Chicago in 1886 that killed seven. The conflicts escalated in 1893, when America fell into its worst depression to date. Massive bankruptcies, extensive unemployment and violent strikes and riots rocked the nation until the economy recovered four years later. At the time it looked to many like the social order was falling apart. A number of reform movements arose in reaction during this period, about which we will hear more later.

These social changes and conflicts engendered a number of architectural challenges and reactions. Most obviously, the consolidation of industry into great enterprises led to larger factories and office buildings than ever before, for which architects needed to find new ideas. The architects themselves formed larger partnerships and offices in order to accommodate these larger and more complex commissions. The class conflicts also split architects between those who happily provided suitable settings for the extravagant rich, and others who pointedly tried to design for the sensible middle classes. Designers of all stripes reacted against the chaos in society by calling for greater cohesion and order in the built environment, leading to less stridently picturesque forms in this period no matter what the style or social audience.

Further unsettling American society in the last decades of the nineteenth century was a massive influx of European immigrants. Over nine million arrived between 1880 and 1900 alone. Unlike the earlier immigrants who came from northern and western European countries and who were mainly Protestant, the new immigrants mostly arrived from southern and eastern Europe, and were mainly Catholic and Jewish. They did not all assimilate easily into the older American culture based on Anglo-Saxon attitudes and traditions, many preferring instead to cluster together in urban ghettos where they could maintain their own traditions. By 1890 those of foreign birth or parentage accounted for one-third of the populations in Boston and Chicago, and four-fifths of that in New York City. In a few short years, America had changed from a land of primarily white Anglo-Saxon Protestants to something more culturally diverse. What now was the core American outlook or set of values? Some praised the new diversity and spoke of the great American melting pot. Others asserted more stridently the priority of the Anglo-Saxon view (land developers partly sold southern California in the 1890s as the last refuge of Anglo-Saxon culture). Architects before this cultural transformation had already struggled to maintain a relationship between a particular style and its commonly understood meanings. Given this richer and more diverse cultural mix, the difficulties involved in finding commonly shared meanings were now even greater. Architects of the period split according to how they handled this problem of meaning, ranging from those who attempted to recover traditional associations, to those who abandoned the quest for shared meaning altogether.

The cities continued to grow at a breathtaking pace in this period. People who complain about the problems of living in areas of high growth today can hardly imagine the urban population explosions in the last decades of the nineteenth century. Chicago tripled in size between 1880 and 1900, while Minneapolis and Denver quadrupled in the same period. At the same time, New York City grew from two to three and a half million people. Many of these urban inhabitants still despised the city, and found themselves there mainly because of economic opportunities. Many who could afford to do so continued to flee the inner city to the suburbs at night. However, the sheer number of people moving to the cities in this period suggests a new enthusiasm for the amenities of urban life. For someone fresh off an isolated farm, the cities offered extensive shopping, bright lights, opportunities for entertainment, and greater chances to socialize. We find in this period a new interest in city life, and in ways to reshape the cities for the common good. The Chicago Exposition of 1893, we will see later, offered a dazzling example of how city centers could be designed in a grand manner, sparking off a City Beautiful Movement that spread throughout the country. Architectural styles in the late nineteenth and early twentieth centuries split sharply on whether they stressed the urban or the rural.

Yet another issue with which America and its architects struggled in the late nineteenth and early twentieth centuries was an increasing realization that America had begun to emerge as a world power. Its population more than doubled in the 35 years from the end of the Civil War to the end of the century, reaching 76 million by 1900. It was now larger than all European countries save Russia. With an extensive home population, a vast continent of natural resources still to exploit, a comprehensive infrastructure of industrial plants, and its own financial center in New York, America had created a largely self-sufficient economy. Although America's per capita production lagged behind the Europeans, the sheer size of its economy made it the largest producer of industrialized goods in the world by 1890. Aware of its new power, America built up the world's third largest navy and joined the industrialized European countries in seeking overseas colonies. The Europeans mainly carved up Africa and Asia, while America rushed for colonies in Hawaii, the Philippines, Alaska and Cuba. Over the latter it fought a short war with Spain in 1898. Although most Americans enthusiastically supported these imperialistic enterprises, a number objected to the incompatibility of colonization with the cherished American principles of self-determinism and democracy. We will find some architects designing for the new empire, and others stressing more humble American values.

Closely related to this question of imperialism was the entire question of nationalism itself. Nationalism provided one of the main driving forces of the nineteenth century, as we have seen, uniting peoples with a common culture and often providing a common purpose for their endeavors. However, by the end of the nineteenth century, the nationalist urge had sometimes reached hysterical proportions. The popular presses screamed for retributions against perceived slights by other countries, while countries took it as a matter of intense pride to best its rivals in whatever competitions it could imagine. Eventually this exploded in the First World War. A number of thinkers, particularly on the political left, began to challenge the concept of nationalism. According to them, the real source of competition lay between the social classes, not between national groups. A worker in France had more in common with a worker in Germany than with a member of the French aristocracy. A movement grew in this period to abandon national groupings as anachronistic and insidious, and to favor instead international groupings without geographical boundaries. This idea of the universal rather than the national lay behind the international socialist and communist movements. It also provided much of the philosophical foundation for the European Modern movement in architecture. The hostility to nationalist ideas set European Modernism at odds with the more nationalistic modern expressions in America, as we will see later.

These issues and challenges, then, comprised the cultural milieu within which the late nineteenth- and early twentieth-century architects had to operate. An almost bewildering number of architectural styles emerged in response, including the ones mentioned earlier like Beaux-Arts Classicism, Gothic Revival, French Chateau, Arts and Crafts, Prairie Style and Modernism. However, behind this multiplicity of styles one can find three broad movements, or clusters of shared concerns. For convenience we will call these movements Academic Eclecticism, Progressivism and Modernism. We easily recognize the term Modernism, because it was originally employed by a relatively small group of proponents to define an unprecedented agenda, and it entered into common usage particularly after the Second World War. The first two movements, however, never received commonly accepted terms either at the time or today. This is probably because they were far more pervasive, and so were employed by many more people with numerous overlapping agendas. They had also evolved from earlier traditions which, over time, had acquired a number of interpretative shadings and stylistic names themselves. At the turn of the century, architects working within these broad traditions were more inclined to see the differences among them than the similarities, and so developed particular stylistic names for their particular outlooks. But in the hindsight of history, we can see how these many styles broadly fell into two camps in terms of their underlying philosophies. Recent historians have proposed a variety of generic names for these two, none of which have yet gained universal acceptance and use. For convenience we will follow Richard Longstreth in calling the one movement Academic Eclecticism, and we will follow several historians including William Jordy and Alan Gowans in calling the other movement the Progressive. Broadly speaking, Academic Eclecticism encompasses most of the traditional styles of the period, while the Progressive encompasses what we formerly conceived of as the proto-modern movements including the Arts and Crafts and Prairie Styles. Along with Modernism, each of these embodies a distinct set of responses to the great issues of the period that we have just examined, although on occasion they overlap. Sometimes individual architects even stepped from one camp to the other according to the project at hand. For the remainder of this chapter we will examine each of these movements in turn.

## Architectural movements at the turn of the century

### Academic Eclecticism

Academic Eclecticism dominated the age. Its proponents gained the most prestigious commissions in America and Europe, designing the bulk of commercial structures, public buildings, and private residences of the period. This movement in its broadest terms continued the revival of traditional styles that we have seen throughout the nineteenth century, so much so that the casual observer is sometimes hard pressed to see the differences between the revived styles of this period and those that preceded it. However, the Academic Eclectics themselves conceived of their movement as something fundamentally different from the work that characterized most of the nineteenth century. They even called their movement a rebirth, an American Renaissance, after the benighted Victorian Age.

The Academic Eclectic movement embraced the widest number of styles and architects in this period, and therefore we find in this movement the widest number of views regarding the great issues of the day. As a general rule, however, the Academic Eclectics stood for the adaptation of the past to the present, rather than for revolution; they stressed order and simplification; on the whole they embraced the city and its design challenges; and while they often claimed to seek the universal rather than local or idiosyncratic, many of them put into practice theories about regional design.

The new movement largely took its inspiration from French Beaux-Arts theory as it had evolved by the 1880s. The architects there had realized that the rapidly changing conditions in the late nineteenth century were no longer adequately accommodated by many of the traditional styles. One simply could not fit a modern office building or a train station into a Greek temple or a Gothic parish church. New conditions required new architectural expressions. But at the same time, the Beaux-Arts theorists did not wish to throw away the entire Western architectural heritage, since it provided cultural continuity and the very basis of good taste and commonly understood meanings. How could they reconcile this increasing conflict between continuity and change?

Viollet-le-Duc had shown the way earlier in the century, when he suggested looking behind the outward appearance of the Gothic style to discover the structural principles upon which the style was based. Once discovered, those principles could generate new architectural forms just as valuable as the Gothic yet adjusted to new conditions. Although he stirred up much controversy at the time, by the 1880s a version of this concept was beginning to shape Beaux-Arts thinking. By the end of the century it had become enshrined in the widely read student textbook, *Eléments et Théorie de l'Architecture* (1901–4), written by the Ecole's professor of theory Julien Guadet. Guadet extended Viollet-le-Duc's structural theory to architectural design generally. Behind all good styles, he claimed, lie several fundamental and universal principles of design including logic, symmetry and proportion. Individual styles are but varying manifestations of these principles. If one understands the principles, then one can design new forms that nonetheless retain the essential character of the revered and commonly understood architectural traditions.

This understanding of principle is what distinguished the new eclectics from the old. From the new perspective, the old eclectics throughout most of the nineteenth century had simply lifted bits and pieces of traditional styles without really under-standing the essential nature of their sources. For this reason Guadet largely dismissed as superficial and irrelevant the entire nineteenth-century battles of the styles. The new eclectic was to concentrate his education on the principles of design, discovered by examining a number of good styles for their underlying commonalities and essences. It is this broad and rigorously academic study of precedents that lends the term 'academic' to this movement. In America, the emphasis on scholarly study as the basis of good design further encouraged the rise of the university-based architecture pro-grams at the expense of the traditional apprenticeship system.

It follows from this view that no one style is particularly better than another, as long as each embodies the universal principles of good design. One might use any style, or combination of styles, according to the particular design problem at hand. The Academic Eclectics consequently ranged widely in their tastes, drawing from a broader selection of architectural traditions than ever before. The point was not to copy, but to adapt these traditions sensitively and creatively to the new conditions they faced. But at the same time, the Academic Eclectics disparaged the kinds of personal expressions and experiments that we saw earlier in Frank Furness. In their view, these idiosyncratic inventions did not derive from the inherent needs of the building or of society, nor did they maintain the essential connection to the uni-versal principles of good architecture. Almost by definition, if one carefully follows the principles from which traditional styles derived, then one's own details and compositional arrangements should correspond closely to those typically found in the originals. Historical accuracy was therefore important. The Academic Eclectics themselves always tried to maintain a decorous and sensible balance between con-tinuity and change, avoiding mere copyism at one extreme and personal expression-ism at the other.

The eclectics tried to select their styles according to the particular circumstances of the design. Often they looked for traditional associations between form and meaning of the kind we have seen throughout the century. An Italian palazzo originally designed for the Renaissance aristocracy might provide the model for a wealthy client's urban mansion, for example. One of the most striking examples of this kind of associationalism is Richard Morris Hunt's Biltmore in Asheville, North Carolina [185]. Designed for George Washington Vanderbilt, whose father Cornelius established the family fortune in water and rail transportation earlier in the century, this vast country estate was modeled after sixteenth-century French châteaux, mostly the royal palace at Blois. The style appropriately expressed the social status and power of the Vanderbilts who, along with the other upper-class Americans of this period, increasingly saw themselves as the aristocracy of a rising world power. The building derives its forms and details from its precedents more accurately than did revivals earlier in the century, reflecting not only the Academic Eclectic reverence for historical accuracy, but also a new attitude to wealth. Compared to the nouveau riche of the immediate post-war generation, the second- or third-generation families of wealth felt less need to proclaim their status loudly; the quieter but more powerful authority of authentic European aristocratic traditions would do nicely. But compared to the generation of the 1870s who were more reticent in their expression of wealth, the upper classes at the end of the century did not hesitate to express through monumental mansions and estates their position at the head of a rising world power. Biltmore's façade is 375 feet long, and it sat in a woodland of 120,000 acres. Although this is the largest of its kind in the nation, other vast mansions and estates can be found scattered throughout the country.

The new sensitivity among the Academic Eclectics to changing social and functional conditions also extended to a new sensitivity to place. As the keeper of the Classical torch, the Ecole des Beaux-Arts had long stressed the universal applicability of their chosen style to any location. A Classical building suitable for Rome would be equally suitable for Paris. But by the 1880s, the French had come more to Pugin's

185 Biltmore, Asheville, North Carolina, 1890–95, Richard Morris Hunt

**186** Ponce de Leon Hotel,
St Augustine, Florida, 1885–87,
Carrère & Hastings

position that different regional settings demand different architectural responses. As Guadet pointed out, buildings designed for the mountains should differ from those designed for the seaside. Yet in reviving an interest in regional character, the Academic Eclectics did not always simply revive local vernacular traditions. Sometimes no suitable local traditions existed, as in the recently settled Midwest in America. Other times local traditions needed extensive modification before they satisfied the all important requirement of embodying universal principles of design. To avoid these difficulties, and to guarantee the respectability of their precedents, many architects selected traditional styles from other similar regions in Europe. For example, one might choose from Alpine chalets for a building in the mountains, or from Italian vernacular buildings for structures in hot, dry climates.

One of the earliest and most striking examples of this adapted regionalism can be found in the design by John Merven Carrère and Thomas Hastings for the Ponce de Leon Hotel in St Augustine, Florida [**186**]. Both architects worked in the office of McKim, Mead and White before undertaking this huge project as their first independent commission. To express an appropriate character for a seaside hotel in formerly Spanish territory, Carrère and Hastings synthesized a number of southern European and French styles including Moorish, Italian Romanesque and various versions of Renaissance Classicism including Spanish. The parts were combined and fused together according to the prevailing Beaux-Arts traditions of axial and rational planning. At a more modest scale in the Southwest, Henry Trost revived Spanish Colonial traditions as shown here in his Second Owls Club in Tucson, Arizona [**187**]. We will recall that the original Spanish missions in this area fused Native American Pueblo traditions with elements of Spanish sixteenth-century Mannerism. Here Trost reinterpreted the idea with thick adobe walls, flat roofs and exposed beam ends (vigas) from the Pueblo tradition, and heavy arcades and mannerist decorations from the Spanish tradition. From this derives the Southwestern style that still flourishes in the region today.

As the population of southern California mushroomed in the 1890s, boosters there also turned to the local eighteenth- and early nineteenth-century Spanish Colonial missions for an instant architectural heritage and an identifiable image that could sell real estate. The style gained a secure foothold when the Santa Fe and Southern Pacific

187 Second Owls Club, Tucson,
Arizona, 1903?, Henry Trost

Railroad line adapted it for all of the company's stations and resort hotels in the West. Unlike the missions in the Southwestern deserts, we will recall, the original eighteenth- and early nineteenth-century California missions drew more completely from Spanish and Mexican traditions than from the Native American Pueblos further east. The revival of the style at the end of the nineteenth century, called the Mission style, consequently employed mostly Hispanic elements like bell towers, ogee gable ends and shallow tiled roofs [188]. After the first decade of the twentieth century, the Mission style gradually gave way to a more comprehensive Mediterranean style, which added a number of other hot climate traditions to the mix including ideas from Mexico, Italy, Greece and North Africa.

The most popular, and hence most widely diffused, Academic Eclectic style derived from ancient Roman and Italian Renaissance Classicism. Despite Guadet's professed willingness to entertain a number of styles, the Ecole des Beaux-Arts still emphasized the continuing tradition of rational Classicism as the one that most fully embodied the valued universal principles of good design. For an increasing number

188 House, Pasadena,
California, c. 1915

189 Pennsylvania Station,
New York City, 1902–10,
McKim, Mead & White

190 Pennsylvania Station, interior

of American architects after 1885, the style further offered appropriate answers to many contemporary challenges. As the social order seemed to crumble around them during the strikes, riots and economic depressions, Classicism offered rationality and clarity in compensation. For a rising world power, the architectural language of the Roman Empire offered an appropriately majestic and powerful image for its public buildings, including the palaces of the new American aristocracy. For the new world-class cities, the style generated sleek and urbane public structures on which the public could focus its pride. This was the architecture of power, of self-assurance, of good and urbane taste.

The undoubted masters and chief propagandists of Beaux-Arts Classicism were McKim, Mead and White. From their initial interest in Colonial Revival, and from McKim's training at the Ecole in Paris, they developed a sure hand at designing Classical buildings for everything from houses to significant public structures. Most impressive of all was their Pennsylvania Station in New York City, which provided one of the key transportation hubs of the emerging American Empire [189]. The largest railway station of the day, it covered two city blocks and provided the major gateway to and from America's premier commercial and financial city. Roman Classicism offered an appropriately majestic setting. A giant colonnade running along the front façade established a suitably grand portal, while at the same time marking the structure on the outside as a major civic building. For the vast concourse within, the architects constructed a 300 feet long by 150 feet high version of the Roman baths of Caracalla, complete with the semi-circular lunette windows in the vaults that flooded the interior with natural light [190]. Travelers in the new empire could not help but be reminded of their connection with a great ancient civilization.

Italian Renaissance Classicism evoked equally appropriate meanings for McKim, Mead & White's Boston Public Library. Sited across Copley Square from Richardson's Romanesque Trinity Church, this library housed what was then the largest public circulating collection in the world [191]. The trustees explicitly asked for a 'palace for the people' that would embody Boston's cultural heritage. The architects consequently designed the library as an Italian Renaissance palace, whose main organization idea is

191 Boston Public Library, Boston, Massachusetts, 1887–98, McKim, Mead & White

192 Columbian Exposition, Chicago, Illinois, Court of Honor, 1891–93, various architects

193 Palace of Fine Arts, Panama-Pacific Exposition, San Francisco, California, 1911–15, Bernard Maybeck

a square block hollowed out to form a courtyard within. In their version, the courtyard transformed into a reading court with the other public areas and the book stacks arranged around it. Just as the Renaissance palaces placed the main reception rooms on the second floor and marked them on the outside with larger windows, the Boston Public Library lights main public rooms on the second floor with a grand arcade of windows. This particular treatment echoes Labrouste's Bibliothèque Ste-Geneviève earlier in the century (see figure 149). Readers in the library could imagine themselves sitting in a fifteenth-century palace during the Renaissance revival of arts and learning, and naturally equate its world with theirs.

This revival of Classicism rapidly spread beyond the East coast in the 1890s, largely thanks to the World's Columbian Exposition held in Chicago in 1893. This prestigious Exposition marked the 400th anniversary of Columbus's voyage to the New World. The Chicago architect Daniel Burnham was appointed as the fair's principal adviser, who in turn invited the major Academic Eclectic architects of the day to design the main Exposition buildings. These architects included Hunt, McKim, Mead and White, Peabody and Stearns, George Post, and Van Brunt & Howe. Five local firms including Adler and Sullivan were also asked to participate. At one of their first meetings, they agreed that each firm would design its own building with an architectural style commonly shared by them all. They settled on Classicism because it was the one language they all knew well. It was also by now the preferred language of the leading Academic Eclectics, for all of the reasons described above. The local architects designed the buildings for a central section of the fair, while the imported eclectics took charge of the formal southern end named the Court of Honor. It was the latter that dazzled visitors [192]. Formally arranged around a central lake and fountain stood gleaming white buildings visually tied together with a uniform cornice height, a regular spacing of arcades, and a shared language of massing and detail. Each building, as well as the entire ensemble, displayed the rational and axial order of Beaux-Arts planning. The 'White City', as it was quickly dubbed, offered a tantalizing vision of a clean, orderly and urbane city in the very same year of the great depression with its attendant unemployment, strikes and violence. Telephones, electric transportation systems, and dramatic electric lighting of the buildings lent further proof that this was the city of a saner and more promising future.

Influential visitors from other parts of the country returned home with grand plans to construct similar urban centers. A 'City Beautiful Movement' swept the country, eventually leading to formally planned Beaux-Arts centers in many American cities from Cleveland to Denver and San Francisco. Most were appropriately comprised of public and civic buildings, including state and local government offices, libraries and art museums. In the undifferentiated grids of many American cities, these offered a central focus not only for public buildings but also for civic pride among those who now valued their cities. In 1911–15 San Franciscans built an academic eclectic setting for the Panama-Pacific Exposition to celebrate the opening of the Panama Canal, and became so enamored with Bernard Maybeck's design for the Palace of Fine Arts that they subsequently rebuilt it in permanent materials. It remains a landmark in San Francisco today [193].

This movement also led to a revival and enhancement of L'Enfant's original scheme for Washington, DC. The Mall in particular had fallen on hard times earlier in the century, encroached upon by Renwick's Smithsonian Institution near the middle of the central axis, and even by a railroad station and tracks. In 1902 a Senate Park Commission advised by Burnham, McKim and Frederick Law Olmsted, Jr proposed a number of changes that rationalized axial alignments, cleaned out inappropriate structures, and established a site for a new memorial to Abraham Lincoln at the south end of the axis extending from the White House through the Washington Monument. In essence, the City Beautiful movement and its accompanying Beaux-Arts Classicism revived the Enlightenment desire to plan rationally for the common good, while rejecting the laissez-faire individualism that had characterized the middle decades of the nineteenth century. The profession of town planning emerged in this period to advance this cause.

To keep this Classical revival in its broader context, it is worth noting that many British architects also turned enthusiastically to the Classical after 1890, for many of the same reasons we have already discussed in America. At first, the leading architects including Richard Norman Shaw, John Belcher, and Beresford Pite resisted French Beaux-Arts ideas because of the historical animosity between the two nations. The intense nationalism of the day encouraged these British architects to revive a suitably English version of Classicism, the Baroque style of Wren, Hawksmoor and Vanbrugh. After 1906 a reaction set in against this style's flamboyance, and a number of architects including Sir Reginald Blomfield, John Burnet, Charles Mewès and Arthur Davis turned to the more austere and rational Beaux-Arts tradition that had previously swept across America.

Although the Classical tradition dominated the Academic Eclectic movement, its traditional conceptual and aesthetic counterpart the Gothic also enjoyed a revival in this period. Gothic never entirely disappeared after the decline of the High Victorian Gothic, even though in the 1880s Romanesque began to challenge its predominance for church designs. Towards the end of the century Ralph Adams Cram revitalized the Gothic by creatively fusing Academic Eclectic ideas with the original moralizing spirit of Pugin. In books and articles written around the turn of the century, Cram argued for the main ideas of Academic Eclecticism. According to him, a number of styles embody the desired timeless principles of good design, these styles should be studied for their underlying essences, and new designs should adapt these essences creatively to the new design challenges. However, where Guadet and the Ecole assumed that these principles would be found most fully embodied in the Classical, Cram contrarily believed they would be found most fully developed in the Gothic. Cram was devoutly religious, and saw the intimate connection between High Church and the Gothic style

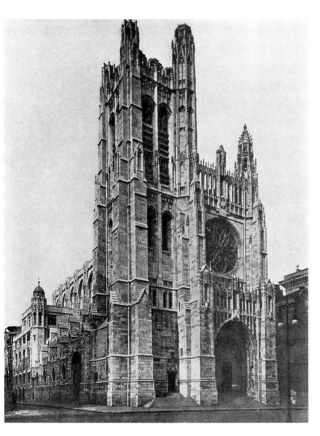

194 St Thomas's Church, New York City, 1906–13, Cram, Goodhue & Ferguson

195 Home Insurance Building, Chicago, Illinois, 1883–85, William Le Baron Jenney

that traditionally supported it. He imagined an idyllic world where Christian virtues once again dominated society, and in which mainly Gothic buildings provided the setting for both religious and secular affairs. Although he admired other styles and even occasionally used them, for most of his buildings he attempted to find modern expressions for traditional Gothic ideas. For example, together with his partners Bertram Grosvenor Goodhue and Frank Ferguson, he creatively combined French and English Gothic ideas for St Thomas's Church in New York City [194]. Compared to Pugin's accurate revivals early in the previous century, this building captures the spirit of Gothic without obviously following a familiar precedent. Compared to the freely interpreted High Victorian Gothic at mid-century, this building displays more decorum and a more obvious affinity to its original roots. Cram's writings and buildings helped spark an academic Gothic Revival throughout America in the first decades of the new century, particularly for ecclesiastic and academic buildings.

Skyscrapers grew dramatically taller after 1885, and were mainly clothed with Academic Eclectic styles. We saw in the last chapter how the first skyscrapers in the 1870s had reached ten stories while continuing to employ traditional load-bearing external walls. A number of experiments with mixed frame and load-bearing constructions finally culminated in the first ever free-standing frame with an attached external curtain wall for an inhabited structure, William Le Baron Jenney's 1883–85 Home Insurance Building in Chicago [195]. Above a solid masonry base he set a metal frame constructed partly in cast and wrought iron, and partly in the newly available Bessemer steel. Cast iron shelf angles at every second floor carried the weight of the external brick and terracotta sheathing back to the frame. Other architects immediately saw the advantages of this system. The walls at the bottom of the structure could remain as thin as those at the top no matter how tall the building grew. Buildings of apparently unlimited height were now possible (later, as we will see, the heights of extremely tall buildings were limited more by wind pressures and potential overturning than by the traditional problem of carrying the weight of the building to the ground). This rapidly became the standard system of construction for tall buildings.

Jenney styled his building with a freely interpreted Classicism. The usual tripartite divisions are expressed with a Richardsonian rusticated base, a middle shaft of intermediate floors and a capping cornice. The intermediate floors are treated like several horizontal Classical buildings piled on top of each other, each one defined by its own Classical pilaster and entablature. Subsequent modernist historians disapproved of this styling, because it pretended to be a load-bearing masonry wall, and did not honestly express the metal frame within. Indeed, for the same reason they disparaged all subsequent framed buildings that continued to use any form of traditional masonry-based styling. For most architects in this period and well into the twentieth century, this was not a problem. From the Renaissance on, as we have seen in this history, most architects adjusted the structure and construction of their buildings to fit their desired image. False parapets hid flying buttresses in Wren's St Paul's Cathedral, plaster ceilings hid the floor and roof structures in Federalist houses, false vaults covered trusses in the first American Gothic Revival churches, and Shingle Style houses hid their wooden skeletons behind a smooth veneer. It was only in the second third of the nineteenth century that Pugin and Ruskin had insisted on 'honesty' of construction, and even then mainly to justify their preferred Gothic style. For most nineteenth- and early twentieth-century architects, decorum and appropriate dress remained more important than frankly expressing one's skeleton. Furthermore, the problems of fireproofing the metal structures meant that they would have to be clad in masonry or clay tiles anyway. Why not continue to use stylistic images derived from masonry's venerable traditions?

Most architects consequently continued to employ traditional styles for their tall steel framed buildings. But by the first decade of the twentieth century, their styling problem had become more acute. Continuing economic pressures and Jenney's system had created skyscrapers over fifty stories tall. The buildings were now so much taller than their width that architects could no longer simply pile up bands of horizontal pieces. They needed to look again for traditional precedents that could express this vertical emphasis. The Metropolitan Tower in New York City [196] shows the use of one popular and useful precedent, the campanile or bell tower at St Mark's Square in Venice. Here the main shaft of the building sweeps up without horizontal interruption, until it reaches what in the original was the arcaded belfry and its steeple roof. Another ingenious answer sheathed the outside of the building in Gothic ribs and pinnacles, as shown here in Cass Gilbert's 52-story Woolworth Building in New York City [197]. The Gothic style answered the aesthetic problem of tall buildings particularly well, because this was traditionally the style of sweeping verticals. The appropriation of the style from its original religious roots was vindicated when the Woolworth Building acquired the moniker the 'Cathedral of Commerce'. Numerous other Academic Eclectic styles were also employed for tall buildings in this period, ranging from Beaux-Arts to Romanesque.

Both the Metropolitan Tower and the Woolworth Building continued to use Hunt's idea of a tower growing out of a lower base, by now a characteristic New York City skyscraper tradition. Many other American skyscrapers in this period, however, rose

**196** Metropolitan Tower,
New York City, 1909,
Napoleon Le Brun & Sons

**197** Woolworth Building,
New York City, 1911–13,
Cass Gilbert

up to their full heights without a break or setback. As these bulky forms proliferated in American cities, they began to cause serious congestion at street level and to block light and air. A number of cities subsequently passed building regulations in the first decades of the twentieth century which included restricting heights, relating heights to a percentage of the area of the site, and requiring setbacks as the building grew taller. These regulations eventually led to skyscrapers which progressively narrowed towards the top, or which stepped back from the edge of the street altogether.

Despite the Modernists' later hostility to Academic Eclecticism, we can see that this architectural tradition seems to have expressed many Americans' conception of the society in which they lived or wished to live. In a period of dramatic change, when Americans struggled through a depression and great social upheaval, many saw in Academic Eclecticism a welcome emphasis on order and urbanity. And as Americans began to face the reality of their growing international presence, many also enjoyed the implied connection with great civilizations and empires past.

### Progressive movements

Although the Academic Eclectic styles dominated American architectural production after 1890, there also arose in this period a number of other styles that diverged markedly from the academic mainstream. Known as Arts and Crafts, Craftsman, Organic and Prairie in their day, they derived from a different set of architectural beliefs, and answered a different conception of society. We will call these the Progressive styles, named not only for the expressed desire of their protagonists to innovate, but also for a contemporary movement of social reform in America named Progressivism that helped shape the mood in which these styles emerged.

In essence, the Progressive styles originated in the Gothic Revival ideas of Pugin and Ruskin. These two offered, we will recall, the most overtly hostile architectural reaction to the Industrial Revolution and the social ills that followed. Both thinkers rejected modern nineteenth-century life and the artificial architectural forms that had grown out of it, offering instead an idyllic image of medieval life when life was more moral, and architecture was in direct consequence more honest and beautiful. They both stressed the importance of building forms naturally deriving from their functions, both praised the virtues of honest structure and construction, and Ruskin also lauded the virtues of hand craft rather than machine production. These ideas passed to the British designer William Morris in the 1860s and 1870s who, like Ruskin, asserted a clear relationship between an ailing society and the poor architectural and product designs it created. As a leading British socialist, Morris actively agitated for a social revolution, insisting that only when society healed would good design emerge again. Healing for him meant a rejection of industrialization and capitalism, and a return to the values and institutions of the Middle Ages. He particularly rejected machine-made goods, because of the dehumanizing effects on the workers who ran the machines. His own firm of artisans produced various arts and crafts for buildings, including stained glass, wallpapers, tiles, textiles, carpets and metal goods, within a setting as medieval as it could manage. Morris's firm attempted to derive its product designs from honest construction and materials without artificial conceit, much as it imagined medieval artisans must have done. The actual designs creatively modified medieval forms and decorative systems.

His architect and friend Philip Webb, whom we will recall helped lead the search for a picturesque style of architecture less strident than High Victorian Gothic, stressed these same ideas in architecture. Conceiving of himself as a humble and anonymous medieval craftsman, he studiously avoided following an obvious style, and hoped that good building forms would naturally derive from function and honestly expressed hand-made construction. Like Pugin, he also appreciated how his favorite medieval buildings varied according to region, both in form and in the materials employed. His own designs offered simplified versions of vernacular medieval traditions with touches from later periods, often constructed in local materials. Common to both Morris and Webb was a fervent belief that one ought to aim for a simple and honest life, expressed through simple and honest architecture and furnishings.

A number of British artists, craftspeople and architects developed these ideas in the 1880s and 1890s into what they called the Arts and Crafts movement. Several of the movement's most important proponents emerged from Richard Norman Shaw's prestigious office, including Edward Prior and William Lethaby. Other advocates included Arthur Mackmurdo, James MacLaren, Charles Annesley Voysey, Edwin Lutyens and Charles Rennie Mackintosh. Like the Academic Eclectics, they wished to avoid stylistic wranglings by focusing attention on the principles behind good architecture. They, too, wished creatively to adapt these principles to the new conditions of the late nineteenth century. However, where the Academic Eclectics derived their principles mainly from rationally geometrical styles like Classicism or Gothic cathedrals, the Arts and Crafts architects looked more to picturesque vernacular medieval traditions. For them, many of the important principles of design had already been established by Pugin, Ruskin, Morris and Webb, including honest and expressive construction, the importance of handcraft, the need to integrate buildings with nature

**198** Munstead Wood,
Surrey, England, 1896,
Sir Edwin Lutyens

and the local setting, the moral and aesthetic value of simplification, and the importance of integrating all the arts. Some like Lethaby acquired Morris's socialist political
views; others like Voysey and Lutyens were either conservative or held no strong
political views, expressing more interest in the aesthetic possibilities of the new direction than in changing society. In keeping with the Gothic Revival origins of these
ideas, however, they established a number of medieval-like guilds including the Art
Workers' Guild where the new ideas could be discussed and disseminated.

The British Arts and Crafts movement derived from the Gothic Revival, which in
turn derived from the Romantic movement of the late eighteenth and early nineteenth
centuries. Given this heritage, the Arts and Crafts architects not surprisingly fell into
the old Romantic paradox regarding the role of the architect. Some like Webb regarded
the designer as humbly responding to the functional requirements and reflecting the
dominant spirit of the times, while others saw the designer as a creative artist who
responds to inner urges even when those urges might conflict with the client's wishes
or the prevailing spirit of the times. Lethaby, for example, proclaimed that his first
duty as an artist is to please himself. When the Royal Institute of British Architects
attempted to professionalize architecture in the early 1890s with more stringent
educational requirements and restrictions on entry to the field, a number of leading
Arts and Crafts architects rejoined that architecture is an art, not a profession, and
left the RIBA in protest. Here we have the beginnings of the adversarial relationship
between architects and their clients that still often plagues the profession today. These
attitudes subsequently ran through most of the American architects who took up the
Arts and Crafts ideas, most especially Louis Sullivan and Frank Lloyd Wright.

The Arts and Crafts ideas spurred a domestic building revival in Great Britain
from the 1890s to the First World War that attracted international attention. Edwin
Lutyens's design for Munstead Wood in Surrey, England, offers a good example of
how medieval vernacular ideas were simplified and clarified, and how much aesthetic
delight derived from medieval construction details like the protruding oak pegs in
the window frame [198]. Voysey took the process of simplification even further, as
we see here in his design for Broadleys, Lake Windermere, England [199]. Although
medieval traditions including steep roofs, tall chimneys, bay windows and bands of

windows obviously provided inspiration for this design, the overtly historical details are stripped away to reveal the underlying essence of the medieval picturesque idea. Around the turn of the century, several British architects led by Mackintosh, Charles Townsend and Charles Holden pressed this concept of simplification to its logical conclusion. They sought what they called a Free Style that would ignore historical styling altogether. Mackintosh's design for the Library Wing of the Glasgow School of Art shows the idea [200]. Although the design is vaguely reminiscent of a number of architectural traditions including Mackintosh's earlier favorite Scottish Baronial, the forms are abstracted, clarified and reduced to richly interlocking geometrical shapes for which there are no obvious precedents.

A number of these ideas caught on in America starting in the late 1880s. Although the more socially conservative Americans shunned the radical socialism of Morris and Lethaby, the moralizing and reforming tone of the Arts and Crafts movement fitted well with an emerging movement of social reform later known as Progressivism. This social movement merged a Populist crusade for agricultural reforms with a middle-class rebellion at the excesses and injustices in late nineteenth-century America. The latter group in particular objected to the extravagances of the upper classes, to the pervasive corruption in civic government, and to the shocking conditions in which the working classes lived. Their moral outrage was helped along by fear of the anarchists and industrial unrest that plagued the 1890s. Better to reform America's social institutions than to lose them altogether through revolution. They established good government clubs, and successfully pressed for mildly socialist reforms including municipal ownership of utilities, unemployment relief and a minimum wage. Middle-class organizations also sent social workers into the cities – still regarded by many as unsavory wildernesses – to work on behalf of the poor. A movement for women's rights also emerged in this period, focusing after 1890 on earning the right to vote (although Wyoming entered the Union in 1890 as the first state to offer full suffrage, American women did not receive the vote nationally until 1920).

The Progressives also agitated for restrictions on big business and the trusts, whose monopolies not only generated glaring disparities between rich and poor, but also worked against the American ideal of individuals rising up on talent and hard work. The Progressive movement accelerated rapidly after 1901, when Theodore Roosevelt became president after McKinley's assassination at the hand of an anarchist. Roosevelt built a stronger central government and established more regulatory powers to counter

**199** Broadleys, Lake Windermere, England, 1898, Charles Annesley Voysey

**200** Library Wing, Glasgow School of Art, 1905–9, Charles Rennie Mackintosh

the excesses of big business. He aimed to provide what he called a 'square deal' for all segments of the American population, although his natural constituency primarily remained the farmers, skilled workers, small businessmen and professionals.

This predominately middle-class movement stood opposed to – or at the very least less enthusiastically embraced – many of the attitudes that had fueled Academic Eclecticism in architecture. The Progressives objected to the idea of an American aristocracy, and its extravagant display of wealth. They valued instead a simple and honest lifestyle. They stressed the priority of democracy and self-determination, many agreeing only reluctantly to America's empire building as a necessary means of self-defense and as an opportunity to extend the virtues of democracy to other countries. They remained ambivalent towards the cities, viewing them mainly as homes for the extremely wealthy and for the underprivileged poor. The middle classes retained the traditional American preference for nature and rural life, seeking the suburbs when-ever possible. And although they had personally benefited economically from the Industrial Revolution, they had also seen how its excesses had dangerously brought the Republic close to ruin. For many the machine was something by which to benefit, but certainly not something to celebrate.

How appealing the British Arts and Crafts ideas must have appeared. Those houses were not extravagant displays of power and wealth, but rather cozy domes-tic settings for family life (even though most of the British houses were designed for upper middle- and powerful upper-class clients). They were designed for the sub-urbs and the countryside, intimately connected to their natural settings. And while they reassuringly reminded one of familiar traditions, their simplified and abstracted forms seemed so sensible, so free from pretension. This was just the right image for the sensible, hard-working middle class that comprised the core of America.

The Arts and Crafts ideas first appeared in Chicago, and not by mere coincidence. Sitting on the intersection of several transportation networks, Chicago had emerged as the economic hub of an Inland Empire in the Midwest. Its speculators and entre-preneurs had built it from a wilderness to a major commercial and industrial city in less than a century. At the same time, it stood in the heartland of American agriculture and housed a large middle-class population, both seedbeds for Progressive ideas. Indeed, the nearby state of Wisconsin led the country in initiating social reforms, causing Teddy Roosevelt to call it a 'laboratory of democracy'. Far from the East coast cities and on the edge of the rapidly closing Western frontier, its character was more boisterous than refined, less constrained by tradition. It was ready to try new ideas.

Two of the central Arts and Crafts ideals, simplification of form and the frank expression of construction, first appeared in Chicago buildings not so much as a con-scious philosophical decision, as much as a pragmatic response to a building boom in the 1880s. Entrepreneurs wanted maximum floor area for minimum financial outlay, and were willing to forgo the niceties of traditional architectural decoration. Jenney's first true frame building that we discussed earlier was developed in this climate. In others of his Chicago buildings he experimented with reducing the outer skin even more. For example, he abridged the façade of his Second Leiter Building to little more than vertical piers, horizontal beams, intermediate window mullions and the barest of traditional details like pilaster capitals and cornices. Glass filled in the rest. For mostly practical reasons, he had arrived at Viollet-le-Duc's conception of the Gothic as a structural frame with glazed infill. The clients for Daniel Burnham and John Wellborn Root's Monadnock Building specifically asked the architects to refrain from applying ornament. Root originally conceived of the building as a simplified version of an Egyptian column, but in the end stripped off any ornamental hints of the precedent. He was left with little more than a massive brick block flared out slightly at top and bottom, and slightly projecting bay windows [201]. Root saw virtue in necessity, and argued the Academic Eclectic view that architecture had to face up to modern realities. New approaches were necessary for the more complex problems of the modern world.

Louis Sullivan tied these early experiments more specifically to the Arts and Crafts and Progressive ideas. Drawn from an astonishing number of sources, his theories are complex, often contradictory, and written in an effusive style that often obscures rather than clarifies. While growing up he acquired an almost mystical appreciation of nature. From reading Greenough, Emerson, Pugin and Ruskin he acquired a broad range of Romantic and Gothic Revival ideas. Walt Whitman, Friedrich Nietzsche, Auguste Comte, Herbert Spencer and Hippolyte Taine contributed ideas about the individual and society. A year's study at MIT and another year at the Ecole des Beaux-Arts in Paris taught him Beaux-Arts theories. A brief stint in Frank Furness's office introduced him to Viollet-le-Duc and Furness's idiosyncratic approach to design. In William Le Baron Jenney's office, and later from his engineer partner Dankmar Adler, he learned about the new techniques for constructing tall buildings. In the German-American community surrounding his partner Adler he became acquainted with the writings of the German architect and theorist Gottfried Semper who, writing at mid-century, blended ideas of structural rationalism with German Romanticism.

Sullivan promulgated his synthesis of these ideas through articles and speeches, through a series of short weekly essays published in 1901–2 in *The Interstate Architect and Builder* entitled the 'Kindergarten Chats', and through later books including *The Autobiography of an Idea* (1922–23). In essence, Sullivan took up the Romantic and Rousseauian idea about the priority of the individual, and about the need to fulfill one's inner potential as a human. Until recently, he went on, Western cultures sub-jugated individuals because society had remained in a Feudal phase characterized by the inequalities and selfish materialism of High Victorian capitalism. Now in America, however, society was entering a Democratic phase where individuals stood on equal ground and could finally achieve their inner potential. Where Morris had hoped for a socialist revolution to improve the lot of individuals, Sullivan asserted that American democracy had already begun the transformation.

This idyllic new society would need its own appropriate architectural expression, an architecture of democracy. Ironically, perhaps, Sullivan viewed the speculative office buildings rapidly rising on the Chicago skyline as the harbingers of the new democratic style. He admired the entrepreneur businessmen as hardy individuals who took risks and reaped rewards while building a better city for everyone. This was American democracy at its best. But what should these tall buildings look like? Turning again to a Romantic idea further developed in the Gothic Revival and British Arts and Crafts, Sullivan asserted that an appropriate architectural style will grow naturally out of the conditions at hand. In some writings, he meant by this the Beaux-Arts idea that a form should logically derive from the nature of the building program. One should be able to read the building functions, he maintained, in the arrangement of the building form. To this he added the Gothic Revival and Arts and Crafts idea that forms ought to express the nature of the construction and structure within. Sullivan summed up these ideas in the subsequently well-used phrase of Modernism, 'form follows function'. In other writings, however, he abandoned these rationalistic ideas in favor of the old Romantic idea that a work of art grows according to its own inner vital force. His architecture was 'organic', he explained, an expansive and rhythmic growth beyond logic. Restating Semper in particular and Romanticism in

general, he claimed that nature is the ultimate source of all beauty, and that the spirit transcends everything else. These two positions reflect the old Romantic paradox regarding outer or inner sources of design ideas. Despite the obvious contradictions, here we have the major Progressive themes including the value of democracy, the importance of nature, the priority of the individual, and the forthright expression of function without extravagance.

So how did this theory translate into architecture? Like Hunt before him, Sullivan recognized that the dominant heights of these tall buildings called for a vertical emphasis. But where Hunt searched for appropriately vertical historical precedents, Sullivan looked for internal functions to suggest the form. Tall commercial buildings logically break into three parts, he noticed. The bottom two floors house entrances, lobbies and retail shops, an indeterminate number of floors above house rentable space which can freely divide in plan, and the top floor houses mechanical equipment. As we see in one of his most famous designs, the Wainright Building in St Louis, Missouri, these functions found expression as a base, a soaring middle section uninterrupted by horizontal lines, and a capping frieze and cornice [202]. Rather than hide the frame structure behind an historical skin, Sullivan frankly expressed it as a series of vertical piers and slightly recessed horizontal spandrels. Although at first glance the boxy form has little to do with nature, on closer inspection we discover elaborate ornamental patterns on the spandrels and in the capping frieze that fuse stylized plant forms with complex geometries, giving the building an organic liveliness. This ornamental system became one of Sullivan's trademarks.

Admiring Sullivan's rejection of historical detail, his emphasis on function, and his honest expression of structure, later Modernists held him up as a pioneer of their own ideas. Yet one might be forgiven for questioning the degree to which Sullivan broke with the past or the consistency with which he implemented his theory. The division into three parts that he supposedly derived from the skyscraper's functions we have seen throughout this book as the traditional Classical tripartite division of base, middle and, employed by countless buildings in numerous traditional and modern societies. The massing of many of his buildings owes much to Richardson's Romanesque, particularly the Marshall Field Wholesale Store, while his distinctive ornamental patterns derive from Romanesque, Gothic, Celtic, Egyptian and Renaissance sources. Furthermore, the honest expression of structure in the Wainright Building turns out to have bent the truth, since only every other pier is actually structural. The other decorative piers were inserted to give the building more vertical emphasis. And is the celebration of commerce and speculative real estate really the highest expression of American democracy?

The Chicago School of commercial architecture, as later historians termed these experiments of Burnham, Root, Sullivan and others, fell out of fashion towards the end of the century. Most clients turned instead to the ideas of the Academic Eclectics, as did some of the Chicago School architects themselves. It was Burnham, we will recall, who brought in the leading Academic Eclectics to design the Chicago Columbian Exposition. Sullivan refused to compromise, and saw his career collapse as few commissions came in except for some banks in small midwestern towns. In these he turned even more thoroughly to Beaux-Arts ideas of massing and axiality, although he continued to develop his highly personal system of decoration in preference to the historical modes [203]. Sullivan bitterly blamed the Columbian Exposition for foisting a Classical lie onto the American public, prophesying that it would set back the course of a proper American architecture by half a century. After Sullivan died penniless and alone in 1924, later Modernists pointed to the tragedy of his life as an example of the heroic struggles at the genesis of their movement. Subsequent generations of Modernist students grew up learning to admire Sullivan's tenacity and to despise his perceived arch enemy, the Classicism at the Columbian Exposition.

The Progressive mantle passed to Sullivan's disciple, Frank Lloyd Wright. Many – including Wright himself – have considered him the greatest architect America has ever produced. Without any formal training, he developed a number of innovative and uniquely American styles throughout a career spanning almost three-quarters of a century. He drew from many sources, but always managed to synthesize these into buildings of uncommon power and unity. Like Richardson, Wright exerted more influence on the European architects than they did on him. Indeed, when his work was first published in Europe it helped instigate there a more thoroughly modern movement than had so far been attempted. Even today his buildings continue to touch a deep nerve among architects and lay people alike, as witnessed in part by the extensive number of books on his work that continue to fill bookstore shelves throughout the country.

Although we have not dwelled on the personal lives of architects in this history so far, in Wright's case the biographical details particularly help explain many of his later design attitudes. He was born in Wisconsin where, except for a short period back East, he spent most of his childhood. We will recall that Wisconsin later became one of the leaders of the Progressive reform movement, and in many ways embodied the values of heartland America. Wright's mother had decided early on that her son would become an architect. She purchased a set of educational play blocks

**203** Merchant's National Bank, Grinnell, Iowa, 1913–14, Louis Sullivan

designed by the great German educationalist Friedrich Froebel, for which Wright later credited his understanding of geometrical shapes and composition. She tried to provide a congenial home life and education that would nurture his talents, despite a moody husband who eventually abandoned the family when Wright was 16. Both these positive and negative influences left Wright with an almost romantic ideal of family life centered in the home. Wright spent summers on his uncle's farm near Spring Green, where he further acquired an intense love of nature and a deep appreciation of the hardy homesteading values that he witnessed in the self-sufficient families of the Wisconsin countryside. The virtues of nature, democracy and family life centered on hearth and home combined in Wright to form the core set of values from which his architectural ideas later sprang.

After a year at the University of Wisconsin studying French and drawing, in 1887 he entered the office of the architect J. Lyman Silsbee in Chicago. There he learned to design fairly conventional versions of the picturesque Shingle and Colonial Revival styles. His first buildings sported high medieval roofs, picturesquely asymmetrical floor plans and turrets. At home and at the university, he had also become acquainted with the great texts of the Gothic Revival movement, including those by Ruskin and Viollet-le-Duc, in which he particularly admired the call for honest expression of material and structure. Wright joined Adler and Sullivan in 1888 where, under Sullivan's tutelage, he found a more comprehensive philosophical foundation and a more appropriate architectural vocabulary for his deeply felt beliefs. He also came into contact with Semper's theories. Besides propounding the now usual idea of expressive structure, Semper described the archetypal house as one with a platform, a fire at its core and a sheltering roof hovering over enclosing walls. These ideas later found their way into Wright's first Prairie houses, although in a form quite unimagined by Semper.

As Wright's star quickly rose within the firm, he was given increasing responsibility for the residential commissions while Sullivan concentrated on the commercial work. Wright continued to work with the usual Shingle and Colonial Revival ideas, although now he began to simplify and rationalize them in the spirit of Richardson and Sullivan. His own house in Oak Park, a suburb of Chicago, shows the new idea [204].

**204** Wright House, Oak Park, Illinois, 1889, Frank Lloyd Wright

As we approach the front of the building, we are confronted with a massive gable front reduced to a primitive geometrical triangle covered in shingles and punctured with a Colonial Revival Palladian window. Like a giant hat, the roof gathers under itself the body of the house and the various protuberances like the bay windows. The embracing, protective roof sums up the idea of shelter. The spaces inside echo the open planning we saw earlier in the Queen Anne and in McKim, Mead and White's Shingle Style Bell House, with a stairwell entry hall giving through a wide opening onto a central living room. A deep fireplace inglenook on the internal side of the living room symbolically and literally places the fire at the heart of the home. Although technological advances in centralized heating had long made the fireplace redundant as a source of heat, Wright intentionally used it to recall a romantic image of a hardy pioneer family gathered around the fire at night, protected at the heart of their cozy shelter.

In 1893 Wright fell out with Sullivan and started a practice on his own. In the same year he visited the Chicago Columbian Exposition, where he had worked with Sullivan on the Transportation Building. There he saw two grand architectural traditions in the flesh that he added to his developing architectural vocabulary. The first tradition was, of course, the Academic Eclectics' Beaux-Arts Classicism in the Court of Honor. Wright had known the Classical language mainly through its Colonial Revival variant, and had even used a few Classical details in his own Oak Park house. Here he saw it in all its glory. Although he followed Sullivan in despising the style itself, the power and grace of its underlying order and geometry clearly made an indelible impression on him, as we will see below. The second architectural tradition Wright encountered at the Exposition was a half-scale reproduction of a Japanese temple, erected by the Japanese government as their official pavilion. Now we have already seen how Japanese ideas infiltrated the Queen Anne and Shingle styles earlier in the century. The British Arts and Crafts architects also explored Japanese ideas of simplicity and expressive craftsmanship in the same period. Wright therefore already indirectly knew a number of these ideas. Now, however, he saw the Japanese tradition in its original form. Its expressive craftsmanship, open planning, horizontal lines, and broad roofs hovering over non-structural walls, all resonated well with the images and ideas he had accumulated and was rapidly assimilating.

After a series of transitional experiments, in 1900 Wright finally synthesized his diverse sources into what we now call the Prairie Style. The main ideas first appeared in two unbuilt designs commissioned by the *Ladies' Home Journal*, as part of a scheme by the journal's publisher to improve the residential design tastes of middle America. The requirements abounded with Progressive ideals, including modest construction costs that the readership might be able to afford, and an insistence on replacing the traditional aristocratic term 'parlor' with the recently fashionable and more family-related term 'living room'. These requirements accorded well with Wright's own Progressive interests, and perhaps helped him find the new expression for which he was searching.

We can see his new style most clearly in the Ward Willitts House designed about the same time, but for a wealthier client [205]. Here is a building unlike anything we have seen before in this architectural history, vaguely reminiscent of many traditions but overtly derived from none. In essence, Wright successfully fused the spirit of the two broad traditions that we have seen weaving in and out of Western architectural history, the rationalism of Classicism, and the picturesque of the Gothic and its Arts and Crafts derivatives. Where the former had traditionally excelled at satisfying our need for intellectual understanding and order, and the latter had excelled at satisfying

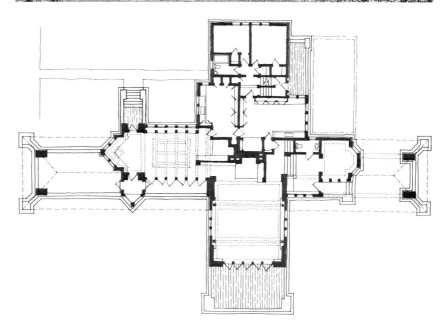

**205** Ward W. Willitts House,
Highland Park, Illinois, 1900–2,
Frank Lloyd Wright

**206** Ward W. Willitts House,
plan

**207** Ward W. Willitts House,
interior

our need for emotional stimulation and variety, Wright managed to answer both equally well in the same building. We see the spirit of Classicism in the axial planning of the various parts, and in the careful arrangement of simple geometrical forms. We see the spirit of the picturesque traditions in the asymmetrical dispositions of the parts, in the piled up massing, in the hint of medieval half-timbering trim, in the meandering sequences of rooms within, and in the massive fireplace core, dark wooden trim and stained glass. We comprehend the overall order while delighting our senses with rich details and varied spatial experiences.

Besides fusing the rational with the picturesque, Wright also took up Sullivan's notion of the organic and fused the building with nature. He accomplished this through several visual devices. First of all, he emphasized the horizontal lines of the composition wherever possible, relating the building to the horizontal lines of the Midwestern prairie (he also described the horizontal as the line of domesticity). From this derives the term Prairie Style. Second, he blurred the distinction between the inside and the outside by constructing covered but open spaces at the building's edges, a terrace on one side and a *porte-cochère* or covered driveway entrance on the other. These intermediate spaces gently encourage one to move from land to building and back again. Interestingly, the organic theory as first developed in Romanticism and as elaborated by Sullivan stressed the idea of a building growing out of the ground like a plant. But in the Prairie houses, Wright emphatically rejected the traditional basement, preferring instead to sit the building on a slab-like base according to Semper's theory. The effect is more like clearing the land at the homestead to provide a flat platform upon which to construct the house. In abandoning the basement, by the way, Wright gave up a useful tradition that provided a cool retreat in the summers and a haven from tornadoes.

Wright cleverly reconciled his new desire for horizontal lines with his earlier preference for the broad sheltering roof. He reduced the roof pitch to something more Classical, but then projected the eaves well beyond the walls. The roof appears to float over the building. The horizontal strips of windows further enhance the hovering effect by disintegrating the load-bearing wall just under the roof soffits. The plan reveals his continuing preoccupation with the symbolic hearth at the center of the home [206]. Here a massive chimney reminiscent of early New England houses stands at the crossing axes of a cruciform plan, with a separate firebox and inglenook pointing to each of the two main wings [207]. The entrance brings us directly to this heart of the house, from which we may see and enter the main reception rooms. Windows at the ends of the main rooms opposite the fireplace provide one of Wright's most delightful effects. On wintry nights one may turn one's back on the cold outdoors and huddle around the fire; on balmy spring days one may leave the dark, cave-like center and move out to the bright windows and landscape beyond. These Prairie houses were so abstracted from their multiple historical roots that they no longer overtly referred to traditional meanings and associations. But at the same time, they embodied deep associations to primeval notions of fire, shelter, family and nature which people without knowledge of the traditional styles would still intuitively understand.

Wright employed a number of medieval and Arts and Crafts details like stained glass windows, expressively interlocking joinery connections, and heavy wooden paneling and trim. However, in one important regard he broke with the Arts and Crafts tradition. Where his predecessors from Ruskin and Morris onwards had stressed the importance of handcraft and had disparaged the machine, Wright contrarily championed machine-made materials like plain milled wood. His enthusiasm derived

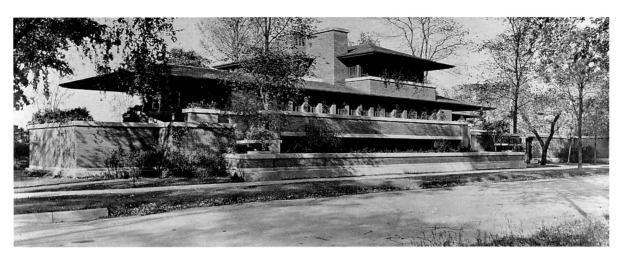

208 Robie House, Chicago,
Illinois, 1906–9,
Frank Lloyd Wright

in part from his early efforts to design affordable houses for the middle classes, where handcraft proved prohibitively expensive, and in part from his aesthetic preferences for the simple and the clean as he saw in the Japanese attitude to materials.

Most famous of all Wright's Prairie houses then and now is the Robie house, whose bold, abstract forms and emphatic horizontal lines summed up Wright's early ideas and expressed the degree to which architecture could divorce itself from traditional styles [208]. Here, however, the Prairie idea is not so compelling. The building sits on a site only slightly larger than the building itself, in the middle of a gridironed residential area, far from the open prairie, and mostly surrounded by traditional buildings. This house also shows the degree to which Wright was willing to bend the usual Gothic Revival and Arts and Crafts insistence on honesty of structure. To project those long floating roofs over the terraces, Wright had to bury massive steel beams inside the roof construction. Like most architects before him, Wright placed greater emphasis on appearance than on ruthless honesty when he had to choose between the two.

In the same period he was developing the Prairie houses, Wright also applied his Progressive ideas and new architectural vocabulary to public buildings. For the Larkin Building in Buffalo, New York, he turned the building in on itself to form an enclosed courtyard surrounded by balconies [209]. In so doing he hoped to create a sense of an extended family and community in the workplace. Elaborate ventilation ducts buried in various vertical piers helped further seal the building against the soot in the building's industrial setting. Unity Temple in Oak Park continued the idea that Wright received from Sullivan, and that Sullivan received from the Ecole des Beaux-Arts, of clearly expressing internal functions in external massing [210]. Here the auditorium and a social hall each received its own independent block, connected together with a low entrance sandwiched between the two. The main blocks themselves divided into smaller blocks according to the functions within. For example, the corner blocks of the main auditorium reflect the stairwells, while the higher block at the center expresses the skylights over the auditorium's square center. All the shapes are reduced to simple geometrical solids artfully composed in relation to each other, just like a giant version of the Froebel blocks with which he played as a child. Creatively responding to a limited budget once again, Wright decided to construct the entire building in inexpensive poured concrete. He livened this somewhat brutal and utilitarian material by exposing the pebble aggregate. Stripped of all traditional detail and material, this building offers visual interest entirely in the play of solid against void, and of highlight against shadow.

Wright first gained fame in Europe, not America. The German Wasmuth Press published a portfolio of his work in 1910, entitled *Ausgeführte Bauten und Entwürfe von Frank Lloyd Wright* (Studies and Executed Buildings by Frank Lloyd Wright), filled with seductive drawings of his projects rendered as Japanese prints by his assistant Marion Mahoney. A subsequent publication in the following year offered photographs of the completed buildings. Many of the younger European architects were electrified by the bold, abstract forms, and by the complete absence of historical detailing. They themselves were searching for a modern idiom, as we will see in the next section, and suddenly they found in Wright an extensive body of work that expressed their desired values of order, simplicity and abstraction. A number of later European Modernists including Walter Gropius and Mies van der Rohe began to experiment with some of Wright's forms, particularly the more abstract ones. Wright also inspired a Prairie School of architects back in the American Midwest, including Marion Mahoney, her husband Walter Burley Griffin, William Drummond and George Grant Elmslie.

Wright also acquired the Arts and Crafts idea that the architect is an artist first and foremost. Where earlier generations of architects worked more in partnership with their clients, Wright insisted on complete control over the entire project from the original conception to the final details of the furniture and finishings. Wright's clients got what he decided to give them. His early career came to an abrupt end in 1909, when he left his family and traveled in Europe with the wife of a client. On his return Chicago society ostracized him, denying him any significant commissions. Wright's story picks up again in the next chapter when, in the interwar years, he revived his career and struck out in new stylistic directions.

Several San Francisco Bay Area architects working in this same period combined more traditional versions of Arts and Crafts ideas with Academic Eclecticism. Ernest

**209** Larkin Building, Buffalo, New York, 1903, Frank Lloyd Wright

**210** Unity Temple, Oak Park, Illinois, 1904–6, Frank Lloyd Wright

Coxhead, A. Page Brown, Willis Polk, A. C. Schweinfurth, John Galen Howard and Bernard Maybeck had moved from back East to San Francisco in the last decades of the nineteenth century, bringing with them rigorous Academic Eclectic educations they had received in school and in the great academic eclectic practices of the day. For example, Maybeck and Howard had attended the Ecole des Beaux-Arts in Paris, Howard had worked for Richardson and McKim, Mead and White, Maybeck had worked for Carrère and Hastings, and Polk had worked for Van Brunt and Howe. Yet like their colleagues in Chicago, they found at this great distance from the eastern tastemakers a new freedom to experiment with the ideas they had acquired in their training. Responding to the special conditions they found in what a contemporary San Franciscan writer called the 'edge of the world', they began to fuse a number of disparate ideas into a distinctive Bay Area style.

Following the prevalent Academic Eclectic theories, they saw stylistic distinctions among buildings of different types and settings. In particular, they often distinguished between buildings for urban settings and buildings for the suburbs or countryside. For the largest buildings and most urban settings, they often chose variations on formal Classicism or Colonial Revival. For more rural areas they often turned to more picturesque styles derived from a number of medieval sources. However, this distinction sometimes blurred under the influence of a Western lifestyle more casual than the architects had experienced back East. Californians had come to revere their rugged natural setting, and valued opportunities to escape into the wilderness where they camped or stayed in small rustic cabins and inns. Inspired by this romantically rustic ideal, the architects began to bring the vernacular images of the countryside back into the city. Coxhead and Coxhead experimented with fusing the Classical and the Shingle style.

At the turn of the century, Bernard Maybeck added more explicit Arts and Crafts ideas to these rustic ideals that had been filtered through Academic Eclecticism. Now Maybeck, it must be remembered, trained at the Ecole des Beaux-Arts and was a highly competent Classical designer as we saw earlier in his Palace of Fine Arts. For major civic projects he usually turned to this tradition. But for smaller or more private buildings, he favored medieval precedents and ideas derived from the Gothic Revival and Arts and Crafts traditions. From Viollet-le-Duc he took the usual idea about expressive structure, as well as a philosophical justification for the rustic. Viollet had praised primitive cultures for their energy and native intuitions about building. Of German descent, Maybeck also read the same passages in Semper that had inspired Frank Lloyd Wright about the archetypal house consisting of a platform, a fireplace, a sheltering roof and an enclosure. For Semper, the steeply pitched medieval vernacular traditions of northern Europe expressed this archetypal idea most completely. Maybeck readily agreed, since he had become enamored of these same traditions while visiting his family's German home.

Maybeck's house for Charles Keeler shows how thoroughly he took up the medieval ideas [211]. He abandoned the usual American balloon frame in favor of the medieval system of a post and beam frame, using the exposed and steeply pitched trusses to provide most of the character of the room. In the spirit of the Arts and Crafts, materials are simplified and expressively joined together. As in Wright's Prairie houses, massive fireplaces derived from medieval sources advantageously and symbolically provide the focal points for 'home life', a key middle-class and Progressive notion widely advocated by Maybeck's client. Just as Viollet-le-Duc described the Gothic structural system, Maybeck reduced the walls in places to glazed infills between the structural frame.

A trip to Europe at the end of the century brought to Maybeck's attention a wider range of vernacular traditions, particularly the shallow pitched roof ideas in the chalets of southern Germany and the hill towns of northern Italy. Inspired both by the Academic Eclectic and the Arts and Crafts desire for appropriate regional design, Maybeck identified these regions as similar in character to the hilly terrain in the Bay Area for which he had to design. On his return, the shallow roof pitches appeared in his design for the Boke House in the Berkeley hills [212]. The roofs project out well beyond the body of the house just like those in Wright's Prairie houses, although Maybeck would also have seen this in the chalet roofs designed to protect from snow. In the hot sun of the semi-arid East Bay, these roofs proved equally useful at shading the building below. The expressive structure, luscious Arts and Crafts detailing, and central fireplace remained from his earlier interests [213]. In his most famous building, Berkeley's First Church of Christ, Scientist, Maybeck brought together his ideas of shallow roofs, expressive structure, Arts and Crafts detailing and medieval imagery in a remarkable synthesis that recalls Gothic ideas without overtly deriving from them [214]. Like Wright in his Unity Temple project, here Maybeck answered a tight budget with innovative uses of material, including asbestos sheets for exterior siding, industrial metal windows, and poured concrete with details picked out in bright paint.

Arts and Crafts ideas diffused more thoroughly into the American middle classes thanks to Gustav Stickley. Stickley ran a furniture-making shop in New York which, after he visited Voysey and Ashbee on a trip to Europe in 1898, he renamed Craftsman Workshops and reorganized as an Arts and Crafts guild. He founded

211 Charles Keeler House, Berkeley, California, 1895, Bernard Maybeck

212 George Boke House, Berkeley, California, 1902, Bernard Maybeck

213 George H. Boke House, interior

**214** First Church of Christ, Scientist, Berkeley, California, 1910, Bernard Maybeck

*The Craftsman* magazine in 1901 at first to advertise his own Arts and Crafts products, but soon he elaborated its editorial content to explain Morris, Ruskin, and Arts and Crafts principles to America. In 1903 Stickley began publishing designs for 'Craftsman Homes', which melded British Arts and Crafts ideas with a variety of American traditions including the California Mission style, log cabins and New England farm houses. These designs were democratic, Stickley said, because they let each individual work out a suitable house plan, and they were regionally appropriate, because they were adapted to the local conditions and building materials of different parts of the country. The Craftsman houses typically amalgamated Shingle style walling, Stick style timbering at the roof, medieval jettying, Maybeck's and Wright's shallow overhanging roofs, and Voysey's casement windows in stucco walls [215]. Unlike the British Arts and Crafts designers and theorists with which he was smitten, Stickley joined Wright in embracing the machine as a cost effective way of producing good designs for a wider audience.

For many families of modest means throughout the country seeking the simple and honest life, the Craftsman style houses offered a simple and honest architectural

**215** Clem House, Dallas, Texas, 1920

setting. Other popular magazines of the day helped disseminate the idea further, including *Ladies' Home Journal*, *House Beautiful*, *Good Housekeeping*, *Western Architect* and *Architectural Record*. After 1905 the Craftsman style as characterized by exposed rafter ends, simple wooden details like triangular knee braces, broad front porches, and shallow overhanging roofs became the dominant style in the country for small houses.

The Greene brothers Henry and Charles in Pasadena, California, offered the high fashion version of the Craftsman style. Both were trained in the manual arts and, after an initial flirtation with the usual picturesque styles available at the end of the century, began to focus on those which derived their character from the expression of structure and good craftsmanship. They drew from the Stick Style, the contemporary English Arts and Crafts, and the Japanese traditions of wooden joinery. We see how this all came together in the David B. Gamble House [216]. The overall effect is decidedly more picturesque than Wright's Prairie houses, with loosely grouped rooms in plan, and asymmetrical massings of shallow pitched roofs. As with Maybeck's houses further north, the broad roof overhangs sheltered the building from the intense Californian sun. Like Wright, the Greene brothers extended the house into the landscape with intermediate spaces roofed but not enclosed. Here the idea fitted the California lifestyle perfectly, because the mild climate allowed extensive outdoor living throughout most of the year. Liberally sprinkled throughout are beautifully conceived and executed wooden joinery details, often rounded over on the edges to hint at great aging. However, like many buildings before it, the honest expression of construction is not quite as honest as first appearances suggest. Wooden pegs like Lutyens's hide screws, while veneers of expensive teak often cover the real beams made of more economical woods. The Arts and Crafts ideals were often adhered to more in the spirit than in the material reality.

It is easy to see why the Progressive styles found such a receptive audience in America at the turn of the century. In their various forms, they stood for the priority of the individual, for honesty, democracy, family values and integration with nature. For those who still espouse these values today, the Prairie and Craftsman houses continue to offer compelling images of how such a life might be lived. Yet ironically, the more the styles adhered to the ideal of spiritually uplifting hand craftsmanship, the

**216** David B. Gamble House, Pasadena, California, 1909, Greene and Greene

more these styles were forced to diverge from their original philosophical intentions. The Arts and Crafts movement had begun as a reaction against the Industrial Revolution and the brutalization of workers, and had attempted to improve the quality of life for modest and lower incomes. But the incredible investment of labor required in something like the Gamble house quickly put the style out of the reach of its originally intended market. Apparent simplicity and honesty increasingly came at a price that the middle classes could not afford. And for the cost of a highly crafted 'rustic' house, the upper middle and upper classes could afford the more refined traditional styles of the Academic Eclectics that they perceived were more suitable to their elevated station in life. The Academic Eclectics had no scruples about using the machine to produce economically the repetitive and well-understood ornaments of the traditional styles. Due in large part to these economic and social realities, the Arts and Crafts movement began to die out in America and Great Britain by the beginning of the First World War.

One more important idea emerged from the reform movements at the turn of the century, the idea of the garden city. The Englishman Ebenezer Howard proposed a new conception of the city in his progressively titled book of 1898, *Tomorrow, a Peaceful Path to Real Reform* (later renamed *Garden Cities of Tomorrow*). He dismissed the modern industrial cities as lost causes, victims of the private ownership of land. This malady induced property values to skyrocket towards the center of town, leading to endless sprawl at the city's edges. Howard proposed to establish new garden cities in the countryside, in which a limited company would hold the land for the common good and prevent real estate speculation. Buildings would be owned privately. Howard conceived of his garden cities as self-contained entities, possessing their own industries, businesses and social amenities like schools and shops, and isolated from other developments by a green belt of rural land. The size of the town would remain sufficiently small to keep all amenities and the rural green belt within walking distance. The first garden cities were developed outside London at Letchworth in 1902, and Welwyn in 1919. After the First World War, as we will see in the next chapter, American planners adapted some of these ideas to the design of the new automobile suburbs.

### Modernism

The last major stylistic movement to appear in this period, the Modernist movement, began on the continent of Europe. Unlike the Academic Eclectic and Progressive movements we have examined so far, the Modernist movement up to the First World War did not catch on with many architects or clients beyond a small circle of the self-appointed avant-garde. Most European continental architects throughout this period joined their American and British counterparts in embracing the principles and images of Academic Eclecticism. French taste still dominated much of the continent, and so the Beaux-Arts ideas as summed up in Guadet's *Eléments et Théorie de l'Architecture* continued to shape most continental European architectural production.

In the 1890s, a number of continental architects joined the American Progressives and British Arts and Crafts architects in seeking a modern style less directly obliged to the usual European traditions. Their first effort, broadly known as Art Nouveau, was characterized by writhing naturalistic plant forms cast in metal. Although many of the young continental architects in search of new directions initially flirted with the style, it remained a decorative idea that did not provide obvious guidance for the spatial planning of buildings, and died away by 1910. A more successful continental strategy at the turn of the century looked to the idea of simplifying the traditional styles in the spirit of Richardson, Sullivan, and the British Arts and Crafts and Free Style architects. The continental architects seeking new directions admired and followed closely the American and British developments. They particularly envied America's relative freedom from tradition, and enjoyed even more than the American architects the plain vernacular forms in the American landscape like grain elevators and factories. Just as Richardson had simplified the Romanesque, Otto Wagner from Vienna and the Dutch architect Hendrik Petrus Berlage, two of the most significant continental innovators, began to distill simplified forms from a number of traditions including the Romanesque, Classical and Byzantine. They still largely followed the Beaux-Arts principles of geometrical organization. At the more picturesque end of the architectural spectrum, the British Arts and Crafts abstractions of medieval British forms inspired a similar German Arts and Crafts movement to simplify central European medieval forms. After the publication of Wright's work in Europe in 1910 and 1911, continental architects in search of a new style pressed this process of abstraction even further. Particularly influential were Wright's cubistic shapes like in the Unity Temple and Larkin Building, his open space planning and his floating roofs.

From this initial Anglo-American impetus towards simplification and abstraction, the continental architects proceeded to push the ideas to greater extremes than were imagined by their original proponents. We find in this period a new taste among the European avant-garde for stridently polemical viewpoints, in which balanced positions gave way to aggressively held and sometimes simplistic extremes. As an example of the new mood, Adolf Loos followed many Arts and Crafts, Progressive, and even some Academic Eclectics in criticizing the contemporary use of ornament. Now where the others had urged the simplification of ornament to avoid visual fussiness or to encourage giving more attention to the underlying forms themselves, Loos attacked the concept of ornament altogether. For one thing, he pointed out, the traditional ornamental systems belonged to the aristocracy, and had no place in modern bourgeois society. For another thing, ornament originally derived from primitive urges to decorate, as in body tattoos and in erotic cave paintings. He described these as appropriate for primitive savages, but degenerate and even criminal in modern society. Loos consequently dismissed ornament as crime, turning its use or not into a litmus test for one's personal morals. No degenerate himself, he ruthlessly stripped all ornament off several of his own designs, leaving plain white box-like surfaces relieved by nothing more than punctured rectangular openings for windows and doors.

The tendency to extremes in this period also led to a striking divergence of views regarding the two aspects of human nature, the intellectual and rational on the one side, and the emotional and expressive on the other. Where Wright had attempted to integrate these two, the continental European avant-garde began to define their positions at the opposite extremes. A group later known as the Expressionists, including Bruno Taut, Hans Poelzig, Hermann Obrist and Rudolf Steiner, stressed the emotive, expressive side of life in projects that intentionally tried to elicit deep, even primeval, responses to spaces reminiscent of dark caves and light crystalline forms [217]. They carried even further the Arts and Crafts idea of the architect as expressive artist, seeing themselves as poets interpreting the present and visualizing an ideal future. Many of them also saw themselves as the leaders of a great social and spiritual uprising that would sweep away the ills of the past and usher in a more socially equitable and spiritually pure future. Like William Morris, they conceived of this idyllic future in terms of something like the medieval past.

At the other extreme, Hermann Muthesius founded an association for designers

217 Goetheanum Building, Dornach, Switzerland, 1913–22, Rudolf Steiner

218 Project for a skyscraper, 1914, Antonio Sant'Elia

and industry named the Werkbund that called for simple, rational forms derived in part from the geometrical essences of Classicism, and in part from mundane functional requirements. Good, simple forms embodied universal types, he maintained, that everyone could understand and appreciate. Muthesius supported such forms because he thought that they would make the products of German industry more attractive and therefore more marketable internationally. He had no interest in artistic expression, or in poetically visualizing the future, or in leading a social revolution. Appreciating the merits of these arguments, the German industrialists invited prominent Werkbund members to design their rapidly expanding line of products and their new factory buildings. The first application of the rationalist modern ideas to architecture, not surprisingly, naturally glorified machine production while seeking an appropriate industrial aesthetic. Walter Gropius's design for a model factory at the Werkbund Exhibition in Cologne in 1914 shows the idea with its simple rational forms, Classical symmetries, extensive use of industrial materials like glass, no traditional ornament, and Wright's hovering roof planes [219]. The Expressionists and these Rationalists fought acrimoniously until the 1920s over the direction of German design, each arguing the virtues of what were often mutually exclusive views.

The Italian Futurists carried the new enthusiasm for machine imagery beyond the design of factories. Italy had only begun to industrialize after 1900, and so had not yet experienced the worst problems of the Industrial Revolution. A group of

219 Administration Building at the Werkbund Exhibition, Cologne, 1914, Walter Gropius

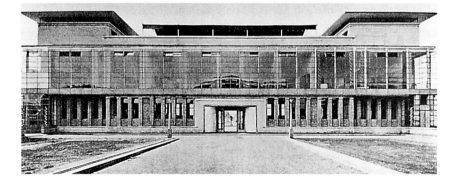

Further east, the socialist movement born in the social strife of the Industrial Revolution finally sparked a Bolshevik Revolution in Russia in 1917. The Bolsheviks overthrew the Czar, withdrew from the 'capitalist' war and, perhaps ironically, established a communist state in one of the least industrialized countries in Europe. The communists rejected the principles of capitalism and nationalism, established state control of the economy for the benefit of the workers, and agitated for an international revolution by the working classes in the rest of Europe. In Italy, economic distress and a fear of a communist revolution led an anxious coalition of industrialists and the middle class to support Benito Mussolini's fascist party. After seizing control in 1922, Mussolini established a state as totalitarian as the communists, yet shrilly championing nationalism over any idea of an international workers' movement. The ideological conflict between these two totalitarian viewpoints began to spill over into the Western democracies including America, the socialists in the democracies hoping for a similar communist revolution in their own country, and the fascists admiring the Italian imposition of order.

The Americans emerged from the war in far stronger condition than the Europeans. Long the second-class citizens in the world, American manpower, matériel, and economic loans had turned the tide in a major European war, and their own President Woodrow Wilson had brokered the peace. The doughboys proudly returned home to a country whose confidence and self-esteem blossomed after this triumphant test on the world stage. While the European economies and industries lay in tatters, the American economy had just geared up for the war and continued to surge forward after the peace. In the 1920s, America enjoyed a period of unprecedented prosperity while Europe struggled to repay its loans and to rebuild its industries and economies.

America had become a world power without quite yet realizing it. On the conclusion of the war, most Americans wished to retreat from international politics and return to their traditional policy of isolationism. President Wilson had convinced the Europeans to establish an international League of Nations charged with arbitrating future disputes among nations, but he could not persuade his own Congress to participate. Americans wanted no part of international bodies meddling in their affairs. Following the now usual pattern, this political retreat from Europe did not translate into a retreat from European architectural fashions. After the few decades of architectural independence and even occasionally leadership around the turn of the century, most American designers after the First World War returned either to following or at least to paralleling European architectural ideas.

Despite the great passions raised by the various political movements of the day, many Europeans and Americans in the 1920s lost interest in public affairs. The Europeans, particularly on the continent, viewed the collapse of order and economic health with considerable cynicism, doubtful that any politicians or social reforms could improve their fortunes. The Americans either felt satisfied with their current good fortune, or tired of trying to solve the great and often intractable public problems which had preoccupied the pre-war Progressive generation. America returned to a philosophy of laissez-faire individualism like that following the Civil War a half century earlier. Rising prosperity encouraged individuals to think that they could manage nicely for themselves without government intervention, and the federal government happily obliged. First Warren Harding and then Calvin Coolidge rolled back many of the pre-war social reforms and regulations, turning the federal government instead to the service of big business. As direct beneficiaries of capitalism and free enterprise in a booming economy, and as advocates of minimal government intervention in personal affairs, most Americans were therefore hostile to the socialist ideas sweeping through parts of Europe. Indeed, the Bolshevik successes in Europe caused a Red Scare in America in 1919 and 1920, leading to witch-hunts, violence towards immigrants and suspected communists, and deportations. When the first European Modernist architects associated themselves with socialism, as we will see later, they guaranteed a hostile reaction to their ideas in America.

In place of social reform or political involvement, many Europeans and Americans in an age appropriately named the Roaring Twenties turned instead to hedonistic pleasures. The pre-war social conventions were now seen as prudish constraints on personal liberties, and were enthusiastically overthrown by many keen to experiment. This was the heyday of Hollywood, jazz, 'decadent' European cabarets, flappers, and a new sexual liberation. This popular desire for a modern world free of traditional convention, as will be seen later, helped generate a popular interest in architectural and interior styles equally liberated from social convention. However, these experiments in cultural and moral license shocked a number of Americans into a conservative backlash. The Prohibitionists successfully agitated for an amendment to the United States Constitution outlawing the manufacture and sale of alcohol, which they believed had caused much of the country's moral decay. A fundamentalist religious movement, particularly in the rural areas, seized upon the evils of modern science as the root cause of America's ills and banned, for example, the teaching of biological evolution in some Southern public schools. In the conservative quarters of America, 'modern' meant decadent.

This period also saw the development in America of the consumer society as we know it today, in which the chief indicator of achieving success and the good life became the possession of material goods. In this period of booming economic growth, many Americans drew higher wages than ever before, and many advantageously participated in the rising stock market. With surplus income in their pockets, with the new business of modern advertising touting the virtues of everything from vacuum cleaners and radios to automobiles, and with easy credit available, Americans bought goods like never before. Interestingly, the new advertisers sold goods not only on function and ease, but also on fashion and status. Since normal wear and tear did not induce Americans to replace their material goods frequently enough, American manufacturers intentionally restyled their products periodically, and then convinced buyers to purchase the latest models in order to remain in fashion and to maintain their status. This popular interest in changing fashions as a way of maintaining social status began to appear in the homemaking magazines like *House Beautiful* in the 1930s, expressed as seasonal fashions in decorating schemes. Like the old aristocratic code of gentility, the new consumer society intimately related social status to design fashion, and demanded ceaseless stylistic change as consumers felt compelled to keep up with their neighbors.

Faced with these often diametrically opposed conceptions of society after the war, architects in Europe and America broadly followed the three main strands of thinking mentioned at the beginning of the chapter. At one extreme, those who stressed a return to pre-war values revived Academic Eclecticism. At the other extreme, those who sought radical change developed the anti-historical Modernist movement. The third strand stood at a variety of points between these two, attempting in various ways to modernize the traditional. In the next sections we will explore each of these in turn.

### Academic Eclecticism

Most American and European architects in the 1920s, just as before the war, turned to Academic Eclecticism. After all, this was the long established and predominant theory of architectural design, and its continuation no doubt helped people recover the civilized values so brutally upset by the world's first fully mechanized war. Architects and builders, both high fashion and vernacular, revived many of the previous styles we have already examined in previous chapters. After the First World War, American builders also perfected a method of attaching a thin masonry veneer to the usual American timber-frame house, allowing designers to recreate more accurately and economically the traditional styles originally constructed in brick or stone.

Like their academic predecessors at the turn of the century, most of the postwar eclectics continued to stress decorum, good taste and restraint over exuberance and personal expression. Even a leader of the pre-war Arts and Crafts movement, Sir Edwin Lutyens, abandoned his earlier enthusiasm for freely composed and inventive vernacular images in favor of the more stately Classical tradition. A number of country houses, banks, public buildings and war monuments he designed in the 1920s carried the Classical language to perhaps its ultimate level of refinement in proportions, massing and detail. Others in England like Sir Charles Nicholson and Sir Giles Gilbert Scott worked equally hard to restore the Gothic idiom and the cultural values it embodied.

Echoing the retreat from social reform in politics, many American architects and builders in the 1920s retreated from the serious moral tone of the pre-war Progressive era. In keeping with the mood of sensual hedonistic pleasures, designers sought light-hearted picturesque effects, particularly for houses. Each issue of the high fashion architectural magazine *Architectural Record* in the 1920s began with a picturesque and atmospheric image of a European village or house, giving architects specific ideas about how to achieve similar effects in their own designs. This and other magazines like the draftsman's companion *Pencil Points* and the homeowners' magazine *House Beautiful* described their featured houses in picturesque terms like 'alluring', 'charming', 'atmospheric', or 'domestic'. Rational, functional or intellectual justifications for designs were not to be found. Some designers in quest of the cozily picturesque devised ways of prematurely aging their buildings, by intentionally sagging the roofline, or by staining the walls, or by laying up patches of irregularly colored and sometimes tilted bricks in a masonry wall. The more extreme versions of these atmospheric buildings David Gebhard aptly described as dollhouses or Hansel and Gretel houses, because they appealed to our childlike delight in playfulness and visual stimulation.

America's foremost designers of high quality traditional homes between the wars were Walter Mellor, Arthur Meigs and George Howe, who masterfully interpreted vernacular domestic European styles for a number of suburban and rural country house estates. They drew mostly from English and French Normandy medieval vernacular forms, sensing in the combination of these two visually powerful and unassuming traditions the possibility of a uniquely American vernacular style. The Francis S. McIlhenny House in Chestnut Hill, Philadelphia, fuses elements of English picturesque planning, French roof shapes, Italian detailing and American shingles with an ingenious circulation system [221]. The visitor passes through a false front door into a dramatically revealed sunken garden, then abruptly turns right to face the true front door, which lines up on axis with the entrance hall and a formal parterre garden beyond [222]. Mellor, Meigs and Howe's favored picturesque medieval forms, with steep asymmetrical gables, dormer windows, high chimneys and sometimes half-timbering, became a de facto American vernacular style between the wars. Known more popularly as the Tudor style, it graces American suburbs around the country and remains today one of the most marketable styles of all.

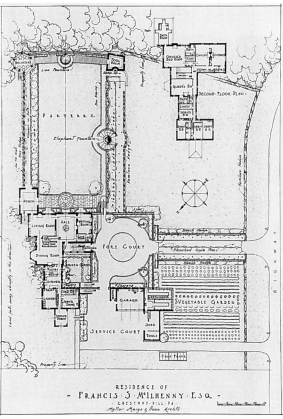

221  Francis S. McIlhenny House,
Chestnut Hill, Pennsylvania,
1918, Mellor, Meigs & Howe

222  Francis S. McIlhenny House
and garden plan

Regionalism remained a popular idea among the Academic Eclectics of the 1920s. For the Broadmoor Hotel at the base of the Rocky Mountains in Colorado Springs, the eastern firm of Warren and Wetmore designed an unusually tall version of Italianate Classicism, with touches of Alpine detailing including a floral painting on the main façade [223]. Like the bold Richardsonian Romanesque buildings on the prairies, this style asserted a strong presence against the backdrop of a powerful natural setting, while at the same time it appeared rooted in the place. For a chain of hotels associated with the Santa Fe Railroad in the Southwest, Mary Elizabeth Colter turned to Native American motifs like Navaho weaving patterns and exposed structures in the Pueblo style.

Spanish Colonial and Mediterranean styles continued to flourish in the country's hot regions, particularly in Florida and California. Perhaps most extravagant of all between the wars was Julia Morgan's design for the San Simeon estate of California publishing baron William Hearst [224]. Morgan was the first woman ever to attend the Ecole des Beaux-Arts in Paris and, after working for Bernard Maybeck, became an accomplished designer in the Bay Area Shingle Style. For the San Simeon project she turned to European hot climate styles and elements like arcades, all organized according to the rational principles of academic composition that she had learned at the Ecole. In the front façade of the main building seen here, we find the twin towers of Spanish Baroque churches combined with the mannerist detailing developed during Spain's transition from the Gothic to the Renaissance, all brilliantly highlighted and shadowed by the intense California sun.

223 Broadmoor Hotel, Colorado
Springs, Colorado, 1918,
Warren and Wetmore

Many Academic Eclectic architects between the wars admired the picturesque qualities, visual harmonies, and historical associations of European towns that had grown up over centuries, and that had adhered to a common regional style. When they had the opportunity, the American eclectics tried to recreate a similar feeling in their own projects. For example, in the 1920s the entire California town of Santa Barbara mandated the Spanish Colonial style for all new future construction. Charles Z. Klauder similarly established an Italian vernacular style for all buildings and future development on the University of Colorado campus [225]. Compared to the uncontrolled and uncoordinated growth of most other American towns and college campuses, projects like these remain as memorable as the European images upon which they were modeled.

The Academic Eclectic buildings of the 1920s captured a dominant mood in America. They expressed ideals which many Americans wished to attain after the upheavals of the war, including domestic bliss, material affluence, and connections to ancient and venerable traditions. Interestingly, throughout the 1920s the buildings which summed up these ideals were to be found both in the architects' journals and

224 San Simeon, California,
1922–26, Julia Morgan

225 University of Colorado
campus, Boulder, Colorado,
Tuscan theme established
1917–19 by Charles Klauder

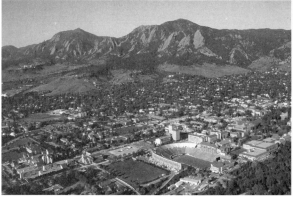

in the homeowners' magazines, clearly indicating that the designers and their clients valued similar ideas. Only a decade later, as we will see, the two kinds of magazines no longer illustrated the same architectural ideas, as the architects began to pursue philosophies and images no longer shared by the bulk of their market.

### The Modernist movement

In the chaotic conditions of post-war Germany, good taste, refined tradition and the cozily picturesque were the last things on the minds of many architects. Their profession largely collapsed with the fall of the Kaiser's regime and the destruction of the economy. With their old bourgeois, industrial and aristocratic patrons and commissions gone, many architects enthusiastically embraced a post-war revival of the Expressionist movement that promised a social and architectural revolution. According to Bruno Taut, Adolfe Behne, and Erich Mendelsohn, among others, the birth of the new Republic marked the beginning of a great spiritual, cultural and artistic uprising, generated deep in the soul of the German people, and led by the avant-garde artists and architects. Many Expressionists aligned themselves with socialism, attacking the bourgeoisie who had abandoned them, and championing instead the cause of the workers who they thought would create a communal society out of the post-war disorder. As before the war, the Expressionists also stressed the priority of individual expression through unprecedented and powerfully emotional forms. Their new enthusiasm for the working classes encouraged them to value handcraft over machine production, although their expressive and handcrafted curvilinear forms often echoed the streamlining of modern industrial machines like ocean liners [226].

Expressionism rapidly fell out of favor in the early 1920s as the avant-garde turned increasingly to the other line of pre-war Modernist thinking, the Rationalism of Behrens and Gropius. This movement, we will recall from the last chapter, insisted on simple, austere forms derived in part from the geometry of Classicism, in part from mundane functional requirements, and in part from the image of the machine. The proponents of this revived view, including László Moholy-Nagy, Joseph Albers and members of the post-war Dutch De Stijl movement, objected to personal expression, to handcraft, to traditional meaning and, indeed, to anything reminiscent of the individual personality. They focused their attention instead on what they claimed were the objective laws of vision, the principles behind all good artistic and architectural composition irrespective of culture, geographical setting, or individual inclination. Although the Academic Eclectics had also sought universal principles of design like these, the Modernists looked for principles far more abstract, and far more divorced from regional variations or the possibility of personal interpretation. Their particular laws of form stressed visual austerity and geometrical clarity, echoing the tendency we saw in the late 1880s to impose order on the built environment when the social order is perceived to have declined.

At the height of the Expressionist movement in 1919, Walter Gropius founded a small school for artists and architects in Weimar, named the Bauhaus after medieval German craft guilds. Although Gropius had helped develop the Rationalist ideas before the war, immediately after the war he enthusiastically supported the Expressionist notion that his students would lead the great social and spiritual uprising in Germany. He prepared them for this role by teaching them design and handcraft in the manner of the medieval apprenticeship system. But always sensitive to changing directions, a few years later he abandoned these Expressionist ideas in favor of the more recently fashionable Rationalism. Now the Bauhaus students learned the objective laws of artistic and architectural form from Moholy-Nagy and Albers, applied those laws to the design of machine-like forms without evidence of handcraft or tradition, and began to conceive of architectural design as a process of 'solving' functional problems. Although the new Bauhaus method of design education exerted little influence on architectural production between the wars, we will see later how Gropius carried these concepts to the United States in 1939 and eventually overthrew the Beaux-Arts system that had long dominated American architectural education.

The Swiss avant-garde architect and propagandist Le Corbusier coalesced a number of these ideas into the classic expression of Modernism in the 1920s. Echoing the pre-war Futurists, he insisted on destroying Europe's old culture in order to create the new. He proposed bulldozing central Paris flat, for example, in order to clear the ground for regularly spaced rows of rectangular Modernist housing blocks. He rejected the concept of a home as a place imbued with meaning and tradition, declaring the house instead as a 'machine for living in'. He designed suitably machine-like, pristine forms devoid of ornament or any other indications of individual personalities living within [227]. Intentionally inverting the Academic Eclectic ideal of a building growing out of its location, Le Corbusier lifted his buildings off the ground with thin columns he called *pilotis*, and painted the entire structure a neutral white to deny any physical, material or color relationship to the surroundings. Le Corbusier, like other proponents of the Rationalism in the 1920s, reduced life and culture to abstractions, and found a suitable architectural expression to match.

Many of the Rationalist Modernists in this period, like the Expressionists, aligned themselves with the political left. They rejected anything smacking of middle-class taste or bourgeois values, associating themselves instead with the working class. Many fervently believed that Modernist architecture would serve as an instrument for ameliorating social ills, and that it might lead to a social utopia based on class equality. They concentrated much effort in the 1920s on designing working-class housing to replace the housing stock destroyed in the war. However, in keeping with their philosophical predilection for abstractions, they conceived of this task as providing generic housing for the working class, rather than as providing homes for individuals. To build quickly and inexpensively, they often mass produced relentless rows of austere houses or flats, conveying intentionally or not the impression of beehives inhabited by workers with anonymous personalities.

Given the Modernists' hostile attitude towards the individual, and their explicit connection to European socialism and revolution, their ideas attracted few American or British architects before the mid-1930s. The first explicitly Modernist buildings in America were designed by two Viennese immigrants, Rudolph Schindler and Richard Neutra. Both had originally trained in Europe, and had learned the ideas of a number of early Modernists including Otto Wagner and Adolf Loos. Both made their way to Chicago at different times, eventually working for Frank Lloyd Wright at the Taliesin atelier in Wisconsin. As Wright's chief assistant during and after the war, Schindler moved to California to supervise a number of Wright's projects there. When his own practice subsequently grew in Los Angeles he was joined by Neutra, who first worked on joint projects and then established a career of his own. In their own ways, each transplanted the Rationalist Modernist style from Europe to America. Neutra's design for the Dr Phillip Lovell House strikingly proclaimed the new style from the top of the hill, with its simple geometric shapes, interlocking volumes, elevating *pilotis*, pure white color, and complete absence of any historical references [228]. However, Wright's influence on this mainly European idea shows in the emphatic horizontal lines, relating the house to the hillside more sympathetically than Le Corbusier would

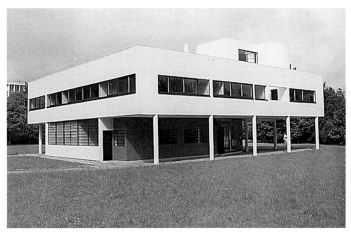

have done. As it turns out, Neutra's borrowing from Wright returned full circle, because Wright used these bold horizontal balconies for his Fallingwater house a decade later. We will discuss Wright's design later in the chapter.

### The traditional modernized

A number of architects in the 1920s found little joy either in the resolutely traditional Academic Eclecticism, or in the stridently anti-traditional Modernist movement. They did not wish to abandon architecture's connection with the past altogether, but the traditional styles had clearly begun to run out of steam. How many more ways can one play out variations on the Tudor style, for example, before visual boredom and clichés creep in? These architects found new energy in the modern world, but they could not relate to the spiritual anguish, the ardent socialism, the suppression of the individual, or the antagonism towards previous Western culture that the continental Modernists insisted had to accompany the modern world. These architects looked for ways to modernize their architectural traditions, gaining the best of both outlooks.

A popular strategy began with designing traditional architectural shapes and arrangements, and then stripping off the traditional ornamental devices like window frames and hoods, and elaborate entablatures. Beaux-Arts Classicism offered the most popular architectural language for this treatment, partly because it was well known, and partly because it had long stressed the importance of the massing and proportion behind the stylistic detail. A number of Classically inclined British architects including Sir Edwin Lutyens and Charles Holden began to simplify their preferred style after the mid-1920s. While some of the stripped Classical buildings from this period appear naked and even brutish, Lutyens infused new life in the traditional forms by experimenting with bolder geometrical arrangements, and by subtly curving the façades with a progression of slight setbacks. In the Midland Bank seen here, only occasional hints of traditional detailing remain in the austere moldings, and in the greatly simplified Classical Order at the top [229].

Stripped Classicism proved equally popular in America, particularly for the monumental public buildings that, in an earlier age, would probably have been designed in the Classical language anyway. For the design of the Lincoln Memorial at the west end of the Washington, DC mall, for example, Henry Bacon pared down his Classical forms to their essence, wrapping a somber Doric colonnade around a plain, minimally decorated box [230]. With only the barest of traditional ornament at the column capitals and in the cornice, we could almost read this monument as an essay in the pure geometries of Modernism. Yet those few remaining details linked the building to a long and – at the time – still valued cultural tradition.

Another influential version of stripped tradition appeared in the Finnish architect Eliel Saarinen's entry for the Chicago Tribune competition in 1922 [231]. Although his entry lost to a more straightforwardly traditional Gothic Revival building by John Mead Howells and Raymond Hood, a number of American architects were favorably impressed by his pared forms. Vaguely reminiscent of the Gothic with its emphatically vertical piers and capping pinnacles, the building nonetheless gains most of its dramatic appearance from the overlapping forms implied by the progressive setbacks at the top of the tower. Like Bacon's Lincoln Memorial, Saarinen's project fuses the visual drama of bold geometry with the barest hints of long traditions. Howells, Hood and other American skyscraper designers later used similar ideas for skyscrapers in this period, including the Rockefeller Center in New York.

229 Midland Bank, Manchester, England, 1929, Sir Edwin Lutyens

230 Lincoln Memorial, Washington, DC, 1929, Henry Bacon

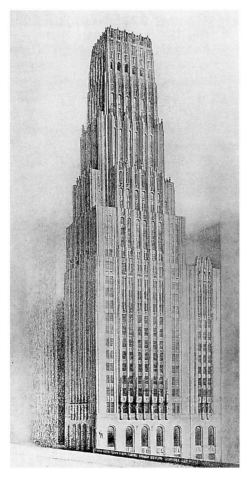

231 Chicago Tribune competition entry, Chicago, Illinois, 1922, Eliel Saarinen

232 State Capitol, Lincoln, Nebraska, 1922, Bertram Grosvenor Goodhue

We will recall from the last chapter that Bertram Grosvenor Goodhue first gained his reputation designing Academic Eclectic Gothic buildings in partnership with Ralph Adams Cram. Just before the war he dissolved his partnership, and began to explore a number of other styles ranging from Spanish Baroque to Persian and Egyptian. He even tried a riotously decorative Churrigueresque style for projects including the California Building at the 1915 Panama-California Exposition in San Diego. But by the 1920s he had discovered the logic and clarity of Beaux-Arts Classicism, and the power of simplified geometrical forms. His design for the State Capitol in Lincoln, Nebraska, offered one of the most striking examples of stripped Classicism in America [232]. Note the simplified decorative figures, the windows treated as punched holes in the wall, the barest of moldings at the cornice, and the subtle layering of surfaces created by slight projections and recessions. These ideas appeared in a number of public buildings in America between the wars.

Stripping the detail off traditional building forms – particularly Classical ones – tended to create powerful, but somber, images. Those architects who sought to capture more of the energy and sensuality of the Jazz Age turned instead to Art Deco. This distinctive style developed first in Europe, as an amalgam of several sources. From the pre-war Viennese Secession movement, it took the idea of simplified Classical forms as a basic armature; from Italian Futurism and German Expressionism it acquired a repertoire of visually dynamic shapes like zigzags, sunbursts and dramatic angles;

and from the frivolous mood of the period it acquired a taste for opulent and glittery materials, and a desire to create buildings as atmospheric as theatrical stage sets. These ideas all came together throughout the early 1920s, gaining wide exposure at the 1925 *Exposition Internationale des Arts Décoratifs et Industriels Modernes* in Paris. An abbreviation of this exhibit title eventually gave the style its name, although between the wars most people referred to it as the modern, moderne or jazz modern style.

Americans imported this style with enthusiasm. For many, it perfectly captured the mood of the age, expressing modernity and freedom from convention without succumbing to the socialist Modernist movement. Its emphasis on glitz, glamour and theatrical atmosphere perfectly suited the new moving picture cinemas springing up around the country [233]. Businesses and corporations liked the style because it expressed progress and modern efficiency, while at the same time the distinctive architectural images helped create an equally distinctive corporate image in this age of marketing and advertising. No building exploited these possibilities more success- fully than the Chrysler Building, which remains one of the distinctive landmarks of New York City, and one of the most familiar of all Art Deco buildings [234]. Designed for the automobile manufacturer Walter Chrysler, the building hawks his products with friezes of automobile tires and hubcaps, and abstracted gargoyles shaped like hood ornaments. The polished metal cap and spire at the top screams energy and movement, with its radiating lines and spiky triangular windows punctuating the semi-circular shapes that progressively burst out of larger ones below.

Art Deco also appealed to wealthy apartment dwellers in the cities, who linked the style to fashionable Paris, to urban elegance and to modernity. For the same reason, many retail shops selling luxury goods quickly remodeled in the new mode. The style began to filter down the social scale and into the builders' vernacular, eventually shaping a number of modest building types from inexpensive apartment

233 Paramount Theater,
Denver, Colorado, 1930,
Temple Hoyne Buell

234 Chrysler Building,
New York City, 1928–30,
William Van Alen

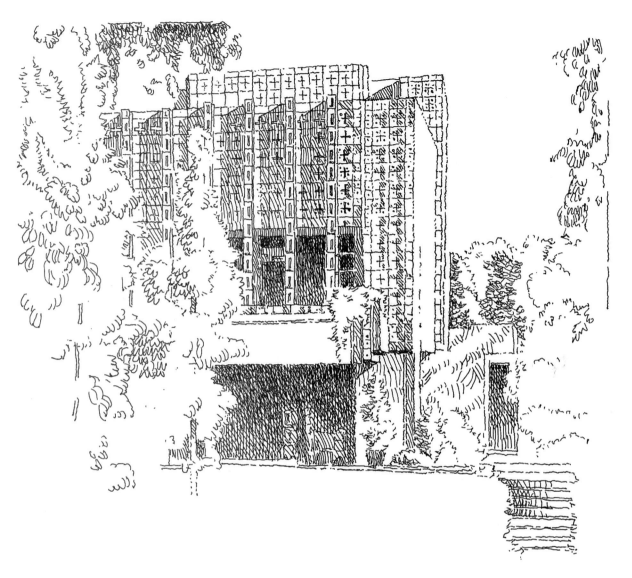

235 Mrs George M. Millard House, Pasadena, California, 1923, Frank Lloyd Wright

buildings to diners. The same masses of Americans who lived a glamorous life vicariously through Hollywood movie stars could also attain some of that glamour through living in Art Deco apartment buildings. The style proved as popular as the Academic Eclectic ones, appearing side by side with the Tudor, Norman, Gothic and Colonial Revival projects in both the professional architects' journals and the popular homeowners' magazines throughout the late 1920s.

As the style developed in America, it drew from an even wider range of sources including Egyptian, Chinese and Mayan. Movie theaters in particular attempted to establish an overall theme with these exotic sources, leading to stage set buildings like Grauman's Chinese Theater in Hollywood, or to the Mayan or Aztec theaters throughout America. Even Frank Lloyd Wright turned to Central America for inspiration in the 1920s. In several house projects including the Mrs George M. Millard House illustrated here, he abandoned his earlier horizontal Prairie house ideals in favor of something more modern [235]. Clearly inspired by the simple cubist and geometrical forms of the European Modernists, but publicly opposed to their philosophies and formulistic images, Wright found an alternative source for boldly geometrical buildings in the Mayan temples and public buildings. In Wright's mind, these offered the further advantage of originating in America, not Europe. The Mayans favored repetitive blocks of stone carved with rich sculptural reliefs, which Wright translated into specially cast concrete blocks piled up into simple cubist forms.

### The suburbs

The mass production of the automobile after the war reduced its cost to the point where, by 1928, more than 20 million cars filled the nation's rapidly expanding network of paved highways. Americans began to rely exclusively on the automobile as their primary means of transportation, particularly in the West and Southwest where distances to travel were greater, and where the traditional modes of public transportation were not as extensively established. Although many Americans living in the suburbs surrounding the large eastern cities continued to commute by train, the great days of the railroads were finished. Owning a car brought individual Americans more intimately in contact with high technology machinery, and with the thrill of speed and individual freedom of movement. This certainly helped spark an enthusiasm for the energized Art Deco style we have just examined, and for the machine-like, streamlined Art Moderne style soon to follow in the 1930s.

Automobiles also began a fundamental transformation of the American cities and countryside. Traffic congestion in the central cities encouraged yet further flight to the suburbs, which were now free to develop wherever a relatively inexpensive highway could run. And since the suburbs no longer needed to cluster within walking distance of the railway stations, they could extend indefinitely in any direction. Suburban sprawl began in earnest in the 1920s. More families than ever before enjoyed the traditional American dream of living outside the cities and closer to nature. Not all families were welcome, however. The white Protestant tolerance for immigrants, Jews, Catholics, Hispanics and Blacks diminished in this period, leading to systematic discrimination and, worst of all, to the scourge of the Ku Klux Klan and its tactics of terror. Developers, financial institutions and real estate agents placed many suburbs off limits to people of the wrong color or religion.

The partnership of Henry Wright and Clarence Stein applied a number of Ebenezer Howard's pre-war Garden City ideas to the design of the new American automobile suburb. After a number of earlier projects, they formed a company in 1928 to build Radburn, New Jersey, a model town projected to hold 25,000 people [236]. From Howard they acquired the idea that the town ought to be large enough to support local amenities like schools and shops, yet small enough to retain its own identity and allow easy access to the surrounding green belt. They also took the idea of retaining rural-like open spaces within the development. To these Garden City concepts they ingeniously added the car by restricting main arterial streets to the periphery of the project, allowing access to individual homes through local dead-end streets, or culs-de-sac. Families were free to wander through the local parks and pathways without fear of encountering heavy automobile traffic, even crossing under major streets through underpasses.

The combined concepts of rural-like settings and houses, local parkways, and the separation of main streets from local culs-de-sac, subsequently inspired countless housing developments in America, in many cases to the present. Although these ideas answered some of the new problems of accommodating automobiles, they also generated new problems of their own. Navigating one's way through the curving,

**236** Radburn, New Jersey, 1928–29, Stein & Wright

often dead-end streets became one of the frustrations of suburban living, while the lack of public thoroughfares past individual houses reduced the number of chance encounters with one's neighbors. The car had begun to isolate individuals from each other. Additionally, the more Americans depended on the car for transportation, the further apart shops and services could be located and still attract sufficient customers to remain economically viable. In many American car-based suburbs, the option to walk to shops or even to one's neighbors diminished, fueling even further dependence on the car. After a while, many suburbs even stopped building sidewalks.

## The Great Depression

### A collapsed economy and society

America built the economic boom of the 1920s on unstable foundations. Such a small proportion of the vast industrial profits trickled down into the pockets of the industrial workers that, at the end of the decade, only 5 per cent of America's population received 30 per cent of the country's personal income. The booming industries eventually produced more goods than Americans could afford to buy, despite easy credit and the lure of advertising. Faced with faltering markets, the industrialists laid off workers and further reduced the market available to which they could sell goods. They also reduced their investments in production, forcing them and their financiers to seek other places to invest their accumulated capital. Speculative loans were made with limited or no collateral, while massive investments in the stock market drove stock prices to ever greater heights. These easy and apparently endless profits, in turn, attracted even large portions of the middle class to invest their life savings in the market. In October 1929 the entire edifice came crashing down. Stock prices plummeted as panic swept through the market, wiping out 40 per cent of the invested capital in less than a month. The American economy spiraled ever downward. The losses in the stock market drastically reduced the money available for purchasing goods or investing in production, which led to further reductions in production and further layoffs, which reduced the markets yet again. By 1932 America's industrial production had fallen 50 per cent, thousands of banks had failed taking further savings with them, fifteen million people were unemployed, and foreclosures on mortgages had thrown Americans off their farms and out of their houses in unprecedented numbers. The European economies had come to depend so much on American loans and trade now dried up that in 1931 they finally collapsed into depression as well.

The Great Depression seriously challenged the American belief in self-sufficiency, and in the ability of an individual to rise up through talent and hard work. Through no fault of their own, millions had fallen on hard times. Even highly skilled professionals like doctors and architects stood in the bread lines and lived in the shanty towns of empty packing boxes and pit houses roofed with corrugated metal. Although no amount of skill or hard work could find jobs that simply did not exist, many Americans raised on the ideal of individualism began to think that a flaw in their own character had led them to their debased condition. Now the American aversion to big government came home to roost. Unlike other industrialized nations in the world, the American federal government provided no social safety nets, and possessed no mechanisms for intervening in the downward spiral of the economy. Local governments and charities struggled desperately and often futilely to provide shelter and food for the millions of destitute Americans.

The hard times and despair following on the Great Depression were accompanied by more political extremes and militaristic agitation throughout the world. Germany handed over control to Adolf Hitler and his fascist party in 1933, upon which he began to implement his policies of rearmament, territorial expansion, and the persecution and ultimately extermination of Jews and others who did not fit into the nationalistic Aryan Germany. Joseph Stalin, who had gained control of the Soviet Union in the late 1920s, imposed a brutal totalitarian regime on the Soviet Union in the following decade. His forced collectivizations and mass exterminations effectively ended the socialist ideals of a free and egalitarian society for which the communists had fought in 1917. The bitter ideological rivalry between the fascists and the communists mounted during the 1930s, first leading to a surrogate war played out in the Spanish Civil War of 1936–39, and then ultimately contributing to the outbreak of the Second World War in 1939.

This hardening of attitudes in the Great Depression did not leave America untouched. Even many formerly moderate Americans condemned the capitalist system and the selfishness of the business leaders who had brought the country to calamity. The American communist party began to attract more supporters to its cause of a social revolution, while the hunger marches, violence and riots in the period compelled some still wealthy Americans to call for a fascist leader like Mussolini or Hitler. These different motivations led to the same conclusion: Americans wanted to abandon their traditional ideology of laissez-faire individualism in favor of a substantial state intervention in the economy and in social life.

On his inauguration in 1932, Franklin Roosevelt moved rapidly to revive the Progressive Era ideals of his distant cousin Theodore, and to re-establish the country's shattered confidence. He and the Congress enacted sweeping reforms in his New Deal for America that gave the federal government greater leadership and substantially stronger control over all aspects of American life. A partnership between government and industry fixed prices, controlled industrial and agricultural production, and set minimum wages. The Social Security Act of 1935 established a national system of unemployment insurance and took responsibility for welfare. A number of agencies with triple abbreviations put unemployed Americans on the federal payroll to undertake public service projects: the Civilian Conservation Corps (CCC) helped clear and develop parks, forests and reservoirs; the Public Works Administration (PWA) built large works like dams and bridges, and took responsibility for clearing the urban slums and for constructing housing 'projects' in their place; and the Works Progress Administration (WPA) built roads and schools, painted pictures and produced plays, wrote guide books and even employed out of work artists and architects to build historical dioramas for museums. A new Federal Housing Administration (FHA) not only guaranteed mortgages and loaned money for house repairs, but also sponsored a number of model communities including greenbelt suburbs. America had acquired its first taste of big central government.

### Depression Era architecture

We have seen throughout this history that particular architectural styles do not directly correspond to particular social or political systems. Classicism enjoyed the patronage of societies as diverse as democratic ancient Greece and absolutist seventeenth-century France, while the Gothic appeared in the feudal Middle Ages and then in the industrialized societies of the nineteenth and twentieth centuries. Each age – or each group in an age – often selectively chose from the associations a style might have acquired in the past, in order to appropriate a style to its own purposes. In other words, cultures see what they want to see in the history of architectural styles. This curious phenomenon of selective stylistic appropriation occurred once again in the Great Depression. While we might have assumed that the substantial change in social outlook would have engendered new styles or substantial revisions of existing styles, what we find is mainly a continuation of pre-Depression styles reinterpreted and turned to new ends.

Nothings shows this tendency more dramatically than the fortunes of stripped Classicism. Although before the Depression this style housed many capitalistic enterprises like insurance companies and banks, in the 1930s its commanding visual presence and affiliation with great Western civilizations appealed to the grandiose plans and self-images of the rising totalitarian states, who were in all other respects hostile to capitalism, to democracy, and even to each other. Hitler's Nazi Germany and Stalin's communist Soviet Union both appropriated the style to assert their authority and control, and to associate their regimes with great empires of the past. Now, however, they constructed their buildings on a scale as grandiose and as brutal as their politics. Most striking – and frightening – of all was Albert Speer's design for the outdoor theater at Nürnberg, in which the Nazi party staged dramatic torchlit mass rallies supporting Hitler's regime and condemning the proclaimed enemies of Germany. The sheer visual power of stripped Classicism constructed on a megalomaniac scale helped convey the sense of unbridled and irresistible forces, while the modernity of the style stressed the totalitarian regimes' 'modern' answers to contemporary society.

Although many now associate stripped Classicism with Hitler's Germany and Stalin's Russia, America and Great Britain continued to use the style throughout the 1930s as well. In the Conservative Britain of Stanley Baldwin and Neville Chamberlain, Charles Holden designed a monumentally severe central administrative headquarters for the University of London that looks like it would fit perfectly in Moscow or Berlin

[237]. Roosevelt's New Deal America also continued to use the style for its public buildings throughout the country, including post offices and courthouses. Even if they did not reach such grandiose scales as the designs of Speer, the American federal buildings were often stripped so severely that they expressed a similar feeling of power and authority. Most imposing of all were the new buildings in Washington, DC, symbolic of Roosevelt's greatly expanded federal government. Monumental projects, including the new Supreme Court building behind the Capitol, the bureaucratic offices in the Federal Triangle beside the Mall, and John Russell Pope's designs for the Jefferson Memorial and for the National Gallery of Art within the Mall itself, used overscaled Classical forms to convey the authority of the country's centralized power. In Pope's work in particular, the Classical language is stripped to its simplest possible underlying geometry, and then sleekly elaborated with the barest of moldings and the slightest of projections and recessions. The visual effect is one of confident refinement, like the self-assured manners of Roosevelt himself [238].

The make-work projects of the federal authorities like the WPA and PWA were intended to employ people indefinitely, not to complete work as quickly or as economically as possible. For some federally funded projects, designers were consequently able to revive labor intensive ideas like those of the Arts and Crafts movement that accompanied the Progressive movement at the turn of the century. Timberline Lodge on Mount Hood in Oregon, for example, designed by the US Forest Service architects under Gilbert Stanley Underwood, returned to the massive stone walls, heavy timber construction and steeply pitched roofs of the Arts and Crafts medieval ideals [239]. Throughout the project, workmen lovingly shaped intricate wooden joints, and carved sculptures of Oregon animals into the structure. This and other federal projects of the 1930s helped turn America's tragedy into substantial contributions to America's heritage.

The shift from the buoyant 1920s to the sober 1930s challenged those designers who had used Art Deco to modernize the traditional. The rich materials and flippantly jazzy details no longer seemed appropriate in an age now hostile to personal ostentation and extravagance. The new mood in the country, exemplified by Roosevelt's pragmatic approach to getting the country back on its feet, stressed practical and

237 Senate House, London, England, 1932, Charles Holden

238 National Gallery, Washington, DC, 1939, John Russell Pope

**239** Timberline Lodge, Mount
Hood, Oregon, 1936–37,
US Forest Service

rational answers to basic problems. Many began to hope that science and technology would rejuvenate the economy and lead to a more humane society, and they began to view the machine as the practical means by which this might be accomplished. The machines in the popular imagination included automobiles, ships, railroad locomotives and airplanes which, from the late 1920s on, had been scientifically improved by aerodynamically streamlining their forms to increase their speed. These so caught the mood and hopes of the period that designers began to streamline static objects which could not possibly benefit functionally from such treatment, including clocks, radios and buildings. The resulting style, known as Art Moderne in product design and Streamline Moderne in architecture, replaced Art Deco as the popular style of modernity in the 1930s. The new image stripped off ornament, rounded the corners wherever possible, typically added horizontal bandings which looked like they had been whipped taut by terrific aerodynamic forces, wrapped bands of windows around corners, and replaced Art Deco's ostentatiously rich materials with more practical and

**240** Thomas Jefferson High
School, Los Angeles, California,
1936, Morgan, Walls & Clements

modern looking materials like chrome, plastic, glass blocks and stucco [240]. Streamline Moderne clearly drew some inspiration from the forms and materials of the German Expressionist buildings like Mendelsohn's Einstein Tower (see figure 226), and it was enthusiastically employed in Europe as well as America. Streamline Moderne quickly passed down from high fashion into the vernacular, shaping everything from store fronts and diners to single family houses and apartment buildings.

Frank Lloyd Wright offered his own version of Streamline Moderne, in the Johnson Wax Administration Building [241]. The functional program echoed that of the Larkin Building three decades earlier, requiring a large secretarial space and a number of ancillary offices. Like the Larkin Building, Wright turned the building inward to create a great community of workers within one dramatic space [242]. Now under the influence of the Moderne, Wright turned to circles for the organizing geometry of the building, rather than to his usual strictly orthogonal arrangements. He developed a forest of columns shaped like giant lily pads, between which skylights admitted natural light to a space he described as inspiring as a cathedral. On the outside he streamlined the corners and wrapped the emphatic horizontal bandings of the Moderne style.

Streamline Moderne helped ease the entry of fully developed European Modernist architecture into America in the 1930s. Although they often drew from different sources and sometimes professed to serve different ends, the two styles had come to share a number of visual motifs including flat roofs, stripped and boldly geometrical forms, horizontal bands of windows, and the use of modern industrial materials like steel and glass. Most Americans were still not willing to embrace the radical socialist program with which the European Modernist movement had been associated, but in Roosevelt's New Deal society the new sense of a common cause rendered the idea less of an anathema than it had been in the 1920s. Furthermore, the Modernists themselves had begun to repackage their theories in a form more acceptable to a wider range of clients and architects. They formed the *Congrès Internationaux d'Architecture Moderne* (CIAM) in 1928, and the Modern Architectural Research Group (MARS) in Britain in 1933, to promote the idea that Modernism was simply the correct way to build for the twentieth century. They said they offered not another style in the long history of architectural styles, but rather the end of style itself. Modernism inevitably resulted, they maintained, when one built functionally, rationally and economically. These sentiments accorded well with the pragmatic mood of the 1930s.

Americans were also more willing to accept the Modernist style after the Museum of Modern Art in New York mounted an influential exhibition on Modern Architecture in 1932. Arranged by Henry-Russell Hitchcock and Philip Johnson, the show displayed recent European and some American Modernist buildings as art objects largely divorced from their original social program or context. In the book which accompanied the show, *The International Style: Architecture Since 1922*, Hitchcock and Johnson attempted to present Modernism as simply a new visual language which was sweeping around the world. Its defining characteristics, they claimed, included an emphasis on volume rather than on mass, an emphasis on expressing the structural frame rather than on composing façades, and an absolute prohibition against ornament and applied decoration. Their presentation further stripped European Modernism of its original socialist agenda, and offered it as an aesthetic language which might be freely adapted by any architects no matter what their political creed. To this day, many Europeans still associate Modernist architecture with a movement of social reform, while most Americans see it as a language of abstract shapes disconnected from a political viewpoint.

241 Johnson Wax Building,
Racine, Wisconsin, 1936–39,
Frank Lloyd Wright

242 Johnson Wax Building,
interior

With the onset of the Great Depression, a number of American architects were more inclined to abandon the old architectural traditions and to strike out in new directions. Old modes of thinking, after all, had brought the Western economy and cultures crashing down. The trickle of European Modernist designs illustrated in the American professional architecture magazines in the late 1920s turned into a flood by the mid-1930s, eventually completely replacing the Academic Eclectic and Art Deco ideas. Instead of the old articles extolling the picturesque and the charming, we find hard-nosed discussions of function, economy and modern construction techniques. The profession had begun its conversion to the new point of view. Significantly, the homeowners' magazines in this period, like *House Beautiful*, did not embrace the new ideas with any enthusiasm. Art Deco and Art Moderne were about as far as they were willing to go towards modernizing the traditional. From this point on, we see an increasing divergence between the tastes and ideals of the professional architects, and the tastes and ideals of their middle-class clients.

Some architects in this period saw a role for both the traditional and the modern. Albert Kahn, for example, accepted the traditional Beaux-Arts idea about a hierarchy of building types ranging from the ceremonial, which are imbued with cultural meaning, to the purely utilitarian, which convey no particular meaning. For designs at the culturally significant end of this spectrum like libraries and houses he continued to use the traditional Academic Eclectic styles, while for utilitarian buildings like factories he happily turned to Modernist images. Kahn particularly disparaged the European Modernists for attempting to make every building type look like a factory. Perhaps ironically, Kahn built his reputation as America's premier designer of industrial buildings even though he personally valued his Academic Eclectic projects. He designed many of the automobile factories in Detroit, received commissions for 521 factories in the Soviet Union, and ultimately built over 2000 factories in his career. To accommodate the new idea of the industrial moving assembly line, Kahn perfected the idea of the factory as a single-story, large span structure lit from above by sawtooth skylights.

Other architects in this period took a harder view, and began to see Modernism as a complete replacement for the traditional ideas no matter what the building type. They saw no possibility of compromise or accommodation between the two architectural philosophies. George Howe was one of the first American architects to abandon his earlier traditions in favor of an uncompromising Modernism. He was, we will recall, one of the partners in Mellor, Meigs and Howe, the premier designers in the 1920s of picturesque Academic Eclecticism. Increasingly dissatisfied with the traditional ideas, he left the firm in 1928 to form a new partnership with William Lescaze, a Swiss immigrant who was well versed in the European Modernist style. For their design of the Philadelphia Saving Fund Society (PSFS), they turned fully to the principles and images of European Modernism [243]. Although the Modernists did not like to admit it, they had acquired from the Ecole des Beaux-Arts the idea that the building masses and parts should reflect the functional program within. Howe and Lescaze duly implemented this idea by designing three distinct parts, a base containing shops and a public banking hall, a shaft of offices and a service tower containing elevators. Each part was given its own materials and window treatment to highlight the programmatic differences among the parts. Unlike the Beaux-Arts preference for formal symmetries, the PSFS was more dynamically arranged as an asymmetrical T-shaped tower, sitting on top of a base which is entered at the corners rather than in the middle [244].

Further following the Modernist precepts, Howe and Lescaze avoided any traditional detailing or ornament whatsoever. To emphasize the important Modernist

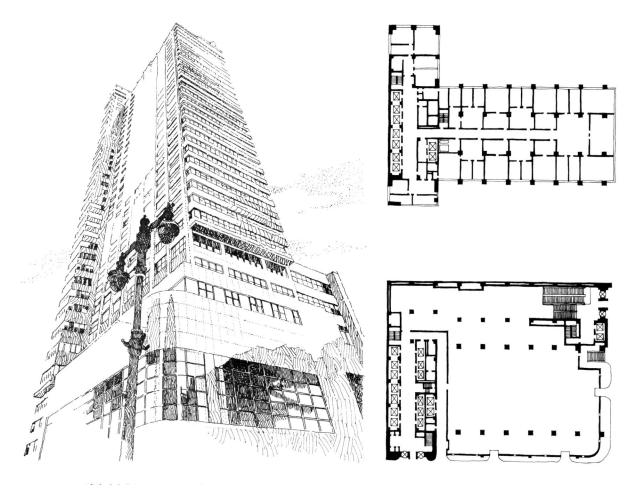

243 Philadelphia Saving
Fund Society, Philadelphia,
Pennsylvania, 1929–32,
Howe and Lescaze

244 Philadelphia Saving Fund
Society, ground floor and
upper floor plans

distinction between the structural frame and the thin weather-excluding wall which is hung from it, they set the windows flush with the outside wall surface, and underplayed the joints in the thin masonry veneer cladding. The structure itself is portrayed as strong vertical piers on the long sides of the office tower, which in turn support horizontal slabs cantilevered out on the short side. Except for slight eccentricities at the middle and at the top, each floor and office window in the main tower block is treated exactly like any other, abandoning the traditional preoccupation in façade design with complex visual rhythms, subdivisions or hierarchies. The PSFS abruptly finishes at the top with only a slight acknowledgment of the penthouse and mechanical equipment housed there; none of the exuberant Art Deco roof caps or spires had a place in this earnest and practical Modernist world.

European Modernism also entered America under the auspices of the federal government in the 1930s. Roosevelt's Public Works Administration (PWA), we will recall, took direct responsibility for clearing slums and constructing new houses when it was clear that private enterprise was no longer willing or able to do so. The PWA might have answered this housing need with any number of ideas including renovating or reconstructing traditional housing arrangements like row houses, but on the whole it did not. Perhaps to provide a visible image of the federal government at work solving people's problems, or perhaps inspired by the mass housing projects undertaken by the Modernists after the First World War, the PWA favored the Modernist idea of designing housing as regular blocks placed in a park-like setting [245]. Here we see the distinctive flat roofs, dominant horizontal lines and complete lack of traditional detail characteristic of low-rise Modernism, while this project even twisted its grid to distinguish itself from the adjoining streets.

When the PWA abandoned traditional housing ideas in favor of these new Modernist notions, they inadvertently set up a number of serious problems which, after the Second World War, ultimately called the entire federal housing program into question. To begin with, the flat roofs and astringent detailing of Modernism led to greater maintenance problems and therefore higher continuing expenses for the public authorities than one would have found in more traditional designs. Second, in pulling the house doorways off the public streets and clustering them around semi-private courtyards, the designers in essence reduced the number of people casually walking by. This, in turn, reduced the informal supervision of the public realm and ultimately contributed to higher crime. As any street savvy person knows, the safest places in a city are in the populated public streets, not in the quiet culs-de-sac or courtyards. Third, by establishing a highly identifiable image for the public housing projects – even restricting access to a few limited entry points – these designs placed those who required federally assisted housing into highly recognizable enclaves. Now one lived 'in the project' with the social stigma which that implied, rather than living on a particular street. Unfortunately, as we will see in the next chapter, the social program of affordable and accessible housing increasingly became inextricably intertwined with aesthetic ideas particularly ill suited to housing.

It was by no means a foregone conclusion that the Modernists would win the day before the Second World War. Most architects still designed in the traditional styles, or in the hybrids stripped Classicism and Streamline Moderne. Most clients were still not willing to embrace the austere European images, or the values for which they stood. However, just before the war, the Modernists in America suddenly gained powerful allies. When Hitler came to power in Germany, he identified Modernist art and architecture with Bolshevism and with moral decadence. Many leading Modernists

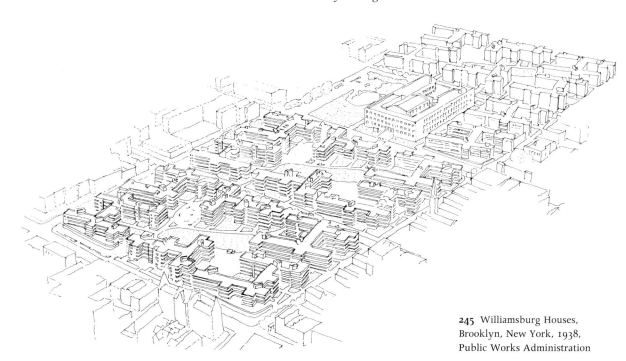

**245** Williamsburg Houses, Brooklyn, New York, 1938, Public Works Administration

saw the writing on the wall and fled the country, settling in more congenial countries including Britain and America. The immigrants to America included Walter Gropius, who was appointed Professor of Architecture at Harvard in 1937; Mies van der Rohe, who from 1938 directed the School of Architecture at the Armour Institute in Chicago; Moholy-Nagy, who directed the New Bauhaus (now Institute of Design) in Chicago from 1937 to 1946; Joseph Albers, who chaired the Department of Design at Yale; and Marcel Breuer, who taught at Harvard from 1937 to 1946.

Holding positions of authority in some of the most prestigious architecture schools in the country, the European Modernists rejected outright the Beaux-Arts system of design education which had dominated American schools since the Civil War, and which had helped support the traditional styles. In its place they substituted the Bauhaus method, claiming that it was not about a particular Modernist style, but rather about a rational method for solving the modern world's new architectural problems. In hindsight, we can now see that the Bauhaus methods inevitably led students to create Modernist buildings and no others. Architectural history was largely ignored, studying precedents other than Modernist ones was discouraged, creativity rather than the refinement of tradition was championed, and the abstractions of the Bauhaus 'language of vision' led to the austere and rational forms of the modernist movement, not to ornamented architectural traditions. After the Second World War, as will be seen in the next chapter, the Bauhaus method eventually replaced the Beaux-Arts system in every American school, just when the schools increasingly controlled entry into the profession. The Modernists shaped the future of American architecture at its source, in the education of the next generation of architects.

Frank Lloyd Wright was appalled at the entry of European Modernist ideas into America in the 1930s. His was the first voice of modernism in America, after all, and his vision stood diametrically opposed to that of the Europeans. They championed universal forms independent of place; he championed forms rooted in a particular site. They argued for the machine and the industrial world that went with it; he still believed in the Jeffersonian ideal of an agrarian America. Wright publicly condemned the International Style as philosophically mistaken and aesthetically limited. In the 1930s – when he was in his seventies – he sallied forth to show America a better way.

Wright explored his alternative vision for America in his Broadacre City project, designed at the beginning of the Great Depression [**246**]. In keeping with his Jeffersonian ideals, he proposed to decentralize America completely. The private automobile, he realized, largely removed the need for core cities. People are now free to travel considerable distances from home to work, shops and entertainment, and therefore do not need to live in crowded, dangerous and spiritually demeaning cities. Wright proposed to spread all future American development evenly over the land, giving each house a one-acre plot. Every American would enjoy a close relationship with the land, gaining not only spiritual sustenance but some economic benefits as well if crop gardens were grown. Linking it all together would be a vast network of roads following the great Cartesian grid of Western America. Although this idea summed up the popular American desires for autonomy and for a connection to the land, critics then and since disparaged the scheme on a number of grounds. Some bridled at the thought of suburban sprawl gradually eating up all of America's rural landscape, eventually destroying the very qualities of unspoiled nature that drove the impulse to rural living in the first place; while others disparaged the idea of a viable culture without cities. As it turns out, American suburban development after the Second World War turned much of Wright's vision into reality despite the

**246** Broadacre City, 1931–35, Frank Lloyd Wright

critics' concerns. Low density housing spreading over the once rural land, dispersed suburban centers of retail and industry, and a vast network of roads linking it all together, have largely defined America's post-war growth.

In the depths of the Depression in the mid-1930s, Wright turned his attention to the design of the small houses that might someday populate Broadacre City, and that would remain affordable for the vast majority of Americans. Until now, he realized, small houses were usually large houses writ small; that is, they usually retained the same spatial arrangements and imagery of large and expensive houses built for the aristocracy or upper classes, and then were simply reduced in size to fit the available budget. For what he called his Usonian houses, Wright started afresh. Unlike the traditional house that turned its best face to the street, the Usonian house turned its back to the street and opened up extensively through glass doors and windows to the rear garden [247]. This idea allowed the small house to extend out into the garden visually, creating a sense of greater space without giving up privacy. To save space in the house itself, Wright abandoned the traditional idea of a separate dining room. A small alcove with a dining table opened onto both the kitchen and the living room, in essence reviving the old medieval idea of a great hall in which most public functions took place. This made new sense in the small servantless house, because the mother could prepare food while watching the children.

To save yet more construction costs, Wright abandoned the basement and the garage, placing the entire house on a concrete slab which floated on the surface of the land. Radiant pipes buried in the slab heated up the entire floor, which then acted like a giant radiator for the house itself. He designed the house on a regular module which allowed economic repetition of similar elements and reduced the amount of labor intensive cutting of materials on the site. For the outside image he turned increasingly to the simple planes of the International Style – built in natural materials like brick and wood, of course – not only for their modern appearance but also because they could be built inexpensively [248]. Like the Modernist housing projects discussed above, however, the simplified details and flat roofs in these Usonian houses were not as durable as the construction details in more traditional designs, ultimately leading to extensive building failures like leaking roofs. Despite the later problems, Wright said he was able to build the first Usonian house in 1936 for $5500 including the architect's fees, where the Robie house had cost $35,000 28 years earlier. Seldom

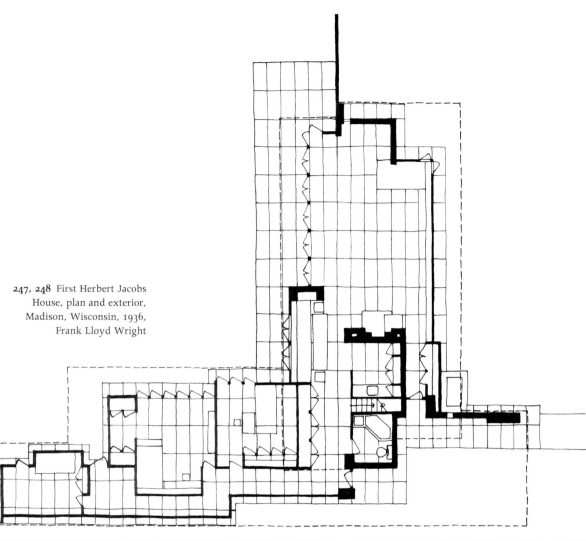

**247, 248** First Herbert Jacobs
House, plan and exterior,
Madison, Wisconsin, 1936,
Frank Lloyd Wright

before or since has a high fashion architect devoted so much attention to the creative design of affordable single family houses.

The commission for Wright's most famous building of all came in the middle of the Depression. He designed the Kaufmann House, or more familiarly the Fallingwater House, for the head of a department store in Pittsburgh whose son had studied in his Taliesin Fellowship [249]. For this weekend retreat, Wright fused his lifelong interest in organic architecture and nature with the International Style images of clean, rational forms. On a rock outcropping over the small waterfall in the Bear Run stream, he built up a series of roughly laid rock walls seemingly grown out of the land. These form an inner core of service rooms like the kitchen, dining area and entry, as well as a massive fireplace whose hearth sits on the exposed rock of the outcropping itself. From this organic anchor, Wright daringly cantilevered a series of overlapping terraces, rendered in the pure shapes and white tones of the International Style, and perhaps influenced by the balconies on Richard Neutra's Lovell house. The house seems to hover weightlessly over the waterfall, apparently defying the obviously heavy nature of the concrete. As in many of his houses, he dramatized the contrast between the deep, dark, cavelike interior centered around the fireplace, and the light, open, outwardly focused windows at the periphery of the terraces. The Fallingwater House masterfully balances a number of other deep

249 Fallingwater, near Mill Run, Pennsylvania, 1936–37, Frank Lloyd Wright

tensions as well, between the natural and the manufactured, the anchored and the soaring, the light and the dark, the fire within and the water without. Fallingwater was widely admired both then and now for its powerful imagery and the way it touches these deep human emotions, even among those who are no fans of Modernist architecture in its other guises.

Unlike the formulistic principles and easily repeatable vocabulary of the International Style, Frank Lloyd Wright's architectural essay at Fallingwater was too idiosyncratic to generate an architectural movement. After the Second World War, as we will see in the next chapter, the architects in America largely ignored Frank Lloyd Wright's ideas in favor of the European Modernist notions for their high fashion designs. However, Wright perhaps understood the American psyche more clearly than many of the architects who succeeded him because, unlike many of the Modernist ideas, a number of Wright's concepts rapidly entered into the American vernacular. Although post-war developers did not specifically follow his vision of Broadacre City, they effectively built much of it while responding to market forces. And while few Americans or their architects built Usonian houses after the war, millions of Americans bought and raised families in the ubiquitous suburban Ranch houses which the Usonian ideas partly inspired.

Standing on the eve of the Second World War at the end of the 1930s, one could hardly have imagined changes more dramatic than those which had swept over Europe and America after the Great War to end all wars. The roller coaster ride of the Roaring Twenties collapsing into the Great Depression, the rise of the twentieth-century's evil totalitarian states, America's unprecedented flirtation with socialism, and American architects embracing styles entirely devoid of any historical meaning; who could have guessed these developments in 1918? But, as will be seen, these were only the beginnings of changes far more sweeping.

# 9

# MODERN CULTURE
## 1945–73

W HEN the atomic bombs fell on Japan in 1945 and finally ended the Second World War, the United States emerged as the economic and political leader of the Western world. Where Americans had long followed European ideas and tastes in cultural matters, now much of the world acquired American tastes in popular music, clothing fashions and speech, and eventually architecture. America after the war abandoned its earlier preference for the historical styles, fully embracing instead the ahistorical and visually austere forms of International Modernism. Most popular at

250 United States in 1973

Major industrial areas ca. 1950

— Interstate highway system ca. 1980

0    250    500 miles

0    250    500 kilometers

U. S. population
1945: 140,468,000
1973: 210,396,000

first were ideas derived from the Europeans Le Corbusier and Mies van der Rohe, the latter of whom settled in Chicago and perfected the rational steel and glass skyscraper in the American context. But in the 1950s, a number of leading Modernist architects throughout the world began to experiment with Expressionist versions of the Modernist language. Without explicitly repudiating the rationalist ideals that had originally driven Modernism, architects like Le Corbusier, Frank Lloyd Wright and Eero Saarinen explored anti-rational and expressively plastic forms like those we first saw in the German Expressionism after the First World War. By the early 1960s, many architects began to see themselves as shapemakers or form-givers, concerned primarily with developing expressive forms outside the bounds of the traditional styles. By the mid-1960s, Modernism dominated the American landscape like no other style before it. A post-war economic and population boom, linked with an unbridled Modernist enthusiasm for bulldozing the old to make way for the new, caused the style to spread rapidly and pervasively. America's prestige in this period also hastened the spread of its official architectural style through the rest of the world. The immediate post-war era largely belonged to America and to Modernism.

A cultural revolution in the 1960s fundamentally questioned or realigned all aspects of society in the Western industrialized countries including America. While Modernism still dominated architectural production in this revolutionary period, a number of movements arose to challenge the architectural status quo. Some critics objected to contemporary Modernism's expressionist divergence from an earlier, purer path, and wished to start afresh with the rational Modernism of the 1920s. Other critics objected to Modernism's abstract and austere forms, and proposed to revive elements of previous architectural traditions. A counterculture movement looking very much like the Romantic movement in the early nineteenth century imagined visionary utopias based in an Arts and Crafts rural past or a space age future. A movement centered mostly in the universities attempted to turn architecture into a rigorous science without personal expression, while an historic preservation movement emerged to defend older buildings from Modernist redevelopment. So while the Modernists at the end of the 1960s still confidently believed that their stylistic revolution had completely won the day, pressures were mounting in their decades of triumph. This chapter will explore how Modernism came to dominate the post-war era, and then why various critics wished to topple it.

## The war and its aftermath

### America's decades

The Second World War was conducted on a scale unprecedented in history, sweeping over every corner of the world and ultimately killing over 25 million people. One small consolation was that the massive industrial production and mobilization of troops required for this effort pulled the world out of the Great Depression. As in the First World War, the conflict devastated Europe, laying to waste not only its cities and countryside, but also destroying its economies and industrial plant. The once dominant European powers emerged from the war exhausted and weakened. Their colonies around the world seized the opportunity, declared independence, and formed dozens of new nations in the decades following the end of the war. The European control of the world stage – which had begun in the Renaissance half a millennium earlier – had begun to wane.

America emerged from the war in far better condition. Although it suffered over a million casualties, no battles were fought on its own mainland. America's farms and industries were consequently left free to produce goods both for itself and for its allies. At the conclusion of the war, just as after the First World War, the American economy surged forward as it continued to produce goods for the world without competition from Europe. American corporations consequently dominated the world markets. And now freed from the austerities of the war economy, Americans at home splurged on consumer goods and further fueled the booming economy. At the same time, the American government stepped into the political vacuum left by the collapse of Europe, taking over the leadership of the world's democratic societies. The world now stood on the threshold of America's decades.

Americans entered peacetime in a jubilant mood, convinced that their traditional values and way of life had won the war. At first, President Truman tried to carry on the big government principles of Roosevelt, including implementing Roosevelt's GI Bill of Rights. This program enormously benefited the war generation, offering returning servicemen inexpensive government loans for a house and a college education, as well as medical care. The American suburbs, as will be seen later, dramatically expanded under this influence. For many Americans, the GI Bill provided an essential boost into a middle-class lifestyle, creating a predominately middle-class culture at the same time as America rose as the pre-eminent international power. Never before – or since – did such a large percentage of the population enjoy such a high standard of living. But despite the personal benefits that millions of Americans accrued from these New Deal ideas, in the 1952 elections they turned away from these experiments with socialism. Under the benign leadership of the war hero President Eisenhower, Americans returned to their traditional beliefs in free enterprise and laissez-faire social arrangements. The great pendulum we have seen swinging back and forth in American life, between eras concerned with the common social good and eras concerned with the individual, had emphatically swung to the latter in the 1950s. This stood in marked contrast to the Europeans after the war, who mostly turned to mild forms of economic socialism allied to democratic forms of government. To this day, the Europeans remain more committed to centrally managed social programs than the Americans.

Interestingly, the 1950s in America were characterized less by the ebullient individualism that we saw after the Civil War and the First World War, and more by a staid conformity to convention and decorum. Perhaps tired of the great public struggles of the previous two decades, most Americans retreated into lifestyles focused on comfort and security. For many, this meant joining the large corporations which offered job security and steady advancement at the price of suppressing individual initiative and toeing the company line. For most, it also meant throwing their greatest energy and enthusiasm into home and family life. Most women either willingly or grudgingly gave up the jobs they had acquired during the war, turning their attentions instead to making homes and raising families. Perhaps reacting against their own parents' sometimes frivolous or even permissive behavior during the flapper era, the post-war generation stressed serious and earnest values like social decorum and personal responsibility while raising their young families. An unanticipated side effect of this emphasis on family was a dramatic population explosion: America's population jumped from 140 million in 1945 to almost 192 million in 1964. Like a pig passing through a python, the baby boom generation surged through post-war American life and substantially helped define the needs and values in each era. In the 1950s, the baby boomers fueled a huge demand for new homes, home-based consumer goods, and schools.

America did not dominate world politics alone for long. Its former ally the Soviet Union quickly emerged as a rival superpower, gathering into its fold the governments of countries espousing socialist or communist systems. Each superpower cluster darkly suspected the other side of attempting to control the world, and fought a series of skirmishes either to test or to block the other. This Cold War ignited a number of confrontations, including the Berlin Blockade, the Korean War, the Cuban missile crisis and, perhaps the most damaging of all for America, the Vietnam War. These conflicts hardened Americans' hostility to socialist ideas, leading to further Red Scares like those following the First World War.

Out of the aftermath of the Second World War, and in the midst of the Cold War, much of the world including America acquired a new enthusiasm for technology which eventually influenced architectural developments in this period. Both wars hastened the development of new technologies, while many people admired how technology and rational problem-solving had helped win the world war. Further, many people had gained first-hand exposure to high technology while serving in the military services or while working in the factories. High technology fully entered most people's lives during the 1950s and 1960s. The first commercial jet airplanes flew in 1958, by 1960 88 per cent of American homes possessed a television, and the space race between the Soviet Union and America landed a man on the moon on prime time television in 1969. These accomplishments were so astounding that many consequently believed science and technology would eventually solve most of the world's problems. The former colonies in the Third World also saw industrialization as essential to survival and eventual prosperity, and enthusiastically mimicked the high technology aspirations of America and Europe. This common attitude encouraged the spread throughout the world of those architectural ideas which were seen to be derived from high technology. There was, however, a darker side to the technological achievements in the post-war era. The Russians developed an atomic bomb of their own, leading to an armaments race and vast stockpiles of atomic weapons which threatened an instant annihilation of the world. Living under the nuclear cloud, many began to fear the consequences of technology out of control. In the 1960s and 1970s, as we will see later, this eventually helped push technology off its high post-war pedestal.

### The triumph of Modernism

All of these developments following the Second World War led to a widespread acceptance of Modernism as the most appropriate architectural expression of the new age. The austere, ahistorical forms now represented a number of ideals which many in the post-war generation admired. First of all, Modernism symbolized a break with the past and seemed to stand for a shiny new age of peace and prosperity after the deprivations and nightmares of the Great Depression and the two world wars. Second, the Modernist emphasis on rational and efficient building technology accorded well with the enthusiasm for high technology in the period. Third, the Modernist conception of design as rational problem-solving appealed to the generation that had similarly used rational problem-solving methods to tackle the logistical complexities of the largest war in history. And fourth, particularly for the government and the private corporations, the visual character of the Modernist style seemed to sum up their own self-images: rational, efficient, the confident possessors of immense power and wealth, and yet not flashy or desirous of individual expression.

As we have seen throughout this history, architectural styles possess no one intrinsic meaning. Different cultures or groups might take up the same style for

251 Unité d'habitation, Marseille,
France, 1946–52, Le Corbusier

quite different reasons. In the 1920s and 1930s, the style of radical Modernism had
stood for socialism and collectivism; now in 1950s America it represented the politically conservative American government and the free market American corporations. Indeed, in the 1950s and 1960s the Modernist style crossed all economic and
political boundaries. The communist Soviet Union, the social democratic Western
European countries, and the developing nations in the Third World all turned to
versions of Modernism. Most probably saw the same virtues in the Modernist style
for the post-war era. Undoubtedly, some valued the style because it was the official
style of America, now the unquestioned leader of the Western world.

Although the prestige of America after the war helped popularize Modernism
around the world, the main architectural ideas still came from Europe or from
European immigrants. Some of the most popular and influential versions of post-war
Modernism were developed by Le Corbusier who, in the years immediately following the war, had begun to experiment with forms more aggressively powerful than
his 1920s International Style white boxes. In a number of projects including the
Maisons Jaoul at Neuilly, the Monastery at La Tourette, and the Unité d'habitation
in Marseille (or the Marseille block), he turned away from his earlier style of thin
stucco walls perforated with openings, in favor of massive concrete structures heavily
modeled with external sun screens and other projections [251]. Pursuing economy,
honesty of construction and a primitive emotional presence, Le Corbusier built these
schemes in roughly cast concrete (known as *béton brut* in French) which frankly

expressed the rough boarding formwork into which the concrete was poured. This construction technique sparked an enthusiasm among many post-war Modernists for raw concrete, and for what was later called the Brutalist style.

The Marseille block in particular influenced much post-war design, since it finally offered a built example of Le Corbusier's pre-war concepts for urban design and housing. We will recall his proposal in the 1920s to bulldoze central Paris to make way for free-standing towers regularly lined up in the landscape. He intended with this scheme to rationalize and to separate the various functions of the city, as well as to form more efficient 'vertical' neighborhoods in place of the traditional horizontal streets. Although no one before the war other than a few ardent Modernists had given much credence to the idea, the extensive war damage to France's housing stock finally provided him with the opportunity after the war to build a prototype in Marseille. He constructed one of what he hoped eventually would become an entire city of housing blocks standing on columns above the sweeping natural landscape, each one intended to replace a traditional neighborhood. Interior 'streets' ran down the length of his prototype on every third floor, giving access to interlocking two-story tall apartments. Le Corbusier provided a variety of unit sizes in the hope that – just like in a traditional mixed neighborhood of apartments and houses – this would encourage a variety of social groups to live together. A shopping arcade in the middle of the block, and playgrounds and a gymnasium on the roof, were meant to provide all of the usual neighborhood amenities within the structure itself. Le Corbusier unabashedly meant to reshape the lives of the people who lived in his structure, insisting that they give up their own traditional manners of living in favor of his own vision of appropriate and healthful behavior. In Le Corbusier's eyes, Modernism still represented a mechanism for re-engineering society.

Although Le Corbusier's Marseille scheme proved too controversial and expensive to merit further expansion, his vision of pristine towers hovering above the landscape caught the imagination of many post-war Modernist architects and urban designers. Housing projects based on the Unité idea sprouted up throughout Europe in the 1950s and 1960s, sometimes in the bomb-damaged centers of cities, sometimes at the peripheries. A popular variation on the theme, known as a point block or tower block, piled more stories on a smaller footprint to create what was in essence a housing skyscraper. These also stood clustered together in the landscape, and often rivaled the old church spires as the most dominant features on the skylines. Many European governments embraced these new forms of housing partly to rebuild the housing stock quickly and inexpensively, partly to control the endless spread of suburbs during the post-war baby boom, and partly to provide affordable, government supported housing for a wider range of social classes.

Although America's cities were not destroyed by bombs, they nonetheless faced serious problems of their own. After decades of white, middle-class flight to the suburbs, many of America's inner cities ringing the commercial cores housed a disproportionate number of poor people, usually racial minorities. Money fled the cities with the middle classes, leaving many neighborhoods with a crumbling housing stock and decaying services. Conditions seemed so dire that President Truman passed the Housing Act of 1949, giving the government the authority to acquire land in the city centers through compulsory purchases. The government then sold or leased the land to redevelopment agencies who constructed state-subsidized housing for the poor. Known optimistically as Urban Renewal, this program represented the continuing legacy of Roosevelt's New Deal efforts to solve public problems with extensive federal government intervention. As in the federal housing projects before the war, the architects and planners chose not to reconstruct traditional rows of houses on streets. Perhaps to create highly visible evidence of federal tax dollars at work, or perhaps thrilled at the prospect of so much land free for development, or perhaps inspired by contemporary European Modernist models, they chose to construct Le Corbusian housing towers in urban parks. Now where Hitler's war machine had cleared the way for many of the post-war urban housing projects in Europe, in America the land was cleared just as emphatically with wrecking balls and bulldozers. Old neighborhoods and streets were completely obliterated to make way for European style tower blocks and Unités. Adding to the destruction of the traditional American city was Eisenhower's Interstate Highway Act of 1956, which built a great interstate highway system linking together most of America's largest cities and towns. These highways shot straight into the commercial centers of the cities, irreparably splitting old neighborhoods in two, and providing an even easier route for those fleeing to the suburbs.

Unfortunately, Le Corbusier's utopian vision of healthy, affordable housing in an urban park quickly succumbed to harsh realities in the American inner cities. Tight budgets for maintenance, and the pervasive use of automobiles, turned his idyllic green landscapes into asphalt parking lots and uncultivated dirt. New apartments in themselves did not remove the underlying causes of crushing poverty in the inner cities, and eventually the housing projects were plagued by vandalism and crime so dire that even the police feared to enter. Although debates continue yet today between those who blame the physical design and those who blame social factors for these ills, the dysfunctional housing projects became tied in the popular imagination to the image of Modernist architecture itself. The failures of the former eventually helped lead to the demise of the latter, as we will see in the next chapter.

In the 1950s, when the Modernist vision still tantalizingly held out promise of a brave new world, another European rivaled Le Corbusier for exerting the greatest architectural influence on America and the rest of the world. Mies van der Rohe was originally apprenticed to Peter Behrens in Germany and, after the First World War, designed a number of Modernist projects ranging from essays in Expressionism to variations on Frank Lloyd Wright. For three years Mies headed the Bauhaus, until the Nazis closed the school in 1933 and encouraged him to emigrate to the United States. From 1938 on he directed the School of Architecture at the Armour Institute (later Illinois Institute of Technology) in Chicago, while developing his distinctive and mature style. Mies was far less interested in the social side of architecture than was Le Corbusier, focusing instead on buildings as technical and visual problems to be solved. He described his philosophy as 'less is more', meaning that he wished to pare architecture down to its most fundamental essence. For him, this usually meant building a simple and rational structural cage, onto which he hung an external cladding system completely subservient to the structure's inherent geometrical grid. Because the cladding system was now reduced to a thin and lightweight veneer of glass and metal panels, it came to be known as a curtain wall, acknowledging that it simply hung like a curtain from the frame to protect the insides of the building from the weather. Although other American architects including Pietro Belluschi and the giant corporate firm of Skidmore, Owings and Merrill had earlier experimented with a number of these ideas, Mies clarified and perfected the concept and its details to create the most striking expression yet of the ancient frame and cover architectural idea.

Mies offered low-rise and high-rise versions of his style. The low-rise idea shows in his design for the campus of the Illinois Institute of Technology. On a rational planning grid he placed a number of free-standing pavilions, each one comprised of simple boxes with flat roofs. Each building, in turn, was strictly planned on a rational Cartesian grid which established the location of the structure, the walls, and openings. The school of architecture building on the campus leaves the entire first floor undivided except for low, free-standing partitions, the whole space spanned over by giant beams above the roof [252]. The high-rise idea shows in his Seagram Building in New York City, designed for a whiskey firm with Philip Johnson as associate architect [253]. Again the design is reduced to a simple box, strictly organized with a regular grid. We look for no visual surprises or complexities here, but rather concentrate on the careful proportions, the studied craft of simplicity, and the inexorable regularity of repeating elements. The building seems to proclaim exactly what it is, without the falsely applied ornament or the misrepresentation of the structural facts that, in the eyes of the Modernists, had blemished earlier skyscraper designs. However, even here everything is not as it seems. Although the structural frame is steel, Mies had to fireproof the steel by encasing it in concrete. The metal we see on the outside of the building is therefore not the real structure, but rather a veneer simulating the structure. Like many buildings we have examined in this history so far, the aesthetic desire for a certain appearance inevitably overcame the philosophical desire to express everything absolutely truthfully.

Like Le Corbusier's projects, Mies lifted the Seagram Building off the ground to form an entry lobby, and to create a sense of the outdoors flowing through the building. He also set the building back from the street and apart from its neighbors on a public plaza, treating it as an isolated object in space rather than as an infill in a continuous streetline of buildings. The practical purpose of the setback was to accommodate New York City's zoning laws, which regulate the amount of light made available to the street. However, Mies could have answered this requirement just like most other New York City skyscrapers, by starting at the street and then progressively setting back higher floors. Since not following this normal pattern meant giving up valuable floor space on expensive property, Mies clearly was answering a higher philosophical or aesthetic urge. In this case, we can infer a strong desire to avoid corrupting his pure vision with the visual clutter of the city around it. If he could not build his rational forms in a park-like campus setting as at IIT, then he would clear out a little park within the city and build his pavilion anyway. So where once only major public buildings like town halls or churches stood apart from the rest of the city in their own plazas or town squares, now Mies had elevated the headquarters of private corporations to the same esteemed status.  ·

Mies applied these same low-rise and high-rise ideas to any number of building types, ranging from convention centers to apartment complexes and office buildings. He largely ignored the nuances of different sites or regions, always preferring to impose the abstracted ideal vision on the local realities. Mies offered a universal solution for every building everywhere. His austere and powerful images of a Modern world inspired so many architects and their clients in the 1950s and 1960s that cities throughout America were recast in the Miesian mold. Shopping centers, schools, office parks, corporate headquarters, apartment buildings, and government buildings sprang up around the country, all based on a rational structural frame and thin curtain wall cladding. Eventually, this model spread to Europe and then to the Third World countries, defining for many the essence of Modernism and pragmatic rationalism. So pervasive was the idea of the curtain walled box that one can be shown a photograph today of a downtown or a suburban office park, and not immediately know if one is looking at Los Angeles, Denver, Atlanta, Houston, Hong Kong or any number of other cities expanded or rebuilt during the heyday of Modernism. The old Academic Eclectic idea of designing differently for different locations held little interest for

252 Crown Hall, Chicago, Illinois,
1950–56, Mies van der Rohe

253 Seagram Building, New York
City, 1954–58, Mies van der Rohe
and Philip Johnson

architects pursuing the Miesian ideals of a rational structure, industrialized construction and perfected proportions.

One Miesian building set back from the streetline stands apart as an isolated jewel; an entire street of Miesian buildings set back on their own plazas radically undermined the familiar conception of an urban street as a continuous façade of buildings. At the time, many admired the manner in which these plazas opened up what they saw as cramped and crowded cities. When a large number of Miesian buildings in their plazas clustered together in a given city, the downtown began to exude the image which Sant'Elia and Le Corbusier had intended: glistening, high technology centers of commerce and industry, unencumbered by the past and looking boldly to the future. For just this reason, a cluster of Miesian skyscrapers downtown became a source of civic pride for many cities throughout America in the Modernist era. Only later, as we will see, did critics begin to attack this Modernist vision as windswept and barren, devoid of the hustle and bustle, sensory richness and spatial enclosure of traditional urban streets.

Even as the Miesian box multiplied across America in the 1950s and early 1960s, a number of architects objected to its severity and austerity. They sensed that it had lost sight of art or beauty in favor of constructional exigency, and complained that it insufficiently expressed the highest cultural aspirations of what was now the most powerful nation on earth. They did, however, recognize the obvious virtues of its rational constructional system. These architects were known as the New Formalists or Neo-neo-Classicists, and explored various ways in which the basic frame and cover box could be elaborated or even decorated to provide a more elegant and commanding presence. As their name implies, many in this group turned to traditional Classical ideas for inspiration. The Classical temple, after all, was based on a rational grid of columns and beams just like a Miesian box, while it offered the further advantage of representing the highest political and aesthetic achievements of Western civilization. Many New Formalists including Edward Durell Stone, Minoru Yamasaki and Philip Johnson consequently played out Modernist variations on the Classical forms. For the American Embassy in New Delhi, India, for example, Stone wrapped a Classical colonnade around a simple box, although he replaced the usual thick stone columns with astringently thin gilded steel supports. He further modernized and dematerialized the walls of the box itself, constructing them of perforated terrazzo blocks which served as sun screens. Perforated screens in masonry and aluminum, and the extensive use of richly gilded surfaces and structures, appeared time and again in buildings constructed in this style.

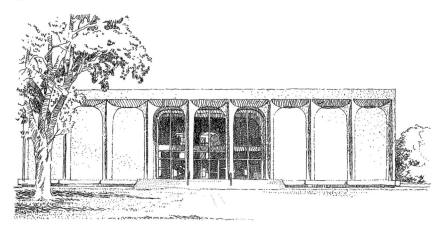

**254** Sheldon Memorial Art Gallery, Lincoln, Nebraska, 1963, Philip Johnson

Philip Johnson also explicitly referred to the Classical temple in his Sheldon Memorial Art Gallery [254]. Here he even hints at a Roman arcade, with the flattened arches smoothly bridging between the sharp edged columns. And yet the overall effect is decidedly modern. Each bay looks like a giant panel stamped out in an industrial process like that which stamps out car doors, while the open bays at the center reveal a Miesian frame and glass infill. Although examples of the New Formalism can be found scattered around the country, the idea never caught on extensively. From the strictly Modernist point of view, the forms returned too explicitly to the discredited traditional styles, and too often disguised or obscured their constructional realities. From the traditionalist point of view, the lack of detail failed to moderate the scale and bulk of what were still in reality large Modernist boxes. Both sides tended to view these buildings as lacking in substance. To be more charitable, we might now view these buildings as tentative precursors to Postmodernism, the architectural movement of the 1970s and 1980s which similarly attempted to bridge between the modern and traditional.

### The suburbs and a triumphant middle class

Given a choice, most Americans in the 1950s and 1960s happily fled the cities in favor of a house in the suburbs. The financial incentives were almost irresistible. Roosevelt's Federal Housing Administration (FHA) still offered inexpensive and insured loans for purchasing single family houses, while returning GIs were allowed to take out a 100 per cent mortgage with no down payment. With little to risk and much to gain, Americans in the millions bought a little piece of what by now had become the American dream. In just four years between 1956 and 1960, 11 million new homes were built in the suburbs. Owning one's own single family detached house on its own plot of land, close to nature and away from the now thoroughly evil cities; this is what many desired and could now possess. Jefferson's rural vision for America – although now much transformed – continued to drive American values and aspirations.

Middle-class families in the suburbs still resisted high fashion Modernist ideas, preferring instead something more reminiscent of traditional styles like Cape Cod or Tudor. For a war-weary generation, these styles no doubt represented welcome stability and a return to normal life. And for the many who had just achieved the American dream for the first time, these represented the proper image of houses they had often seen around them, but never believed they could afford. However, these traditional styles were modified by post-war conditions into something more modern. The affordable housing in the suburbs usually came at the price of simplification, in order to keep the construction costs down. Steep Tudor roofs were flattened, most ornament and decoration was stripped off, and forms were reduced to a box with perhaps a few protruding bay windows or gable ends. So although these post-war suburban houses derived from traditional ideas, the resulting effect of constructional economy was a less detailed and hence more modern look.

Particularly popular in the 1950s and 1960s was the Ranch style, first developed in California in the 1930s and derived from earlier precedents including the Spanish Colonial, the Craftsman, and Wright's Prairie and Usonian ideas [255]. Trying to capture the rural spirit of a rambling hacienda out in the countryside, the American Ranch house placed all of the rooms on the ground floor in long ranges of wings. A long, low, overhanging roof capped and further emphasized the horizontal composition. Ranch houses were set well back from the street and placed lengthwise on a wide lot, portraying a rural and genteel image of a large house on a sweeping lawn. These wide lots were made possible by the now universal use of the automobile, since houses

255 Post-war Ranch house

no longer had to cluster closely together to reduce the walking time to the local train station or streetcar stop. Where garages before the war typically stood detached at the back of the lot, now in the post-war suburban houses the garage proudly attached to the house at the front or side. A popular variation on the Ranch house known as the tri-level or split level placed the garage under the main house, with another wing attached halfway up between the two levels. Although the Ranches offered little detailing compared to the traditional styles of the previous generation, they usually added a vestigial wrought iron grill or roof support from Spanish precedents, or decorative shutters from the British colonial tradition.

Most of these suburban houses mentioned so far were designed and built speculatively by developers. When architects designed custom homes for particular clients in this period, many also turned to a version of the Ranch house sometimes known as the Contemporary style. This higher fashion style also arranged the rooms in long wings on one and occasionally two floors, capped with long, low roofs. Many exposed the roof beams or other structural members in the spirit of the Craftsman tradition. The architects' Contemporary style typically favored less traditional shapes and offered less traditional detailing than the builders' Ranch houses. A few architects removed a pitched roof altogether and designed in the cubistic forms of International Modernism, although they tended to prefer the American wood tradition to the European white stucco, and they followed Wright in integrating the house with the landscape.

In the years following the Second World War, American houses whatever their style largely abandoned their traditional front porches in favor of a rear patio. From the Colonial period onward, as we have seen in this history, front porches provided congenial places to sit on a balmy evening and chat with passing neighbors. Now in the anti-urban, anti-public, and family-centered mood of the post-war era, Americans preferred to enjoy the balmy evenings in the privacy of their own backyards. Even if one were more inclined to socialize with neighbors, few walked by anymore in a neighborhood dominated by cars.

Large-scale tract house developers like Levitt and Sons perfected methods of mass production in the post-war years, in which prefabricated building components and materials were shipped to the site and assembled like in a factory into rows of similar houses. So efficient was the construction method, and so great was the demand, that these post-war tract developments spread rapidly out into the countryside. In areas of the largest growth like California, cities and towns which were once separated by farmland eventually grew together into a great urban sprawl. Now one drove for miles through undifferentiated and continuous development, with only a small roadway sign to note that one had entered a different town.

The old central business districts no longer conveniently provided the retail and service needs for these widely flung suburbs. The old downtowns were now a long distance away and, with the demise of much public transportation after the war, accessible only by car. Unfortunately, the old downtowns were not designed for a massive influx of automobiles, since their narrow streets could not easily accommodate the traffic or provide sufficient parking. More convenient answers came in the form of strip malls, which were first developed between the wars, and regional shopping malls which were invented just after the war. Located along the broad avenues criss-crossing the suburban areas, the strip malls set a row of shops back from the street, leaving a broad expanse of asphalt between the buildings and the street for free parking. To attract the notice of cars passing by at 35 or 40 miles an hour, the strip malls erected large signs advertising their wares and joining their competitors' signs in a visual cacophony of information. The architectural character of the buildings could hardly be seen – indeed, hardly mattered – in this brave new world of automobile shopping.

The regional malls carried this idea even further. A number of developers and designers seem to have hit on the idea of the regional mall immediately after the end of the Second World War, and a number claimed credit for the main idea or essential pieces of it. The honor seems to go to John Graham, who in 1950 completed the Northgate Regional Shopping Center in Seattle, Washington, with the concept that still defines most malls today [256]. He pulled his building back from the street altogether, placing it in the center of a vast parking lot. This arrangement maximized the parking area while minimizing the walking distance between cars and building. Graham arranged the shops in his mall along a central pedestrian 'street', directly under which ran a service tunnel that provided access for delivery trucks to the shops. He placed two large department stores at the middle of the mall in order to generate foot traffic there, and a third department store at the end of the mall to pull pedestrians down the street and past the smaller specialty shops lining the way. Later malls refined the concept by placing large department stores at either end of the mall, thereby generating maximum foot traffic along the entire length of the mall, and by roofing over the central 'street' to create a weather-controlled interior. As the malls grew increasingly larger, they eventually offered most of the essential shops and services in one convenient location, including dentist and doctor offices, movie theaters, car repair centers, restaurants, bookstores, beauty parlors, and a wide variety of specialty and general retail stores.

The strip and regional malls answered the realities of the car and the retail needs of the suburbs so successfully that they began to threaten the continuing viability of the traditional downtowns. The central business districts throughout America fell on hard times in the midst of the post-war economic boom, while an entire generation of Americans grew up with the local mall as the only location for public social interactions and the celebration of public events. Privately owned centers of commerce had taken over the traditional role of public streets, town squares and parks in providing a setting for a public life in America.

The American middle class came of age in the 1950s. In the Eisenhower era, fully 60 per cent of Americans lived in households whose incomes were defined as middle

**256** Northgate Regional Shopping Center, Seattle, Washington, 1950, John Graham and Company

class. Where once the upper classes had defined the country's taste, and where once middle Americans were happy to mimic on a reduced scale the values of the rich and famous, now the middle classes were conducting their lives in unprecedented settings largely invented for their own realities and convenience. The baby boomers and their parents, by sheer weight of numbers and by virtue of a shared suburban culture, had begun to define their own characteristic lifestyle. So where movies between the wars had tended to focus on glamorous urban settings and upper-class lifestyles, now in the 1950s and 1960s the popular television shows portrayed middle-class family life in the suburbs. Looked at pessimistically, this new middle-class culture resulted in diminishing standards of taste as a crass popular culture began to dominate American life; looked at optimistically, we might see this as a newly confident middle-class culture seeking standards which were simply different from those that the upper-class tastemakers had long asserted.

### Renewed Expressionism

Just as the rational versions of Modernism were gaining widespread acceptance throughout the world in the early 1950s, a number of high fashion architects turned to the Expressionist strand of Modernist thinking that we have seen cropping up now and again throughout the twentieth century. Le Corbusier shocked his followers by designing the chapel of Notre-Dame-du-Haut at Ronchamp in France, whose richly sculpted shapes reflected the designer's personal artistic imagination more than they rationally answered universal problems [257]. Le Corbusier admitted that he found inspiration for the form not in the functions, as was required by the now orthodox Modernist view, but rather in a crab shell he had picked up on the beach. For a number of projects ranging from planetariums and gift shops to art museums, Frank Lloyd Wright also ignored function in favor of an unusual shape which had begun to preoccupy him before the war. In his interwar projects (as we saw in the Johnson

Wax building, for example) he turned increasingly to circles and triangles rather than to rectangles for his underlying geometry. In his quest for greater spatial effects and more powerful organic forms, Wright began to extrude the circle into the third dimension, forming a great spiral tapering upwards. This spiral became all things for all projects. In an unbuilt planetarium project in 1925, he proposed using the spiral as an approach ramp for automobiles. In a gift shop designed for V. C. Morris in San Francisco and built after the war, the ramp provided access to the second floor of display space. And in one of his most famous projects of all, the Solomon Guggenheim Museum in New York City, the ramp became the gallery itself [258]. Although the Museum offers a delightful spatial experience with its great skylight at the top of the spiral flooding the interior space with light, and with its dramatic spiral sweeping up and away from the center, it clearly did not derive from the functions of an art museum. As Wright originally designed it, the art patron would have had to stand on an incline while viewing a painting, which would have been hung sloping backwards on a curved wall. Wright had become infatuated with a shape, and then fitted various functions to it however awkwardly.

Eero Saarinen similarly sought sculptural effects for his TWA Terminal building at Kennedy Airport in New York City [259]. In looking for a rationale for his invented forms, he revived the eighteenth-century French idea of *architecture parlante*, in which a building is expected metaphorically to express its function and character. He conceived of his airport terminal as an expression of flight, manifested as a great bird-like form. Unfortunately for his intended image, though, he decided to build these curvilinear forms out of reinforced concrete, whose weight conveys a feeling on the inside more of a massive cave than of a lightweight structure about to fly away. The Modernist language of design had freed architects from traditional meanings, and had therefore allowed them to invent their own; but, as we see here, inventing one's own architectural meanings for each new building easily runs the risk of misinterpretation through unfamiliarity or miscues.

Skidmore, Owings and Merrill (SOM), who in all other respects were Miesian, also toyed with Expressionism for their Chapel at the United States Air Force Academy in Colorado Springs [260]. Where the academies at West Point and Annapolis for the older branches of the armed services were built in traditional collegiate styles like the Gothic, the newcomer Air Force founded its academy in the heyday of Modernism. SOM resisted calls to design an equally traditional campus design, finally winning approval for a Miesian campus of flat roofed and curtain walled pavilions laid out on a gridded campus plan. Only in the cadets' non-denominational chapel did the archi-

**257** Notre-Dame-du-Haut, Ronchamp, France, 1950–55, Le Corbusier

**258** Guggenheim Museum, New York City, 1956–59, Frank Lloyd Wright

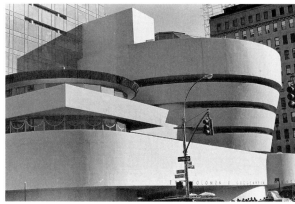

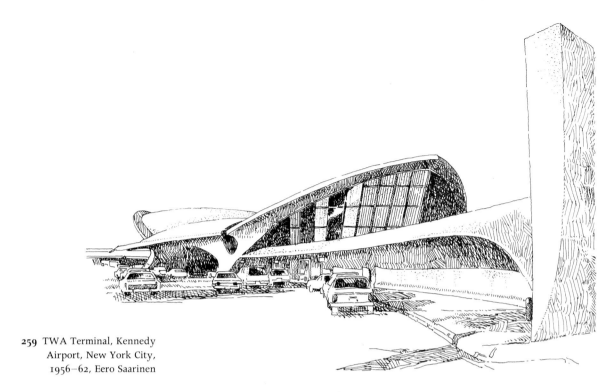

259 TWA Terminal, Kennedy
Airport, New York City,
1956–62, Eero Saarinen

tects permit themselves to deviate from this orthodox rational Modernism in favor
of something more expressionist. Like Saarinen, they sought some rationale for an
unusual shape by reviving the idea of *architecture parlante*. The high technology
spires of metal and glass seem vaguely reminiscent of high technology aeronautics,
and they point to the skies over the academy through which the cadets endlessly

260 Chapel, US Air Force
Academy, Colorado Springs,
Colorado, 1956–62, Skidmore,
Owings and Merrill

circle in practice flights. But they also partly revived the nineteenth-century idea of associationalism, in which a building explicitly refers to a traditional architectural style whose meanings are already familiar to an informed public. In this case, the relentless repetition of spiky bays refers to the nave and spires of a Gothic church, bringing with it the inevitable meaning of a religious setting. For the architectural cognoscente, the spiky glass shapes also refer to the German Expressionist crystalline forms popular after the First World War with designers like Bruno Taut.

Why did the Modernist architects in the 1950s suddenly revive Expressionism, when their predecessors between the wars had fought so hard to banish anything smacking of the idiosyncratic or the subjective? One reason we might infer is that which eventually undermined Academic Eclecticism between the wars: boredom with predictable solutions. Just as designers of Tudor houses eventually ran out of fresh ideas so, too, did the post-war generation run out of new things to do with the austere International Style box. Mies himself was content to refine the same ideas over and again, seeing no virtue in novelty for its own sake, but other designers proved to be more restless. The latter were probably more in tune with the mood of the 1950s, since by then America had largely defined itself as a consumer society. The admen between the wars had done their job well. By the 1950s the American dream had become intimately tied up with purchasing the latest versions of consumer goods, defined as much by styling as by technological improvement. A society that enthusiastically awaited the new model year at the car factories in Detroit was not going to remain content for long with the same austere International Modernist buildings.

Furthermore, despite the predominately staid and conformist mood of the Eisenhower era, there were undercurrents of Expressionism in the popular culture. Some of the youth who objected to the conspicuous affluence and social conformity of the age joined the 'beat generation', and enjoyed tweaking the noses of their parents by pursuing offbeat lifestyles, clothing fashions and musical expressions. Even the mainstream Americans, who in all other respects followed the bland norms of the period, enthusiastically drove the ostentatious cars of the period with their giant fins and loads of chrome. A society that could love these showboats was going to love a building that looked like a giant bird.

Finally, the Modernist revolution against traditional styles between the wars had started architects down a slippery slope to subjectivity that they could not resist for long. The early Modernists had rejected the rules and meanings inherent in the traditional styles, but to avoid complete subjectivity they had attempted to replace these with guidelines of their own, including deriving the form from the function or honestly responding to constructional and structural necessities. They also attached new meanings to the new forms, seeing their preferred aesthetic style as the inevitable expression of the modern age and, for many, as the proper expression of socialist reform after the First World War. But when Hitchcock and Johnson stripped the Modernist language of its socialist associations in order to popularize it in America between the wars, they inevitably weakened the connection between the forms and their shared meanings. They treated Modernism as simply a popular language of shapes which happened to follow the few rules they elucidated. But why these particular rules, subsequent architects could reasonably ask. And if the forms were now largely divorced from any inherent or shared meanings, then why could one not entirely invent one's own meanings? Forms without inherent meanings or rules can obviously become whatever the designer wishes them to be, since no one can object that the form was used improperly. Some like Saarinen and SOM still tried to attach understandable meanings to forms, while others like Le Corbusier and Frank

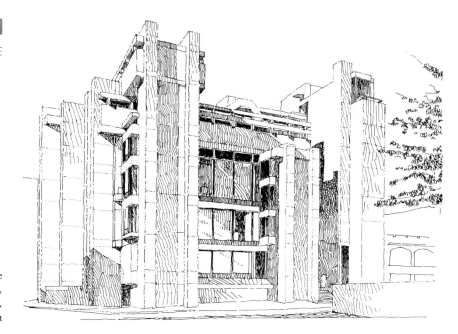

**261** Art and Architecture
Building, Yale, New Haven,
Connecticut, 1958–64,
Paul Rudolph

Lloyd Wright saw the full consequences of the Modernist idea and enjoyed making unprecedented shapes which answered no demand other than their own judgment of aesthetic delight. By the 1950s, the Modernist revolution for many had largely culminated in a conception of architecture as aesthetic shapemaking.

Many of the first Expressionist buildings in the 1950s favored the curvilinear forms we have just seen in the Ronchamp chapel, the TWA Terminal and the Guggenheim Museum. Other architects found expressive possibilities in the assertive rectilinear forms of Le Corbusier's post-war projects like the Marseille block. They admired the brutal monumentality of the forms, the thick and expressively constructed details, and the frank exposure of raw concrete. A school of architects in England known as the New Brutalists, including James Stirling, James Gowan, and Peter and Alison Smithson, experimented with similar bold forms and raw materials. In America, a good example of this expressive brutalism can be found in Paul Rudolph's Art and Architecture Building at Yale, where he was the Director of the architecture program [**261**]. Here Rudolph piled up layers of vertical and horizontal boxes, elaborately interlocking them like giant children's building blocks. Although the building is seven stories tall, the number of different levels created by these interlocking boxes approaches forty. Like Le Corbusier and the British New Brutalists, Rudolph formed the building out of cast in place concrete. But rather than leave the concrete as a frank expression of its simple boarded formwork, Rudolph elaborately prepared the forms ahead of time to shape vertical ribs on the surface of the cast walls, and then later hammered off portions of the ribs to create an even stronger texture. The guileless and inexpensive expression of constructional realities had been turned into a painstaking and expensive search for a brutal aesthetic effect. Rudolph conceived of architecture as the art of making expressive forms, publicly dismissing the functionalism of his teacher Gropius, and noting that even Mies attempted to solve only a few carefully chosen functional problems.

Just as visually expressive, but perhaps more philosophically conceived, were the later works of Louis Kahn. Kahn arrived in America from Estonia in 1905, and later studied Beaux-Arts Classicism under Paul Cret at the University of Pennsylvania in the 1920s. After years of working for other architects and struggling to find his own direction, by the 1950s he had begun to see how he could reconcile his Beaux-Arts training with Modernist principles. Like the great Classical theorists Durand and Guadet before him, he conceived of architecture as the composition of additive elements according to clear geometrical rules. Kahn updated this traditional idea by describing a plan as a society of rooms. Although he did not stress an overall bilateral symmetry as emphatically as his Classical predecessors, he nonetheless symmetrically organized many of his individual elements as well as large components of his compositions. Kahn was therefore not favorably disposed to the flowing spaces and asymmetrical compositions of many of his Modernist colleagues. Like his Classical predecessors, he also looked for suggestions within the functional program for the types of elements to be combined, and for the rules of their combination. He restated this traditional notion for modern ears by asking the question, 'what does the building want to be?'

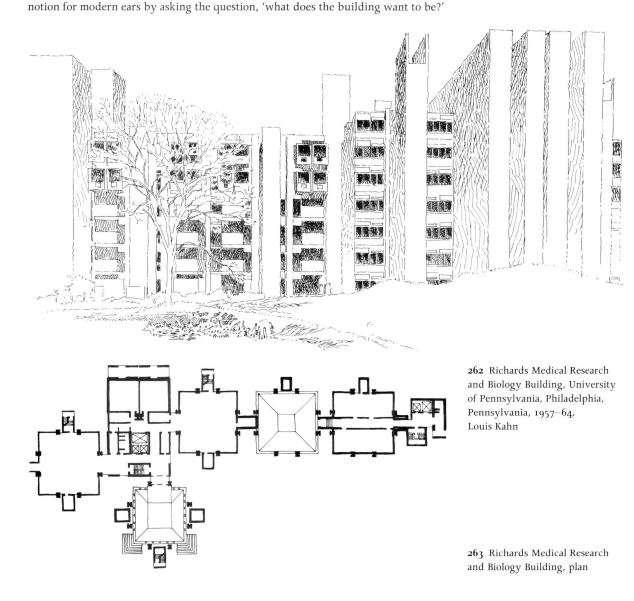

**262** Richards Medical Research and Biology Building, University of Pennsylvania, Philadelphia, Pennsylvania, 1957–64, Louis Kahn

**263** Richards Medical Research and Biology Building, plan

In the Richards Medical Research and Biology Building at the University of Pennsylvania, Kahn decided that the building wanted to be a cluster of six linked towers [262]. Each tower housed a 47 foot square laboratory space on each floor, intentionally kept small to encourage an intimate working environment for groups of researchers. We see in the plan how Kahn combined both the axial arrangements of Classicism, and the asymmetrical pinwheel arrangement popular with earlier Modernists like Gropius [263]. Also modern was his realization that a contemporary building like a research center had to accommodate a vast web of vertical and horizontal service pipes and ducts. Rather than bury these within the fabric of the building as most traditional and even many modern architects had attempted to do, Kahn celebrated them by bundling them together into prominent brick service towers standing adjacent to the laboratories themselves. Kahn described the two types of towers as 'servant' and 'served', a distinction which he used a number of times in other buildings. To provide horizontal runs for the services at each floor, Kahn and his engineer August Komendant devised an elaborate structural system of Vierendeel trusses which work without diagonal struts, and which therefore allow more room for the passage of large ducts and pipes. These trusses also allowed Kahn to pull the vertical supports back from the corners of each tower, in essence dramatically cantilevering the corners into space. Even though each component of the building logically derived from solving a particular functional problem, the overall effect of the total composition was a visually complex, delightfully picturesque form. Although Kahn spoke and wrote about architecture in terms of cryptic and sometimes indecipherable aphorisms, he nonetheless sought philosophical, functional and technological reasons for his expressive forms. In this regard, he stood in marked contrast to other form-givers of the 1950s like Rudolph, who offered little justification for their invented shapes other than personal visual delight.

## The revolutionary 1960s

### Culture in turmoil

The Expressionist challenges to the orthodoxy of mainstream International Modernism in the 1950s anticipated a fundamental reorientation of cultures and values throughout the world in the 1960s. While the 1950s – particularly in America – were characterized by a retreat from social idealism and a general adherence to conservative cultural conventions, the next decade swung to the opposite extreme. Cultural conventions were questioned, social injustices were attacked, and radical new ideas were proposed for all aspects of society, ranging from flamboyant Mod and hippie clothing fashions to visionary proposals for walking cities and rural communes. This remarkable period of great energy and zeal fundamentally realigned American culture and eventually its architecture.

The new mood swept in with John F. Kennedy's election as President in 1960. Objecting to the social complacency of the Eisenhower years, he called on Americans to revive their sense of idealism. Although he enjoyed only limited success before his assassination in 1963, his successor Lyndon B. Johnson moved quickly during the period of national mourning to enact a number of sweeping reforms and federal programs which he coined the Great Society. His updated version of Roosevelt's New

Deal included a Civil Rights Act banning racial discrimination, national health programs for the old and poor, a National Foundation for the Arts, a federal department of Housing and Urban Development (HUD), and a War on Poverty which redistributed income to those at the bottom of America's economic ladder. Johnson received a compelling mandate for these social programs in 1964 by winning the largest election victory since Roosevelt's in 1936.

However, this domestic program was soon overshadowed by the escalating war in Vietnam. Like his post-war presidential predecessors, Johnson believed that America had to stop the spread of communism wherever it appeared. Confident in the technological superiority of America, he committed American troops to the defense of South Vietnam against the efforts of the North to reunify the country under communism. By 1968, over half a million American troops had been deployed, and one and a half times more bomb tonnage had been dropped on Southeast Asia than on all fronts in the Second World War. But America's technology did not prevail. As the war dragged on with no end in sight, as the television news brought the carnage nightly into American homes, and as the war's cost drove up domestic inflation, America split bitterly between the hawks and doves. The former urged further escalation of the war to bring it to a decisive conclusion, while the latter doubted that America had any national security at stake and urged peace. Violent anti-war protests erupted throughout America in the last three years of the decade, particularly after young white middle-class Americans were drafted to join the poor whites and blacks on the battlefields. American culture seemed to unravel even further in 1968, when the assassination of the civil rights leader Martin Luther King spurred violent race riots from Detroit to Los Angeles, and when John Kennedy's brother Robert was assassinated during a political campaign.

These upheavals both reflected and exacerbated a broad mood of rebellion in the 1960s, which eventually found its way into ideas about architecture. The call to idealism unleashed powerful expectations that society could be improved and inequities banished, particularly among the baby boomers who came of age in the 1960s. Anything that stood in the way of such an obviously virtuous goal as social equality was seen as repressive or reactionary, and was vigorously attacked or dismissed. Further fueling this rebellious attitude was a rising cult of personal individualism. Perhaps paradoxically in this age of heightened concern for fellow human beings, many sought first and foremost to fulfill their own personal potential and to seek their own happiness. Anything that stood in the way of this was also seen as constraining and repressive, even those shared norms of behavior which had evolved to help people live together in some social accord. Although this conflation of individualism and heightened social cohesion is paradoxical, it is not unprecedented; we saw it before in the nineteenth-century Romantic movement. And so for a complex mix of social and personal reasons which sometimes harmonized and sometimes clashed, virtually every social institution and cultural assumption was challenged in the 1960s. The popular youth culture erupted in a cacophony of wild sights and sounds, turning upside down every traditional assumption about dress, music and behavior. A counterculture movement sought alternatives to the traditional family structure, and developed communes like those which we saw in the utopias at the beginning of the nineteenth century. The civil rights movement and an emerging women's movement highlighted more forcefully the continuing social inequities in American culture, demanding sweeping changes in American attitudes and laws. A new environmental movement focused attention on the alarming consequences for the natural environment of uncontrolled technology. These confrontational attitudes inevitably sparked a conservative backlash, distressingly splitting the country along racial, sexual, political and generational lines.

The mood of rebellion challenged not only the social and political status quo, but also the claim of professionals to possess special expertise beyond the comprehension of lay people. Many individuals began to realize that professional judgments often involved making decisions about values, and values are not matters to be left to professionals alone. Indeed, the bitter conflicts over society's fundamental values during this period led many people to suspect the values to which their professionals adhered. The decisions of military leaders, doctors and architects, among others, were increasingly challenged as ideologically tainted. Since its inception, the Modern Movement in architecture had attempted to reshape the built environment without consulting those whose lives would be transformed in consequence, all the while claiming that the design professionals knew best. As the professions in general came under attack, the resistance to this paternalistic attitude mounted both within the architectural profession itself and in society at large. Eventually, as we will see, the profession and its beliefs substantially transformed in response.

### Modernism and its critics

By the 1960s, the Modern Movement had come to represent the establishment. It was the official style for the government, for banks and corporations, for churches, and for the houses of successful business people and middle-class suburbanites. Indeed, Modernism had so thoroughly entered the mainstream of architectural thinking and social acceptance that its proponents no longer felt compelled to offer philosophical or functional justifications for its use. Furthermore, the schools of architecture had so thoroughly shifted to the Modernist point of view that students were hardly aware of the earlier architectural traditions overthrown in the Modernist revolution. Yet in this period of clashes between the status quo and the forces of change, the once revolutionary movement itself became a target of reform. A number of alternative architectural movements sprang up in the 1960s to challenge the Modernists on a number of grounds ranging from aesthetic to social. The story of architecture in the 1960s is therefore one of Modernism at the zenith of its success, and a number of reform movements barking at its heels.

The prominent Modernists in the 1960s, including Skidmore, Owings and Merrill, Kevin Roche and John Dinkeloo, and I. M. Pei, continued to develop forms according to the broad principles which we have seen informing Modernism since its inception. They valued technology and its expressive possibilities, they studiously avoided any reference to historical styles or familiar forms, and they preferred minimal detailing and plain surfaces. Since the Expressionist movement of the 1950s had legitimized the idea of architecture as personal expression, the prominent Modernists in the 1960s and early 1970s mostly conceived of design as sculptural form-making for which there were few – if any – universally accepted rules or guiding principles.

Few mainstream Modernists in the 1960s and early 1970s followed Saarinen in developing an explicit *architecture parlante*. That is, they did not seek forms which metaphorically expressed the building's functions like a bird in flight, but rather wished instead to treat architecture as abstracted form without obvious or previously understood meanings. At the same time, many Modernists sought striking and memorable images for each building they designed. The Transamerica Pyramid in San Francisco by William Pereira Associates summed up this attitude [264]. Here the

264 Transamerica Pyramid,
San Francisco, California, 1972,
William L. Pereira Associates

form was so unprecedented that no one could attach a pre-existing meaning to it, yet it was so distinctive that the corporation it housed could and did use it as a readily identifiable trademark. The architects had invented a new form and a meaning which attached to it alone. No justification for this unusual shape other than visual distinction can be advanced, since the shape gave away valuable floor space and achieved little more structural stability than could have been achieved with a rectangular box.

Many Modernists in this period continued to celebrate technology, and often looked for forms as logical by-products of dramatic structures or constructions. For the Federal Reserve Bank Building completed in 1972 in Minneapolis, Minnesota, for example, Gunnar Birkerts avoided columns in the basement by suspending the entire building from two catenary cables which were slung from concrete towers 275 feet apart. Buckminster Fuller proffered even more radical technological ideas. Between the wars he had proposed the mass production of houses based on systems like those used for automobile manufacturing. After the war he expanded his vision of a high technology society to include covering entire cities with geodesic domes in order to control their climates. Although geodesic domes offer a particularly elegant structural system in that they provide maximum strength for minimum weight, Fuller's idea for artificial climates now seems like an elegant solution in search of an unperceived problem. Nonetheless, he had an opportunity to build a prototype of the idea for the US Pavilion at the Montreal Exposition in 1967, where it represented America's continuing faith during the 1960s in high technology [265]. An equally

**265** US Pavilion, Montreal Exposition, Montreal, Canada, 1967, Buckminster Fuller

**266** Sears Tower, Chicago, Illinois, 1970–74, Skidmore, Owings and Merrill

impressive technological achievement was the Sears Tower in Chicago, Illinois, by Skidmore, Owings and Merrill [266]. For a time the tallest building in the world at 1450 feet, the Sears Tower resisted the considerable forces acting to overturn it by bundling together a variety of structural tubes of different heights. Built just after the remarkable accomplishment of landing a man on the moon, the Sears Tower represented one of the last efforts in Modern America to push building technology to its limits.

While these expressive and technologically derived forms dominated commercial architecture production in the 1960s, a number of other movements emerged to challenge the status quo. One attack came from Peter Eisenman, Richard Meier, Charles Gwathmey, Michael Graves and John Hejduk, who bridled at the lack of intellectual rigor and at the apparently capricious Expressionism in contemporary Modernism. Calling themselves the New York Five, they retraced the route of Modernism back to a fork in the road where they believed the movement had gone astray, and then attempted to follow a truer path. For them the truer path led from Le Corbusier's austere white houses of the 1920s, including the Villa Savoye at Poissy, and the Stein House at Garches. They admired the rational clarity, the powerful geometry in plan and elevation, the play of the enclosing wall against the regular grid of columns and the intellectual rationales which Le Corbusier had used to justify his forms in the early fight for Modernism. For them, this was architecture with logic, purpose and a powerful presence. Richard Meier's Smith House shows how this Le Corbusier revival restated the precisely controlled cubic forms, and recreated an image of an intellectually pure and manufactured object standing in contrast to nature [267]. Nothing in the building seems willful or capricious; everything seems to follow from a logical or conceptual idea. For example, the entire building divides into two zones, a solidly walled back which encloses private functions like bedrooms and bathrooms, and a glazed front which encloses the more public living spaces [268].

Peter Eisenman derived even greater abstractions from this tradition. He conceived of architecture as a grand game of geometrical transformations. He might begin with a pure cube, for example, then twist another gridded cube at 45 degrees, and then slice the ensemble with planar walls [269]. Into the resulting form he then fitted functions which were intentionally secondary to the logical system itself [270]. A column might crash through the middle of a room, or a floor might split apart along the lines of a grid. In this sense the forms were just as willful as the Expressionist mainstream to which the Le Corbusian revival had reacted, although they seemed to follow inexorably from a logical geometrical system.

A more fundamental challenge to the Modernist mainstream came from Robert Venturi. Where the New York Five had objected to the lack of intellectual clarity in contemporary design, and had opted for a more austere and rational flavor of the Modernist idiom, Venturi objected to the aesthetic assumptions and tastes of Modernist architecture altogether. In 1962 he wrote a 'gentle manifesto' which he published in 1966 as *Complexity and Contradiction in Architecture*. Claiming to speak only as a practicing architect and not as a critic or theorist, he chastised the Modernist movement for its rejection of tradition. He reminded architects that we live in a cultural heritage which not only nourishes us, but also provides useful precedents upon which new design ideas can be based. In defending the essential role of tradition, he rejected one of the most fundamental principles upon which Modernism had fought its revolution. Venturi then attacked another cherished principle of Modernism, that simplicity and rational clarity are the essential hallmarks of the modern twentieth

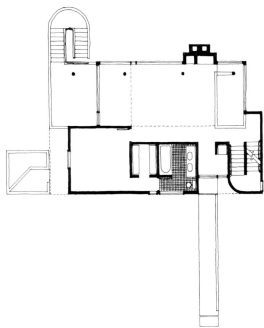

267 Smith House, Darien,
Connecticut, 1965–67,
Richard Meier

268 Smith House, plan

century. He wrote that he personally preferred the visually complex periods like the Mannerist, Baroque and Rococo, where 'messy vitality' prevailed over order, and where the 'diverse and sophisticated' predominated over the primitive and elementary. For Venturi, ambiguity, complexity, and contradiction more accurately reflected the modern age. His book offered numerous examples from history of buildings which possessed these qualities, and then presented a few of his own designs as evidence of how these visual principles might be updated.

The New York Five largely wished to treat architecture as form without content. For them, designing consisted of manipulating geometry and shapes, without concern for the meanings that might have attached to forms in the past, or that might be read into their new forms in the future. Aesthetic pleasure came from one's intellectual and visceral reactions to these abstract shapes alone. Venturi, in contrast, revived an interest in architectural meaning. He explicitly referred to traditional forms and images which, through familiarity and convention, had attached to themselves commonly understood meanings. A prominent gable roof means 'house', for example, or a giant billboard means 'shop'. For Venturi, the aesthetic joy came from unusual juxtapositions or inversions of familiar forms, in much the same way that we obtain pleasure from poetry. So where the New York Five wished to restrict architecture's language to syntax alone, Venturi wished to add in the rich vocabulary accumulated over centuries of architectural history. In essence, Venturi proposed to revive the manner in which architects had designed since ancient times. Before the Modernist revolution, we will recall, most architects in history chose a style or a particular detail with its conventional meanings well in mind. In the 1960s, the two views represented by the New York Five and Venturi came to represent two fundamentally different ideas about the direction in which architecture should head. The debate was polemically framed at the time as the Whites versus the Grays.

Venturi's house for his mother shows how far his ideas took him from the mainstream Modernists and the Whites [271]. Here we have a design that refers so

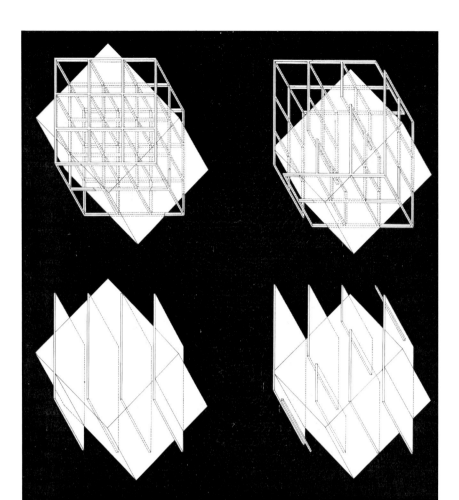

**269** House III: Miller House, Lakeville, Connecticut, 1969–70, Peter Eisenman

**270** House III: Miller House, exterior

**271** Vanna Venturi House,
Chestnut Hill, Pennsylvania,
1962–65, Robert Venturi

explicitly to a traditional gable roof house form that it almost parodies the idea. The gable has become the entire house, which stands only one room deep behind the façade. And yet all is not what it seems. The symmetrical entry opens onto a blank wall, which forces the visitor to turn abruptly right and discover the true front door hidden at right angles behind the façade. Another turn once inside the building brings one onto an axis parallel to, but offset from, the one running through the symmetrical middle. This was a favorite device of Sir Edwin Lutyens for elaborating the path through the building, and for enhancing the visual delights and surprises within. The overall symmetry also broke down in the placement of the windows, in which a horizontal strip window on one side balanced a small and large rectangle on the other. Defiantly challenging the Modernist prohibition against applied decoration and ornament, Venturi ran a thin horizontal band around the building, and sprang a false and broken arch over the entry. The latter explicitly revived the Mannerist sensibilities of the sixteenth century, because it perversely juxtaposed an arch onto a beam which carries its weight according to an entirely different structural principle. Many Modernists were bewildered and even angry about this little house that pointedly subverted the tenets they had long held dear. Although few architects in the 1960s followed Venturi in pursuing these sometimes arcane visual effects, we will see in the next chapter that these ideas eventually helped engender the Postmodern movement in the late 1970s.

While the Modernists had long decried the visually messy shopping strips and suburbs that had mushroomed after the war, Venturi pronounced the architecture of the American Main Street 'almost all right'. His *Learning from Las Vegas*, written with his wife Denise Scott Brown and Stephen Izenour in 1972, highlighted the rich visual possibilities in the contemporary American built environment. The authors admired these commonplace – and sometimes even kitsch – images partly because they embodied the desirable qualities of complexity, ambiguity and contradiction, and partly because they represented a straightforward and 'ordinary' approach to design. Where the Modernists had long attempted to redesign the world through heroic and grandiose schemes, and had long ignored or despised the values and tastes of those who would live with the consequences, Venturi and his co-authors directed unprecedented attention to the contemporary American vernacular environment where those values and tastes had already found expression. This not only represented one of the first influential shots across the bows of Modernism's paternalistic

attitude, but also gave an intellectual stamp of approval to a reality which many Americans had by now thoroughly taken for granted.

This enthusiasm for the vernacular in this anti-heroic age found further expression in the early works of Charles Moore, Donlyn Lyndon, William Turnbull and Richard Whitaker (MLTW). Working in northern California, they inherited from Maybeck, Coxhead, William Wurster and Joseph Esherick a continuing interest in local vernacular traditions and a regionally appropriate style. For the Sea Ranch condominiums north of San Francisco, they sought an image expressive of a ranch on the windswept California coastline, and found it in the local vernacular wooden barns [272]. The picturesque jumble of mono-pitched forms clad in weathered wood conveyed an aura of a utilitarian compound which had stood at the top of the cliffs for generations. At first glance, the hand of a sophisticated architect is intentionally nowhere to be found. Yet on closer inspection we find striking spatial effects at play. Taking a clue from Kahn's concepts of the servant and served, and of forms within forms, MLTW inserted free-standing platforms on columns into each condominium. These functionally provided bedrooms on the platform and living spaces underneath, while aesthetically they offered rich and unexpected surprises within the utilitarian box. The mono-pitched roofs and weathered boarding of Sea Ranch subsequently inspired a slew of 'vernacular' forms throughout America, most notably in the Western resort towns.

Like Venturi, Moore enjoyed the sophisticated effects of the Baroque and Rococo, and explored how they might be accomplished with modern materials and within modest budgets. Along with Venturi, he helped develop what is sometimes called the Pop Architecture movement. This paralleled the 1960s Pop Art movement of artists like Roy Lichtenstein and Andy Warhol, who had reacted against the Abstract Expressionist movement of the 1950s by building sophisticated images out of elements taken from popular culture. The architectural equivalent of posterized soup cans and Marilyn Monroe portraits became, in the hands of Moore, bold supergraphic paintings and neon tubing on equally bold cardboard-like cutout forms [273]. Although the forms are constructed of the cheapest possible material in the quickest possible way, the layering and fusion of spaces and surfaces clearly recall similar spatial effects in the Baroque tradition. MLTW's design for the University of California's Kresge College in Santa Cruz attempted to create a small village in the forest with a meandering medieval street lined by dormitories and classrooms, all formed out of walls like stage sets [274].

272 Sea Ranch, Sonoma County, California, 1964–65, Moore Lyndon Turnbull Whitaker

273 Sea Ranch, interior

274 Kresge College, University of California, Santa Cruz, California, 1972–74, Moore Lyndon Turnbull Whitaker

Despite their aesthetic and philosophical differences, the New York Five, Venturi and Moore were all still mainly interested in the sophistications of high fashion design. Others in the 1960s responded more fully to the energy and revolutionary spirit of the counterculture movement, which deeply distrusted elitism and fashion. Like the Romantics in the nineteenth century with which this movement had much affinity, the participants in the counterculture movement wished to heal the ruptures in contemporary life between man and nature, and between individuals and society. They also espoused social egalitarianism. How they proposed to accomplish these goals varied as much as similar efforts in the nineteenth century. At one extreme, some members of the counterculture retreated from urban society into rural settings, where they could be closer to the land. Many formed communes which they believed would foster closer social integration and equality. Like their nineteenth-century predecessors, they preferred hand-made arts and crafts to the artificialities of polished society and high technology. Some found their role models in the traditional Native American cultures, and even lived in tipis. Others built funky cabins and communal structures of roughly hewn and sometimes elaborately carved wood. These rustic works represented a romantic look back to an idyllic past when everyone was thought to have lived in harmony with nature and with each other.

At the other extreme, some members of the counterculture took on a visionary role, and imagined an equally idyllic future utopia when their social agenda had been achieved. The English architectural group called Archigram, including Peter Cook, Ron Herron and Mike Webb, turned to a futurist technology rather than to the arts and crafts for their ideal images. They conceived of society as loose clusters of high-tech nomads, roaming from city to city and from pop concerts to Woodstock happenings. Drawing on images of Modernist megastructures, pop culture fashions and space age technology, they designed cities that walked on giant legs, electric tomatoes into which one could plug in and turn on, personal spaceship-like pods that provided one's entire shelter and nourishment, and cities to which components could be added or removed as needs changed [275]. This was sci-fi technology placed in the service of the tune in, turn on, and drop out generation. In the United States, Paolo Soleri combined the sci-fi and the arts and crafts visions for his Arcosanti settlement in the remote Arizona desert. He conceived of a future communal civilization

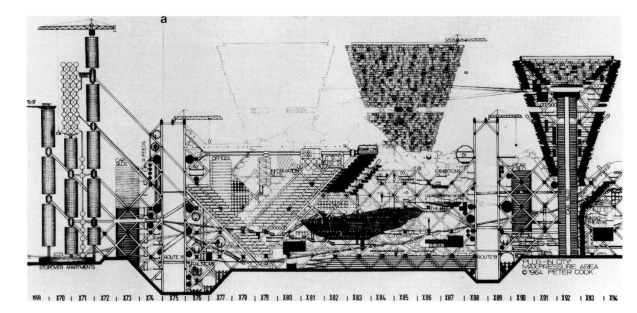

living in harmony with nature, and inhabiting a variety of hi-tech cities designed like futurist space stations [276]. He named these 'arcologies' to signify their close integration with the natural ecology. Despite the space age imagery of his drawings, he began constructing the first prototype at Arcosanti with low-tech technologies and a distinctly arts and crafts character.

The aesthetic preoccupations of the high fashion architects came under even more sustained attack from two new initiatives called the Environmental Design and Design Methodology movements. As part of the social concerns of the 1960s, a number of thinkers – particularly in the universities – stressed the social nature of architecture. Pressing the functionalist argument of the Modernists to its extreme, they conceived of architecture as a deterministic system in which certain spatial arrangements inevitably caused certain social and personal behaviors. The right environments lead to healthful behaviors, the wrong ones foster social ills. These

**275** Plug-in City, 1964, Peter Cook

**276** Arcology, 1969, Paolo Soleri

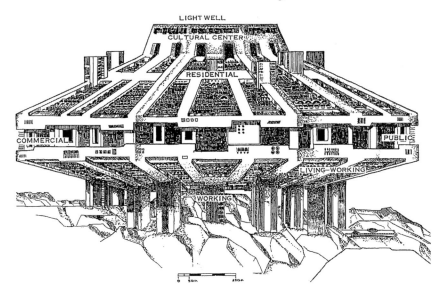

had nothing to do with style or aesthetics; indeed, concerning oneself with image meant that one was not attending to the more serious social and behavioral issues at stake. Advocates of this view proposed to abandon architecture's traditional alliance with the arts, and to redefine it as a rigorous science.

They proposed to move on two fronts. First, they would develop a body of scientific knowledge about the relationships between people and their environments. What spatial configurations would encourage people to talk to each other, or feel happy, or become more productive? The new functionalists banded together with sociologists and psychologists to study people and settings, the results of which were published in the newly established academic paraphernalia of scholarly journals and conferences. In 1970, Harold Proshansky, William Ittelson and Leanne Rivlin compiled the first generation of this work in *Environmental Psychology: Man and his Physical Setting*. Second, the new functionalists would develop methods of design by which this body of information could be rationally applied to what they now called design 'problems'. The first methodologists based their ideas on notions gleaned from the philosophy of science, and from the operations research developed during the war. Horst Rittel initiated much of this work in Germany in the 1950s, while an English school including Christopher Alexander, Geoffrey Broadbent, Tom Markus and J. Christopher Jones elaborated the ideas in the early 1960s. When Rittel and Alexander emigrated to the United States, the movement put down roots in a number of American schools of architecture, most notably MIT and Berkeley. Alexander's 1964 *Notes on the Synthesis of Form* provided the inspiration for many subsequent methodologists and designers who also sought a rational design method independent of aesthetics. His method divided design into two parts, an initial analysis of the functional requirements and their logical relationships, and a subsequent synthesis of these requirements into architectural form. By the late 1960s, architecture students throughout the country were following some variation on this idea even when, as it turned out, the method did not generate convincing architectural forms. Student projects based on this method usually remained abstract diagrams of relationships. Nonetheless, the design methodologists remained confident at the end of the decade that they would eventually find a workable scientific method free of art.

Although the Environmental Design movement continued to place its faith in science and technology, others in American society in the latter half of the 1960s began to have doubts. The Cuban missile crisis and the nuclear arms race between America and the Soviet Union brought home for many the very real threat of annihilation by technology. The vast technological superiority of America in the Vietnam War seemed increasingly incapable of bringing the war to a conclusion. And the emerging environmental movement had shown how industrial processes polluted and defoliated the planet. For many, technology was less something to be celebrated and now more to be feared. This changing perspective caused many to look at their built environment afresh. Urban Renewal and Modernist redevelopment had swept away large parts of the central cities in the name of technology and progress, but the results were nothing to celebrate. Life in the housing projects had deteriorated further still, while the Modernist buildings once celebrated for their brutal frankness and simplicity now seemed shoddy and inhuman. Many began to prefer a run-down warehouse with some style and character to a modern replacement with blank walls and stained concrete. The historic preservation movement emerged in this period, to fight redevelopment and to protect and preserve America's earlier architectural heritage. Sometimes this meant preserving old buildings as museums, more often it meant adaptively reusing and updating old buildings for new purposes.

277 Ghirardelli Square,
San Francisco, California, 1965,
Bernardi and Emmons with
Lawrence Halprin Associates

In San Francisco, Bernardi and Emmons along with Lawrence Halprin and Associates rebuilt an old chocolate factory into an upscale shopping center, complete with
a traditional plaza [277]. Throughout America, people rediscovered the aesthetic
virtues of the pre-Modern styles, and restored older homes to their original character
rather than modernizing or replacing them altogether. Particularly popular in this
exuberant period were the gingerbreaded Victorian piles, the stylistic antithesis of
everything for which Modernism had stood.

We have seen in this chapter how the revolutionary Modernist movement – long in
gestation – finally triumphed throughout the world in the post-war era. Its success
coincided with a dramatic economic and population boom that allowed it to reconstruct much of the built environment in its own image. By the end of the 1960s
it seemed so securely ensconced in the schools of architecture and in professional
practice that its proponents could believe they had permanently won the war to
replace the traditional styles. But in the moment of their triumph, movements were
afoot to revive the very ideas which they had worked so hard to overthrow. As we
will see in the next chapter, the end of Modernist dominance came more quickly
than anyone at the time could have imagined.

# POSTMODERN CULTURE
## 1973–98

INTERPRETING the recent past, as many historians have pointed out, is an enterprise often doomed to failure. With insufficient historical perspective, one cannot yet see which contemporary trends will quietly fade away, and which will provide the foundations for significant and lasting developments. It is always entertaining for this reason to read the final chapter of histories written over a decade or two ago, and to see how often they misjudged the significance of recent developments in their own time. Architectural histories finished in the early 1970s often

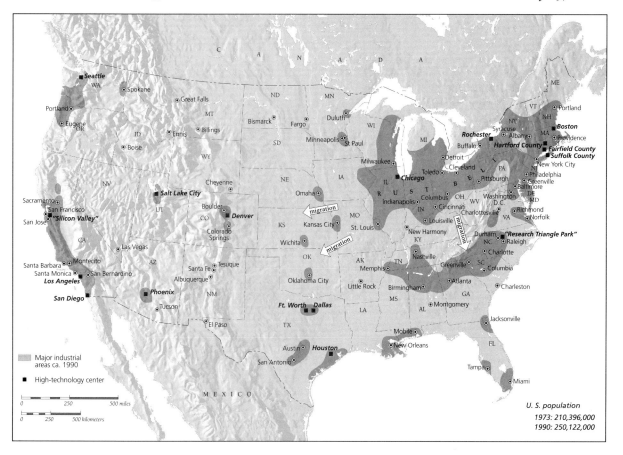

Major industrial areas ca. 1990

■ High-technology center

0    250    500 miles

0    250    500 kilometers

U. S. population

1973: 210,396,000
1990: 250,122,000

portrayed Modernism as a healthy movement in its prime, for example, when in fact the style rapidly declined only a few years later. I am fully aware that this final chapter will similarly entertain future generations, who will wonder how I could have failed to see the true significance of cultural and architectural developments in the last quarter of the twentieth century.

With this reality in mind, I will nonetheless sketch out the major trends that seem to have shaped American culture and architecture in the last two decades. Broadly speaking, American society entered a new stage of development in the early 1970s, whose architectural expressions we now call Postmodern. This name attempts to convey the idea that the architecture in this period superseded Modernism in some respects, while still continuing to accept some of its underlying tenets in others. Although some Modernist notions continued in this period, the Modernist paradigm no longer dominated architectural thinking or production as thoroughly as it had done since the end of the Second World War. And with the Modernist king dead, a number of philosophical and stylistic movements arose to claim the throne. At the time of writing, American culture and its designers face an almost bewildering number of architectural choices, many overlapping and several diametrically opposing each other. This chapter will try to unravel some of the complexities.

## The deflated 1970s

### Cultural retrenchment

The energy driving the cultural revolution in the 1960s rapidly burned out at the beginning of the next decade, for several reasons. First of all, the Vietnam War continued to tear the country apart over fundamental questions about America's role and responsibilities. Richard Nixon won the 1968 election partly by appealing to the 'Silent Majority' who resented the cultural upheaval, and partly by pledging to end the Vietnam War as soon as possible. To achieve 'peace with honor' he nonetheless escalated the war, sparking even more violent student protests in 1970 that resulted in six shooting deaths on university campuses. Warfare seemed to be breaking out between the generations and between the hawks and doves. And yet for all the trouble it caused at home, the military escalation could not turn the tide. America ignominiously lost its first war on the collapse of Saigon in 1975. Recriminations over this unprecedented defeat soured the country's mood, while the returning veterans were either pointedly ignored or treated with contempt. America lost confidence in its abilities when its vast technology seemingly failed to prevail against a peasant society.

Further contributing to America's sour mood in this period were a series of scandals in the Nixon administration, ranging from his Vice President's conviction for tax evasion, to his own involvement in a 'dirty tricks' campaign waged by his staffers against his political enemies. Nixon's attempted cover-up of illegal activities in the Watergate affair led to articles of impeachment in the Congress and finally to his forced resignation in 1974. Although the system of checks and balances in the American government had successfully reined in an imperial president who had extensively abused his power and authority, the scandal caused many in the country to lose faith in America's most fundamental institutions. The governmental authority that had pulled America through the Great Depression and the Second World War was no longer to be trusted. In addition, the social idealism and the high expectations for reform which had inspired many Americans in the 1960s came hard up against coarser human realities in this period of scandals, leading to profound disappointment and then cynicism.

As if this were not enough, America's support for its traditional ally Israel in the 1973 Arab-Israeli war led to a devastating oil embargo by OPEC (Organization of Petroleum Exporting Countries). America's post-Second World War economic boom and lavish lifestyle demanded so much energy that by the 1970s 6 per cent of the world's population consumed one-third of the world's fuel. Most of this came from non-renewable mineral resources including petroleum and natural gas, of which 30 per cent was imported from the Middle East. When OPEC suddenly turned off the pipeline, America's boom finally busted. The price of fuel soared, the value of the dollar fell, inflation rose to 12 per cent, and America suffered the worst recession since the Great Depression. The technology that once was going to solve the world's problems had seemingly ground to a halt, held hostage to politics half a world away. Even a concerted effort to build nuclear power plants as replacements for oil came to grief after a potentially catastrophic accident at the Three Mile Island nuclear reactor plant near Harrisburg, Pennsylvania in 1979.

All of these factors fundamentally changed America's outlook after the mid-1970s. The country turned to more conservative domestic policies, rejecting the big government ideas of Roosevelt, Kennedy and Johnson. It retreated from its international obligations, chastened and angry at its defeat. It turned away from social idealism, disappointed at the limited successes and tired of exerting the personal energy it required. And it cooled its love affair with high technology after the setbacks in Vietnam, the tribulations of the 1973 oil crisis, and the nuclear energy disappointments. President Carter described this dour mood as a 'crisis of the American spirit'. In the more conservative social climate, many attempted to revive the traditional values that were questioned or overthrown in the rebellious 1960s. The 'Moral Majority' that helped sweep Ronald Reagan into power in 1980 espoused a conservative social agenda including reviving prayer in schools and outlawing abortions, for example. Many others resented the civil rights and the women's movements for attempting to alter the balance of social power.

However, these conservative tendencies did not turn back the clock altogether. The 1960s had permanently broken down the cultural conventions of the 1950s, allowing more Americans to develop and follow their own codes of conduct in matters of speech, clothing and behavior. Although some exercised their new freedoms more responsibly than others, few were willing to give up the liberating spirit of individuality for what they now saw as artificially imposed and constraining conventions. And once the racial minorities and women had tasted greater equality of opportunity and treatment, the former were not going to return to the back of the bus, and the latter were not going to return to the kitchen unless they chose to. Both groups capitalized on their new freedom to enter businesses and professions from which they had formerly been discouraged or excluded. The number of women earning professional architecture degrees multiplied from 3.3 per cent of the total in 1963 to 37.6 per cent in 1993.

This continuing emphasis on individual freedom inevitably broke down the old idea of America as a melting pot into which everyone happily assimilated, and encouraged instead greater cultural diversity. People began to pursue their own agendas, and were more forthright in demanding that their needs be attended to. Many began to identify themselves secondarily with some abstract idea of America, and primarily with subgroups in the country with whom they felt more cultural affinity. Now one was Italian-American, or Native-American, or African-American. The class structures also hardened in this period. For many, the reduced economic opportunities destroyed the American dream that one could always achieve a higher standard of living through hard work. For the first time, the younger generation of Americans could not reasonably expect that they would achieve a higher standard than their parents, much less achieve the standard in which they had grown up. Many began to realize that they belonged to a particular social class from which they would not be able to move, and whose values were quite distinct from the others. If ever there were a common American outlook, by the late 1970s it had been replaced by a number of competing and often acrimonious viewpoints. The multiplicity of architectural styles in the 1970s and 1980s, which we will discuss below, derive in no small part from this multiplicity of values in the society at large.

### Modernism in eclipse

So where did these substantial cultural changes leave the Modernist architectural style? It had closely associated itself with technology and progress, and now both were suspect. It saw itself as an instrument for social change and improvement, and now America had grown tired of reform movements. It mostly celebrated a rational, orderly world, but Americans had just suffered upheavals most irrational and disorderly. And although the orthodox Modernist theory stressed objective and universal truths which held true for all places and people, now America had begun to celebrate cultural diversity. Modernism was about to be hoist with its own philosophical petard. The Modernist movement had correctly recognized that the world changed in the beginning of the twentieth century, and had demanded a new architectural expression commensurate with the new outlook. They explicitly con-nected a world view with its own appropriate architecture. However, it never occurred to most Modernists in the heat of their revolution that the world might change again. Their fundamental values and outlook now stood in relation to the 1970s and 1980s as Beaux-Arts Classicism stood in relation to the 1940s. By their own argument, the culture needed a new architectural expression.

We saw in the last chapter how a few avant-garde architects and theorists in the mid-1960s had begun to challenge Modernist forms and theories. By the early 1970s a wider spectrum of Americans and Europeans turned against the style. People complained about their bland and even ugly Modernist environments, while social critics like Oscar Newman blamed the forms and layouts of the style for the rise in crime in Modernist housing projects. In 1972, the city of St Louis blew up its Modernist Pruitt-Igoe housing project. Originally designed in 1951 by Minoru Yamasaki accord-ing to Le Corbusier's principles of housing and urbanism, the project consisted of the usual Modernist high-rise slab blocks with 'streets in the air'. And although it won an award from the American Institute of Architects when it was first designed, by the early 1970s the crime and vandalism had so escalated out of control that the city decided it would be cheaper to demolish the project than to continue throwing money at it. The architectural critic Charles Jencks later dated the death of Modern architecture to the precise moment when Pruitt-Igoe exploded, because the event publicly and violently acknowledged the failure of the entire Modernist agenda.

Less melodramatic but no less significant was the failure of the Design Methodo-logy and the Environmental Design movements. Although these movements origin-ally emerged as critiques of contemporary Modernism, they nonetheless attempted to fulfill the original Modernist promise of functional architecture based on scientific principles. Unfortunately, a decade of research in American and European university departments of architecture, psychology and sociology did not produce methods or a body of knowledge that substantially helped practicing architects to design better buildings. The methods never adequately captured the complexities of the design process; and although the empirical research offered a clearer understanding of how people use buildings, it was not presented in a form that architects could easily employ when designing new buildings. Even architects who had originally supported this research agenda eventually grew disillusioned with the results. Its failure therefore seemed to demonstrate even further the collapse of the Modernist point of view.

No style ever suddenly finishes overnight. Architects and the building industry have usually invested heavily in certain ideas, and individual clients do not always change their own values in lockstep with broader cultural changes. Many architects consequently continued to build in the Modernist style well into the 1970s and 1980s. However, these final expressions of Modernism sufficiently changed in the new era that we can recognize them as a distinct subcategory of the Modernist style, which we typically call Late Modernism. One of the first changes appeared in the curtain walls of office buildings. In the mid-1970s, a number of buildings acquired smooth skins of reflective glass apparently attached with minimal or no window frames. To a certain extent these mirrored surfaces resulted from technical innovations in the production of glass, in which sandwiches of glass and other materials helped control temperature and light. But we can also see this fashion as a changing attitude about a building's relationship to its immediate environment. Where Modernist buildings had long ignored their surroundings in order to highlight their own distinctive personalities, now these Late Modern buildings seemed more interested in literally reflecting their immediate environment than in standing out themselves. The buildings hid their personalities behind the reflective walls just as one might hide one's feelings behind reflective sun glasses. A good example can be found in Cesar Pelli's Pacific Design Center in Los Angeles, California [279]. Here sheets of blue reflective glass wrap smoothly around a form that looks like it has been extruded in some gigantic industrial process. We have no sense of the scale, the structure, the construction, or the contents of the building within. Despite the vast bulk, the building

279 Pacific Design Center, Los Angeles, California, 1976, Cesar Pelli

seems curiously self-effacing and enigmatic. Numerous other reflective buildings in this period wrapped their skins around even simpler rectilinear forms, deflecting commensurately more attention to the buildings and landscapes surrounding them. It is as if the architects of these reflective buildings could no longer think of something novel to say, and deferred politely to their neighbors. We see here little of the brash self-confidence of orthodox Modernism.

Other Late Modernist architects tried to shake off this malaise, and stepped forward to reaffirm the Modernist vision of a high technology society. Norman Foster and Richard Rogers in England led what was called a High-Tech movement, in which the building forms derived almost exclusively from expressively engineered structures and prefabricated building components. Projects like the Pompidou Centre in Paris, and Lloyds Insurance in London, looked like giant engineering works – oil refineries or space rocket gantries – inserted into the medieval city street pattern. In America, Helmut Jahn built similarly bold high technology projects like the State of Illinois Center in Chicago [280]. Here a lacy structural frame wraps around a dramatic

280 State of Illinois Center, Chicago, Illinois, 1980–85, Helmut Jahn

multi-story atrium, all sheathed on the outside with glass panels. Like a giant Gothic traceried window, the frame casts a complex web of shadows on the interior surfaces, obscuring the forms and creating a mood reminiscent of a science fiction stage set. Technology in these Late Modernist projects became more flamboyant and even mannered than in orthodox Modernist buildings like those of Mies van der Rohe. The image of the building no longer derives from a rational and efficient use of technology, but rather the technology is exaggerated to create a high-tech looking image. For example, Rogers suspended the roof of his Inmos Microprocessor Factory in South Wales with cables from an elaborately engineered central spine, when in fact sufficient structural support could have been built into the exterior walls and the roof trusses to carry the load without any suspension structure at all. Helmut Jahn's project also looks highly technological, but it sufficiently dematerializes the structure that it feels more like an open weave gauze whose means of support is not immediately obvious. These Late Modernist buildings stand in relation to Modernism much as the Mannerist buildings of Michelango stood in relation to the High Renaissance. They appear at first glance to continue the language of the previous style, but then exaggerate or distort it for more expressive visual effects.

Richard Meier in this period continued to develop his Le Corbusian revival forms. At the Atheneum in New Harmony, Indiana, we broadly see the same language of 1920s International Modernism, with pristine white forms, sharp contrasts of solids and voids, clear distinctions between structure and enclosure, and *pilotis* raising the building off the ground [281]. However, as Meier continued to refine this language, he obscured its original intellectual clarity in favor of something visually more luscious. For example, given a choice between a pleasing juxtaposition of shapes, on the one hand, and a Le Corbusian philosophical imperative to lift the entire building up on *pilotis*, on the other hand, Meier happily let the building drop to the ground in places. Furthermore, where Le Corbusier might have inserted one curving wall into an otherwise rational orthogonal geometry, Meier enriched this originally austere palette with complex curves, diagonals and slight skews. We are less aware of a rational organizing principle – like the distinction between the enclosed private and the open public spaces in his earlier Smith House – than we are of richly interlocking and flowing spaces. So where Meier and his New York Five colleagues had once objected to the willful qualities of expressionist Modernism in the early 1960s, and had sought clearer reasons for their own forms, by the 1980s the power of rational clarity seemed less compelling than sculptural effects.

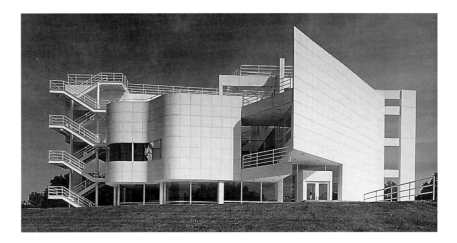

281 Atheneum, New Harmony, Indiana, 1975–79, Richard Meier

### The revival of traditional styles

While the Late Modernists adapted the Modernist style to the changed mood of the 1970s, other architects became disillusioned with the style altogether. No longer convinced of the philosophical ideas which lay behind it, and bored with its abstract forms, these designers began to search for alternatives more commensurate with the new age. They found their new direction in the traditional styles which the Modernists had long banned from use. In the 1960s, as we saw in the last chapter, architects like Robert Venturi and Charles Moore had already begun to cast their eyes backwards to the traditions before Modernism, and had tentatively revived forms ranging from the Baroque to the vernacular. In the mid-1970s the stylistic floodgates opened. Architects developed a keen curiosity about the traditional styles which they had long been forbidden to use, and about which they had learned little during their perfunctory architectural history classes in the Modernist schools. The Museum of Modern Art in New York mounted a major exhibition on the architecture of the Ecole des Beaux-Arts in 1975–76, introducing an astonished younger generation to the visual riches and spatial complexities of the Classical language, and to a standard of drawing which most young architects did not even know was possible. Sir Edwin Lutyens, who was left out of the Modernist history books and who was therefore largely unknown to a younger generation, received his own major retrospective at the Hayward Gallery in London in 1981–82. Publishers in this period rushed to reprint the forgotten works of other notable traditional architects including Karl Friedrich Schinkel, McKim, Mead and White, and Mellor, Meigs and Howe.

Why the revived interest in the traditional styles and architects? It is conceivable, after all, that architects in the 1970s might have dismissed the tenets of Modernism without necessarily returning to the traditional styles. Perhaps rebellion consists partly in valuing those things that the previous generation rejected. Perhaps designers saw in the traditional styles those very qualities that were noticably missing in mainstream Modernism, including character, human scale and detail. Or perhaps the architects responded to the more conservative mood of the period, which had begun to revive traditional values after the revolutionary 1960s. People sought cultural roots after the uproar, and the sense that they belonged to something stable and meaningful. Architects began to appreciate that the traditional architectural styles expressed desired continuities, not revolutions. A semiotics movement in the early 1970s also indirectly lent further credence to the traditional forms. Led by architectural critics and theorists including Umberto Eco, Charles Jencks, Geoffrey Broadbent and Dick Bunt, this movement applied linguistics theories to the study of meaning in architecture. Where Modernism had focused on the syntax of architectural form without regard for its semantics, the semioticians revived the ancient idea that forms can convey commonly understood ideas. Although they eventually hoped to 'decode' all architectural forms including Modernist ones, in the process the semioticians highlighted how effectively the traditional forms transmit well-understood meanings.

The first revivals of traditional forms in the mid-1970s were not archeologically correct reproductions of old ideas. In this period of continuing individualism, few architects were willing to give up personal artistic license in favor of strictly following stylistic conventions. Furthermore, architects in this period still accepted the Modernist idea that an architectural form ought to express its own time, and they were therefore disinclined simply to mimic forms that originated in earlier eras. So although the Academic Eclectics in the first half of the twentieth century rejoiced if their designs were mistaken for something reassuringly familiar and much older, the new revivalists would have been disappointed if their new forms did not express the 1970s or reveal the distinctive hand of the author. Somehow, they had to reconcile the conflicting tendencies of individualism and contemporaneity on the one hand, and cultural convention and timelessness on the other.

The first revivalists in this period answered this dilemma by reviving the spirit of Mannerism even more thoroughly and self-consciously than had the Late Modernists. Michelangelo, we will recall, also tried to reconcile stylistic conventions with his own expressionistic tendencies by playing witty games with the Classical language. He employed conventional forms like the Five Orders in unconventional and even perverse ways, using enough of the traditional language to establish conventional expectations, and then inverting or contradicting their usual meanings. We see this same spirit in an early Postmodern house by Michael Graves [282]. At first glance, the design has completely repudiated Modernism's austere, rational forms in favor of traditional shapes and details. We seem to recognize many familiar elements of the Classical language, including a rusticated base, columns and capitals, and even a keystone from an arch. But on closer inspection, the elements are not at all what we conventionally expect. The keystone seems to have been pushed by a giant invisible hand out of its customary position over the front door, and onto the hill behind the house. It is grossly out of scale with the rest of the design. The columns left flanking the front door carry no load at all, while other columns on the side façade appear to support little glass windows which cannot themselves carry any of the load from the wall above. So even though the design *feels* more familiar and traditional than an equivalent Modernist house, it quickly denies our efforts to understand it in familiar terms. And just as we could not easily mistake Michelangelo's Laurentian Library stairs for a project designed earlier in the High Renaissance or later in the Baroque, Graves's house could not easily be confused with traditional styles from other periods. It is distinctly of the 1970s. In addition, the uses of the Classical language are so intensely personal and idiosyncratic that even casually knowledgeable viewers could readily identify a number of projects in this period as coming from the hand of Graves.

**282** Plocek House, Warren Township, New Jersey, 1977–79, Michael Graves

**283** Portland Public Services Building, Portland, Oregon, 1980–82, Michael Graves

Graves's winning competition entry for the Portland Public Service Building explored similar ideas for a large public building [283]. The programmatic requirements of the project demanded a conventional office building, with a row of offices wrapped around a service core on each floor, and an elevator lobby at ground level. A tight budget also demanded conventional frame and infill construction and inexpensive materials. Now ever since this building type and construction had been perfected in the 1950s, the external walls had become little more than a weather-protecting skin. Although the Modernists decorated their own skins to look techno-logical and rational, Graves realized that there was no compelling reason why the skin could not be decorated according to a different stylistic principle. He chose to develop his favorite keystone motif, in this case by applying a giant fake keystone over equally giant applied pilasters. Vaguely Art Deco garlands frozen in mid-flap added additional ornament to the side façades, while a stylized classical temple capped the top. A bronze statue of the city's emblem Portlandia kneels on a podium at the front of the building, emphatically rejecting the Modernist preferences for abstract sculpture in favor of the older tradition of figural public statuary. And compared to Modernism's muted and usually primary colors, Graves employed a broader palette of what we now regard as quintessentially Postmodern colors: sometimes saturated and other times pastel versions of complexly mixed colors like rusts, ochres, steely blues and purples. This project so blatantly attacked the cherished assumptions and beliefs of the Modernists that it ignited a firestorm of letters in the local paper. The Moder-nists strongly objected to its historicism, and to its superficially applied ornament that bore no relationship to the underlying structure or construction. Gleefully rebel-lious, the Postmodernist supporters disparaged the old Modernist tenets as outdated.

**284** House, Greenville, Delaware, 1983, Venturi, Rauch and Scott Brown

**285** Piazza d'Italia, New Orleans, Lousiana, 1978–79, Charles Moore and Perez & Associates

**286** PPG Plaza, Pittsburgh, Pennsylvania, 1982, Johnson & Burgee

Robert Venturi was the first to revive and update traditional styles back in the 1960s. He and his partners John Rauch and Denise Scott Brown continued to explore these ideas in the Postmodern period. Their house in Delaware places a temple front on a gabled main block, just like numerous colonial and Federalist houses of the eighteenth century [284]. On closer inspection, however, we find that the temple front is nothing more than a stage-set cardboard cutout, with overly wide but completely flat columns. A cluster of sash windows intrude on the right side of the symmetrical temple front, agonizingly chopping off the roof eave and half of the last column. We see here Venturi's continuing fascination with visual complexity and contradiction, only now the forms refer more explicitly to obvious architectural icons like Doric temples, Roman arches and Gibbsian temple fronts. Like Graves's house discussed above, we clearly recognize the historical references while never mistaking this for a product of an earlier age.

Charles Moore also turned to more explicit stylistic references in the 1970s. His Piazza d'Italia in New Orleans, designed for the local Italian-American community, recalled the Italian contribution to high art with a Classical colonnade standing over a fountain shaped like the boot of Italy [285]. Like his Postmodern contemporaries, he indulged in witty commentaries on the traditional Classical themes. Cascading water forms a column, jets of water replace the acanthus leaves on a Corinthian capital, and busts of Charles Moore himself spew water out of their mouths into the fountain below. The neon tubing of American commerce picks out the salient lines of the composition. Moore's enthusiasm for the Classical was shared by most of the Postmodern revivalists, although the firm of Johnson/Burgee revived its conceptual counterpart, the Gothic. For the PPG Plaza (Pittsburgh Plate Glass Industries), the architects wrapped a conventional frame office building with a Late Modernist mirrored curtain wall [286]. They crinkled the mirrored surface to form thin, vertical projections which vaguely referred to Gothic buttresses, and which burst beyond the top of the box to form Gothic pinnacles. Although few architects have so far followed them in reviving the Gothic, the alternating popularity of the Classical and Gothic throughout Western architectural history suggests that we may yet witness a more sustained Gothic revival in the Postmodern age.

We have seen how a number of these early Postmodern designers enjoyed witty architectural jokes, like the missing keystone or the waterjets substituting for acanthus leaves. Despite Venturi's call for architecture based in part on popular taste, these witticisms were clearly directed to a small, fairly elite group of knowledgeable architectural critics. In the early days of these revived styles, most architects hardly knew the traditional rules which these projects set up and then violated. The general public with no architectural education missed the references altogether. So why the fondness for inside jokes and allusions? In part this followed from Venturi's own personal preferences, first spelled out in *Complexity and Contradiction*, for the sophisticated visual devices of Mannerism and the Baroque. Architects in those periods also played to a knowledgeable audience who could appreciate the inversions of convention (although one might argue that the spatial effects of the Baroque were readily apparent to those with no architectural knowledge). The taste for insider jokes might also have followed from the dynamics of a stylistic revolution. In the face of hostility from the Modernists, the early pioneers in the new style wished not only to distinguish themselves from their antagonists, but also to club together for mutual support. A new visual code conveniently served as a password for inclusion in the group, and also set the group apart from the Modernists as possessing a different kind of knowledge. For some Postmodernists, no doubt, the joking approach to the traditional forms allowed them to dabble with long forbidden ideas without looking like they had yet wholeheartedly embraced them. Expressing an unpopular idea with a slight laugh allows one to say 'I was only kidding' if reproachful reactions prove too severe.

Eventually, like puns, the visual jokes paled. At the same time, architects had begun to study the traditional languages more carefully, and had discovered sophisticated visual and spatial systems that could stand on their own without ironic or witty commentary. Just as the first tentative 'Gothick' follies in the eighteenth century eventually led to a full-blown Gothic Revival in the next century, the jokey Postmodern buildings at the end of the 1970s eventually gave way to more accurate revivals of the traditional styles in the 1980s. In Europe, Leon Krier decried the jokes, popularized Neoclassical ideas based on Karl Friedrich Schinkel, and argued for traditional town plans with squares, arcades, and distinguishably different public and private structures. A number of Classicists emerged in England, following the lead of Quinlan Terry [287]. Terry had quietly designed accurate Georgian revival houses from the 1960s onward, at first with his mentor Raymond Erith and then independently. Younger Classicists like Robert Adam and John Simpson subsequently revived a number of other traditional English variants on the Classical language, including those developed by Soane, Gibbs and the Neo-Palladians.

In the United States, architects including Thomas Gordon Smith, Thomas Hall Beeby, Allan Greenberg and Robert Stern also turned to more accurate Classical traditions. Most popular were those versions of Classicism that had captured the imaginations of Americans in previous centuries, including the Tuscan, Gibbsian and Jeffersonian. Robert Stern's Observatory Hall Dining Room on the University of Virginia campus gave him a perfect opportunity to match Jefferson's quietly inventive use of Classical elements [288]. Compared to the earlier mannered Postmodern designs we discussed above, this building follows more completely and sympathetically the organizing principles and ornamental details of Classicism. The columns logically and obviously stand at the corners of the structural bays, a heavier masonry base visually supports the lighter glazed section, and the Tuscan Order obeys the conventional proportional and ornamental rules without jokes or aberrations. Propriety and stylistic convention here dominate personal expression, in marked contrast to most of Modernism and much of early Postmodernism. We certainly do not see the personality of the architect in the design to the same degree that we saw it in Michael Graves's buildings of about the same time. Nor are we any longer sure in which decade or even century this building was designed. Only the lack of a strong visual center and subordinate wings suggests that it was probably not designed in the eighteenth or nineteenth centuries, when such massing conventions were typically followed.

Christopher Alexander, who had helped lead the Design Methodology movement of the 1960s with a rigorously mathematical model of the design process, also discovered the virtues of architectural precedents in this period. His earlier work had advised against studying other buildings because, he said, they represented old solutions to defunct problems and therefore could not reliably guide new solutions to new problems. But by the early 1970s he had changed his mind, calling his earlier attitude a mistake. He discovered what he called a desirable 'quality without a name' in the traditional buildings and towns of many world cultures. According to Alexander, people who inhabit these traditional environments live their lives more fully than those who are doomed to use Modernism's artificial and life-suppressing environments. It intrigued him that, even without professional designers or explicit theories

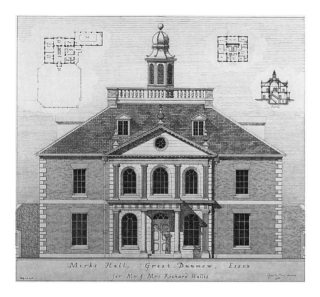

287 Merks Hall, Great Dunmow, Essex, England, 1981, Quinlan Terry

288 Observatory Hall Dining Room, Charlottesville, Virginia, 1982–84, Robert Stern

of design, individuals throughout history were able to design their surroundings according to what he called this 'timeless way of building'. Unfortunately, Alexander went on, the modern world has blunted our senses and suppressed our natural design intuitions. To help us regain the 'quality without a name', he spent the better part of a decade studying traditional architectural and town planning forms in order to discover their underlying principles.

His *A Pattern Language*, published in 1977 with co-authors Sara Ishikawa, Murray Silverstein, Max Jacobson, Ingrid Fiksdahl-King and Shlomo Angel, offered 253 patterns for the design of the built environment, ranging from a proposal for independently governed regions, down to a proposal for basing one's interior furnishing on things from one's own life. Each pattern studied a particular design problem, and then offered specific examples from around the world where the desired 'quality' was present and where it was not. It then tried to isolate the specific design elements which attended the former and which were missing in the latter. In a pattern for successful courtyards, for example, Alexander and his team identified three essential components: the circulation pattern of the building passes through the courtyard, a veranda or arcade provides a covered open space halfway between inside and outside, and an opening provides views to spaces beyond the courtyard. They then offered psychological or sociological reasons why these components were essential, based on the research of the previous decade. Like the stylistic revivalists of this period, Alexander and his team saw a deep and satisfying meaning in traditional buildings and towns; but unlike the revivalists who had typically mimicked the specific rules of particular styles like Classicism, Alexander and his team hoped to discover the deeper essences of which traditional styles were variations. At the time of writing this book, almost 20 years after *A Pattern Language* was published, Alexander's work remains popular with people who are looking for design guidance without necessarily following a particular style.

Common to most of the architectural movements in the 1970s, excluding High Tech and Meier's Le Corbusian revival, was a renewed interest in the context in which the building would sit. Mirrored Late Modernist buildings literally reflected their surroundings, while the Postmodern traditional revivals – both mannered and accurate – often tried to restate the massing, color and detail of the buildings around them. Many saw this as antidote to the arrogance of Modernism, which had pointedly dismissed all existing buildings and traditions as lacking in merit. By the early 1980s the idea of context had become so well established that most workaday architects felt compelled to 'fit the context' in some fashion, picking up the lines of cornices and string courses, or matching the massing, texture and scale, or mimicking details on the adjacent buildings.

Another kind of interest in context – the context of the natural environment – derived in part from the environmental movement of late 1960s, and in part from the energy crisis of 1973. To reduce its dependence on foreign oil, America developed a dual strategy of finding alternative energy sources while reducing demand through conservation. Accelerated construction of nuclear power plants and a federally mandated national speed limit of 55 miles per hour both followed from this plan. Many designers and builders also rose to the occasion, seeking creative ways to make buildings more energy efficient, or to remove buildings from the public energy grid altogether. Reviving the ancient idea of the pit house, some builders experimented with burying their buildings entirely or partly underground to take advantage of the earth's natural insulating properties. Others rediscovered the natural properties of a massive masonry wall, and developed systems whereby a massive wall within the building would absorb the sun's heat during the day, and then slowly radiate heat back out to the building at night. Many buildings began to sport large solar collectors on their roofs, while others directed large mono-pitched light scoops towards the south. Even architects who did not want their buildings to look so obviously 'solar tech' nonetheless paid more careful attention to the natural conditions of sun and wind, and orientated their designs accordingly. When energy costs restabilized, however, Americans' enthusiasm for energy efficient designs faded away. They neither wanted to pay for expensive systems like solar collectors, nor did they want their buildings to look so strange.


## To the present


### The Reagan revolution

Ronald Reagan swept into the White House in 1980 with an agenda to put America back on its feet after the malaise of the 1970s. Conditions had worsened in the last years of the Carter Administration. Inflation rose 40 per cent from 1976 to 1980, accompanied by usury interest rates of 20 per cent, high unemployment, and an economic recession. Despite the first shock of the oil crisis in 1973, America blithely continued to import even more oil, over 40 per cent of its annual supply by 1979. When the Shah of Iran fell in 1979, a theocratic regime hostile to America cut its oil exports and caused more gas shortages. And when Carter's commandos failed to rescue 50 Americans who had been taken hostage in the coup, it seemed once again that America could no longer project its power even when its own vital interests were at stake.

Just when it looked like the American empire was headed for its final decline, Reagan offered a rosy picture of America's resurgence. He boostered America's ability and willingness to fight the 'evil empire' of the Soviet Union, claiming the moral superiority of the American vision against its communist adversary. He backed up the claim with the largest increase in military spending in America's peacetime history. His defiant opposition to the Soviets, and limited military incursions into Granada and Libya, played on many Americans' patriotic sentiments and helped remove the funk of the 1970s, although many were appalled at the strongarm tactics. On the home front, Reagan revived the old American ideal of individual entrepreneurialism, rejecting the idea that government would take care of people's problems. His views in this regard closely paralleled those of Margaret Thatcher, who had undertaken a similar conservative agenda on her election as Prime Minister of Great Britain in 1979. Both saw government and its regulations as actively interfering with individuals making their own successes, and both subsequently privatized industries which had been nationalized in earlier, more socialist, generations. Reagan also deregulated a number of industries and services ranging from banking to telecommunications and nursing homes. To spur the private development of natural resources, his Secretary of the Interior tried to sell off the still substantial public lands owned by the federal government in the western states, and to remove the regulations that had emerged in the last decades to protect the natural environment.

To encourage the entrepreneurial spirit, Reagan also began to dismantle the social programs like welfare and food stamps which he believed had discouraged the poor from improving their circumstances. At the same time he provided extensive tax cuts for the rich, in the belief that this would encourage them to invest in businesses from which all would eventually profit. America had turned again to the Gospel of Wealth that we saw in the period following the Civil War. Unfortunately, the benefits of this 'trickle down' theory did not materialize. Savings, investments and productivity actually grew at a slower rate compared to the previous decade. The combination of massive military spending, tax cuts, and reduced tax revenues during a bad recession in 1982 created the largest national deficit in America's peacetime history, which is just beginning to moderate at the time of writing. The economy revived in 1982–83, but America turned from the world's largest creditor in 1980 to the largest debtor in 1988. The country's balance of trade also steadily worsened in this period, leading to extensive imports of foreign goods and the ensuing decline and even collapse of traditional American manufacturing industries.

The entrepreneurial spirit freed from regulation often turned to greed in this period. The mood shifted away from social responsibility, since social problems were now perceived by many as the personal failures of individuals rather than as institutional or cultural failures. Moral responsibility also fell by the wayside, as it became increasingly respectable to get as much as one can, regardless of the methods or the consequences for others. Fraud and scandals rocked America's government and economic institutions. Government officials took kickbacks as they privatized industries, stockmarket traders defrauded investors, and corruption in the banking industry led to a collapse of savings and loan institutions. Corporate high flyers found it more profitable to invest their capital in buyouts, takeovers and speculation than in the production of goods, even if it meant stripping a company of its assets and laying off its workforce. The implied social contract in the 1950s between a company and its workers – that the company would look after its loyal employees – no longer operated in this free-for-all atmosphere. All of these changes divided America even further along class lines. The rich got richer, while increasing numbers of the poor sank into a chronically impoverished underclass. Many in the skilled working class, who had steadily climbed into a middle-class standard of living since the Second World War, found themselves out of work and facing limited prospects. Even the fortunes and job security of the middle classes declined in this period, leading many to fear the impending collapse of America's traditional backbone. Distrust among these groups mounted, with the rich fearing a violent underclass, the poor bitterly resenting their reduced circumstances and lack of opportunity, and the working and middle classes wondering if they would sink into poverty next. So while Reagan's era helped America regain its confidence, it also exacerbated the plurality of views and divisions which we saw emerging in the previous decade.

### The architecture of individualism and angst

What happened to architecture in this period? We have already seen how the greater conservatism in the 1970s helped lead to a revival of traditional forms, and even to the rejection of individualism in favor of shared cultural conventions. These architectural revivals continued throughout the socially conservative 1980s. However, a new architectural movement also arose in this period which claimed to engage more explicitly some of the complexities of the 1980s. In particular, it expressed the social anxieties of the period while also celebrating the renewed individualism of Reagan's laissez-faire outlook.

Known broadly as Deconstructivism, this movement drew its inspiration from several diverse sources. First of all, many of its visual images derived from Russian Constructivism, an avant-garde Modernist movement in art and architecture which had flourished in Russia in the 1920s. Inspired by the recently successful Communist Revolution, and anticipating the utopian new society which the revolution had promised, the original Constructivists set out to invent a new language of architecture that would not only express, but also encourage the development of, their new society. Like their immediate predecessors the Futurists, they envisioned images of high technology and massive engineering works which they thought would accompany the new social order. And like the Arts and Crafts architects at the turn of the century, they were interested in the expressive qualities of materials and their construction. When these two ideas were combined with a fascination with time and motion, the Constructivists invented a number of distinctive projects like Vladimir Tatlin's *Monument to the Third International* [289]. In this project, several helixes spun around each other at different heights, each supported on a lightweight frame of angled supports. A tilted vertical support thrust through the middle caused the entire structure to look like it was about to spring away. The Deconstructivists in the 1980s revived the spirit of this dynamic visual vocabulary, as we will see, as well as some of its specific elements.

The Deconstructivist movement in architecture also drew inspiration from the Deconstruction movement in literary theory, which had begun to sweep through the art and literature departments of universities in the late 1970s and early 1980s. The French philosopher and critic Jacques Derrida developed the ideas behind the movement as a critique of Western philosophy in general, and of Western literary criticism in particular. He pointed out that most Western philosophy believes it can uncover ultimate and objective truths about the world; and by extension, most literary criticism believes that it can discover the author's true meaning in a text. But restating a view first formulated by the late nineteenth-century philosopher Friedrich Nietzsche, Derrida denied that one could ever discover these objective truths, because they do not exist. We artificially impose order on the world and on literature where no inherent order resides. To prove his point, Derrida 'deconstructed' a number of important texts in the history of Western philosophy, including those by Plato and Rousseau. He highlighted the contradictions in their logic, trying to show that they

**289** Project for a Monument to the Third International, 1919–20, Vladimir Tatlin

never say what they mean or mean what they say. Although Derrida thought that we could never entirely escape this human tendency to impose order on what is in fact a chaotic world, his followers in a number of fields were more willing to draw the nihilistic consequences of his idea. Deconstruction came to mean a radical critique of existing concepts without necessarily supplying new concepts in their place. In the arts, the Deconstructionists demolished traditional distinctions between high art and low, or good taste and bad. They meant to show that everything means anything, and vice versa. They also 'deconstructed' the concept of the autonomous self, thereby dismissing the role of the artistic personality in the creation of art.

So how did 1920s architectural Constructivism and 1970s literary Deconstructionism combine to form architectural Deconstructivism in the 1980s? A number of architects thoughout Europe and America, including Bernard Tschumi, Frank Gehry, Daniel Libeskind, Zaha Hadid and Peter Eisenman, began to develop forms which they thought radically critiqued or completely overthrew the traditional idea of order in architecture. We live in a chaotic world, they insisted, and so architecture should express this essential reality rather than artificially impose structure where no structure exists. Eisenman further wanted to 'dislocate' the users of his buildings, by subverting their usual expectations and making them face the discomfort of their existential condition. For inspiration, many Deconstructivists turned to the visual language of Russian Constructivism, where they appropriately found fragmentary forms crashing into each other and expressing powerful forces almost out of control.

Zaha Hadid, a London-based architect, shocked the architectural world in the early 1980s by winning an international competition for The Peak Project in Hong Kong with an astonishing composition of colliding and hovering slabs. The design looked more like a geological formation than a building, followed no obvious geometrical ordering system, and appeared as if it had resulted from random natural forces and even pure chance. The lack of obviously purposeful design decisions left the viewer wondering if a rational human being had played any part in its conception and development. This project probably remains the clearest expression yet of the nihilistic aspect of Deconstructivism. Frank Gehry also experimented with crashing forms and planes slicing through each other, as we see here in his own house [290]. Gehry frankly employed cheap industrial materials like corrugated metal sheets and plywood, partly for cost, and partly to find aesthetic interest in what

290 Gehry House, Santa Monica, California, 1978–79, Frank Gehry

**291** Wexner Center for the
Visual Arts, Columbus, Ohio,
1989, Peter Eisenman

we conventionally regard as ugly or utilitarian. Like the Deconstructionist agenda in philosophy and art, he intentionally blurred the traditional distinctions between high art and utilitarianism, good taste and bad.

Peter Eisenman also took up the Deconstructivist cause, eventually becoming its chief spokesman and theorist. His designs were less chaotic and random than those of Hadid or Gehry, displaying more geometrical order and even overtly geometrical elements like Cartesian grids. Indeed, his Deconstructivist projects still owe a great deal to his earlier studies in complex geometrical transformations. As we see here in his design for the Wexner Center for the Visual Arts, the building arranges itself around two intersecting axes, one solid and the other an open three-dimensional Cartesian grid [**291**]. These overlap and interfere with each other, just at the point where they slam through the middle of the entire composition. Here we find less of a celebration

**292** Crawford Residence,
Montecito, California, 1988,
Morphosis

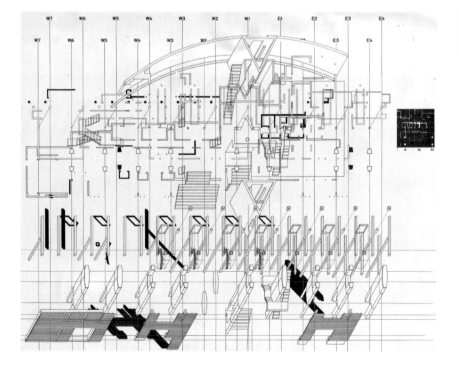

of chaos, and more of an attempt to play on the viewers' perceptions of space and order. The two axes do not intersect at an obvious and conventional angle like 90, or 45, or 30 degrees. They twist so slightly in relationship to each other that the viewer is not immediately aware of the shift, or of the fact that the one has imperceptibly intruded on the other. Instead, the viewer gains a slightly uneasy feeling that something has not quite lined up. Taking explicit clues from Derrida's methods of literary analysis, Eisenman explored complex concepts like *différance*, the space or notion between complementary objects. 'Smooth' means the opposite of 'rough', for example, in which the presence of the one requires the absence of the other. But in order to judge an object as 'smooth', one must simultaneously have in mind the notion of 'rough'. 'Rough' is present in its absence. In the Wexner Center, Eisenman played on similar perceptions by contrasting the open grid and closed surfaces. Why would one want to use a literary concept like this for creating architectural form? To a large extent, we can see this as yet another version of Mannerism, in which conventional perceptions are intentionally inverted, confounded, or commented on, in order to force the viewer to see things in a new light. Yet where others like Michelangelo, Venturi and Graves played their visual games with a commonly understood language of conventional forms and meanings, Eisenman manipulated our deeper expectations of order itself.

The Morphosis partnership of Thom Mayne and Michael Rotondi also experimented with geometries so richly complex that the viewer could not immediately see the underlying logic. Their axonometric study of the Crawford Residence appears at first glance like an incomprehensible jumble of elements [292]. But on closer inspection, we see an underlying geometrical grid and a series of repeating elements like clerestory windows and structural columns which subtly control the complexity. The entire design almost reads like musical notation, with a regular bass line providing order, and a number of richly interweaving guitar riffs providing complexity and

**293** Kate Mantilini Restaurant, Los Angeles, California, 1987, Morphosis

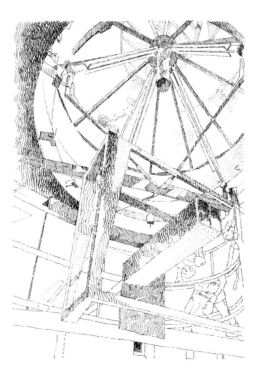

variety. Morphosis also explored the Arts and Crafts side of Russian Constructivism, celebrating the expressive aesthetic possibilities of structure and construction. They exposed structure in places, and lovingly crafted connections with prominently displayed bolt heads and fittings. One can see how things are put together, and how the structural forces are transmitted to the ground. After the applied decoration of the Postmodernist stylistic revivals, this seemed to bring honesty of structure and construction back into architecture, and it inspired countless students in the schools of architecture to design equally expressive details. However, this was not exactly the structural and constructional honesty for which hardcore Modernists might have hoped, after the indignations they suffered in the Postmodernist revivals. Sometimes fake structural forms were applied like free-standing ornaments to the outside of buildings, while details were often elaborated or overscaled beyond the constructional requirements of the job at hand. Construction was elaborated for its sculptural possibilities, just like the Russian Constructivist projects. In the Kate Mantilini Restaurant, Morphosis brought the idea forcibly home by building a Constructivist sculpture in the middle of the space [293].

The Deconstructionists in literary theory clearly wished to disparage the concept of the individual, and therefore to downplay the role of the artist or writer in creating the art object or text. But what about the architectural Deconstructivists? If we did not know the theory from which their designs were supposed to have derived, and if we simply look at the visual qualities of their designs alone, we might be forgiven for viewing them as Expressionists celebrating the individual perception or personal artistic expression. The Deconstructivists' bold and dynamic shapes seem to reveal the personality and energy of the architect as much as Mendelsohn's Einstein Tower or Le Corbusier's Ronchamp Chapel, particularly when we compare them to a style less personally expressive like Classicism. Indeed, the Expressionist tendencies of the Deconstructivists are revealed in a concept which they helped popularize in the architecture schools, the 'gesture'. In the 1980s, teachers and students who employed Deconstructivist images spoke of the essential gesture in buildings, by which they meant an expressive underlying line or visual movement upon which the entire design is based. The Chmar House, by Scogin Elam and Bray Architects, shows evidence of gestural lines, with broadly sweeping curves and a feeling that all of the parts are lining up according to an invisible force, just as iron filings line up to a magnetic field [294 and 295]. Even elements at opposite ends of the project, which no vantage point could see at the same time, are aligned with each other according to an underlying gestural line. These lines not only help animate the project by giving it a sense of movement and liveliness, but they also literally reveal the hand of the artistic creator in the design. We can almost feel the sweep of the designer's pencil across the paper as the lines are first established. Theodor Lipps at the turn of the century had described this phenomenon as a process of empathy, in which we project human characteristics into an inanimate object so that we may empathize with the psychical processes we see there. This is why we talk of 'movement' in a line, or 'stress' in a gesture. The architectural Deconstructivists' enthusiasm for such lines put them at odds with the literary Deconstructionists who wished to disparage the individual's role in artistic creation.

The architects were probably more in tune with the times. Their emphasis on personal artistic expression accorded with the mood of the Reaganite and Thatcherite years, which favored individual initiative over the collective and shared. Deconstructivism's aggressive, dynamic images also captured the energy of the go-go 1980s, when many hustled to create new fortunes in the deregulated economy. In this

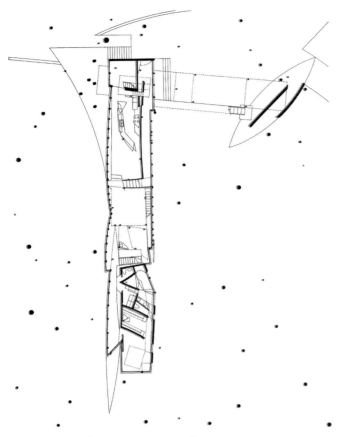

**294** Chmar House, Atlanta, Georgia, 1989, Scogin Elam and Bray Architects

**295** Chmar House, exterior

respect, Deconstructivism is not so very different from the exuberant architecture that accompanied the equally freewheeling post-Civil War era. And yet, there seems to be a darker tone to the Deconstructivist architecture. Its forms are unmistakably violent, with elements crashing into each other, or slicing through each other, or aggressively penetrating each other, or forming knife-like edges. The new forms were meant to undermine our traditional understandings of order, and maybe even to explore the nature of chaos, but do these two philosophical agendas necessarily lead to a celebration of violence? A lack of order could equally well be expressed with benign elements randomly arrayed. The aggressive Deconstructivist forms paralleled increasing aggression in the broader culture, as seen in the decline of traditional manners, in the increased class hostility, in more violent television programming, and in the rise of frightening street crimes like drive-by shootings. Since no Deconstructivists advocated violence, we might see these forms as expressing the general cultural angst that accompanied these unsettling times.

It is interesting to note, by the way, that violent times do not necessarily lead to violent or chaotic forms. Just after the first millennium, when life was arguably more violent and brutish than today, designers developed the highly rational and geometrical Romanesque style. And in the 1890s, when America suffered through a period as violent and as economically unsettling as the 1980s, designers championed the Classical style which was then eagerly embraced by the general public. In those periods, designers compensated for disorder in society by offering greater order in the built environment. There is more than a little irony in the fact that the Deconstructivist buildings were mainly designed by high fashion architects for well-to-do clients who were least touched by the violence and angst. Would this style have been as well received by the skilled factory worker, or the middle-class manager, who had been laid off during the shakedown of the American economy? It is also interesting to note that, once again, a particular architectural vocabulary has been used for almost diametrically opposed purposes in different cultures and times. The language of Constructivism was used in the 1920s to express a boldly optimistic view of an emerging communist utopia, while a variation of it was used in the 1980s to express a more pessimistic, even nihilistic, view of the world falling apart.

### Regionalism, environmentalism and social idealism

The 1980s and early 1990s also saw a revival of interest in regional architecture. In the first quarter of the twentieth century, we will recall, numerous architects including Frank Lloyd Wright, Bernard Maybeck, Julia Morgan, Trost and Trost, and Mellor, Meigs and Howe, had tried to derive their designs at least in part from the special conditions of the building's site and climate. The Academic Eclectics mostly looked for historical precedents in the region which represented tried and tested solutions to the local conditions and, if these were not available, they looked for precedents in other regions of the world with similar geological or climatological conditions. Frank Lloyd Wright tried a more fundamental approach, by innovating unprecedented forms that still answered the climate and geographical setting, and that seemed to fit the mood of the particular place. The buildings which derived from these concerns were not easily interchangeable with other regions or even with other sites within the region.

We will also recall that the Modern Movement strenuously attacked these regional ideas during its stylistic revolution in the 1920s. Many of Europe's intelligentsia were repulsed by the belligerent nationalism leading up to the First World War, which they believed served the upper classes mainly at the expense of the working classes. Many hoped to avoid these problems in the future by abolishing national entities in favor of international groupings. They wished to stress the noble qualities of universal mankind, rather than what they saw as the less noble characteristics of local national groups. This idea helped drive the international socialist workers' movement, the Russian Revolution and the League of Nations. The early Modernist architects closely allied themselves with this internationalist notion, insisting that architecture ought to answer universal human needs rather than individual predilections or localized circumstances. With this emphasis on the international, they disparaged architectural regionalism as insufficiently broad in its scope, and as pandering to local, parochial concerns.

When Hitchcock and Johnson stripped International Modernism of its socialist roots in the 1930s to sell it to a more conservative American audience, they still stressed the international character of the style. This interest in the universal and international at the expense of the regional continued to underpin the Modernist movement throughout most of its subsequent history. Modernism had identified itself with the spirit of rationality, science and technology which, after all, are universal notions not bound by national or regional borders. Only occasionally throughout the middle third of the twentieth century did we find architects exploring regional design ideas. William Wurster, Joseph Esherick and Charles Moore studied local vernacular traditions for stylistic inspiration, for example, while the environmental and solar technology movement born out of the early 1970s energy crisis studied how local climatological conditions might shape architectural forms. But when the first Postmodernists revived traditional styles in the later 1970s, they implicitly restated the Modernist preference for the international over the regional by mainly reviving that older international style, Classicism. And the Deconstructivists certainly showed little enthusiasm for regional issues, since they were addressing larger questions of order and chaos in the world at large.

On first impression, one might expect that the internationalist and universalist impulses would have continued to preoccupy the Postmodern world. Dramatic improvements in transportation and telecommunications allowed quick and easy movement of people and ideas around the globe, while international trade and the flow of international capital inextricably linked national economies together. And yet, just as these technological and economic forces worked to pull people into a closely knit international community, the mood around the world in the 1980s increasingly turned against internationalism and towards regional autonomy. The Soviet Union increasingly struggled to maintain control of its client states in Eastern Europe, many of whom had begun to feel more affiliation with their own regional and ethnic groupings than with a great communist world order. Poland, East Germany and the Baltic and Balkan states agitated for local control and even independence, under the increasingly benign eye of the Soviet President Mikhail Gorbachev. In 1989 the communist bloc suddenly collapsed, poignantly symbolized by the East and West German citizenry literally pulling down the Berlin Wall together. The euphoria following this dramatic end to the Cold War was tempered somewhat when multi-ethnic Yugoslavia fell into a bitter civil war among its religious and ethnic groups, each trying to carve out an ethnically pure and geographically defensible state. For their part, Americans continued to rebel against a large federal government, many insisting that money, power and responsibility should be transferred back to the individual states and local authorities. At the time of writing, a sizable number of Americans wish to retreat from international relations by erecting trade barriers and by blocking further immigration. People around the world increasingly sought to affiliate with smaller political entities, in which they felt they could regain control over their own lives, and in which they could affiliate with others possessing a similar outlook.

We find in the 1980s and 1990s a number of architects who began to explore regional design issues once again. For his office building in California, Robert Stern revived the Spanish Colonial style that many Californian architects in the pre-Modernist age had employed as an appropriate expression of the Californian climate and culture. The familiar elements are here, including the ogee curved pediment, the intensely sunlit stucco, the railing balconies across the second-floor windows, and a street arcade. It is difficult to see this building as sited anywhere but in California, given the stylistic conventions to which it explicitly refers. Antoine Predock in New Mexico explored the adobe traditions of the Southwest, finding strong correlations between the abstractions of Modernism and the simple forms of the Pueblos [296]. Predock often painted his buildings to pick up the distinctive colors of the desert and sky, and hence to link the building intimately to the special character of the place. Phil Korell's house for a ranch in Montana fused elements of Frank Lloyd Wright's Prairie houses with vernacular traditions in the Rocky Mountain region, including Spanish haciendas and log and fieldstone cabins [297]. From these disparate sources Korell derived a striking image of a home able to withstand the severe Montana winters while expressing a distinctive Western ranch lifestyle.

Throughout much of this history, as we have seen, settlers new to an area usually transplanted their familiar culture and architectural styles from back home; but in the 1990s many Americans moving to a new region of the country wished to savor the special lifestyle and sense of place in their adopted home. They sought instant roots in the region's traditions. New York stockbrokers and Hollywood stars built 'rustic' ranch houses in Aspen, Colorado, while tract homebuilders around the country offered styles historically appropriate for a region, like the Colonial or Georgian for the eastern seaboard. Often, the new transplants embraced regional traditions more vigorously than the natives. Even when individuals did not explicitly seek a local regional style, this desire for a special sense of place drove many housebuyers to choose designs with a noticeably distinctive character. American suburban houses in all regions began to sprout traditional picturesque devices like asymmetrical massing, complexly interlocking roof planes, and extensive dormer windows. Given a choice, few wished to live anymore in the blandly uniform housing tracts of the 1950s.

This renewed interest in a special sense of place combined in the 1990s with a renewed interest in environmental issues. Continuing population growth and industrialization put further pressure on the natural environment, gobbling up open spaces for suburbs, polluting the air and, alarmingly, heating up the world's climate and thinning the atmosphere's protective ozone layer. Even Americans who espoused less federal regulation and bureaucracy in their economic and social lives were not willing to remove the regulations put in place to protect the environment. Conservation efforts like recycling became a commonplace for millions of families. The American Institute of Architects set an ambitious agenda for 'sustainable architecture', by which they meant buildings that were ecologically responsible. Such a building would not use products derived from non-renewable resources, like petroleum, or products requiring extensive energy to produce, like aluminum. Sustainable architecture would also require buildings to work in sympathy with their local climates, one of the key issues of regionalism. We have seen in this history how many buildings before the Industrial Revolution had evolved in response to local climatological conditions, employing a compact form to retain heat in cold climates for example,

**296** New Mexico house,
New Mexico, 1983–85,
Antoine Predock

**297** Ranch house, Ennis,
Montana, 1992, Phil Korell

**298** Seaside, Florida, 1986– ,
Duany & Plater-Zyberk

and a thin form to allow cross-ventilation in hot, humid climates. We also saw how subsequent technical innovations like artificial lighting, central heating and air conditioning had removed these natural constraints on forms. Designers were able to put any building form in any climate and simply rely on the brute force of energy intensive technology to keep it inhabitable. But by the mid-1990s, many felt that the economic, political and environmental costs of this design strategy were simply too high to continue. The sustainable architects set out to relearn the ecological lessons of their pre-industrial predecessors.

The interest in a special sense of place also fueled a movement in the 1990s called the New Urbanism. Leon Krier, we saw earlier in the chapter, had proposed in the 1980s to revive the traditional town plans of pre-Modernist Europe. Like Christopher Alexander, he believed that traditional town layouts encouraged a more wholesome social life than one could obtain in a typical Modernist city. Since houses and shops in the traditional towns were clustered together rather than zoned apart, one could easily walk down to the local corner shop and chat with one's neighbors on the way. Town squares and plazas provided further congenial settings for public gatherings, where one could feel an integral part of a community. This cozy image of a closely-knit community inspired a number of New Urbanists in America, including Duany & Plater-Zyberk. They objected to the way in which American suburbs had been isolated from the public domain and taken over by the car. Remote shops force individuals to drive everywhere, rather than to walk by their neighbors, while streets designed for the convenience of cars speeding by at 40 miles an hour further discourage pedestrians who try. For lack of public squares and plazas, the only places to see other people are in the private shopping malls where the emphasis is on spending rather than conversation. The New Urbanists offered instead the romantic image of the small American town, where people know their neighbors and feel like they belong to the community [298]. These designers proposed street layouts like Krier's, with public buildings standing in squares at the crossing of important boulevards, and with shops mixed in with houses. To diminish the impact of the car, they proposed pushing garages away from the front of the house and back into the rear yard, and reducing the width of streets. They also advocated building small workshops or offices over the garages, so people could integrate their home and work lives. In the new age of international telecommunications and automated manufacturing, according to this vision, people no longer needed to commute to central places of work. Here we return full circle to the typical pre-industrial village, where the local artisans lived over their shops and participated in the daily life of their neighborhood while pursuing their livelihoods.

One could hardly imagine a wider range of architectural ideas than the ones we have just examined. One group insists on returning to order and tradition, while the next group attacks the idea of order itself. Some designers in this period continue to advance a conception of architecture as high art isolated from real life, while others wish to save the souls of communities or the world's ecology. Beaux-Arts Classicism, the Baroque, the Gothic, Spanish Colonial, rustic cabins, High Tech, Arts and Crafts, Frank Lloyd Wright, and vernacular European villages, among others, have all competed for architects' attentions in the last third of the twentieth century. Will we live forever more with this astonishing stylistic diversity, or will one or two ideas eventually emerge to dominate the turn of the millennium? The history of styles suggests that we are probably living in a transitional period between dominant architectural movements, but then never before has America so thoroughly institutionalized such wide-ranging cultural diversity. Perhaps the eclecticism and stylistic diversity that we saw mounting throughout the nineteenth century – and that reached a similar crescendo at the turn of the twentieth century – will remain with us forever more. The dominance of the Modernist paradigm at mid-century might have been only a temporary aberration in the larger picture of post-Enlightenment stylistic plurality. Only time – and a future historian – will tell.

# Glossary

Words in **bold** are defined elsewhere in the glossary. Numbers refer to illustrations.

**Academic Eclecticism**   An architectural approach popular in the last decades of the nineteenth and the first decades of the twentieth century; adapted a wide range of traditional architectural styles to new conditions.

**adobe**   Sun-dried bricks of mud and straw, used extensively in hot, treeless regions.

**adze**   A tool of ancient heritage, used for working wood. Similar in shape and use to a hoe, it is swung to chop timbers flat and square.

**aisle**   In a **basilica** church plan, the spaces on either side of – and parallel to – the central **nave**; usually separated from the nave with rows of columns or piers. See **12, 15**.

**altar**   Used in religious rituals, a table upon which are placed sacrificial offerings to a deity.

**Anglo Palladianism**   A style popular in the first decades of the eighteenth century in England, and in the latter half of the eighteenth century in America. Closely identified with the British Whigs, who wished to establish a new national architectural style based on the austere **Classicism** of Andrea Palladio and Inigo Jones.

**apse**   A recess in a wall, usually semi-circular or polygonal in plan; also, the projection on the outside of a building caused by an apse which is deeper than the wall thickness. Ancient Roman **basilicas** typically placed officials' chairs in an apse; when the Christians took over the basilica form for their churches, they placed the **altar** near the apse at the east end of the church. See **11**.

**arcade**   A row of arches carried by **columns** or **piers**; by extension, a covered passageway with an open arcade on one or both sides.

**arch**   A fundamental construction device used to span masonry over openings. Based on curves or portions of circles, an arch is typically built with wedge-shaped segments called **voussoirs**, the central one of which is called the **keystone**. An arch carries its load by pressing each voussoir against the next, until the load passes down the side of the opening. Styles of architecture based on the arch are called **arcuated**; compare to **trabeated**. See **11, 18**.

**archeological style**   Any architectural style that tries to reproduce accurately an earlier architectural tradition.

**architecture parlante**   A concept of architecture espoused by the eighteenth-century French visionary architects Étienne-Louis Boullée and Claude-Nicolas Ledoux. Buildings were meant to 'speak' ('parler' in French) their purpose so that, for example, a house for a cooper might look like a giant barrel.

**architrave**   The lowest decorative division in a Classical **entablature**; also, the molding around a door or window.

**arcuated**   Any style of architecture that is largely dependent upon the arch. Compare to **trabeated**.

**Art Deco**   A style popular in the late 1920s and the 1930s; inspirations included Jazz, Italian Futurism, German Expressionism, Viennese Secessionism, Egyptian and Mayan architecture. Named after the 1925 *Exposition Internationale des Arts Décoratifs et Industriels Modernes* in Paris where it was first given wide exposure.

**Art Moderne**   A style popular in the 1930s, closely related to **Art Deco**; inspired by the aerodynamic streamlining of contemporary machines like automobiles, steamships and airplanes. Sometimes known as Streamline Moderne in architecture.

**Artisan Mannerism**   A vernacular style popular in England in the late sixteenth and early seventeenth centuries; derived from sixteenth-century Italian and Low Countries **Mannerism**.

**Arts and Crafts**   A style popular in the last quarter of the nineteenth and the first quarter of the twentieth centuries. Growing out of the **Gothic Revival**, it advocated simplified medieval and vernacular forms, handcraft, and the frank expression of structure and construction.

**asymmetrical**   Not equally balanced in features on either side of an axis.

**atelier**   A studio space or room.

**atrio**   Spanish term for the **atrium** or courtyard in front of a Spanish-American Church.

**atrium**   An enclosed courtyard open to the sky.

**axial**   A building composition whose spaces or massing are organized along an imaginary straight line, or axis.


**balcony**   A projection of an upper floor beyond the outer wall, enclosed by a rail.

**balloon frame**   A method of timber-framed construction using light wooden members – usually 2 × 4 inches – spaced 16 inches to 24 inches apart. In a balloon frame, the vertical members rise unbroken from the foundation to the roof, and the horizontal members are hung off the verticals. Compare to **platform frame**. See **151**.

**baldacchino**   A canopy over an **altar**, tomb or throne, meant to give added significance and visual prominence to an important spot in a building.

**balustrade**   A series of thin posts (balusters) supporting a rail.

**banding**   Horizontal striping of color, texture or projection, encircling a structure.

**bargeboard**   A piece of trim on the gable end of a roof; sometimes decorated with carving or scrollwork.

**Baroque**   A style of art and architecture popular throughout the seventeenth century and, in some places, throughout the first half of the eighteenth century. Originally used as a term of derision for the more animated styles that replaced the austere and rational **Classicism** of the Italian **Renaissance**.

**barrel vault**   A **vault** formed by extruding a semi-circular **arch** lengthwise, resulting in a half cylinder. See **11**.

**basilica**   Originally, a large Roman structure used as law courts or for commerce. The form consisted of a high nave running down the center of a rectangular plan, with lower aisles flanking either side of the **nave**. The nave walls rose above the roofs of the **aisles**, and were opened with clerestory windows to admit light into the space below. The early Christians appropriated this form for their churches. See **12**, **15**.

**battlement**   A parapet with alternating solid and open sections; typically used in castles to provide defensive cover for archers. Also called crenellation.

**Bauhaus**   An influential school of art and architecture founded in Germany after the First World War; closely identified with the **Modernist** style.

**bay**   A module of a building which typically repeats down the length of a wall; each bay is defined by vertical elements like **columns**, **pilasters**, windows or **piers**.

**bay window**   A recess in a room, causing a projection beyond the plane of the external wall; filled with windows.

**beam**   A horizontal structural member whose loads are applied at right angles to its long axis. Compare to **column**.

**belfry**   The uppermost room in a bell-tower, containing the bell.

**béton brut**   A French term for concrete cast in rough wooden **formwork** and then left exposed as the building's final finish.

**bifurcate**   To divide into two.

**board and batten**   A method of forming a wall surface on a wooden frame building. Consists of wide boards whose joints are covered by narrow trim pieces called battens; usually the joints run vertically.

**bracket**   A small structural piece that supports the weight of a projection above. Also see **corbel**.

**bric-à-brac**   A collection of small decorative objects, often of sentimental value.

**Brutalism**   A style popular in the 1950s and 1960s; inspired by Le Corbusier's use of crudely formed raw concrete as a finished material.

**buttress**   A mass projecting from a masonry wall, designed to give the wall additional support.

**Byzantine**   The eastern part of the Roman Empire which flourished from the fourth to the fifteenth centuries, and which was governed from Constantinople (originally the Greek town Byzantium, now Istanbul). By extension, the art and architecture of the Byzantine Empire.

**capital**   The topmost part of a **column**, often embellished or ornamented; transfers the load of the **beam** above onto the main shaft of the column.

**cardinal points**   The four directions of the compass, north, south, east and west.

**Carolingian**   A dynasty which ruled central Europe from the seventh to the tenth centuries, whose most famous emperor was Charlemagne. **Classical** Roman and **Byzantine** architectural forms were combined in this period in an effort to revive the glories of the Roman Empire; later evolved into the **Romanesque** style.

**carpenter Gothic**   A style popular in the middle third of the nineteenth century; a wooden version of the **Gothic Revival** typified by scroll-saw cut details.

**Cartesian grid**   Named after the seventeenth-century French philosopher René Descartes, a system of uniformly spaced parallel and perpendicular lines. In mathematics, used to give any point a unique set of coordinates relative to an origin; in architecture, used to lay out a regular spacing of rooms or structural elements; in surveying, used to subdivide land into regular pieces irrespective of local geographical conditions.

**cartouche**   An ornamental panel, often placed in a prominent location in a **façade**, and often designed to look like a scroll of paper or a heavily ornamented picture frame; typically bears an inscription or a date.

**casement window**   A window which is hinged on the side, usually taller than it is wide.

**castle**   The heavily fortified residence of a feudal lord; typical features include **battlements**, slot windows, massive masonry walls, and a moat.

**catenary cable**   A cable suspended from two points that is allowed to take the form naturally caused by gravity.

**chamfer**   The beveling or cutting away of the sharp edge of a column or block, usually at a 45-degree angle.

**chancel**   The end of the church reserved for the clergy and the altar.

**chancel rail**   The railing that separates the chancel from the rest of the church.

**chapel**   A small building, or a small room within a larger structure, that is dedicated to worship.

**château**   A feudal **castle**, or later a large country house, in France.

**Chicago School**   An architectural movement in late nineteenth-century Chicago, which espoused a new aesthetic for skyscrapers.

**Chicago Window**   A window type popular with proponents of the Chicago School; a large window fills an entire **bay**, and is subdivided into a fixed pane of glass at the center and narrower sash windows on either side.

**chickee**   A Native American house type which evolved to accommodate the hot, humid climate of the southeastern region of present day United States; floors are raised up on poles to allow the free flow of cooling breezes. See **30**.

**Churrigueresque**   A style popular in Spain and the Spanish colonies in the late seventeenth and early eighteenth centuries, named after the Churriguera family; characterized by writhing, overpowering ornamentation.

**cladding**   The exterior covering of a building.

**clapboard**   A system of **cladding** on a wooden frame building, in which long horizontal boards overlap each other. Called weatherboarding in Great Britain.

**Classicism**   Also Classical. Refers to the system of construction and ornamentation developed in ancient Greece and Rome. See **Orders**.

**clerestory window**   The windows in the upper wall of a church **nave**, above the roofs of the adjacent **aisles**; by extension, any windows high up in a wall.

**cloister**   The interior court of a church or monastery, surrounded by covered passages called ambulatories.

**colonnade**   A row of **columns**.

**column**   Any vertical structural element that carries its load down its long axis. Compare to **beam** and **pier**. The columns in **Classical** architecture were always circular in cross section and gradually tapered in the top third of their length. Compare to **pilaster**. Classical columns were designed according to specific rules called **Orders**.

**Composite**   See **Orders**.

**concrete**   A building material made of cement and aggregate, which is poured into molds and then allowed to solidify.

**corbel**   A short block of masonry like a **bracket** that projects from a wall to support a **beam** or other horizontal member.

**corbel table**   A series of **corbels** located below the eaves of a building, typically used in the Romanesque style.

**Corinthian**   See **Orders**.

**cornice**   An ornamental molding that projects from the top of a building or wall; also, the upper-most molding of the Classical **entablature**; also, a molding between a wall and a ceiling.

**crenellation**   See **battlement**.

**cross-ventilation**   Providing for air movement through a structure by placing openings in opposite walls.

**cruciform plan**   A building plan formed of two intersecting rectangular shapes, like a cross; sometimes the rectangles are equal in length, other times one rectangle is longer than the other.

**cul-de-sac**   A dead-end street often found in suburban developments; intended to slow and reduce traffic within a residential neighborhood.

**cupola**   A small tower-like element, often with a round or polygonal base and a domed roof, which accents the roof of a building.

**curtain wall**   A non-load-bearing exterior wall hung on the outside of a structural frame.

**curvilinear**   A plan or massing comprised of curved or organic shapes. Compare to **rectilinear**.

**dimensional lumber**   Pre-cut lumber available in standardized sizes like 2″ by 4″, 2″ by 6″, 2″ by 8″, etc.

**dome**   A circular-based **vault** formed by rotating an **arch** about a central point. See **11**.

**Doric**   See **Order**.

**dormer**   A vertical window and its housing which projects above a sloping roof to provide additional living area and light within the roof space.

**double pile**   A rectangular house with a row of reception rooms on each side of a corridor running down the center of the long axis; first developed by Sir Roger Pratt in the seventeenth century for his house Coleshill.

**drum**   The circular or polygonal base of a **dome** or **lantern**.

**earthworks**   Large-scale sculpting of the landscape, involving the movement of large quantities of earth.

**eave**   The underside of the part of the roof that overhangs the exterior wall.

**Ecole des Beaux-Arts**   An influential school of art and architecture in Paris, which taught the principles of **Classical** architecture throughout the nineteenth and first half of the twentieth century.

**elevation**   A drawing which shows the vertical face of a building or an interior wall as if projected onto a flat plane; by extension, the design of the **façade**.

**entablature**   The horizontal **beam** in **Classical** architecture, ornamented according to the rules of the five **Orders**. It is decoratively divided into three horizontal parts: the **architrave** at the bottom, the **frieze** in the middle, and the **cornice** at the top.

**entasis**   The gradual reduction in the diameter of a classical column in the top third of its length; intended to correct the optical illusion of concavity and top-heaviness that results from columns of constant diameter along their full length.

**Expressionism**   Any art or architectural movement that seeks to express the artist's emotions or emotional reactions to objects.

**façade**   The outside face of a building.

**Federalist**   The style of architecture popular after the American Revolution; largely based on the **Classicism** of the British architects Robert Adam and Sir William Chambers.

**fluting**   Vertical grooves carved into the shaft of a **pilaster** or **column**.

**flying buttress**   A free-standing arch or half-arch which projects perpendicularly from a masonry wall; used to provide structural support to the wall while allowing the walls to remain relatively thin and often open. Widely used in **Gothic** architecture. See **17**.

**formwork**   The temporary structure into which concrete is poured, which is then removed when the concrete sets.

**frame-and-infill**   A fundamental construction technique of ancient heritage. A frame constructed of stick-like members carries the structural loads but does not weatherproof; while an outer cover or an infill keeps out the weather but does not carry any structural load. This technique has been used for prehistoric huts as well as modern skyscrapers. Compare to **load bearing**.

**frieze**   The horizontal band, often decorated with sculpture, located between the **cornice** and **architrave** of a **Classical entablature**; by extension, any wide decorative band on a wall.

**gable**   The triangular part of the end wall under a **gable roof**.

**gable roof**   The most usual roof form, with two inclined planes meeting at a ridge line. The two triangular walls at the ends are called **gables**. Compare to a **hipped roof**.

**gallery**   An upper floor space which opens on one side onto an interior court or room.

**gambrel roof**   In Great Britain, a **hipped roof** which terminates in a small gable at the top. In America, a **gable roof** which breaks the inclined planes into two horizontal parts, giving the lower part a steeper pitch than the upper part; compare to **mansard roof**.

**Georgian**   A term commonly used to describe a popular British architectural and furniture style of the late seventeenth and early eighteenth centuries, even though George I ascended to the throne a half-century after the style was first developed. A refined and austere version of **Classicism**, often combining stone Classical details with brick walls.

**gilded**   Covered with a thin layer of gold.

**Gothic**   A style of architecture popular from the twelfth to the sixteenth centuries; evolved from the **Romanesque** style, its characteristics include **flying buttresses**, **pointed arches**, and large sheets of stained glass.

**Gothic Revival**   A style based on medieval **Gothic** architecture, popular from the latter half of the eighteenth century into the first decades of the twentieth century; inspired the **Arts and Crafts** movement.

**Greek Revival**   A style popular in the first half of the nineteenth century, it favored the Greek version of **Classicism** over the Roman. This meant eschewing **arches** in favor of **post and lintel**, basing forms on the Greek temple, and using the Greek versions of the **Orders**.

**gridiron**   A town plan based on a regular grid of streets. See **13, 69**.

**groin vault**   A vault formed by intersecting two **barrel** vaults. See **11**.

**hacienda**   A large estate in a Spanish-speaking country; by extension, the main house on the estate.

**half-timbering**   A variation on the **frame-and-infill** structural system, particularly popular in the Middle Ages. The frame is constructed of widely spaced large section wooden beams and columns, usually joined with **mortises** and **tenons**; the frame is then infilled with brick, **wattle and daub**, or plaster, leaving the wooden structure exposed. Compare to **balloon frame** or **platform frame**. See **14**.

**hall**   In medieval domestic architecture, the main room which served as the dining, entertainment and often sleeping room. In post-Renaissance domestic architecture, the main entrance room in which is often found the main staircase. See **50**.

**hipped roof**   A roof with four inclined planes, leaving no gable ends. On a square plan, the four planes meet at a point if the pitches are equal; on a rectangular plan, the two longer planes meet at a ridge line if the pitches are equal. Compare to a **gable roof**.

**hogan**   A Native American house type which evolved to accommodate the hot, dry climate of the southwestern region of present day United States; typically, insulating soil is placed over a heavy structure of wooden members. See **24**.

**International Style**   An architectural style popular in the 1920s and 30s which rejected the traditional styles altogether. Characterized by cubic forms, flat roofs, and a rejection of ornament, detail and color.

**Ionic**   See **Orders**.

**Italian Futurism**   An avant-garde architectural movement before the First World War which rejected traditional styles, and which championed instead futuristic images based on the motion and machines of modern life.

**Italian vernacular**   Broadly refers to styles of architecture which are inspired by the vernacular forms of rural Italy; characterized by shallow pitched roofs, roof tiles, and simple stone or plaster walls.

**Italianate**   An architectural style popular through much of the nineteenth century, which drew its sources from vernacular Italian farm houses; characterized by rambling, asymmetrical plans, square towers, and ornate **brackets** under the **cornices**.

**joinery**   The art of joining pieces of wood together.

**keep**   A fortified tower which served as the stronghold of a castle.

**keystone**   The topmost **voussoir** in an **arch**, often decorated.

**kiva**   A Native American ceremonial and religious structure, partly or fully underground and usually round.

**knee brace**   A diagonal brace set in the corner of a rectangular frame, meant to resist the frame from racking.

**lantern**   A small turret atop a roof or **dome**, usually with windows on all sides.

**latticework**   A screen of crossed thin wooden members.

**load bearing**   A fundamental system of construction of ancient heritage; structural loads are carried onto thick continuous walls, usually of stone or brick. Compare to **frame-and-infill**.

**lintel**   A horizontal **beam** over an opening.

**longhouse**   A Native American house type which evolved in the woodlands covering the northeastern region of present day United States; typically a light wooden frame was covered with sheets of bark. See **30**.

**lunette**   A semi-circular window or wall panel, often framed by an arch.

**Mannerism**   A style of sixteenth-century art and architecture which followed the Italian **Renaissance** and anticipated the **Baroque**; characterized by mannered exaggerations and deliberate corruptions of the **Classical** rules. By extension, any artistic or architectural styles that distort commonly accepted rules.

**manor**   A unit of the feudal system of land organization; governed by a lord and worked by serfs who were legally tied to the land. By extension, the lord's house on the manor.

**mansard roof**   A **hipped** roof which breaks the inclined planes into two horizontal parts, giving the lower part a steeper pitch than the upper part. Named after the seventeenth-century French architect François Mansart. Compare to **gambrel roof**.

**massing**   The overall arrangement of a building's forms.

**metope**   In the **frieze** of the Doric **Order**, a decorative element which alternates with the **triglyphs**.

**minstrel's gallery**   A **gallery** overlooking a medieval **hall**, upon which musicians played.

**Mission style**   A style of architecture and furniture which is derived from the Spanish missions in the southwestern region of present day United States.

**Modernism**   Also Modernist. An approach to art and architecture that emerged in the first decades of the twentieth century, rose to prominence after the Second World War, and then gave way to **Postmodernism** in the 1980s. In architecture, characterized by its absolute rejection of traditional styles, by its rejection of **regionalism** in favor of universal applications, and by its abstract forms devoid of ornament and detail.

**molding**   A decorative strip used to ornament a surface or to cover a joint in building materials.

**mono-pitch roof**   A roof with one pitch. Also known as a shed roof.

**mortise and tenon**   A joint used for connecting two pieces of timber or other materials. The mortise is a cavity cut into the surface of one member, while the tenon is a projection on the other member which slots tightly into the mortise.

**mosaic**   A surface decoration consisting of small colored pieces arranged to create a larger design.

**motif**   A dominant idea in a design; also, a repeating element in a design.

**mullion**   A vertical element dividing a window into panes.

**nave**   The central space of a **basilica** or church, flanked by the side **aisles**. See **12, 15**.

**Neoclassical**   An art and architectural movement of the late eighteenth century, which rejected the sensual qualities of **Rococo** in favor of a severely rational version of **Classicism**.

**niche**   A small recess in a wall, often containing art.

**obelisk**   A monumental shaft, square or rectangular in plan, which tapers as it rises and is topped with a pyramidal form; used in ancient Egypt and later in a nineteenth-century Egyptian revival.

**ogee**   A standard profile for architecture and furniture moldings; a concave surface in the upper half flows into a convex surface in the lower half.

**Orders**   Classicism's five archetypal systems of decoration for columns and beams. The five Orders comprise an ordered system, ranging from the most plain and squat to the most ornamented and attenuated (see **10**.) Each Order contains specific rules of proportion and detailing for a vertical **column** and a horizontal **entablature**, or beam. The column is divided into a base, a shaft and a **capital**, while the entablature is divided into an **architrave**, a **frieze** and a **cornice**. See **10**. The five Orders are:

1. **Doric.** Named after the Dorian region of Greece, the Greek Doric Order is the most squat. It can be identified by the lack of a base, the emphatic **entasis** in the column, and the **triglyphs** and **metopes** in the **entablature**. The later Roman version of the Doric also used triglyphs and metopes, but added a base and slimmed the proportions.

2. **Tuscan.** Developed by the Romans, the Tuscan is identified by the lack of flutes in the columns, and by the poverty of ornamental detail.

3. **Ionic.** Named after Ionian Greece, now the west coast of Turkey, the Ionic Order is identified by the volute or scroll in the capital.

4. **Corinthian.** Named after the Corinth region of Greece, this Order is the slimmest and most richly ornamented. It is identified by the rows of stylized acanthus leaves in the capital.

5. **Composite.** The Romans combined the Ionic and the Corinthian to form the Composite. It is identified by its capital, which juxtaposes the Ionic volute with the Corinthian acanthus leaves.

**oriel window**   A **bay window** on an upper floor, usually supported by a **corbel** or **bracket**.

**orthogonal**   Mutually perpendicular lines.

**overhang**   The projection of the roof past the vertical plane of the exterior wall.

**palazzo**   A large Italian residence.

**Palladian window**   A window arrangement with a large arched central opening flanked on either side by smaller rectangular openings.

**Palladianism**   An architectural style inspired by the buildings or writings of the sixteenth-century Italian Classicist Andrea Palladio.

**parapet**   A low wall which protects a large drop-off, like at a bridge or a roof-top. Also, when a roof lies hidden behind an exterior wall rather than hanging over it, a parapet is that part of the wall that extends above the roof.

**parlor**   A room in a house used primarily for the reception and entertainment of guests. See **50**.

**parterre**   A formal garden with paths between planting beds.

**pavilion**   An accessory building, often open to the air. Also a projecting subdivision of a building that asserts its own identity as separate from the whole, usually at the ends or middle of a **Classical** composition.

**pediment**   A **gable** in **Classical** architecture, also often used as a decorative element above doors and windows.

**pendentive**   A structural device used to support a circular **dome** on a square base below. Usually, a curved surface that starts as a point in the corner of the base, and then expands upward and around to meet the lower edge of the dome.

**picturesque**   A valued quality in the eighteenth-century Romantic reaction against rationalism; stressed ruggedness and asymmetry.

**pier**   A vertical structural support, typically thicker than a column and rectangular or polygonal in plan. Compare to **column**.

**pilaster**   A square **column** or **pier** that only slightly projects from a wall; in **Classical** architecture, usually decorated according to one of the **Orders**.

**pilotis**   Structural **columns** that raise a building off the ground, allowing the ground to continue under the structure.

**pinnacle**   The uppermost termination, usually a tapered and ornamented cap, on towers or **spires**.

**pitch**   The slope of a roof.

**pit house**   A prehistoric building form, which partly buries the building into the ground for insulation. See **2**.

**plan**   The arrangement of a building relative to a flat ground plane. Also, the drawing showing that arrangement, usually shown as a section cut a few feet above the floor.

**platform frame**   A method of timber-framed construction using light wooden members – usually 2 × 4 inches – spaced 16 inches to 24 inches apart. In a platform frame, the vertical members rise only one story to support the platform of the floor above, and then more vertical members rise to support the next floor, etc. Eventually replaced **balloon frames** when it was no longer possible to obtain the long timbers required for the latter.

**plaza**   A public open space, typically surrounded wholly or in part by buildings and shops.

**pointed arch**   An **arch** formed by two arcs which intersect at the middle of the span, creating an acute angle; widely used in **Gothic** architecture. See **18**.

**polychromy**   The use of multiple colors on a building, usually by employing different colored building materials.

**porch**   A covered entrance to a building, often used as an outdoor living space when weather allows.

**portal**   A door or passable opening.

**portales**   Spanish term for an **arcade**.

**porte-cochère**   A porch usually adjacent to an entry, through which motorized or horse-drawn vehicles may pass.

**portico**   A covered porch, usually **Classical**, which provides the main visual interest of a façade. Usually topped with a **pediment** and framed by **columns**.

**post and lintel** (or **post and beam**)   A system of construction using vertical posts or **columns** and horizontal **beams**.

**Postmodern**   In architecture, the style that supplanted **Modernism** in the 1980s; usually characterized by a return to more traditional modes of expression, often with **Mannerist** twists. More broadly, the artistic and literary movements of the 1980s and 1990s that espouse complexity and disorder.

**Prairie Style**   A style of architecture closely identified with Frank Lloyd Wright's designs in the first decade of the twentieth century; it stresses horizontal lines, broad and shallow overhanging roofs, and natural materials.

**presidio**   A Spanish military post.

**proportion**   The ratio of one part to another. Many architectural styles, both traditional and modern, championed certain proportions as more harmonious or beautiful than others.

**pulpit**   An elevated platform from which a sermon is given.

**pueblo**   A Native American settlement in the southwest of the present day United States, characterized by closely packed adobe dwellings. See **25**.

**pyramid**   A geometrical shape with a square base and four sides sloping equally to meet at an apex; also, any structure of broadly pyramidal shape.

**quatre-foil**   A geometrical pattern used for ornament or to define the shapes of windows; roughly looks like a four-leaved clover.

**Queen Anne**   A style of furniture, interiors and architecture popular in England in the first half of the eighteenth century, based on Classicism; also a style of architecture popularized by Norman Shaw in the 1870s which was drawn from English vernacular traditions of the sixteenth and seventeenth centuries. In America, Shaw's style evolved into one of the first uniquely American styles, with large turrets and front porches, and large decorated gables.

**quoin**   A decorative detail at the corner of usually **Classical** buildings; slightly projecting stones or bricks give emphasis to the corner, often alternating between narrow and wide up the height of the wall.

**Ranch style**   A house style developed between the wars, and extensively built in the post-war housing boom; derived from **Spanish Colonial**, **Arts and Crafts**, and Frank Lloyd Wright's ideas. Usually one story with rambling asymmetrical wings and a shallow pitched roof.

**rationalism**   Broadly, a philosophical or aesthetic view which stresses rational clarity, logic and order. In architecture, any style or approach that values clear and simple geometry.

**rectilinear**   A plan or massing comprised of straight lines and right angles. Compare to **curvilinear**.

**relief**   A surface decoration characterized by slightly projecting ornaments or figures.

**regionalism**   In architecture, any style or approach that tries to fit the building to the culture, climate and geography of a particular place.

**Renaissance**   A broad movement in fifteenth century Italy that wished to revive the glories of ancient Rome by reviving the ancient Roman modes of cultural expression. In architecture, the movement revived Roman **Classicism**.

**Renaissance Revival**   A style in the nineteenth century which revived the **Classical** forms of the Italian **Renaissance**.

**ribs**   Relatively thin strips of masonry which were initially raised to form the arches in **Romanesque** and **Gothic** vaulting. Infilling between the ribs subsequently finished the structure. By extension, any bandlike protrusions on ceilings and vaults which give the appearance of a structural frame behind. See **17**.

**Richardsonian Romanesque**   The personal style of the nineteenth-century American architect H. H. Richardson, who revived the **Romanesque** style and gave it a particularly bold expression.

**ridge**   The horizontal line at the top of a roof, formed by the intersection of the roof planes.

**Rococo**   A delicate and refined style of architecture and decoration in the early eighteenth century, which succeeded the bolder forms of the seventeenth-century **Baroque**.

**Romanesque**   A style of architecture which followed from the **Carolingian**, and which rose to prominence in Italy and Western Europe after AD 1000. It roughly revived the forms of Roman **Classicism**, but gave them a more distinct vertical emphasis.

**Romanticism**   A broad cultural movement of the late eighteenth and nineteenth centuries, which first reacted against the **rationalism** and **Classicism** of the post-Renaissance era, and later against the Industrial Revolution. The movement stressed originality and genius, the natural and organic, and emotional responses to objects.

**rood screen**   A screen separating the chancel from the nave in a church.

**rotunda**   A circular building or room, usually roofed by a **dome**.

**rustication**   Masonry characterized by roughly finished edges and faces and set with deep joints.

**salt-box**   A characteristic house form of the early American colonial period. Adjoining a two-story rectangular box with a **gable roof** is a one-story addition, such that the gable roof on one side continues to sweep down to one story over the addition.

**sash window**   A window divided into an upper and lower unit, each of which slides vertically in grooves in the window frame. Also called a double-hung window.

**Scottish Baronial**   A name broadly given to the grander medieval vernacular buildings and castles of Scotland.

**screens passage**   In a medieval house, a circulation space separated from the main hall by a screen or colonnade, and giving access to the buttery, kitchen and pantry. See **50**.

**Second Empire**   A mid-nineteenth-century style of furniture, interiors and architecture closely associated with the reign of Napoleon III in France. In architecture, characterized by opulently decorated **Classicism** and by prominent **mansard roofs**.

**setback**   A building regulation that establishes a minimum distance between a building and a property line; meant to avoid overcrowding.

**shed roof**   See **mono-pitch roof**.

**Shingle Style**   A style of mostly domestic architecture in America in the 1870s and 1880s, originally influenced by Norman Shaw's revival of English medieval vernacular architecture; characteristically covered the entire skin of the building with shingles.

**siding**   An external skin for a building, usually made of overlapping horizontal pieces.

**sipapu**   A shallow indentation in the ground of a Native American **kiva**, meant to symbolize the place where deities emerge from the earth.

**spandrel**   In traditional architecture, the roughly triangular space between two arches in an **arcade**; also, the space beside one arch. In modern high-rise construction, the horizontal panel between rows of windows.

**Spanish Colonial**   Any style which derives from the architectural traditions of the Spanish Colonial period.

**spindle**   A long, thin, usually decoratively turned, element; usually combined with others to form a screen or a railing.

**spire**   A tall, pointed structure rising from a roof or tower, usually with a conical, pyramidal or polygonal shape.

**Stick Style**   A style of architecture popular in the mid-nineteenth century; grown out of the **Gothic Revival**, it boldly expressed wooden structural elements like **half-timbering**, **brackets**, and exposed timber roofs.

**strapwork**   A decorative motif designed to look like interweaving bands or leather straps, first developed in sixteenth-century Netherlands and popular in Elizabethan England.

**Streamline Moderne**   See **Art Moderne**.

**string course**   A slightly projecting horizontal band set into an exterior wall, usually used as a visual device to tie together façade elements like windows and doors.

**strut**   A structural element, usually employed in **trusses**, which helps brace one part against another.

**stucco**   Plasterwork.

**style**   A particular kind of architecture, with identifiable characteristics of form, material and detail; as in the **Classical** style.

**surround**   The ornament, detail and molding surrounding an opening like a door or window.

**Swiss chateau**   Broadly, a style based on the vernacular houses of the Swiss Alps; characterized by a simple box-like form with a shallow, widely overhanging **gable roof**.

**symmetry**   Equally balanced in features on either side of a center line or axis.


**tenon**   See **mortise and tenon**.

**tensile**   A force that acts to pull a structure apart, or a structural member that resists tensile forces.

**thatch**   A roofing material made of straw, hay or other reeds.

**tipi**   A conical Native American structure, constructed of a light, demountable wooden frame and a removable skin covering. See **32**.

**trabeated**   Any style of architecture that is largely based on a **post and lintel** construction system. Compare to **arcuated**.

**tracery**   Ornamental decoration used in **vaults**, **arches**, screens and in details, often around and above windows.

**transepts**   The transverse arms of a cruciform church plan.

**travois**   A Native American device for carrying loads behind a horse.

**triglyph**   In the **frieze** of the Doric **Order**, a decorative element which simulates the ends of **beams**, and which alternates with a **metope**.

**tripartite division**   The division of any architectural element or **façade** into three parts, either horizontally or vertically.

**truss**   A structural device used to span spaces wider than would be possible with a single beam. A truss is comprised of a number of small **beams** and **struts** all acting together as a single structural unit.

**Tudor arch**   An **arch** created with four centers. See **18**.

**Tudor style**   Broadly, any style derived from the court architecture of the sixteenth-century English Tudor period; characterized by **Tudor arches**, patterned brickwork, steep roofs and tall, decorated chimneys.

**turret**   A small and thin tower.

**Tuscan**   See **Orders**.

**vault**   A fundamental structural device used to span large distances. A vault is formed by extruding an **arch** shape down the length of a building, and thus carries its loads according to the same structural principle as an arch. See **11**.

**veneer**   A thin surface, usually of fine or costly materials, applied to a base of more common materials.

**vernacular**   In architecture, the buildings which evolved in a particular place over a long period, and whose forms and details entered into the common vocabulary of local builders; as opposed to the high fashion designs of professional designers.

**vestibule**   A room which acts as a transitional room to a larger room; by extension, a room which links the exterior to the main rooms of a building's interior.

**vigas**   In **Pueblo** and **Spanish Colonial** architecture, the ends of the **beams** which project beyond the face of the exterior wall.

**voussoir**   The wedge-shaped units used to construct an **arch**.

**wattle and daub**   A building cladding where clay or mud (daub) is pressed onto and into laths (wattle).

**wigwam**   A Native American structure, comprised of a wooden frame and a skin of bark, rush mats or skins. See **30**.

**window crown**   See **window hood**.

**window hood**   A device placed on the wall above a window to help shed water away from the window.

**zapatas**   Carved brackets which serve as capitals in **Spanish Colonial** architecture.

**ziggurat**   A **pyramid** in the ancient Near East, usually with ramps ascending to a truncated top.

# Bibliography and further reading

Alexander, Christopher (1964), *Notes on the Synthesis of Form*, Cambridge, Mass., Harvard University Press.
—— (1979), *The Timeless Way of Building*, New York, Oxford University Press.
—— , Sara Ishikawa, Murray Silverstein, Max Jacobson, Ingrid Fiksdahl-King, and Shlomo Angel (1977), *A Pattern Language: Towns, Buildings, Construction*, New York, Oxford University Press.
Andrews, Wayne (1964), *Architecture, Ambition and Americans; A Social History of American Architecture*, New York, Free Press of Glencoe.
Baker, John Cordis, ed. (1906), *American Country Homes and Their Gardens*, Philadelphia, John C. Winston Company.
Baker, Paul R. (1980), *Richard Morris Hunt*, Cambridge, Mass., MIT Press.
Banham, Reyner (1960), *Theory and Design in the First Machine Age*, London, The Architectural Press.
—— (1971), *Los Angeles: The Architecture of Four Ecologies*, New York, Harper & Row.
Bayer, Herbert, Walter Gropius and Ise Gropius (1938), *Bauhaus 1919–28*, New York, The Museum of Modern Art.
Betsky, Aaron (1990), *Violated Perfection: Fragmentation in Modern Architecture*, New York, Rizzoli.
Billington, Ray (1960), *Westward Expansion: A History of the Western Frontier*, New York, The Macmillan Company.
Bishir, Catherine (1990), *North Carolina Architecture*, Chapel Hill, University of North Carolina Press.
Blum, John, *et al.* (1993), *The National Experience: A History of the United States*, 8th edn, Fort Worth, Harcourt Brace.
Blunt, Anthony (1940), *Artistic Theory in Italy 1450–1600*, Oxford, Oxford University Press.
—— (1980), *Art and Architecture in France 1500–1700*, 4th edn, Harmondsworth, Penguin Books.
Bourassé, L'abbé J.-J. (1885), *Châteaux Historiques de France*, 5th edn, Tours, Alfred Mame et Fils, éditeurs.
Boutelle, Sara Holmes (1988), *Julia Morgan: Architect*, New York, Abbeville Press.
Boyer, M. Christine (1983), *Dreaming the Rational City: The Myth of American City Planning*, Cambridge, Mass., MIT Press.
—— (1985), *Manhattan Manners: Architecture and Style 1850–1900*, New York, Rizzoli.
Brawne, Michael (1994), *University of Virginia: The Lawn: Thomas Jefferson*, London, Phaidon Press.
Briggs, Martin (1974), *The Architect in History*, New York, Da Capo Press.
Brogan, Hugh (1985), *The Pelican History of the United States of America*, Harmondsworth, Penguin Books.
Brown, Glen (1900), *History of the United States Capitol*, Washington, DC, Government Printing Office.

Brownlee, David B. and David G. De Long (1991), *Louis I. Kahn: In the Realm of Architecture*, New York, Rizzoli.

Burchard, John and Albert Bush-Brown (1961), *The Architecture of America: A Social and Cultural History*, Boston, Little, Brown and Company.

Bushman, Richard L. (1992), *The Refinement of America: Persons, Houses, Cities*, New York, Vintage Books.

Campbell, Colen (1715–25), *Vitruvius Brittanicus*, London.

Choisy, Auguste (1899), *Histoire de l'Architecture*, Paris, Gauthier-Villars.

Clark, Clifford Edward, Jr (1986), *The American Family Home, 1800–1960*, Chapel Hill, University of North Carolina Press.

Clausen, Meredith (1984), 'Northgate Regional Shopping Center – Paradigm From the Provinces', *Journal of the Society of Architectural Historians*, XLIII: 144–61.

Coe, Michael (1968), *America's First Civilization*, New York, American Heritage.

Coffin, Lewis A., Jr and Arthur C. Holden (1919), *Brick Architecture of the Colonial Period in Maryland & Virginia*, New York, Architectural Book Publishing Co.

Conant, Kenneth (1966), *Carolingian and Romanesque Architecture 800 to 1200*, Baltimore, Penguin Books.

Condit, Carl (1960), *American Building Art: The Nineteenth Century*, New York, Oxford University Press.

—— (1961), *American Building Art: The Twentieth Century*, New York, Oxford University Press.

—— (1961), *The Chicago School of Architecture: A History of Commercial and Public Building in the Chicago Area, 1875–1925*, New York, Oxford University Press.

Coolidge, John (1942), *Mill and Mansion: A Study of Architecture and Society in Lowell, Massachusetts, 1820–65*, New York, Columbia University Press.

Creese, Walter L. (1990), *TVA's Public Planning: The Vision, The Reality*, Knoxville, Tenn., University of Tennessee Press.

Cronin, William (1991), *Nature's Metropolis: Chicago and the Great West*, New York, W. W. Norton.

Curl, Donald (1984), *Mizner's Florida: American Resort Architecture*, New York, Architectural History Foundation; Cambridge, Mass., MIT Press.

Davey, Peter (1995), *Arts and Crafts Architecture*, London, Phaidon Press.

Davis, Alexander Jackson (1837), *Rural Residences*, New York.

Davis, Mike (1990), *City of Quartz: Excavating the Future in Los Angeles*, New York, Random House.

De Long, David (1979), *Historic American Buildings, Texas*, New York, Garland Publications.

Donnelly, Marian (1968), *The New England Meeting Houses of the Seventeenth Century*, Middletown, Conn., Wesleyan University Press.

Drexler, Arthur, ed. (1977), *The Architecture of the Ecole des Beaux-Arts*, New York, The Museum of Modern Art.

Eckert, Kathryn (1993), *Buildings of Michigan*, New York, Oxford University Press.

Eisenman, Peter (1988), *The House of Cards*, New York, Oxford University Press.

Embury II, Aymar (1913), *The Dutch Colonial House*, New York, McBride, Nast & Company.

—— (1914), *Early American Churches*, Garden City, New York, Doubleday, Page & Company.

Engelbrecht, Lloyd C. and June-Marie (1981), *Henry C. Trost: Architect of the Southwest*, El Paso, El Paso Public Library Association.

Fabos, Julius, Gordon Milde, and Michael Weinmayr (1968), *Frederick Law Olmsted, Sr*, Amherst, University of Massachusetts Press.

Fiedel, Stuart (1993), *Prehistory of the Americas*, 2nd edn, Cambridge, Cambridge University Press.

Fitch, James Marston (1972; orig. pub. 1947), *American Building: The Environmental Forces that Shape It*, Boston, Houghton Mifflin Company.

—— (1973; orig. pub. 1947), *American Building: The Historical Forces that Shaped It*, New York, Shocken Books.

Fletcher, Banister (1987), *A History of Architecture*, 19th edn, ed. John Musgrove, London, Butterworth.

Foy, Jessica and Thomas Schlereth (1992), *American Home Life, 1880–1930: A Social History of Spaces and Services*, Knoxville, University of Tennessee Press.

Franciscono, Marcel (1971), *Walter Gropius and the Creation of the Bauhaus in Weimar: The Ideals and Artistic Theories of Its Founding Years*, Urbana, University of Illinois Press.

Garner, John S., ed. (1992), *The Company Town: Architecture and Society in the Early Industrial Age*, New York, Oxford University Press.

Gayle, Margot (1974), *Cast-Iron Architecture in New York: A Photographic Survey*, New York, Dover.

Gebhard, David (1976), *Bay Area Houses*, New York, Oxford University Press.

—— and Gerald Mansheim (1993), *Buildings of Iowa*, New York, Oxford University Press.

—— and Robert Winter (1985), *Architecture in Los Angeles*, Layton, Utah, Peregrine Smith Books.

——, Eric Sandweiss and Robert Winter (1985), *Architecture in San Francisco and Northern California*, Salt Lake City, Peregrine Smith Books.

Gelernter, Mark (1995), *Sources of Architectural Form: A Critical History of Western Design Theory*, Manchester, Manchester University Press.

Germann, Georg (1972), *Gothic Revival in Europe and Britain: Sources, Influences and Ideas*, London, Lund Humphries with the Architectural Association.

Gibbs, James (1728), *A Book of Architecture*, London.

Girouard, Mark (1977), *Sweetness and Light: The Queen Anne Movement, 1860–1900*, New York, Oxford University Press.

Goldberger, Paul (1981), *The Skyscraper*, New York, Knopf.

Gowans, Alan (1976; orig. pub. 1964), *Images of American Living: Four Centuries of Architecture and Furniture as Cultural Expression*, New York, Harper & Row.

—— (1992), *Styles and Types of North American Architecture: A Cultural History*, New York, Icon Editions.

Gray, Robert (1979), *A History of London*, New York, Taplinger Publishing Company.

Greiff, Constance, ed. (1971), *Lost America From the Atlantic to the Mississippi*, Princeton, NJ, Pyne Press.

—— (1972), *Lost America from the Mississippi to the Pacific*, Princeton, NJ, Pyne Press.

Gropius, Walter (1956), *The Scope of Total Architecture*, London, George Allen & Unwin Ltd.

Guadet, Julien (1909), *Eléments et Théorie de l'Architecture*, 4th edn, Paris, Librairie de la Construction Moderne.

Hamilton, Charles (1995), *Nineteenth Century Mormon Architecture*, New York, Oxford University Press.

Hamlin, Talbot (1955), *Benjamin Henry Latrobe*, New York, Oxford University Press.

—— (1969; orig. pub. 1944), *Greek Revival Architecture in America*, New York, Dover.

*Hammond's Atlas of United States History* (1995), Maplewood, NJ, Hammond, Inc.

Handlin, David (1985), *American Architecture*, London, Thames and Hudson Ltd.

Hatton, Hap (1987), *Tropical Splendor: An Architectural History of Florida*, New York, Alfred A. Knopf.

Hayden, Dolores (1976), *Seven American Utopias: The Architecture of Communitarian Socialism, 1790–1975*, Cambridge, Mass., MIT Press.

—— (1981), *The Grand Domestic Revolution: A History of Feminist Designs for American Homes, Neighborhoods, and Cities*, Cambridge, Mass., MIT Press.

Hays, Michael and Carol Burns, eds (1990), *Thinking the Present: Recent American Architecture*, New York, Princeton Architectural Press.

Hearn, M. F., ed. (1990), *The Architectural Theory of Viollet-le-Duc: Readings and Commentary*, Cambridge, Mass., MIT Press.

Hewitt, Mark (1990), *The Architect and the American Country House, 1890–1940*, New York, Yale University Press.

Heyer, Paul (1993), *Architects on Architecture: New Directions in America*, New York, Van Nostrand Reinhold.

Hines, Thomas S. (1974), *Burnham of Chicago: Architect and Planner*, New York, Oxford University Press.

—— (1982), *Richard Neutra and the Search for a Modern Architecture*, New York, Oxford University Press.

*Historic American Buildings Survey* (1971), catalog of the measured drawings and photographs of the Survey in the Library of Congress, New York, B. Franklin.

*Historical Atlas of the United States* (1993), Washington, DC, National Geographic Society.

Hitchcock, Henry-Russell (1973), *In the Nature of Materials, 1887–1941: The Buildings of Frank Lloyd Wright*, New York, Da Capo Press.

—— (1975), *The Architecture of H. H. Richardson and His Times*, Cambridge, Mass., MIT Press.

—— (1977), *Architecture: Nineteenth and Twentieth Centuries*, Harmondsworth, Penguin Books Ltd.

Hoffman, Donald (1973), *The Architecture of John Wellborn Root*, Baltimore, Johns Hopkins University Press.

Jencks, Charles (1980), 'Post-Modern Classicism', *Architectural Design*, 5/6, London.

—— (1988), *Architecture Today*, New York, Harry N. Abrams, Inc., Publishers.

Jennings, Jan, ed. (1990), *Roadside America: The Automobile in Design and Culture*, Ames, Iowa, Iowa State University Press for the Society for Commercial Archeology.

Jennings, Jan and Herbert Gottfried (1988), *American Vernacular Interior Architecture, 1870–1940*, New York, Van Nostrand Reinhold.

Johnson, Eugene J., ed. (1986), *Charles Moore: Buildings and Projects 1949–86*, New York, Rizzoli.

Jordy, William H. (1972), *Progressive and Academic Ideals at the Turn of the Twentieth Century*, vol. 4 of *American Buildings and Their Architects*, Garden City, New York, Doubleday & Company, Inc.

—— (1972), *The Impact of European Modernism in the Mid-Twentieth Century*, vol. 5 of *American Buildings and Their Architects*, Garden City, New York, Doubleday & Company, Inc.

Kamerling, Bruce A. (1993), *Irving J. Gill, Architect*, San Diego, San Diego Historical Society.

Kaufmann, Edgar and Ben Raeburn, eds (1960), *Frank Lloyd Wright: Writings and Buildings*, Cleveland and New York, Meridian.

Kaufmann, Edgar, ed. (1970), *The Rise of an American Architecture*, New York, Praeger Publishers.

Keeler, Charles (1904), *The Simple Home*, San Francisco, Paul Elder & Co.

Kelly, Barbara M. (1993), *Expanding the American Dream: Building and Rebuilding Levittown*, Albany, NY, State University of New York Press.

Kennedy, Roger G. (1989), *Greek Revival America*, New York, Stewart, Tabori & Chang.

—— (1994), *Hidden Cities: The Discovery and Loss of Ancient North American Civilization*, New York, Free Press; Toronto, Maxwell Macmillan Canada; New York, Maxwell Macmillan International.

Kidder Smith, G. E. (1976), *Architecture in America: A Pictorial History*, New York, American Heritage.

—— (1996), *Source Book of American Architecture*, New York, Princeton Architectural Press.

Kidney, Walter C. (1974), *The Architecture of Choice: Eclecticism in America 1880–1930*, New York, Braziller.

Kimball, Fiske (1968), *Thomas Jefferson: Architect*, New York, Da Capo Press.

Kirker, Harold (1968), *The Architecture of Charles Bulfinch*, Cambridge, Mass., Harvard University Press.

Kostof, Spiro, ed. (1977), *The Architect: Chapters in the History of the Profession*, New York, Oxford University Press.

—— (1995), *A History of Architecture: Settings and Rituals*, 2nd edn, New York, Oxford University Press.

Krinsky, Carol Herselle (1989), *Gordon Bunshaft of Skidmore, Owings & Merrill*, New York, Architectural History Foundation; Cambridge, Mass., MIT Press.

Kubler, George (1972; orig. pub. 1942), *The Religious Architecture of New Mexico in the Colonial Period and Since the American Occupation*, Albuquerque, University of New Mexico.

—— and Martin Soria (1959), *Art and Architecture in Spain and Portugal and Their American Dominions, 1500–1800*, New York, Penguin Books.

Lafever, Minard (1856), *The Architectural Instructor, Containing a History of Architecture from the Earliest Ages to the Present Time*, New York, Putnam.

Lane, Mills (1993), *Architecture of the Old South*, New York, Abbeville Press.

Lapsansky, Emma Jones (1994), *Neighborhoods in Transition: William Penn's Dream and Urban Reality*, New York, Garland Publications.

Latour, Alessandra, ed. (1991), *Louis I. Kahn: Writings, Letters, Interviews*, New York, Rizzoli.

Laugier, Abbé Marc Antoine (1753), *Essai sur l'Architecture*, Paris.

Le Corbusier (1946), *Towards a New Architecture*, London, The Architectural Press.

Limerick, Jeffrey, Nancy Ferguson and Richard Oliver (1979), *America's Grand Resort Hotels*, New York, Pantheon Books.

Limerick, Patty Nelson (1987), *Legacy of Conquest: The Unbroken Past of the American West*, New York, Norton.

Littlejohn, David (1984), *Architect: The Life and Work of Charles W. Moore*, New York, Holt, Reinhard and Winston.

Longstreth, Richard (1982), *Academic Eclecticism in American Architecture*, Winterthur Portfolio, Spring.

—— (1983), *On the Edge of the World: Four Architects in San Francisco at the Turn of the Century*, New York, Architectural History Foundation; Cambridge, Mass., MIT Press.

McAlester, Virginia and Lee (1992), *A Field Guide to American Houses*, New York, Alfred A. Knopf.

McAndrew, J. (1965), *Open Air Churches of 16th Century Mexico*, Cambridge, Mass., Harvard University Press.

McCoy, Esther (1960), *Five California Architects*, New York, Reinhold.

Makinson, Randell L. (1979), *Greene and Greene: Architecture as Fine Art*, Salt Lake City, Peregrine Smith.

Manson, Grant (1979), *Frank Lloyd Wright to 1910: The First Golden Age*, New York, Van Nostrand Reinhold.

Miller, Everard (1968), *Richard Upjohn: Architect and Churchman*, New York, Da Capo Press.

Millon, René, ed. (1973), *Urbanization at Teotihuacán, Mexico*, Austin, University of Texas Press.

Moos, Stanislaus von (1987), *Venturi, Rauch, and Scott Brown: Buildings and Projects*, New York, Rizzoli.

Morgan, William M. (1994), *Ancient Architecture of the Southwest*, Austin, Texas, University of Texas Press.

Morrison, Hugh (1952), *Early American Architecture: From the First Colonial Settlements to the National Period*, New York, Oxford University Press.

—— (1962), *Louis Sullivan: Prophet of Modern Architecture*, New York, W. W. Norton.

Mumford, Lewis, ed. (1972), *Roots of Contemporary American Architecture: 37 Essays From the Mid-Nineteenth Century to the Present*, New York, Dover.

Musgrove, John, ed. (1987), *Banister Fletcher's History of Architecture*, 19th edn, London, Butterworth.

Nabokov, Peter, *et al.* (1993), *The Native Americans: An Illustrated History*, Atlanta, Turning Publishing, Inc.

Nabokov, Peter and Robert Easton (1989), *Native American Architecture*, New York, Oxford University Press.

Ockman, Joan, ed. (1993), *Architecture Culture 1943−68: A Documentary Anthology*, New York, Columbia Books on Architecture/Rizzoli.

O'Gorman, James F. (1987), *H. H. Richardson: Architectural Forms for an American Society*, Chicago, University of Chicago Press.

—— (1991), *Three American Architects: Richardson, Sullivan and Wright*, Chicago, University of Chicago Press.

—— and George E. Thomas (1973), *The Architecture of Frank Furness*, Philadelphia, Philadelphia Museum of Art.

Ould, E. A. (1904), *Old Cottages, Farm Houses, and Other Half-Timber Buildings*, London, B. T. Batsford.

Peck, Ameli (1992), *Alexander Jackson Davis: American Architect 1803−92*, New York, Rizzoli International Publications, Inc.

Perrault, Claude (1683), *Ordonnace des Cinq Espèces de Colonnes selon la Méthode des Anciens*, Paris, Jean Baptiste Coignard.

Pierson, William H., Jr (1970), *The Colonial and Neoclassical Styles*, vol. 1 of *American Buildings and Their Architects*, Garden City, New York, Doubleday & Company, Inc.

—— (1978), *Technology and the Picturesque: The Corporate and the Early Gothic Styles*, vol. 2 of *American Buildings and Their Architects*, Garden City, New York, Doubleday & Company, Inc.

Piranesi, Giovanni Battista (1760), *Carceri d'Invenzione*, Rome.

Podmore, Frank (1907), *Robert Owen: A Biography*, New York, D. Appleton.

Poppeliers, John C., S. Allen Chambers and Nancy B. Schwartz (1983), *What Style Is It? A Guide to American Architecture*, Washington DC, Preservation Press.

Price, C. Matlack (1916), *The Practical Book of Architecture*, Philadelphia & London, J. B. Lippincott Company.

Pugin, A. Welby (1843), *The Present State of Ecclesiastical Architecture in England*, London, Charles Dolman.

Quimby, Ian (1978), *Material Culture and the Study of American Life*, New York, W. W. Norton & Company, Inc.

Ramsey, Charles and Harold Sleeper (1981), *Architectural Graphic Standards*, 7th edn, New York, John Wiley and Sons, Inc.

Rensselaer, Mariana Griswold van (1969; orig. pub. 1888), *Henry Hobson Richardson and His Works*, New York, Dover.

Reps, John W. (1965), *The Making of Urban America: A History of City Planning in the United States*, Princeton, Princeton University Press.

—— (1967), *Monumental Washington: The Planning and Development of the Capital Center*, Princeton, Princeton University Press.

Reynolds, Donald Martin (1994), *The Architecture of New York City*, New York, John Wiley & Sons.

Robinson, Cervin and Rosemarie Haag Bletter (1975), *Skyscraper Style: Art Deco New York*, New York, Oxford University Press.

Robinson, Willard Bethurem (1977), *American Forts – Architectural Form and Function*, Urbana, Published for the Amon Carter Museum of Western Art, Fort Worth, by the University of Illinois Press.

Rocheleau, Paul and June Sprigg (1994), *Shaker Built: The Form and Function of Shaker Architecture*, New York, Monacelli Press.

Roth, Leland (1979), *A Concise History of American Architecture*, New York, Harper & Row.

—— (1983), *America Builds: Source Documents in American Architecture and Planning*, New York, Harper & Row.

—— (1983), *McKim, Mead & White, Architects*, New York, Harper & Row.

Ruskin, John (1989; orig. pub. 1849), *The Seven Lamps of Architecture*, New York, Dover Publications, Inc.

Saint, Andrew (1976), *Richard Norman Shaw*, New Haven, Conn. and London, Yale University Press.

Schinkel, Karl Friedrich (1866; orig. pub. 1819), *Sammlung Architectonischer Entwürfe*, Berlin, Ernst and Korn.

Schulze, Franz (1985), *Mies van der Rohe: A Critical Biography*, Chicago, University of Chicago Press.

—— (1994), *Philip Johnson: Life and Work*, New York, Albert A. Knopf.

—— and Kevin Harrington (1993), *Chicago's Famous Buildings: A Photographic Guide to the City's Architectural Landmarks and Other Notable Buildings*, Chicago, University of Chicago Press.

Scott, Pamela (1993), *Buildings of the District of Columbia*, New York, Oxford University Press.

Scully, Vincent J. (1971; orig. pub. 1952), *The Shingle Style and the Stick Style: Architectural Theory and Design from Richardson to the Origins of Wright*, New Haven, Conn., Yale University Press.

—— (1974), *The Shingle Style Today or the Historian's Revenge*, New York, George Braziller.

—— (1988), *American Architecture and Urbanism*, New York, Henry Holt and Company.

—— (1989), *The Architecture of the American Summer: The Flowering of the Shingle Style*, New York, Rizzoli.

Soleri, Paolo (1969), *Arcology: The City in the Image of Man*, Cambridge, Mass., MIT Press.

Southworth, Susan and Michael (1978), *Ornamental Ironwork: An Illustrated Guide to its Design, History & Use in American Architecture*, Boston, D. R. Godine.

Stanton, Phoebe B. (1968), *The Gothic Revival and American Church Architecture: An Episode in Taste, 1840–56*, Baltimore, Johns Hopkins University Press.

Stegner, Wallace (1987), *The American West as Living Space*, Ann Arbor, University of Michigan.

Stern, Robert (1977), *New Directions in American Architecture*, New York, Braziller.

——, Gregory Gilmartin and John Montague Massengale (1984), *New York 1900: Metropolitan Architecture and Urbanism 1890–1915*, New York, Rizzoli.

——, Gregory Gilmartin and Thomas Mellins (1987), *New York 1930: Architecture and Urbanism Between the Two World Wars*, New York, Rizzoli.

——, Thomas Mellins and David Fishman (1995), *New York 1960: Architecture and Urbanism Between the Second World War and the Bicentennial*, New York, Monacelli Press.

Stevens, John Calvin and Albert Winslow Cobb (1889), *Examples of American Domestic Architecture*, William T. Comstock.

Storrer, William Allin (1993), *The Frank Lloyd Wright Companion*, Chicago, University of Chicago Press.

Sturgis, Russell (1903), *How to Judge Architecture*, New York, The Baker & Taylor Co.

Sutro, Dirk (1994), *West Coast Wave: New California Houses*, New York, Van Nostrand Reinhold.

Sullivan, Louis (1956), *Autobiography of an Idea*, New York, Dover.

—— (1979), *Kindergarten Chats and Other Writings*, New York, Dover.

Summerson, John (1979), *Architecture in Britain 1530–1830*, Harmondsworth, Penguin Books Ltd.

Sweeting, Adam W. (1996), *Reading Houses and Building Books: Andrew Jackson Downing and the Architecture of Popular Antebellum Literature, 1835–55*, Hanover, University Press of New England.

Sweetman, John E. (1987), *The Oriental Obsession: Islamic Inspiration in British and American Art and Architecture, 1500–1920*, Cambridge and New York, Cambridge University Press.

Tatum, George (1961), *Penn's Great Town: 250 Years of Philadelphia Architecture*, Philadelphia, University of Pennsylvania Press.

*The Architecture of McKim, Mead & White* (1990), Mineola, NY, Dover Publications, Inc. Originally published in 1915–20 as *A Monograph of the Work of McKim, Mead & White 1879–1915*.

Thomas, George E., Michael J. Lewis and Jeffrey A. Cohen (1991), *Frank Furness: The Complete Works*, New York, Princeton Architectural Press.

Thomson, David (1966), *Europe Since Napoleon*, Harmondsworth, Penguin Books.

Treib, Marc (1993), *Sanctuaries of Spanish New Mexico*, Berkeley, University of California Press.

Turner, Frederick Jackson (1920), *The Frontier in American History*, New York, H. Holt and Company.

Twombly, Robert (1978), *Frank Lloyd Wright: His Life and Architecture*, New York, John Wiley.

—— (1985), *Louis Sullivan: His Life and Work*, New York, Viking.

Upton, Dell, ed. (1986), *America's Architectural Roots: Ethnic Groups that Built America*, Washington DC, Preservation Press.

Venturi, Robert (1966), *Complexity and Contradiction in Architecture*, New York, Museum of Modern Art.

Venturi, Robert, Denise Scott Brown and Steven Izenour (1972), *Learning from Las Vegas*, Cambridge, Mass., MIT Press.

Webb, William S. and Raymond S. Baby (1957), *The Adena People*, Ohio Historical Society, No. 2, Columbus, Ohio State University Press.

Wheeler, Mortimer (1964), *Roman Art and Architecture*, Thames & Hudson.

Whiffen, Marcus and Frederick Koeper (1981), *American Architecture 1607–1976*, Cambridge, Mass., MIT Press.

—— (1981), *American Architecture Since 1780: A Guide to the Styles*, Cambridge, MIT Press.

Whitaker, Charles, ed. (1925), *Bertram Grosvenor Goodhue, Architect and Master of Many Arts*, New York, Press of the American Institute of Architects.

Williamson, Roxanne (1973), *Austin, Texas: An American Architectural History*, San Antonio, Trinity University Press.

Willis, Carol (1995), *Form Follows Finance: Skyscrapers and Skylines in New York and Chicago*, New York, Princeton Architectural Press.

Wilson, Richard Guy, ed. (1979), *The American Renaissance: 1876–1917*, New York, Pantheon.

—— (1985), *McKim, Mead & White, Architects*, New York, Rizzoli.

Wilson, William H. (1989), *The City Beautiful Movement*, Baltimore, Johns Hopkins University Press.

Wischnitzer, Rachel (1955), *Synagogue Architecture in the United States: History and Interpretation*, Philadelphia, Jewish Publication Society of America.

Wister, Owen, *et al.* (1923), *A Monograph of the Works of Mellor Meigs and Howe*, New York, Architectural Book Publishing Company.

Woodbridge, Sally B. (1976), *Bay Area Houses*, New York, Oxford University Press.

—— (1992), *Bernard Maybeck: Visionary Architect*, New York, Abbeville Press.

—— and John M. Woodbridge (1992), *San Francisco Architecture: The Illustrated Guide to Over 1000 of the Best Buildings, Parks and Public Artworks in the Bay Area*, San Francisco, Chronicle Books.

Wright, Frank Lloyd (1910) *Ausgeführte Bauten und Entwürfe von Frank Lloyd Wright*, Berlin, Verlag Ernst Wasmuth A. G.

—— (1943), *An Autobiography*, New York, Duell, Sloan and Pearce.

—— (1953), *The Future of Architecture*, New York, Horizon Press.

Zabel, Craig and Susan Scott Munshower, eds (1989), *American Public Architecture: European Roots and Native Expressions*, University Park, Pa., Pennsylvania State University.

# Index

Note: See general categories under church design; house design; construction forms; settlement patterns. Number in bold indicates an illustration.